I0828432

HISTORIC PHOTOS OF
OAKLAND

TEXT AND CAPTIONS BY STEVEN LAVOIE

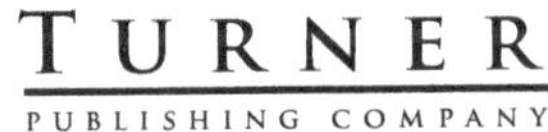

Photographer Carleton Watkins produced this photograph of the nursery of Wright F. Kelsey situated where Telegraph Avenue and 23rd Street now intersect. The image, with its display of the bounty of Kelsey's land, was published widely alongside articles promoting California's rich agricultural potential.

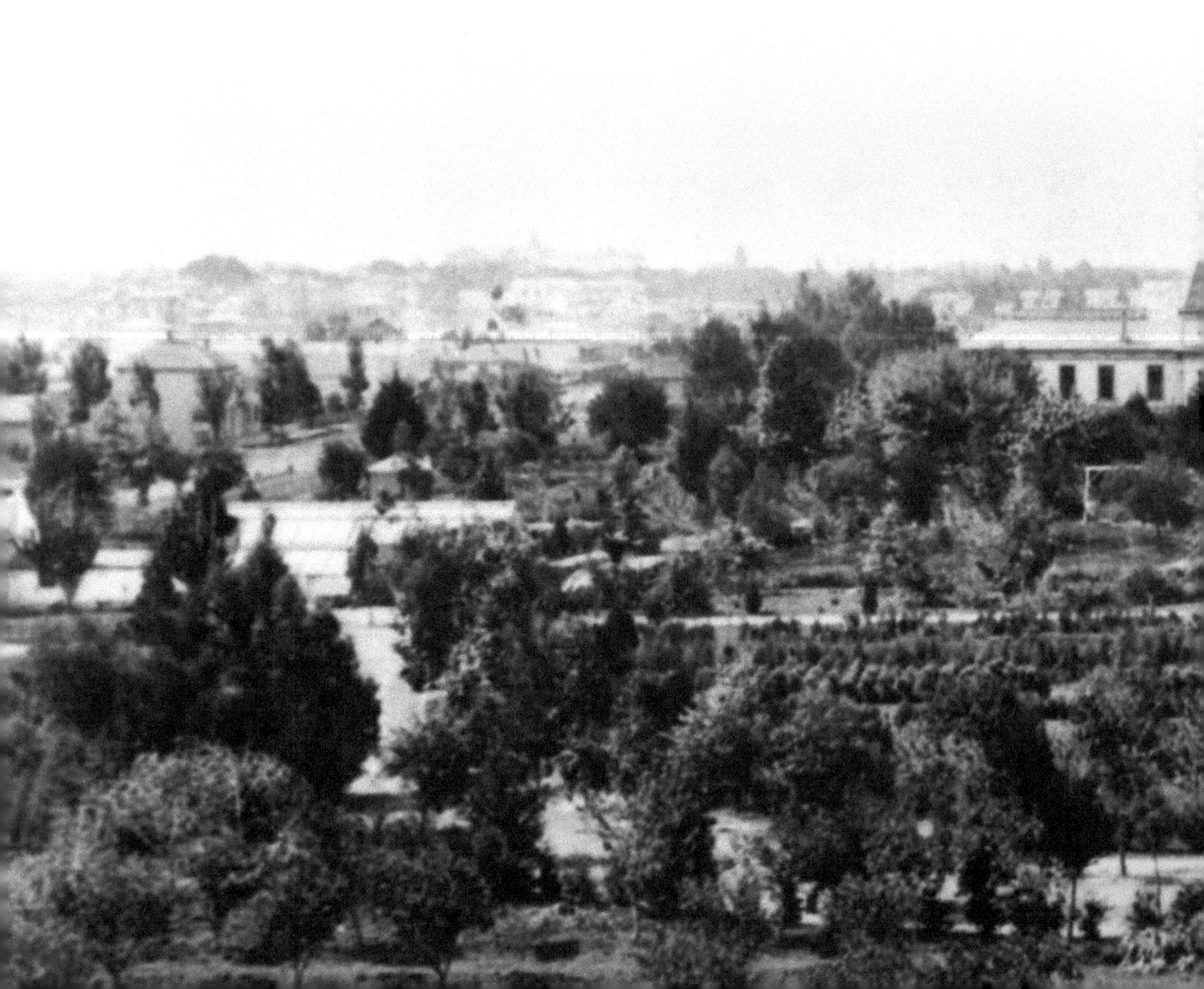

HISTORIC PHOTOS OF
OAKLAND

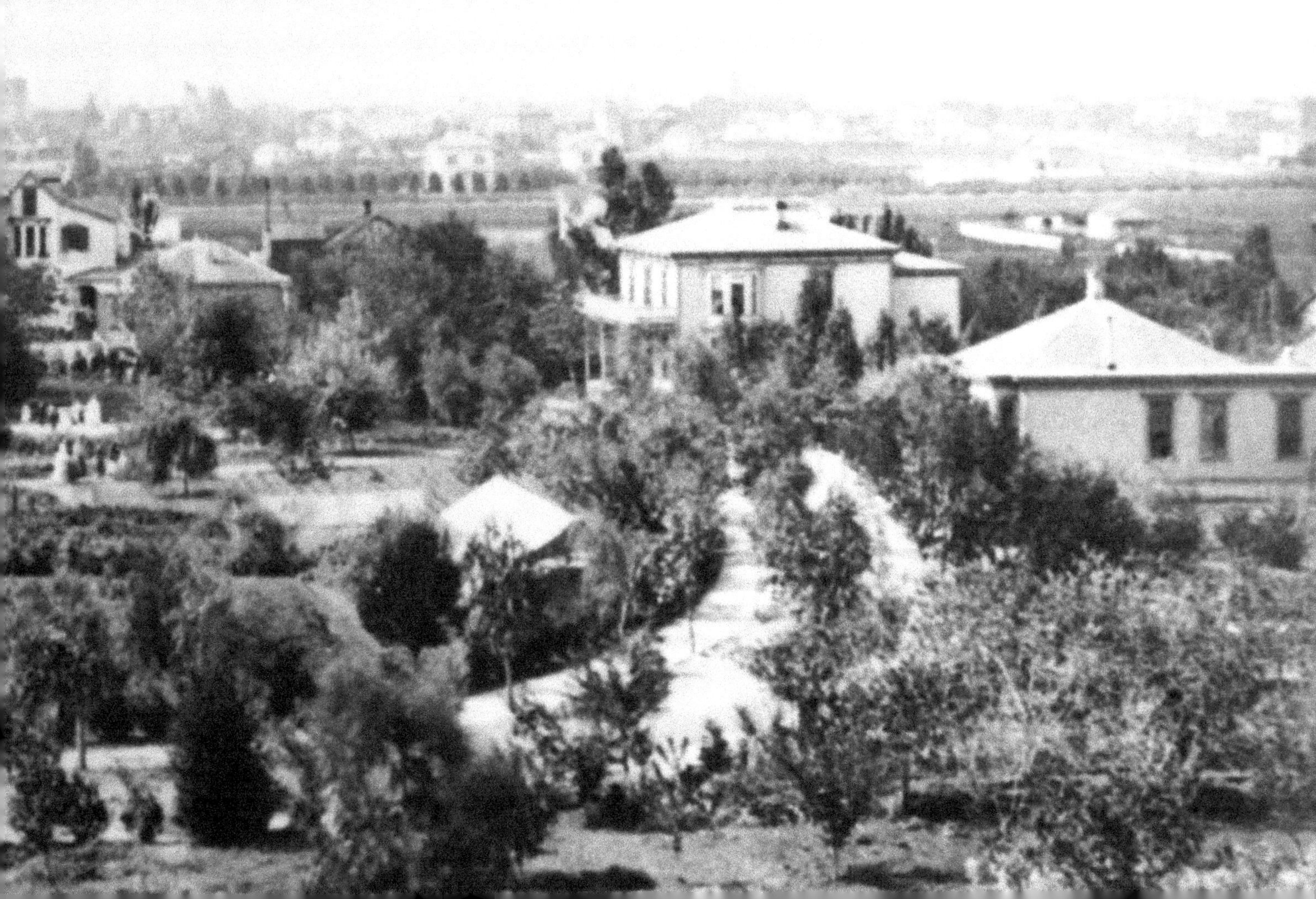

Turner Publishing Company
www.turnerpublishing.com

Historic Photos of Oakland

Library of Congress Control Number: 2009921191

ISBN-13: 978-1-59652-529-0

Printed in the United States of America

ISBN 978-1-68442-085-8 (hc)

Contents

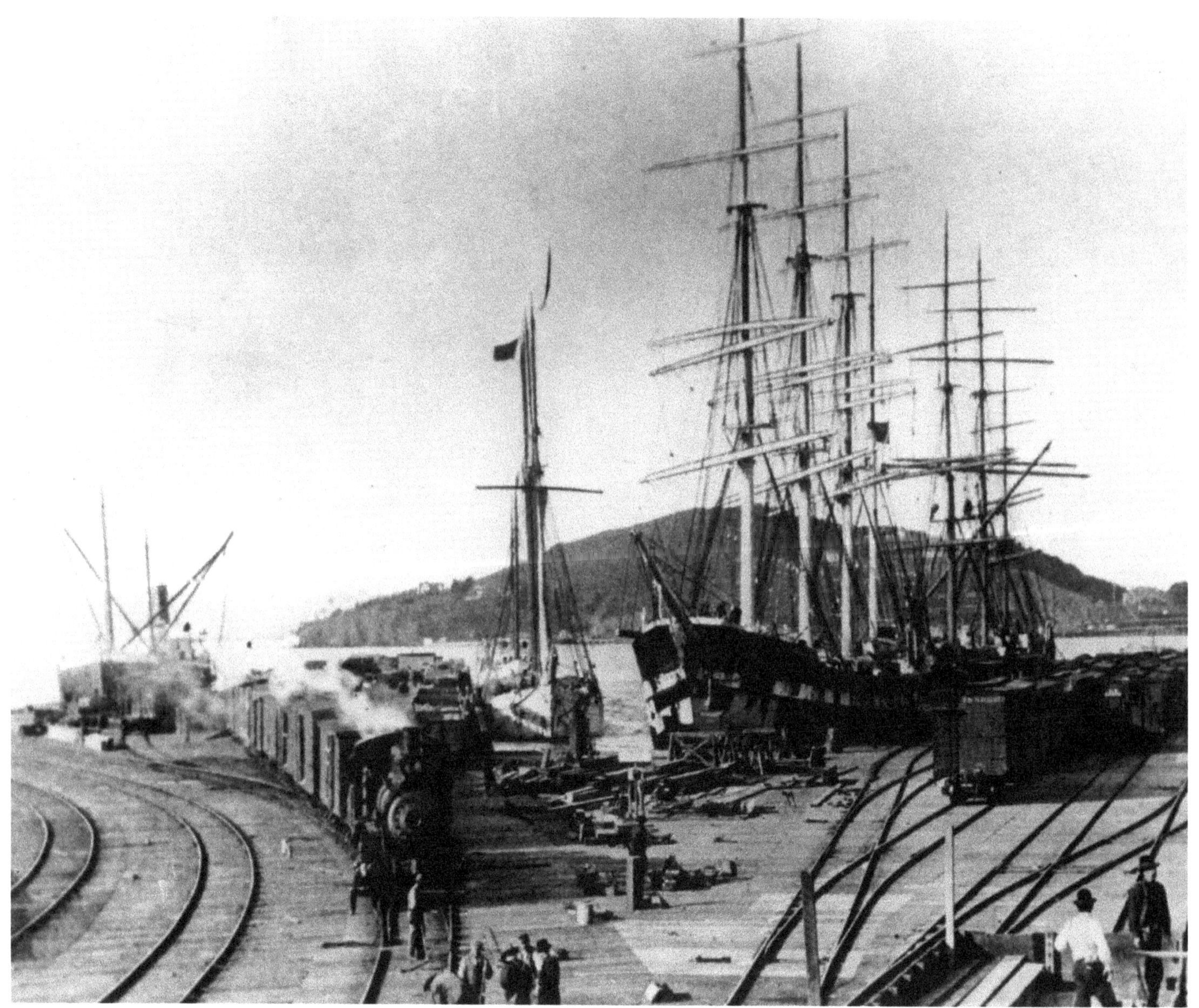

The western terminus of the Transcontinental Railroad, shown here in the 1890s, transformed Oakland from a sleepy cattle town to an international center of commerce and industry.

Acknowledgments

This volume, *Historic Photos of Oakland,* is the result of the cooperation and efforts of many individuals and organizations. It is with great thanks that we acknowledge the valuable contribution of the Oakland History Room at the Oakland Public Library and the Library of Congress for their generous support.

Sincere gratitude for the work and vision of my predecessors and colleagues at the Oakland Public Library, especially the past and present staff in the Oakland History Room, and to Tony Molatore of Berkeley Giclée.

—*Steven Lavoie*

This project represents countless hours of review and research. The researchers and writer have reviewed many hundreds of photographs in numerous archives. We greatly appreciate the generous assistance of the individuals and organizations listed here, without whom this project could not have been completed.

The goal in publishing this work is to provide broader access to this set of extraordinary photographs, as well as to inspire, provide perspective, and evoke insight that might assist citizens as they work to plan the city's future. In addition, the book seeks to preserve the past with adequate respect and reverence.

With the exception of touching up imperfections that have accrued with the passage of time and cropping where necessary, no changes have been made. The focus and clarity of many images is limited by the technology and the ability of the photographer at the time they were taken.

PREFACE

Although it sits at dead center of one of the nation's major metropolitan areas, visible to tens of thousands of travelers moving by car, by sea, by rail, and by air, Oakland remains seldom seen by outsiders. Even its own photographers, some of the most proficient and prolific in the field, have been unable to make scenes of Oakland instantly recognizable such as those of other great cities of the world.

From its hills, cameras capture spectacular views of one of the world's most scenic urban landscapes, with views across the San Francisco Bay and out through the Golden Gate to the Pacific Ocean. On its streets, the world's broad range of human form—and economic circumstance—reveals itself daily. A city plan of great ambition, instituted well ahead of other cities, provided Oakland with a coherent and aesthetic urban core, with busy, colorful, and attractive neighborhood commercial districts and a downtown center rich with architectural treasures.

Along with its shimmering light and consistent sunshine, Oakland would appear to be a prime source of postcard views to attract the attention of photographers. It has certainly provided photojournalists and documentary photographers an abundance of material, situated at the vanguard of nearly every boom and bust, fad, trend, and social phenomenon to emerge on the West Coast, while history carried on in the events of the day. Watershed moments in aviation, in sports, in commerce, in the literary and visual arts, in women's rights, and civil rights were taking place in Oakland, obscured too often by the long shadow cast by the high-profile city across the bay.

Novice photographers, too, had familiar surroundings and interesting if commonplace lives to document with their Kodak Brownies, Instamatics, and Polaroid Swingers. A camera in the hands of an amateur or hobbyist provides a much different angle on the passage of time than it might in the hands of artists and professionals.

The work of women is unequivocally strong in Oakland's photographic heritage. At the turn of the twentieth century, Anne Brigman emerged as a leading member of the Pictorialist photographers from her backyard studio in Oakland that would serve the next generation as a gathering spot for the modernists of Group f/64, best known for the work of Ansel Adams.

Brigman was followed by Imogen Cunningham and Dorothea Lange, who represented far different approaches to their subjects, with Oakland a popular setting for their work. The work of both Brigman and Lange is represented here with images that serve to document important moments of the city's history.

The great earthquake of 1906 provided the opportunity for Oaklanders "Doc" Rogers and Charles Estey to establish their lasting reputations as photographers. Rogers, who enjoyed a long career with the *Oakland Tribune,* was particularly stubborn about adopting new technology and continued the use of glass negatives until supplies ran out during World War II.

A prolific Jewish photographer, Moses Cohen, left a particularly valuable visual record of his city's development during a long career that lasted most of the twentieth century. He took pictures for publicity campaigns launched by merchants, car dealers, movie theaters, real estate brokers, city agencies, corporate offices, and promoters of fairs, festivals, parades, sports contests, and other special events. He took jobs at weddings and photographed municipal projects. Albert "Kayo" Harris carried on that tradition, along with numerous others who covered the news and recorded the activities of Oakland's public agencies, its schools, Chamber of Commerce, and its military commands.

Numerous factors went into the selection of the images included here, causing much to be left out and much that may not seem as significant to be included. Every photograph is part of the collection of a public library or a public museum. If there is intrinsic social benefit in a common understanding of the past, the images reproduced here will attest to the value of those collections and to the institutions we have established to sustain them.

—*Steven Lavoie*

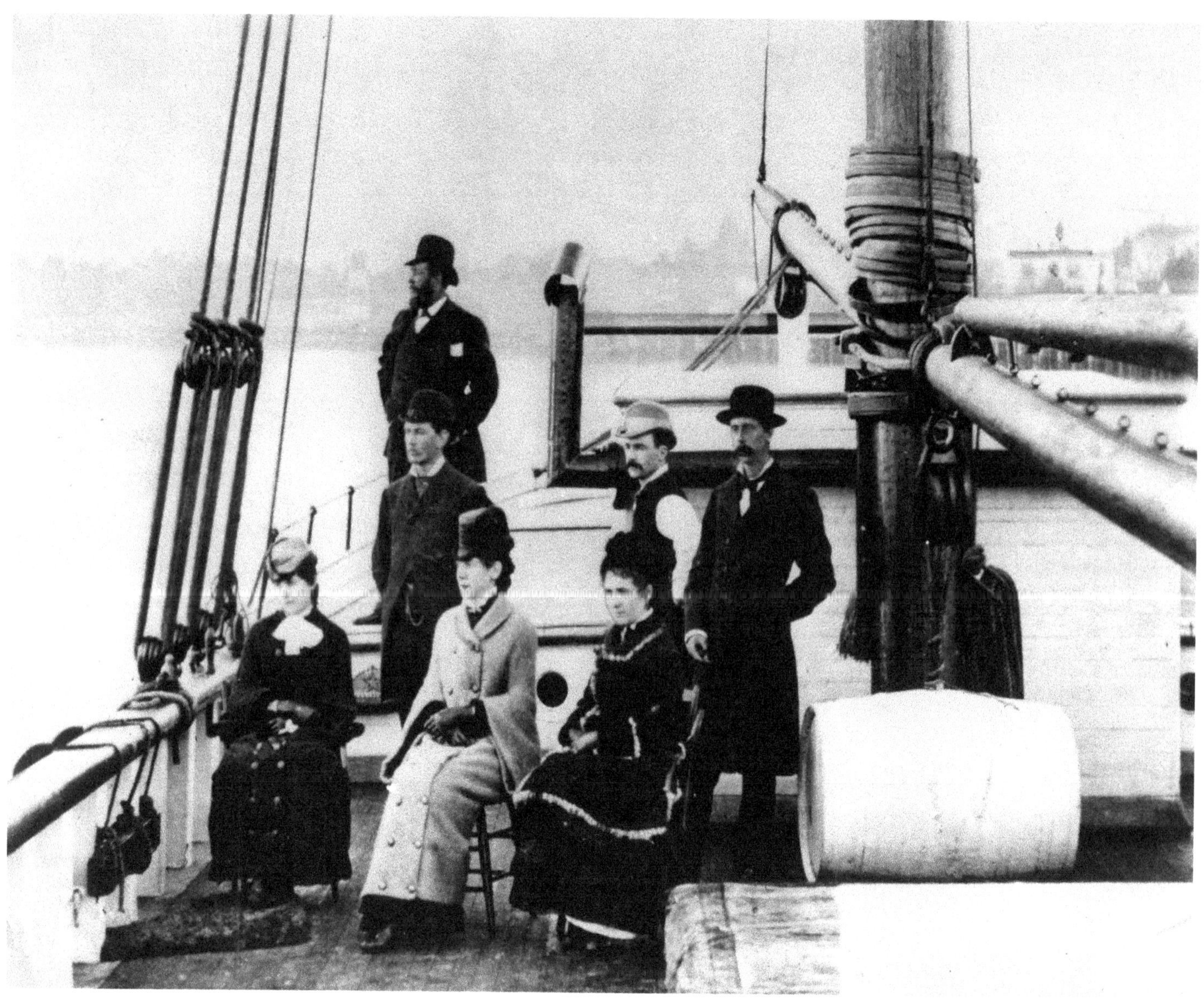

Love lured the great Scottish novelist Robert Louis Stevenson to Oakland, in pursuit of his sweetheart, Fanny Vandegrift Osbourne, whom he met on a visit to the artists' colony at Barbizon, France. The couple married and had settled in Oakland in 1869 to raise children where they encountered Samuel Merritt. A photographer captured an image of the Stevensons with others aboard Merritt's yacht *The Casco* in the Oakland harbor. Merritt stands behind his guests in the bowler hat.

VISIONS OF A GREAT METROPOLIS

(1850s–1899)

Sparsely populated California was a virtual terra incognito when it suddenly caught the world's attention in the late 1840s with a report of rich deposits of gold in the hills. The story grabbed newspaper headlines around the world. The ensuing rush of fortune hunters to the west coast of North America ensured an end to the pastoral existence of the first colonists, a few thousand subjects of the Spanish throne who came up the coast to settle the remote northern frontiers of Mexico, along with that of the surviving indigenous North Americans who had once roamed the land far and wide.

While the gold claims in the mountains and the foothills were up for grabs, the property rights for the pastures, farmlands, woods, and home sites along the Pacific coast were, for the most part, very much established under the treaty that turned California over to the United States in 1848. That small detail had little impact on the newcomers, many of whom found a career in mining far too rigorous, or whose luck in prospecting just went bust. Others saw a rich future in other fortunes California could provide in more refined forms of commerce, such as real estate, agriculture, or retail trade. Towns and cities resulted, among them San Francisco, nearest the Pacific Ocean, and across the bay to the east, Oakland.

By 1869, Oakland had been chosen as the western terminus of the Transcontinental Railroad and was a convenient haven from the lawless city opposite the bay for families wishing to put down roots amid a bounty of educational opportunities and other amenities. A romance lured Scottish novelist Robert Louis Stevenson to help carry on the city's literary legacy, begun by author Bret Harte before him. Oakland's scenic beauty attracted artists, too, including painters Thomas Hill, William Keith, and others, who would inspire a uniquely Californian visual style. The great naturalist John Muir endured urban life in Oakland to complete some of his most enduring literary work.

Rapid growth came with the railroad as great wealth continued its flow out of the Sierra Nevada. Lake Merritt, created with a dam built across a slough, served as a scenic place of residence for the newly well-heeled of the West Coast. For average people, the city's lake, its waterfront, and its pastoral landscape provided a convenient Sunday getaway from city life—and the wide open spaces offered unprecedented opportunity for real estate developers and the newly emerging industries of the modern era. By the end of the nineteenth century, a great metropolis had arisen.

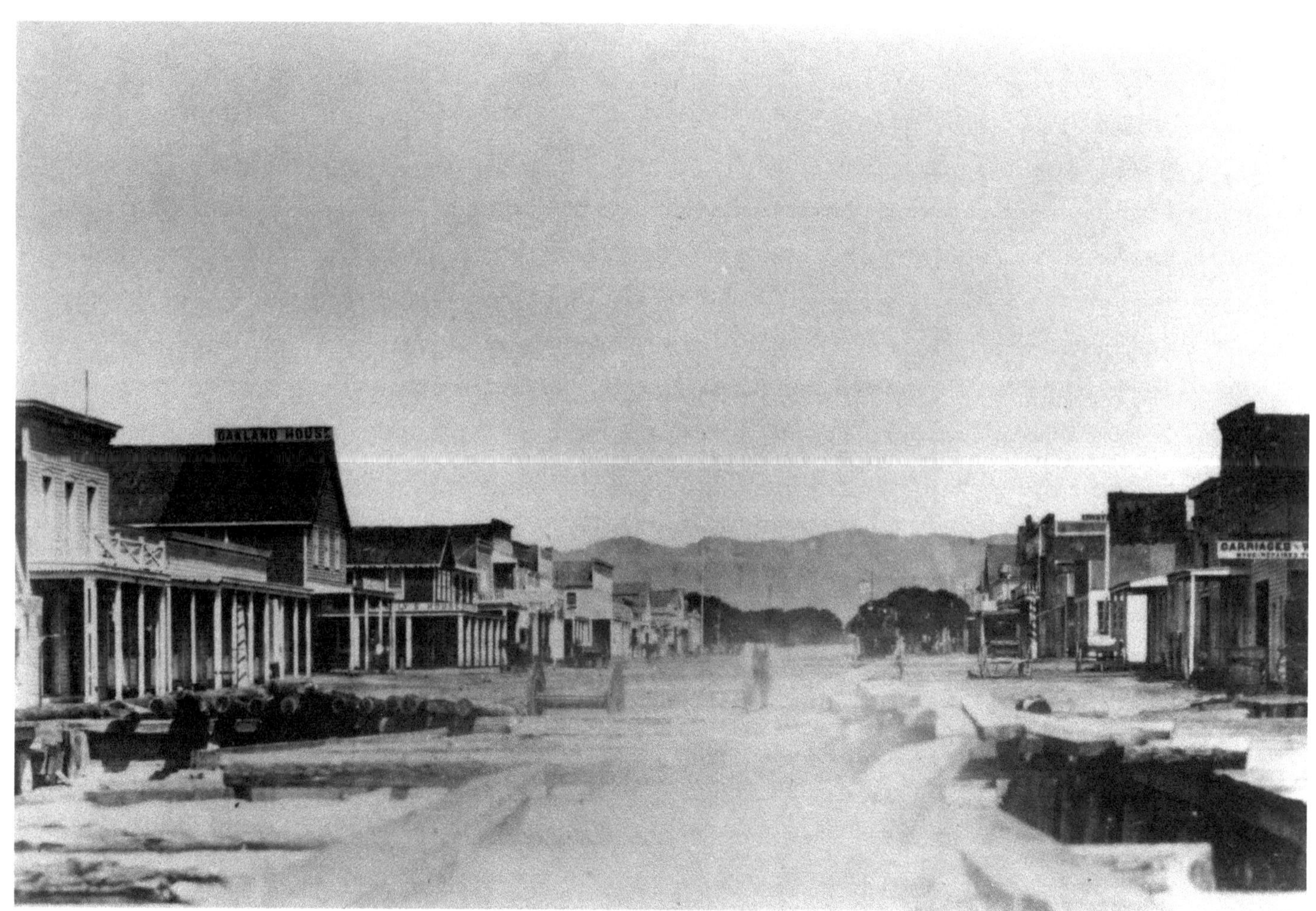

The earliest-known photograph of Oakland looks north up Broadway from the pier in 1857. A thick stand of the city's trademark oaks are visible in the background in front of the treeless Contra Costa Range. The image was included in an album of photographs attributed to George R. Fardon, who developed his own photographic method using salt.

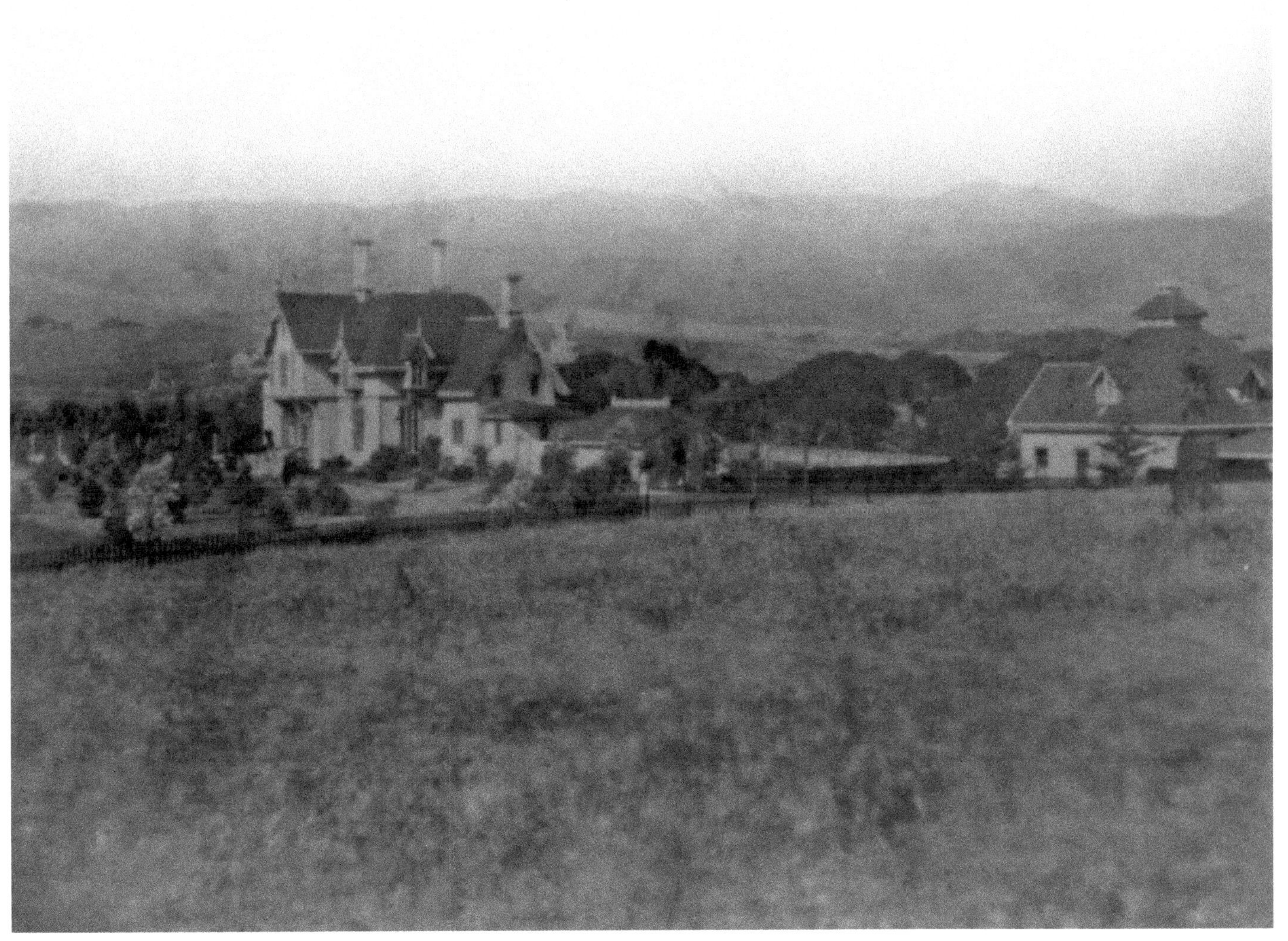

The hills behind Oakland supported little vegetation when the first lawman in the area, Sheriff Harry Morse, built his estate just beyond the current southern boundary of the city. The property is shown here around 1866. Morse's legacy as a lawman included the arrest of some of California's most wanted outlaws, among them stagecoach robber Black Bart.

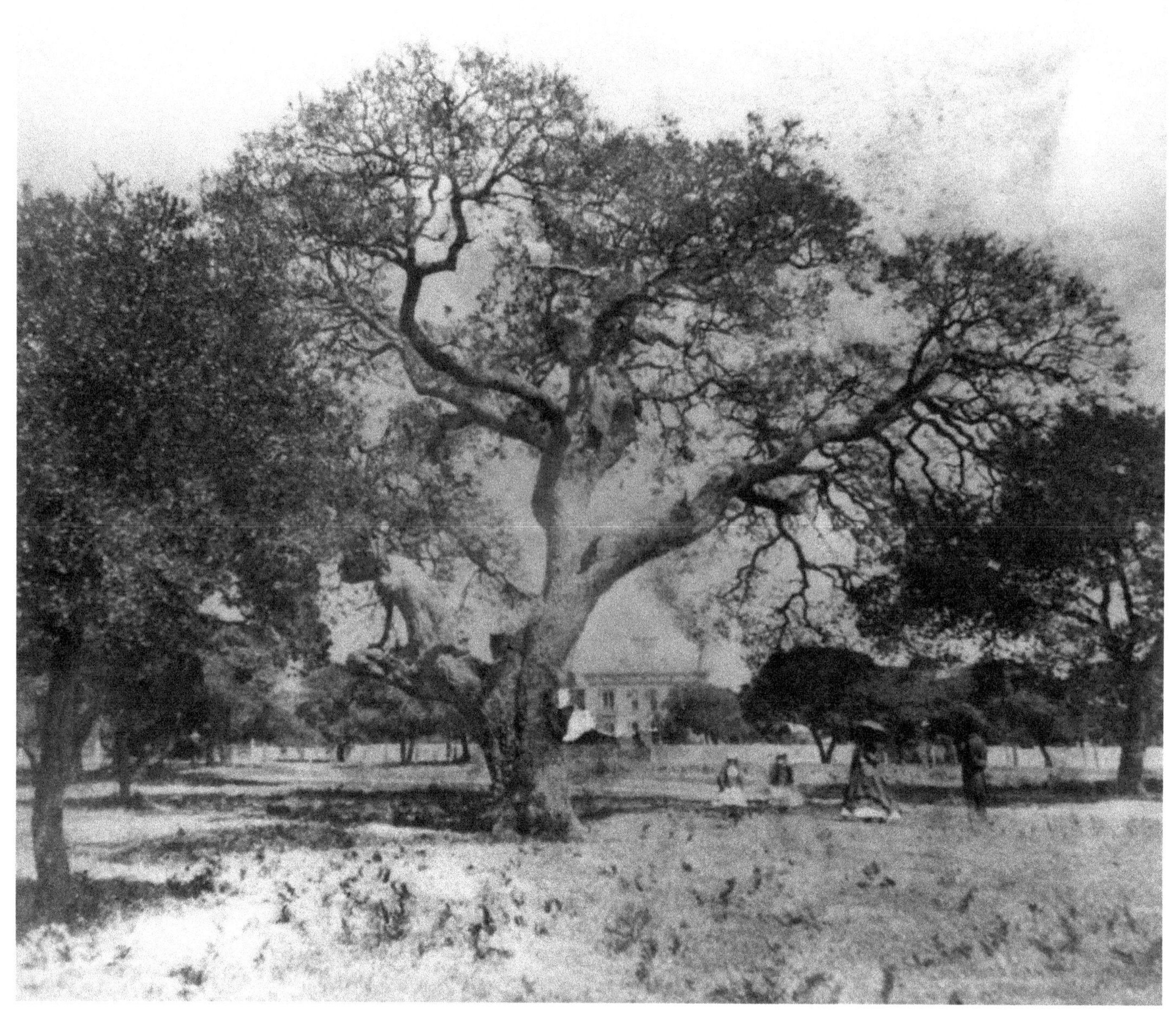

Central Oakland became a refuge from the lawless and corrupt city across the bay for many of the newcomers from the east who sought a place to raise a family. Major Ralph W. Kirkham, a veteran of the Mexican War, acquired for his estate an entire city block on Oak Street between Seventh and Eighth streets.

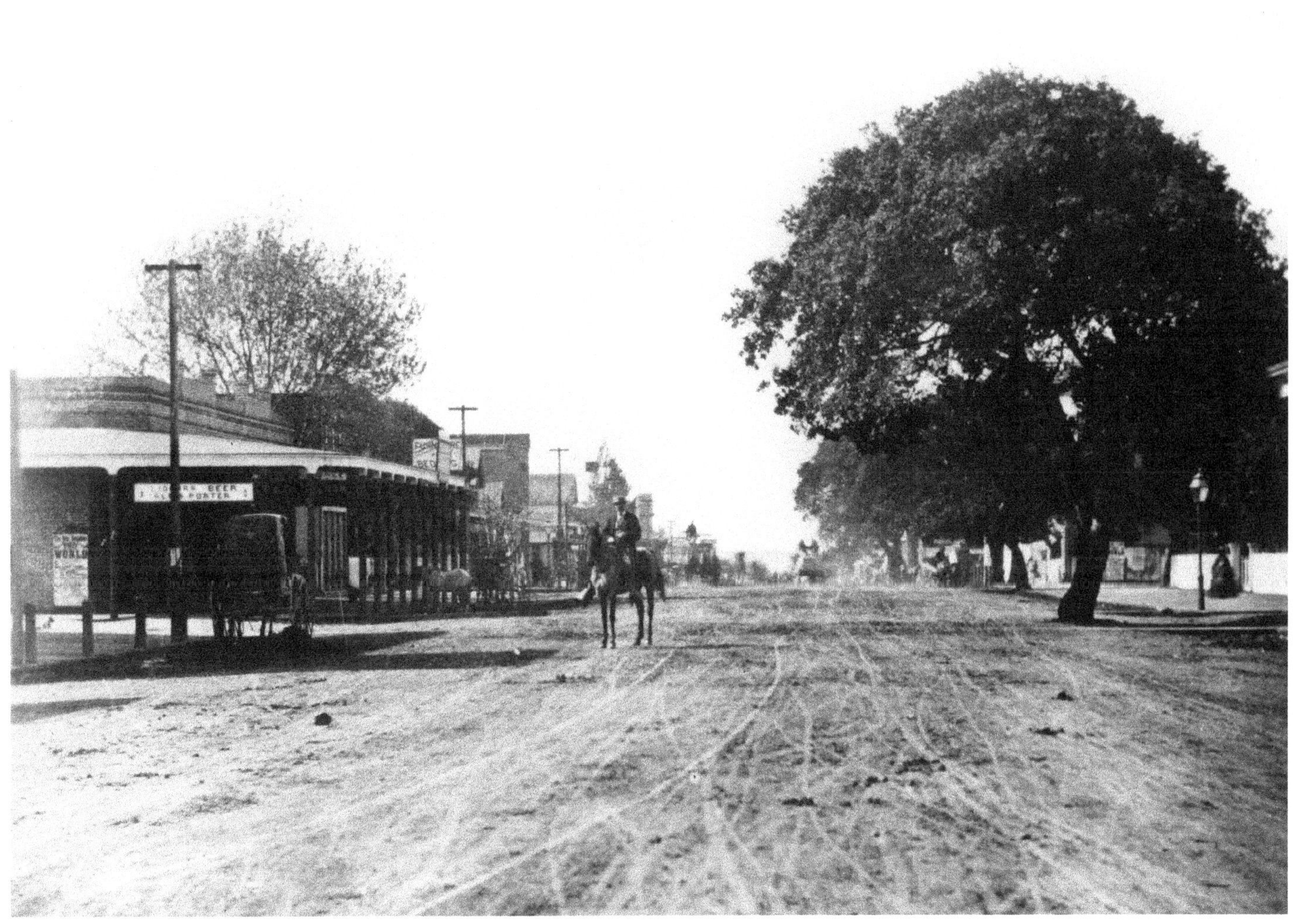

Oaks were left unmolested by official policy in early Oakland, even when they grew in the middle of the street. The long exposures required for the photographic methods available when this image was recorded, around 1869, meant that the man on the horse posing for the shot had to remain nearly motionless for up to 20 minutes to prevent blurring the image.

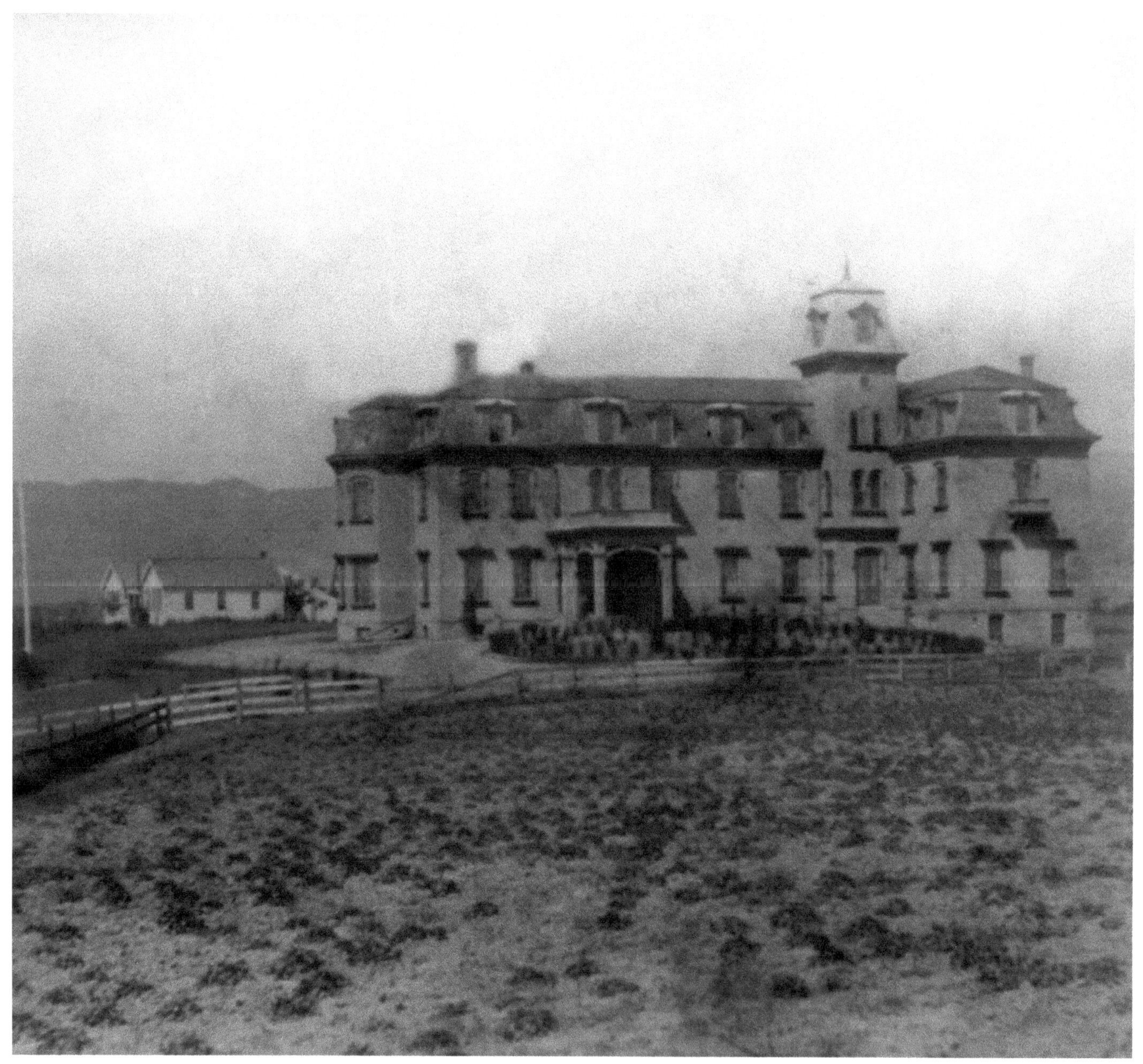

The San Francisco firm of Lawrence & Houseworth published this photograph of the Female College of the Pacific, the first of its kind in California, established in 1863 on the northwest edge of the growing city. It began Oakland's development into the West Coast's primary center of higher education.

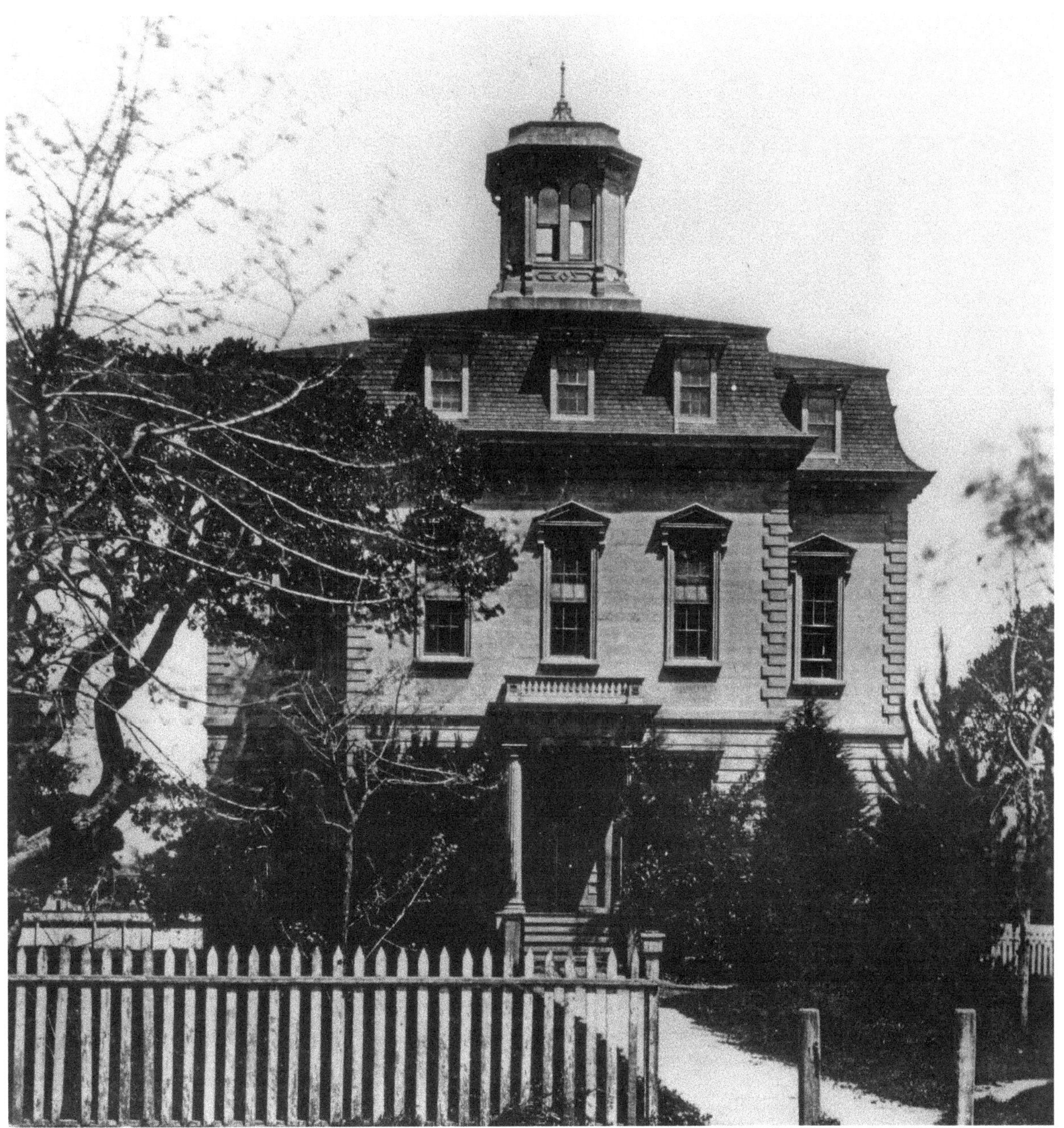

The school founded during the Civil War in this downtown Oakland building by Isaac H. Brayton would expand into the College of California. The college would later be selected as a land-grant institution under a successful federal program in the 1860s and relocate to Berkeley as the University of California, the nation's largest public institution of higher education.

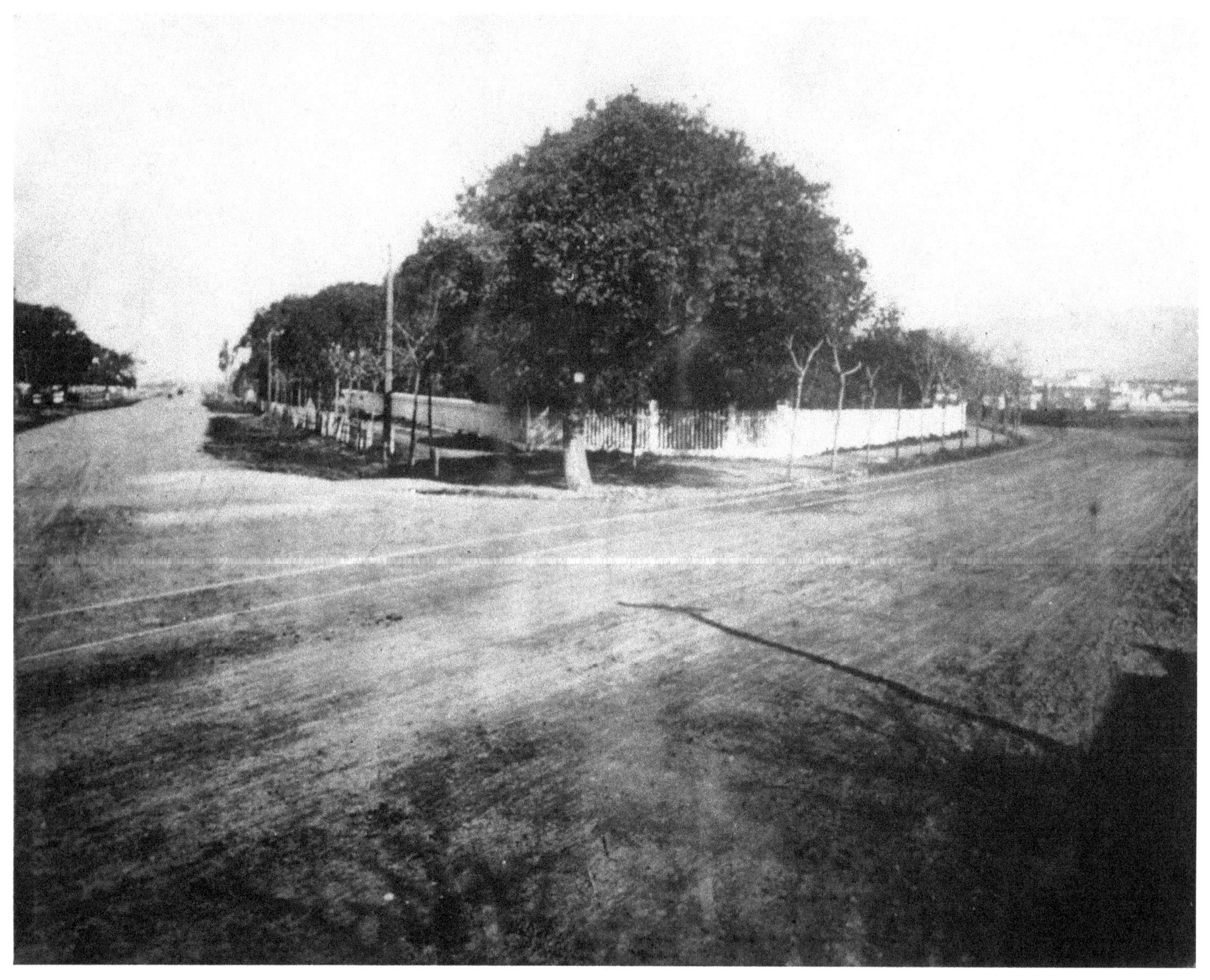

The poles seen at left-center in this image, from around 1869, show the route of the telegraph line past the Oakland residence and gardens of George C. Potter and his family at the former junction of Telegraph and San Pablo avenues.

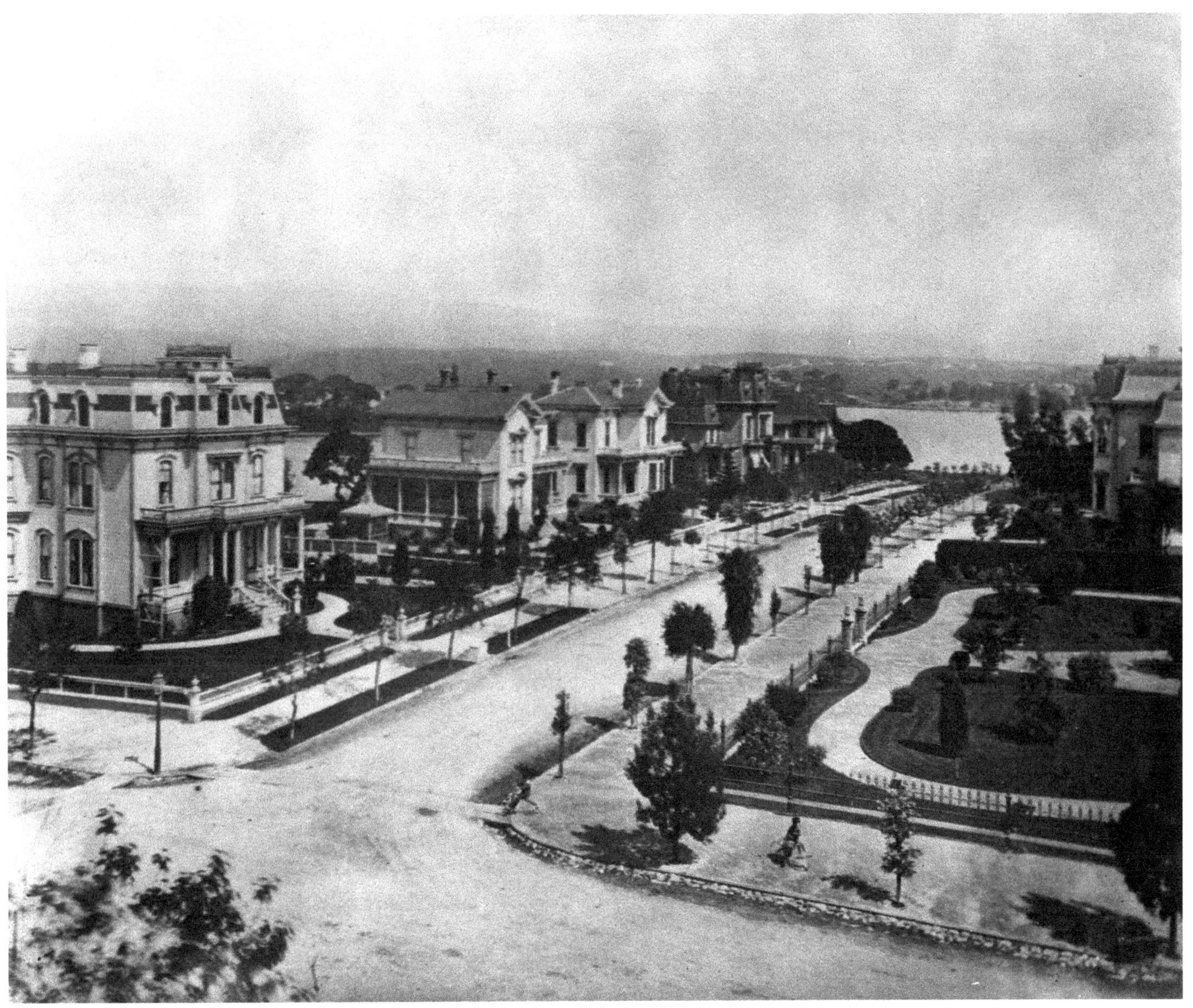

On the western shore of Lake Merritt, some of the West coast's wealthiest residents constructed elegant Victorian houses on broad tree-lined streets. This photograph by Carleton Watkins shows a stretch of these residences along Lake Street (now known as 17th Street) between Madison and Oak streets in the 1870s.

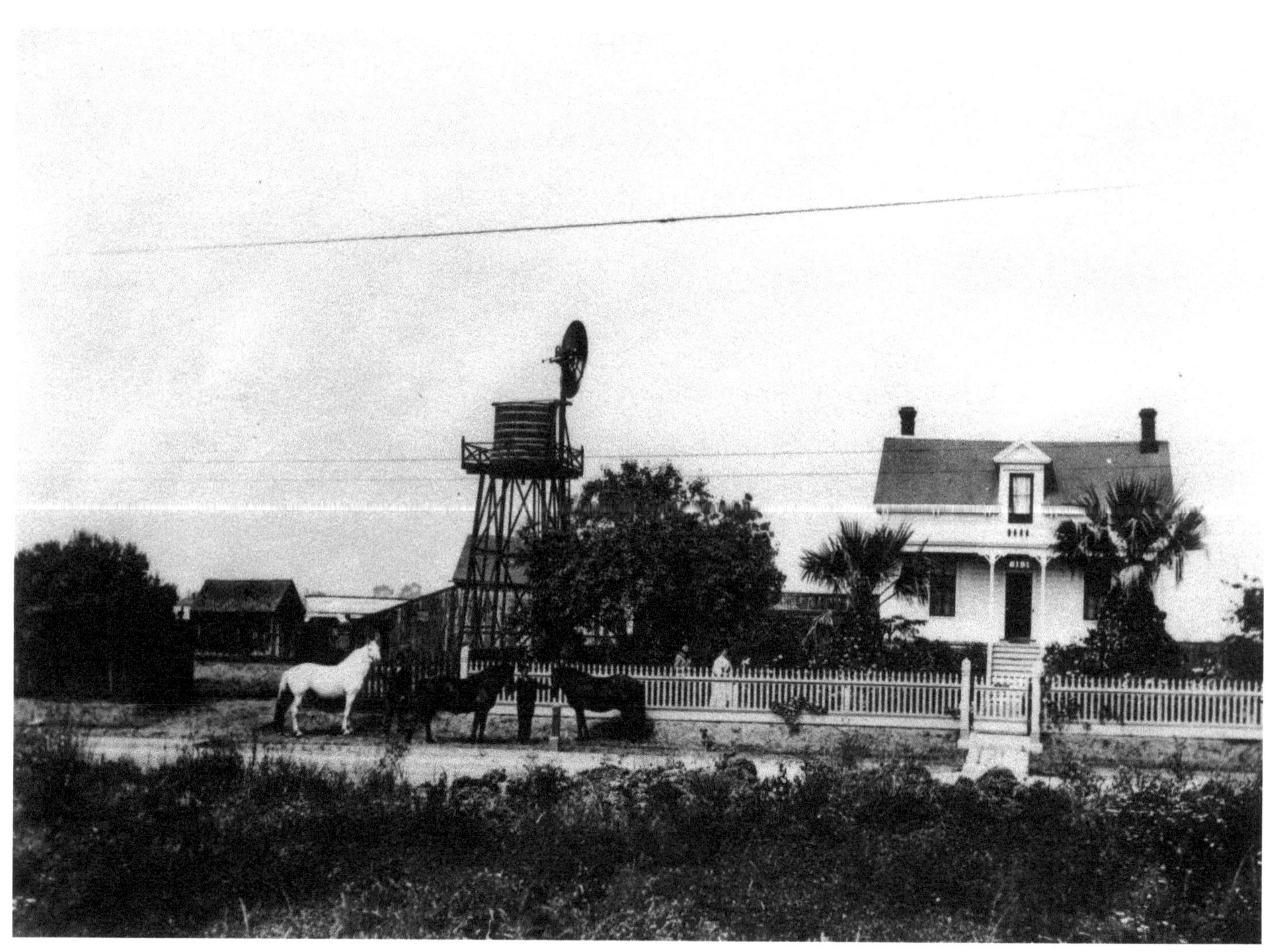

Jean Baptiste Poirier, a member of the Sons of Liberty (Fils de Liberté), fled from Canada after a rebellion in 1837 against British rule there. He came west to settle on land north of the original town of Oakland that he acquired from Vicente Peralta. The first structures were built in 1851 and are visible left of the main house in this photograph by Carleton Watkins, around 1872.

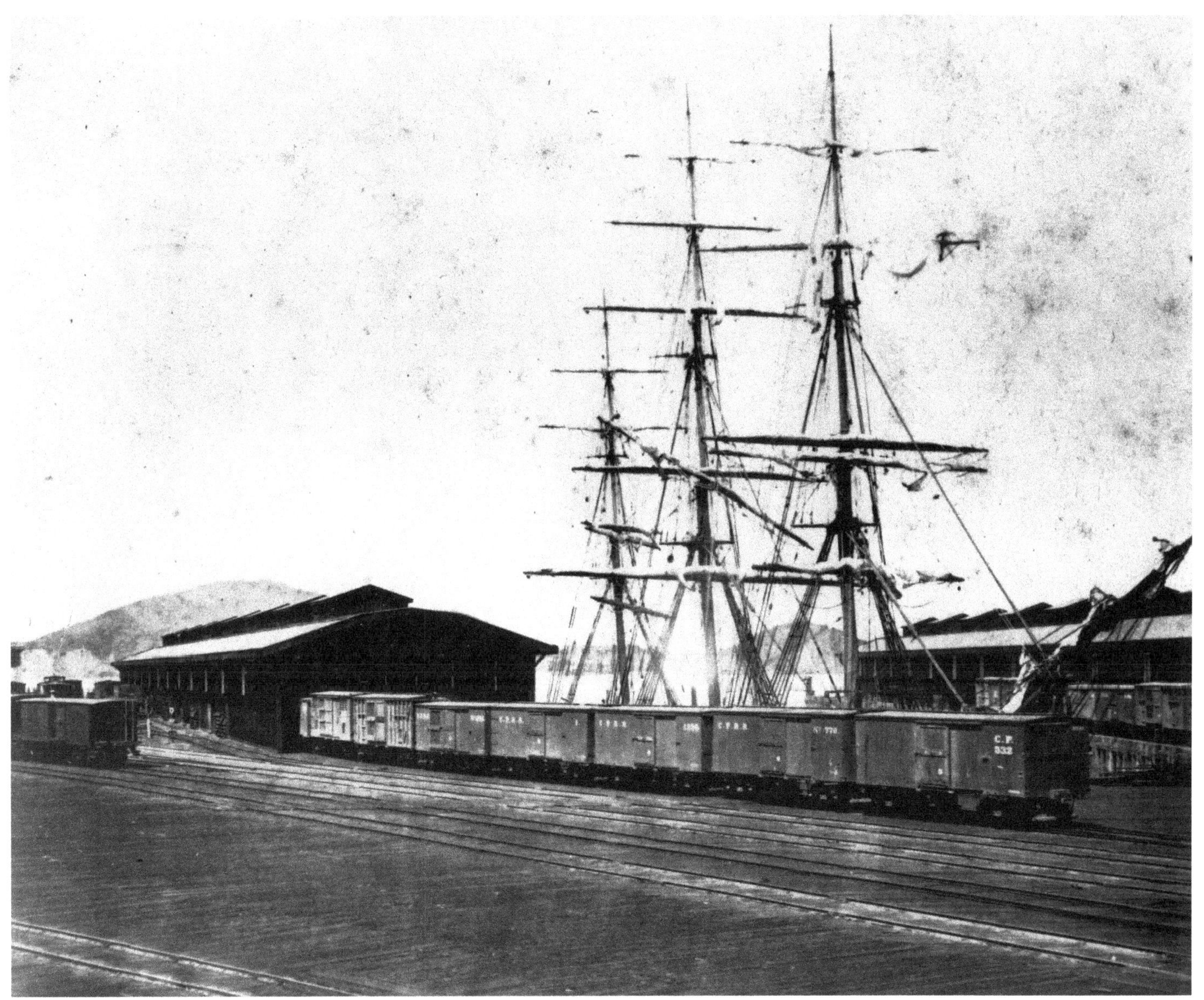

Abraham Lincoln made it a campaign pledge to bring a railroad across the west to reach the Pacific Ocean. The Civil War would interrupt those plans, but only five years after the surrender of the Confederate forces, Lincoln's promise was realized, with Oakland chosen as the western terminus for the railroad. The transcontinental trip ended at this modest wooden wharf. A camera documented the scene there sometime in the early 1870s.

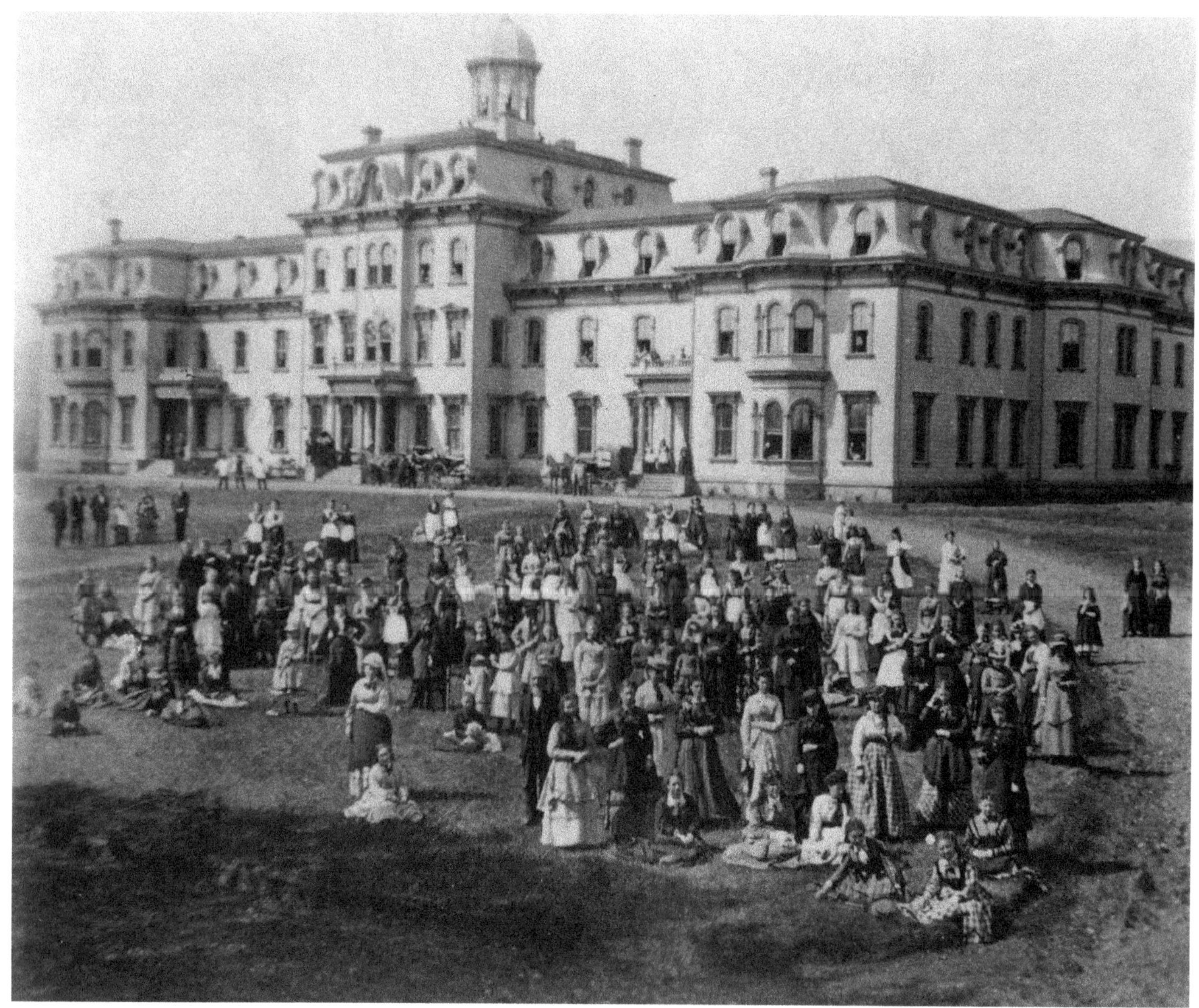

Presbyterian minister Cyrus Mills and his wife, Susan, moved their seminary from Benicia to a new campus in what is now East Oakland in 1871. The new campus and its student body are shown in this photograph from 1873. The building remains the centerpiece of the campus of Mills College, one of the nation's most prestigious women's colleges.

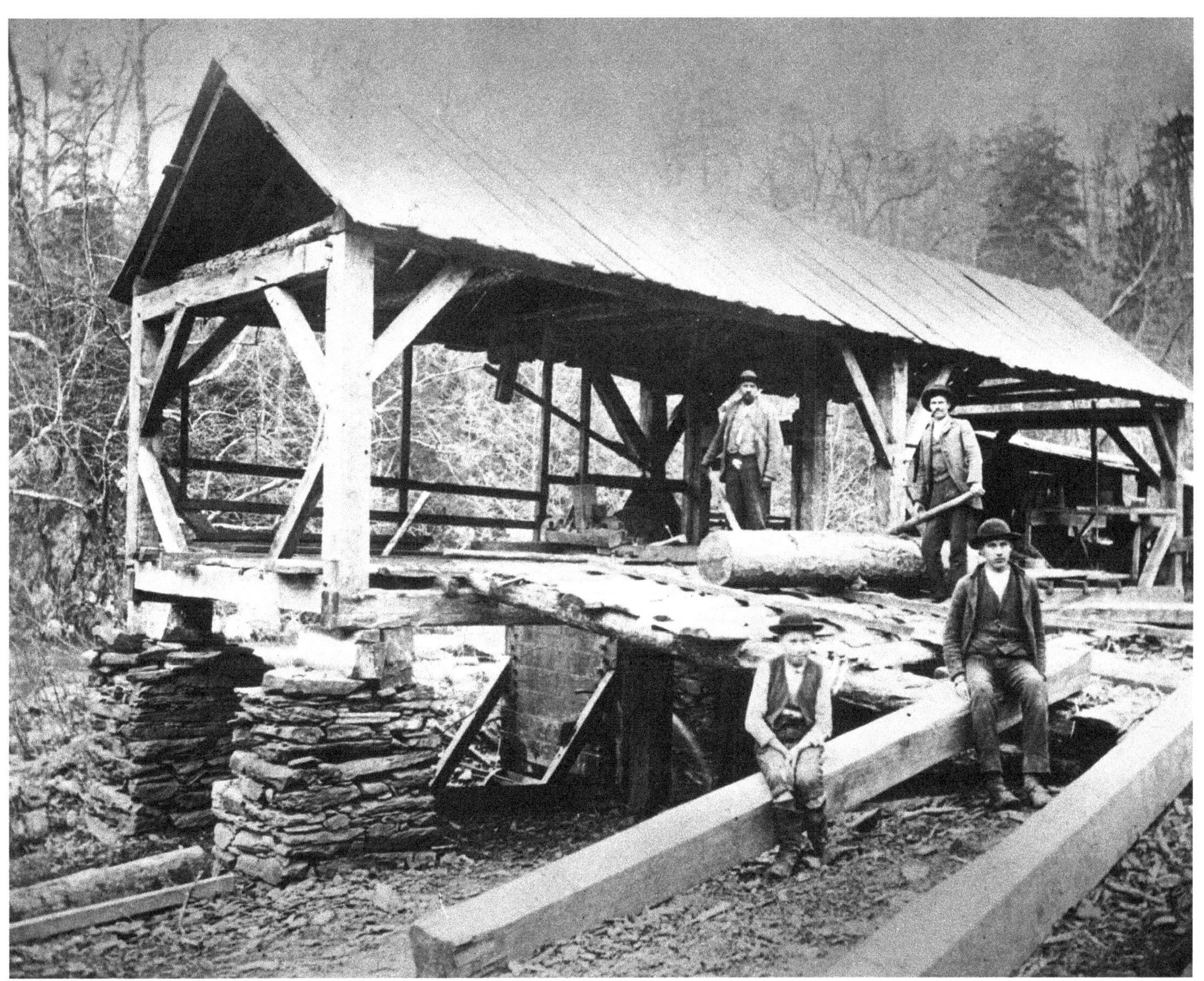

The big trees had all been cut when a photographer captured this image of the sawmill on Palo Seco Creek in the hills above East Oakland. It was used to mill the giant logs harvested from an extensive forest of coastal redwoods, some more that 2,000 years old with heights estimated to exceed 200 feet. The old-growth redwoods were cut by 1860 with the lumber used to build, and then rebuild, San Francisco as fires continued to sweep through the city.

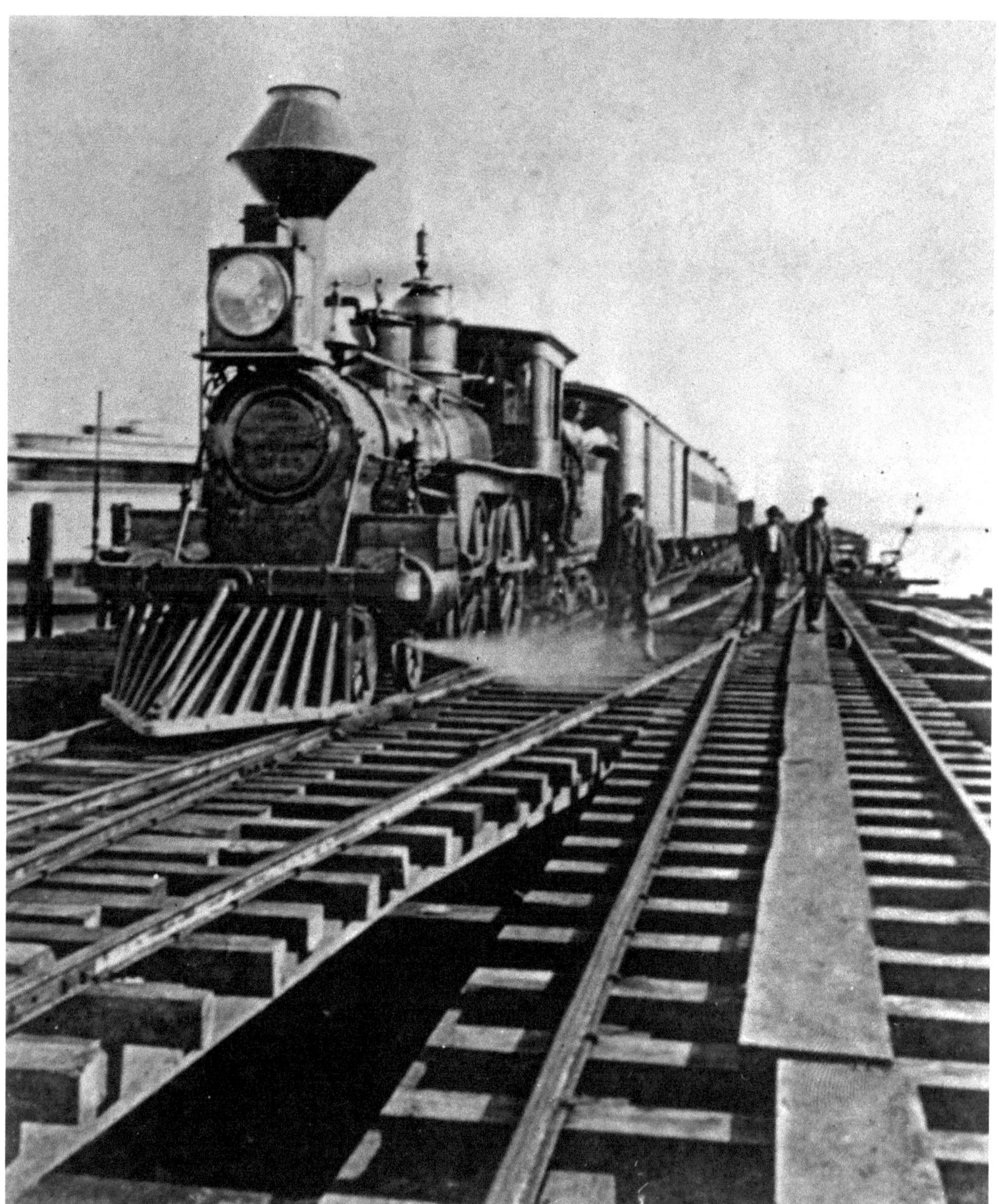

A ferry brought passengers from the wharf in Oakland the rest of the way to San Francisco. To shorten the ride by ferry, a wooden pier was extended far out into the bay. A train is shown as it prepares to head through Oakland for points east sometime in the 1880s.

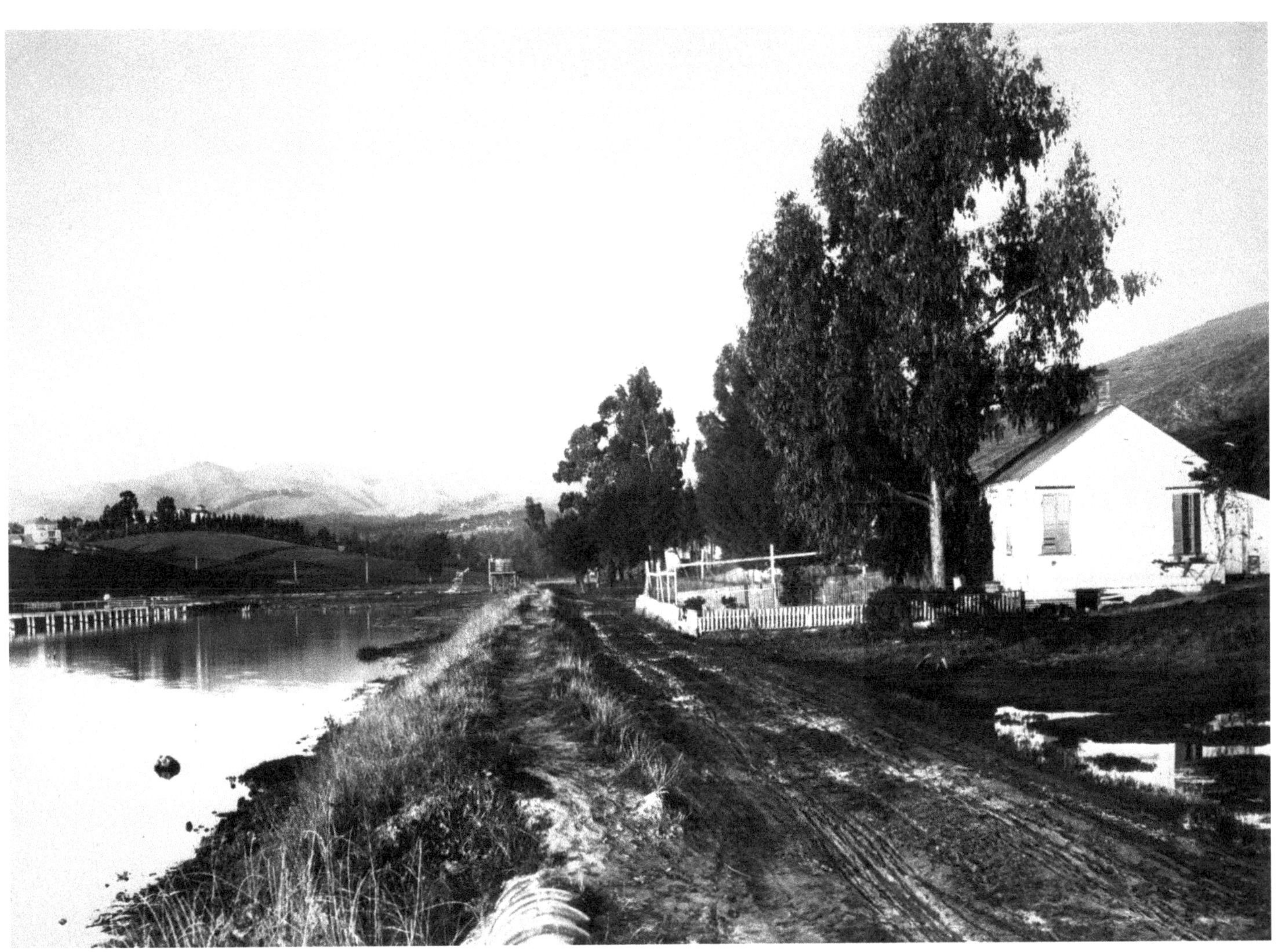

A dam erected in 1869 interrupted low tides, converting a slough formed by the convergence of several creeks flowing from the foothill slopes of the Contra Costa Range into the brackish but beautiful Lake Peralta, a name that never stuck. Its shores became a prized location for wealthy settlers, including this home, attested to be that of one of the city's earliest millionaires, dam builder Anthony Chabot. Photographer Frank B. Rodolph captured this scene in the early 1880s.

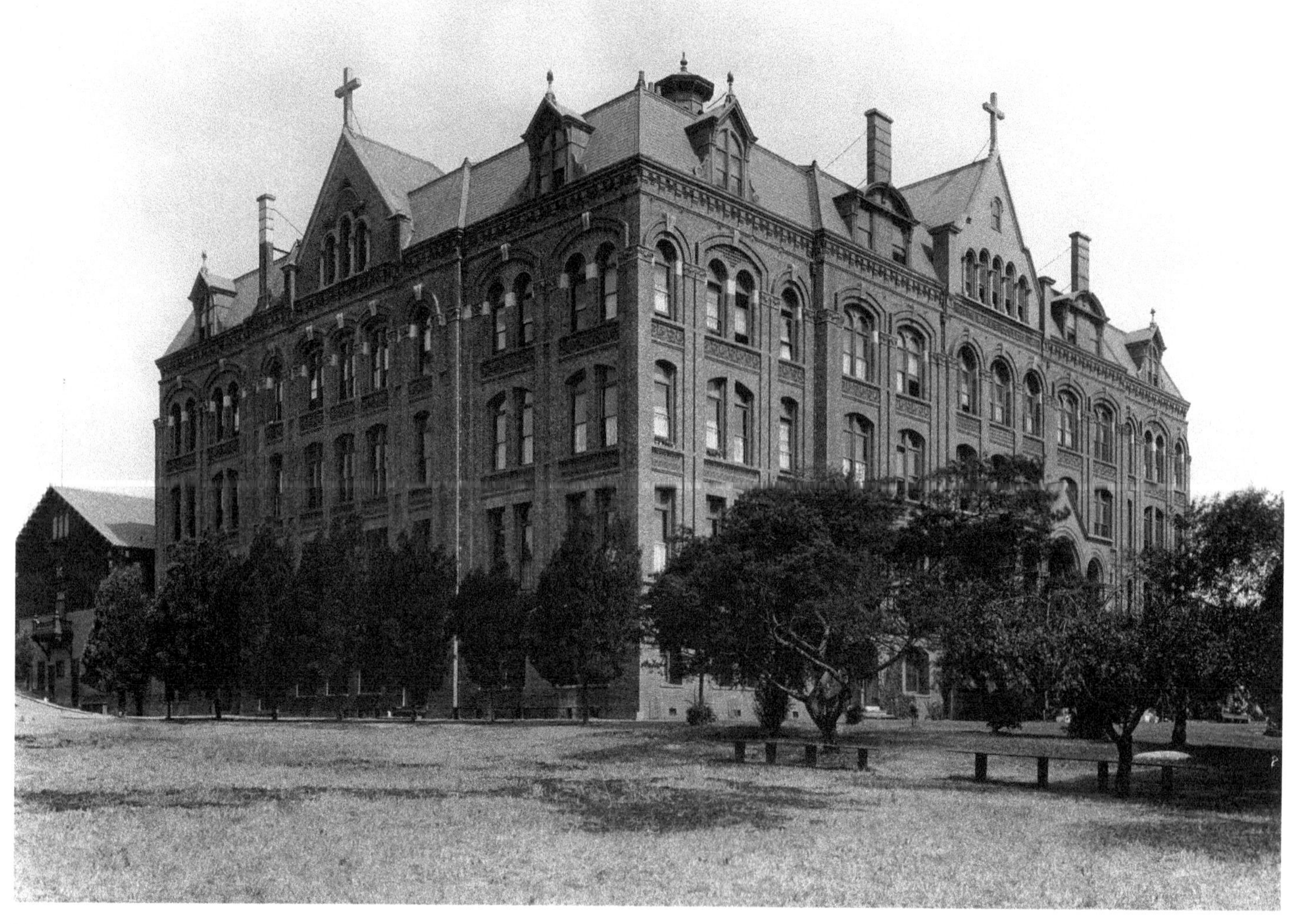

The campus of St. Mary's College of California moved to Oakland in 1869, into a regal structure on Broadway known affectionately as "the Old Brickyard." It quickly became known for its athletes. Harry Hooper went on to the Boston Red Sox, earning a spot in the Baseball Hall of Fame. Coach Slip Madigan made his "Galloping" Gaels a dominant force in college football during the 1920s.

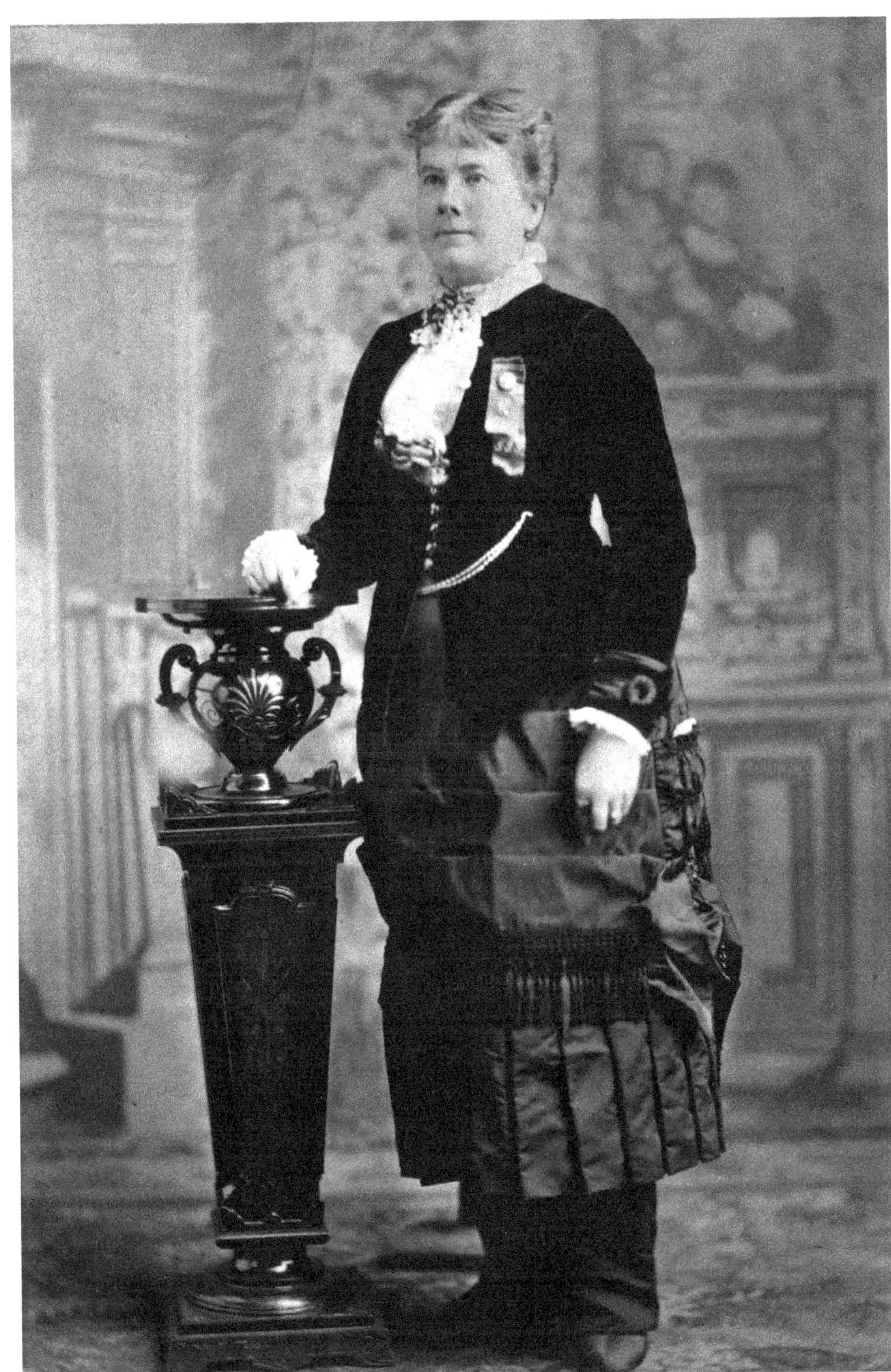

Suffrage for women achieved broad-based support in Oakland. One of its leading proponents, Marietta "Lizzie Bell" Stow, launched a campaign for vice-president of the United States from her Oakland home, joining the ticket of the Equal Rights Party alongside presidential candidate Belva Ann Lockwood in 1884.

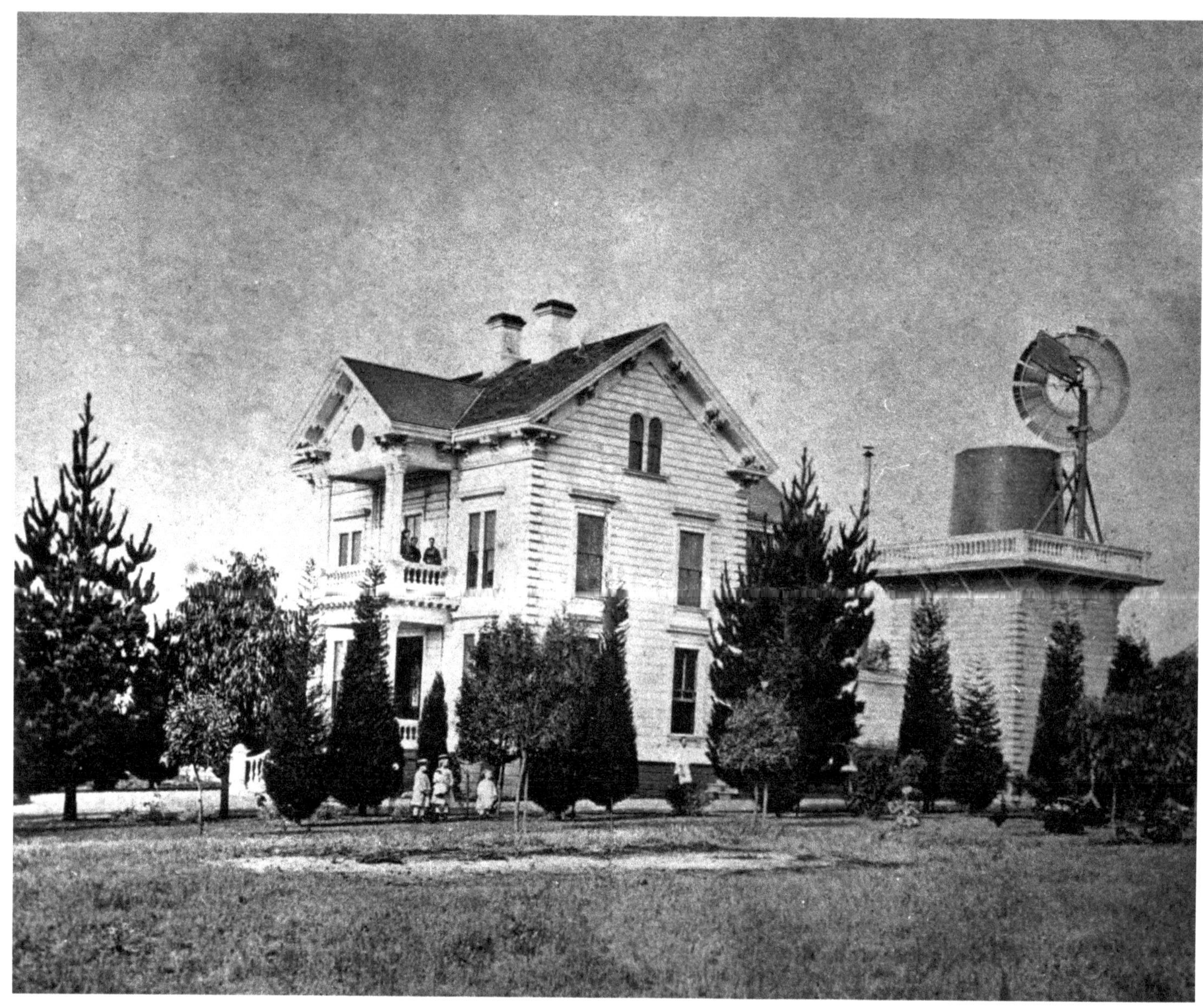

Oakland's scenic beauty attracted a growing community of artists, including painter Thomas Hill, who occupied this house near a creek that flows from the city's oldest cemetery. Hill was an important contributor to a school of landscape painters who produced glowing and romantic representations of California scenery that helped to lure newcomers from the east.

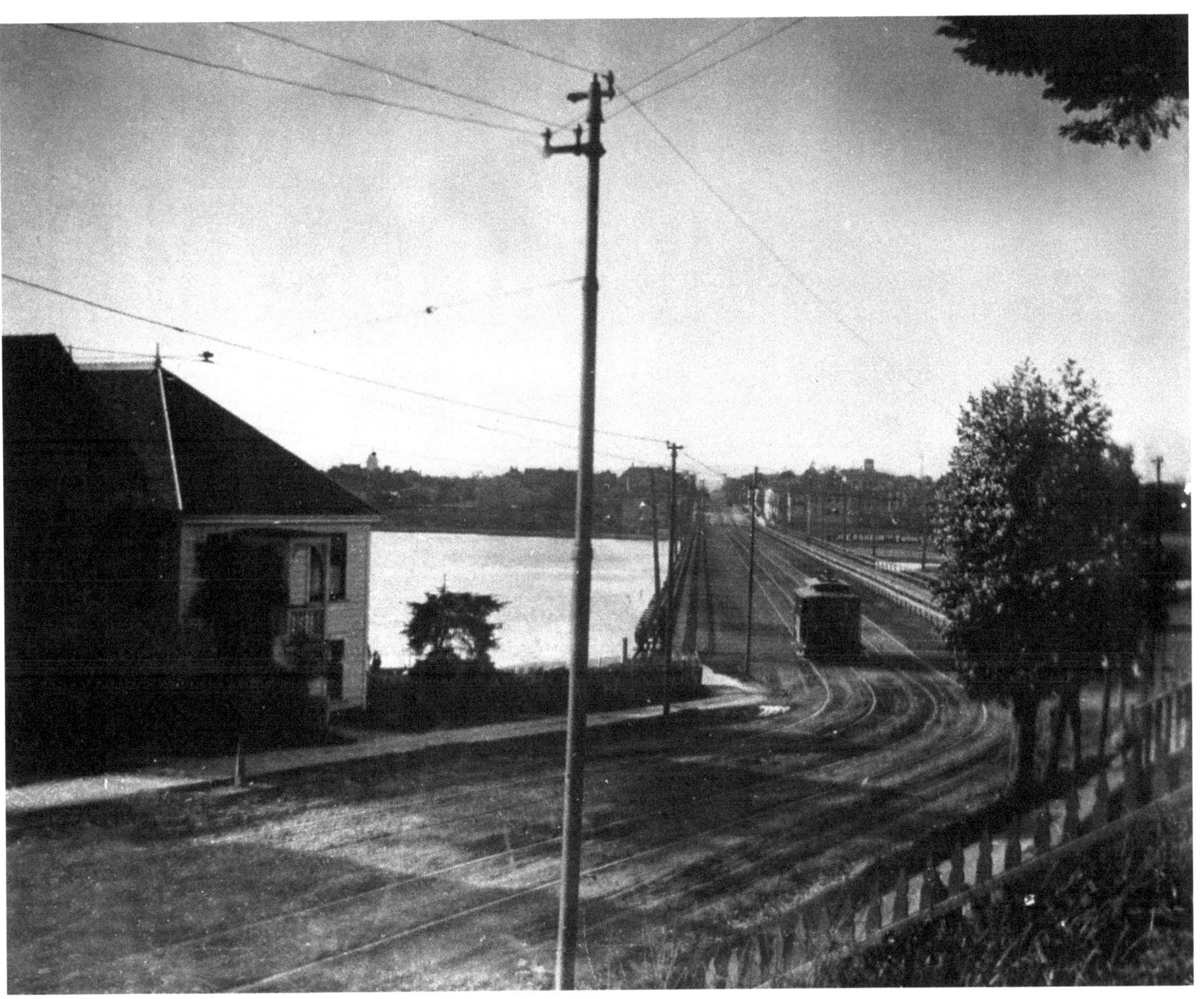

Public funding built the Eighth Street bridge to allow free passage to the east from downtown Oakland. It freed residents from the exorbitant tolls charged by an earlier alternative at 12th Street, financed by Oakland's first mayor to bolster his personal fortune. The bridge at Eighth Street quickly diverted all of the city's traffic from the old bridge, including the local streetcars.

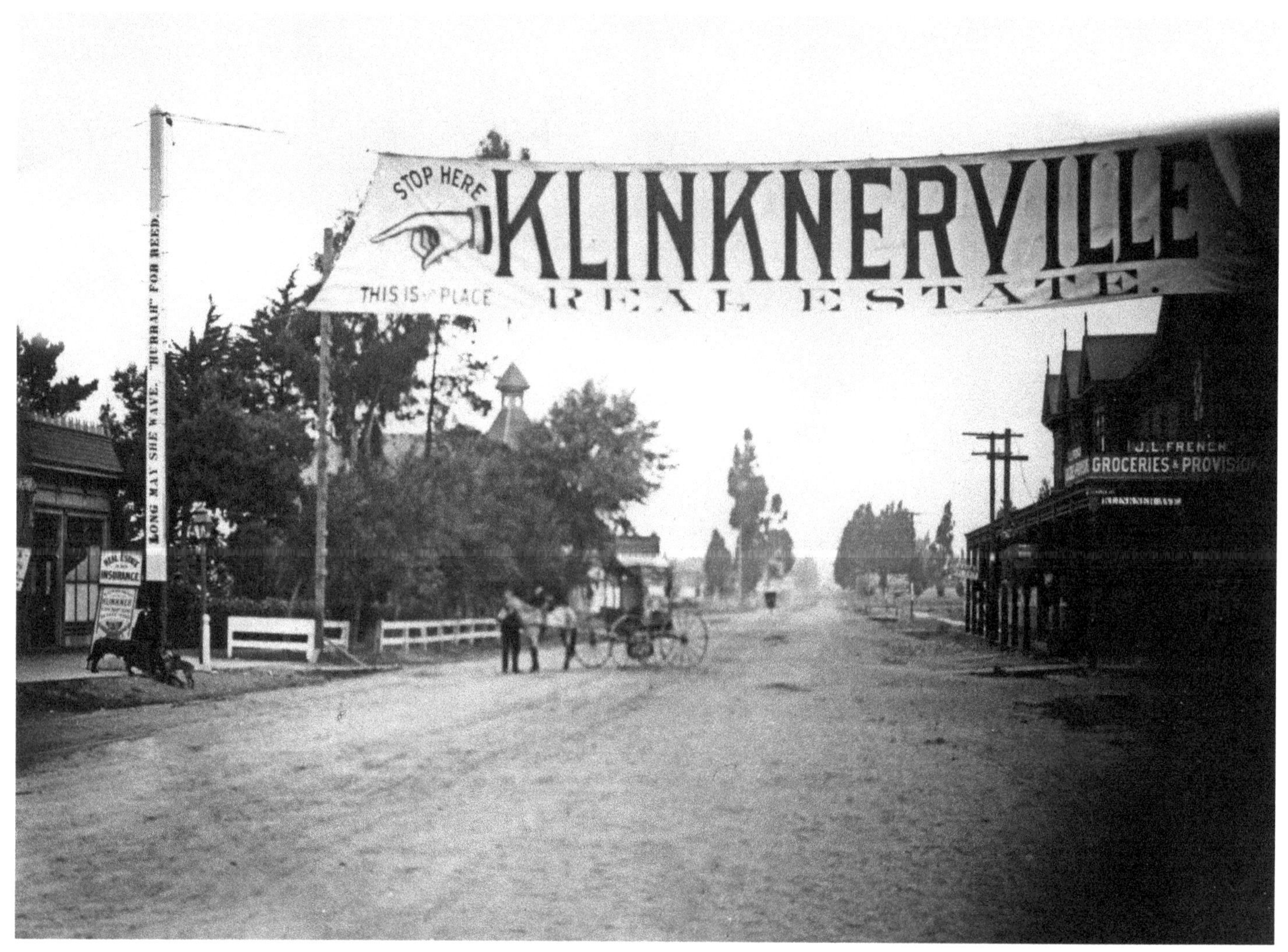

California has attracted more than its share of eccentric visionaries, Charles A. Klinkner among them. After earning a surprisingly large fortune manufacturing rubber stamps in San Francisco, Klinkner acquired a large tract of pasture land on the northern edge of Oakland, proclaimed it a town that he named for himself, and subdivided the land into home sites. The town was never realized and the houses were quickly absorbed into Oakland.

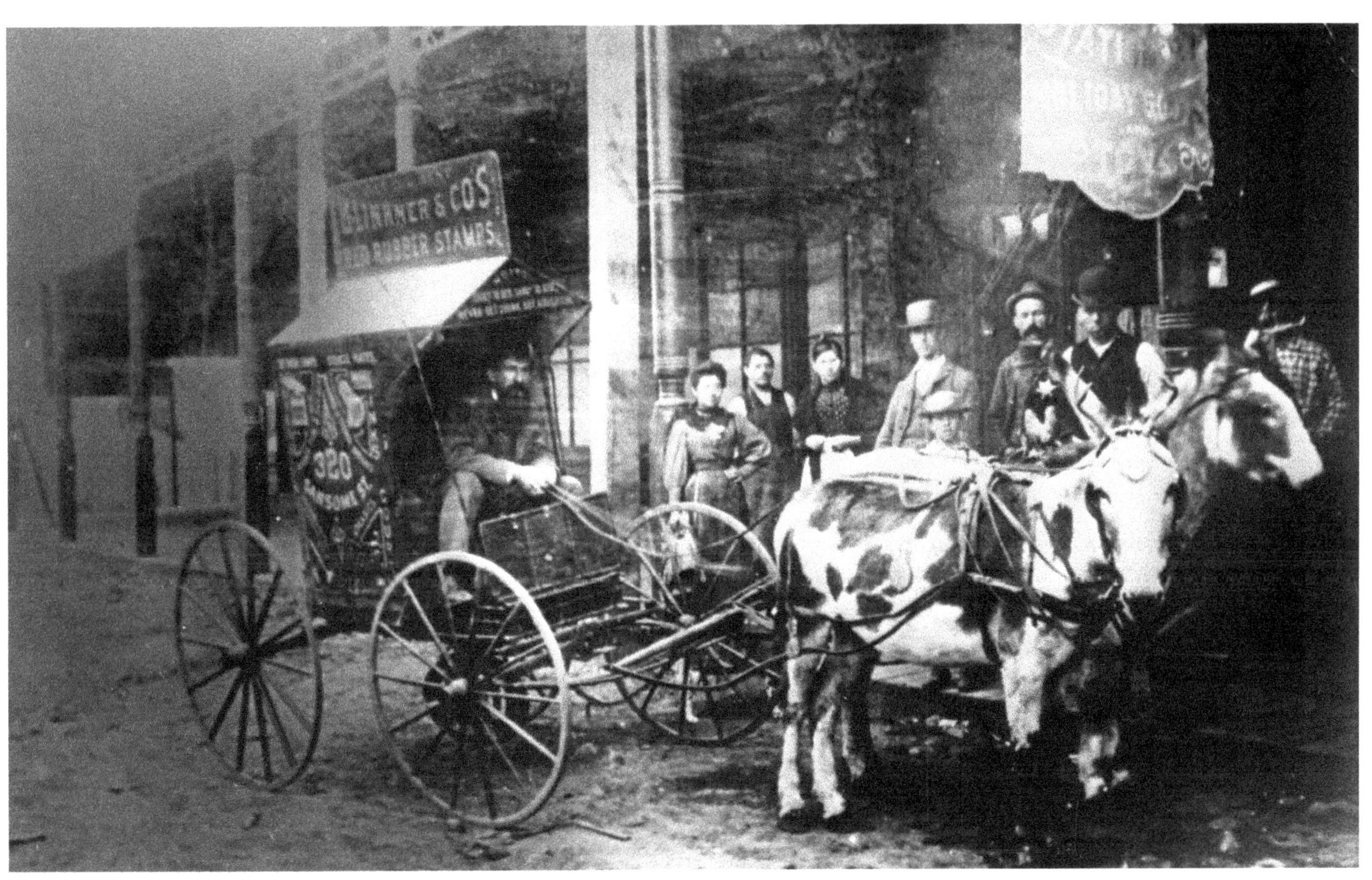

Every Fourth of July, Charles A. Klinkner would hitch up his wagon bearing signage that advertised his rubber-stamp business, paint his mules red, white, and blue, and parade through Oakland. On St. Patrick's Day, the mules were painted green. Klinkner poses here with the wagon and his family for a photographer sometime in the 1880s.

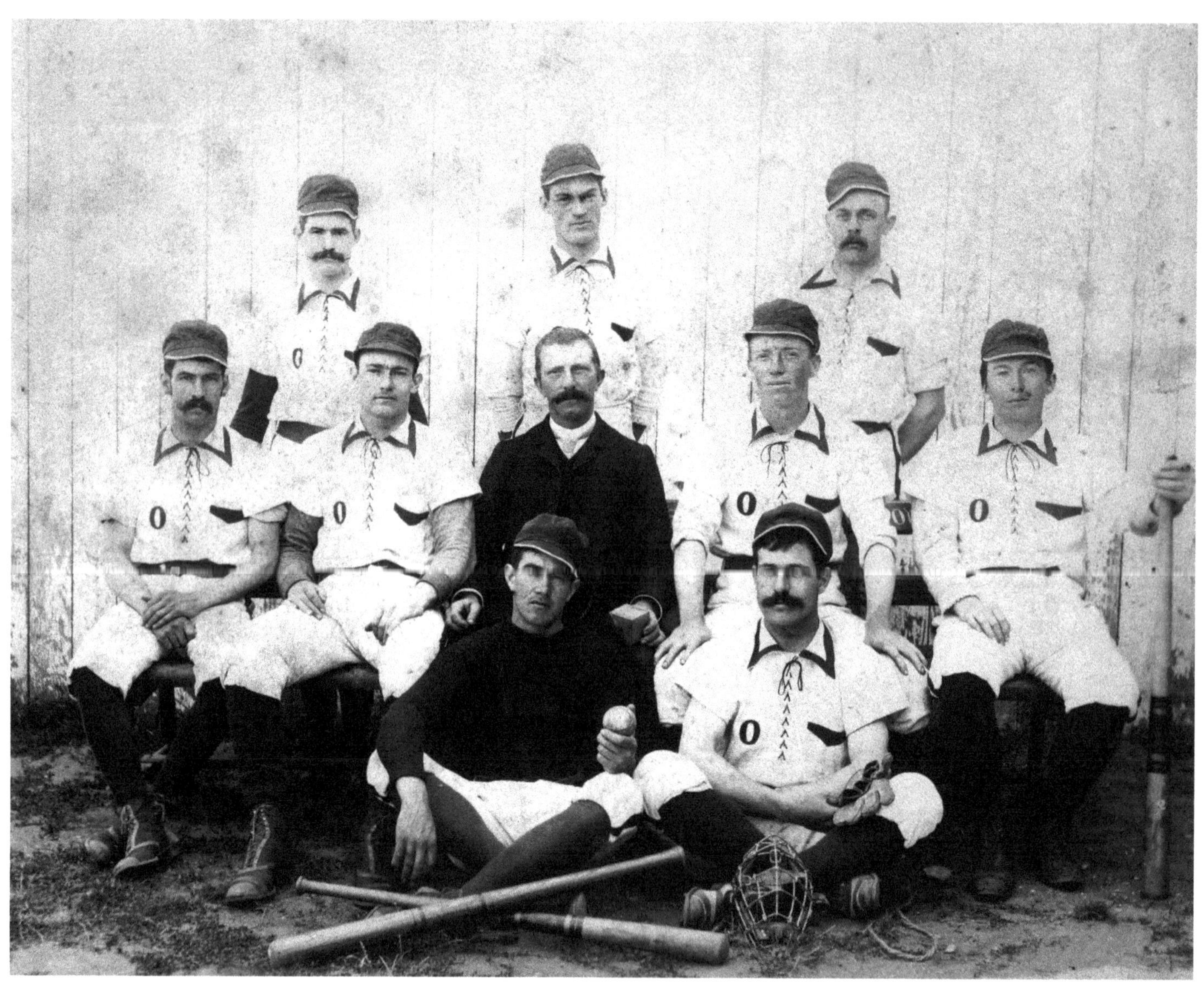

The baseball team sponsored by Oakland retailers Greenhood & Moran won repeated championships in the early Pacific leagues. Its ace pitcher, George van Haltren of West Oakland, went east as "the California Wonder," quickly endearing himself with the fans and reaching superstar status.

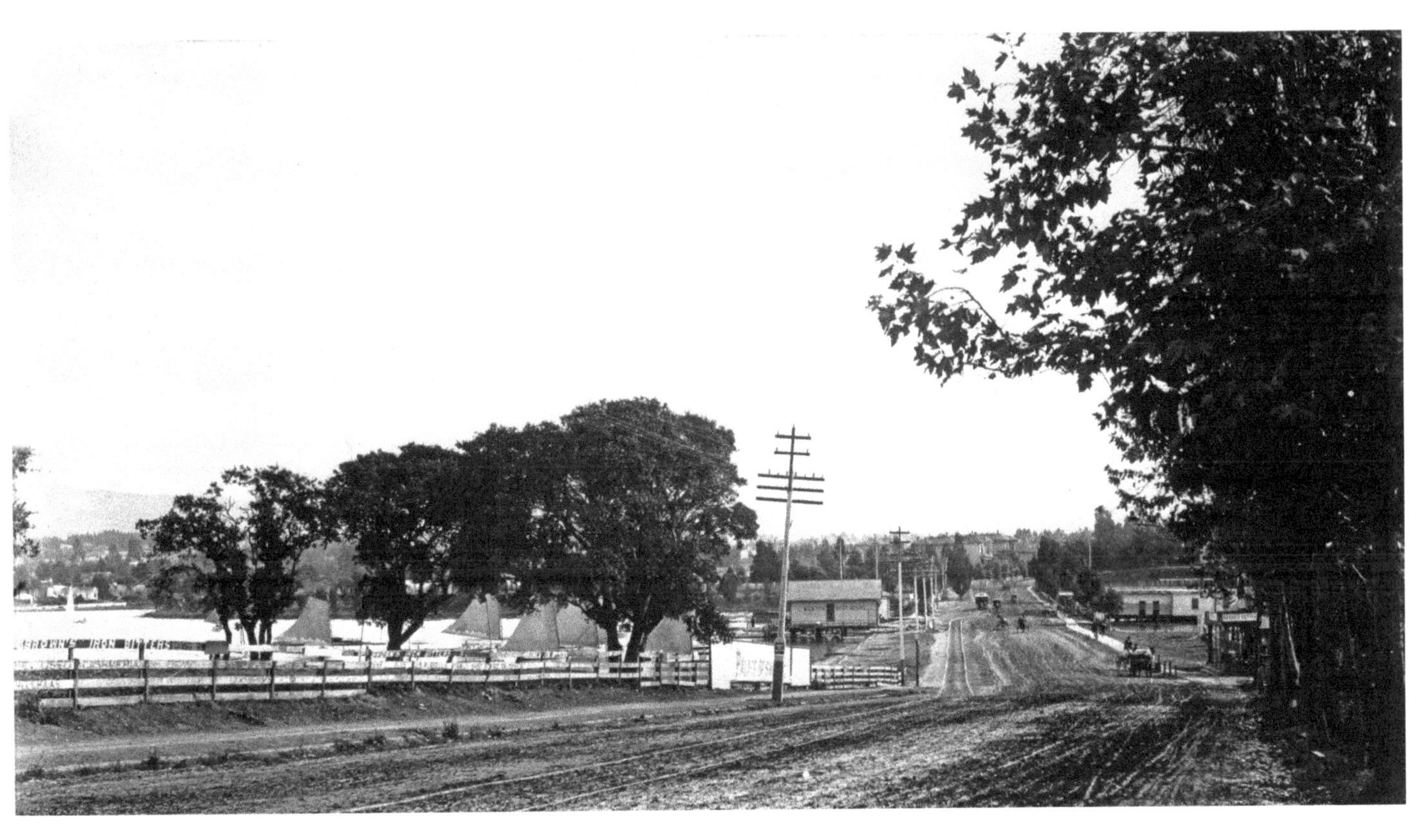

Improvements to the dam that formed Lake Peralta made it the primary east-west traffic artery. Residents preferred to call the lake for the builder of the dam, a very large local physician named Samuel Merritt. In view are the Bon Ton Boat House at center, Rosso's Cottage at right, and signage along the board fence at left advertising the remedy Brown's Iron Bitters.

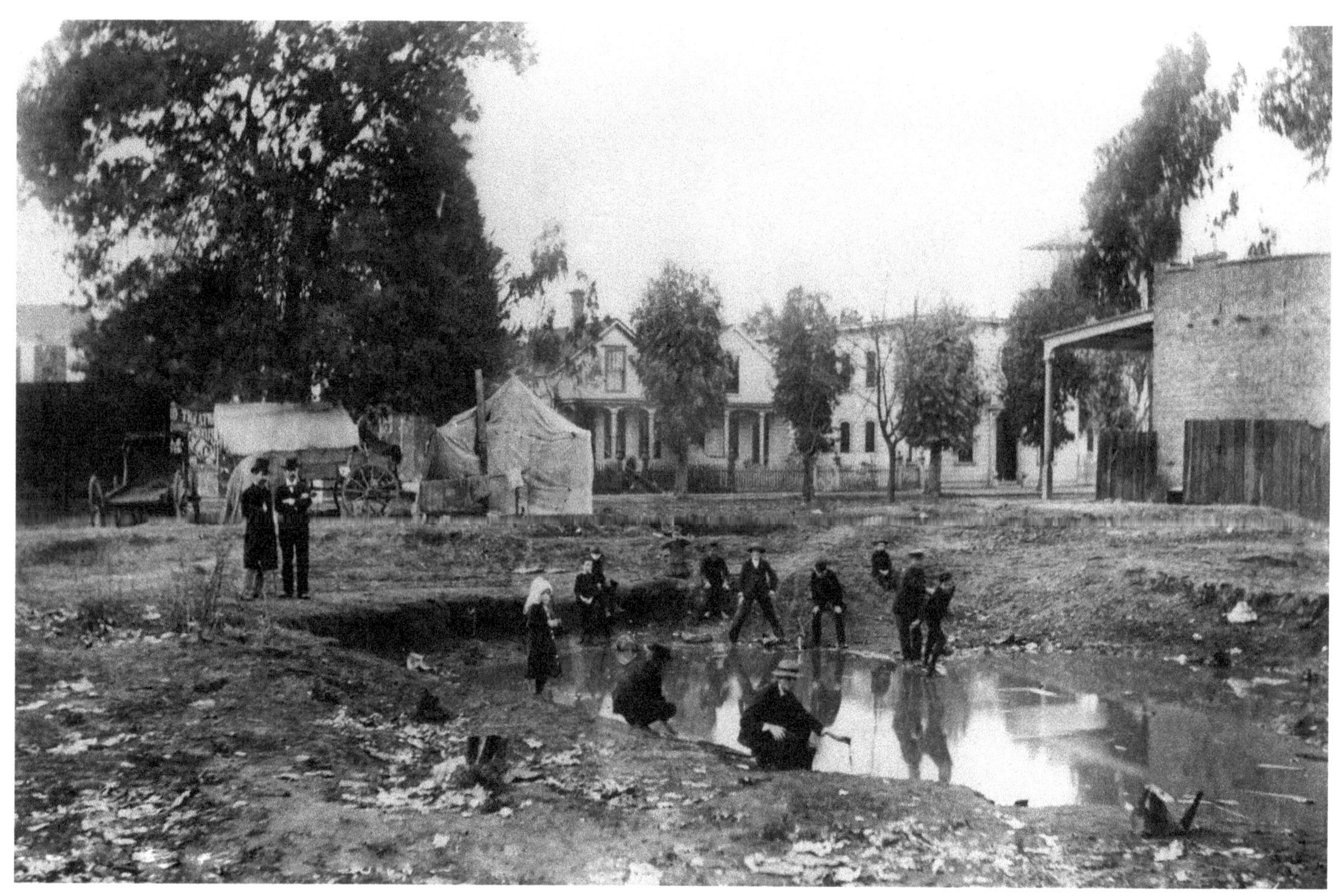

The city's playgrounds were not yet in place in 1880 when this picture was taken, so the city's children found their own opportunities for recreation, appropriating this pond at Tenth and Washington streets for their adventures.

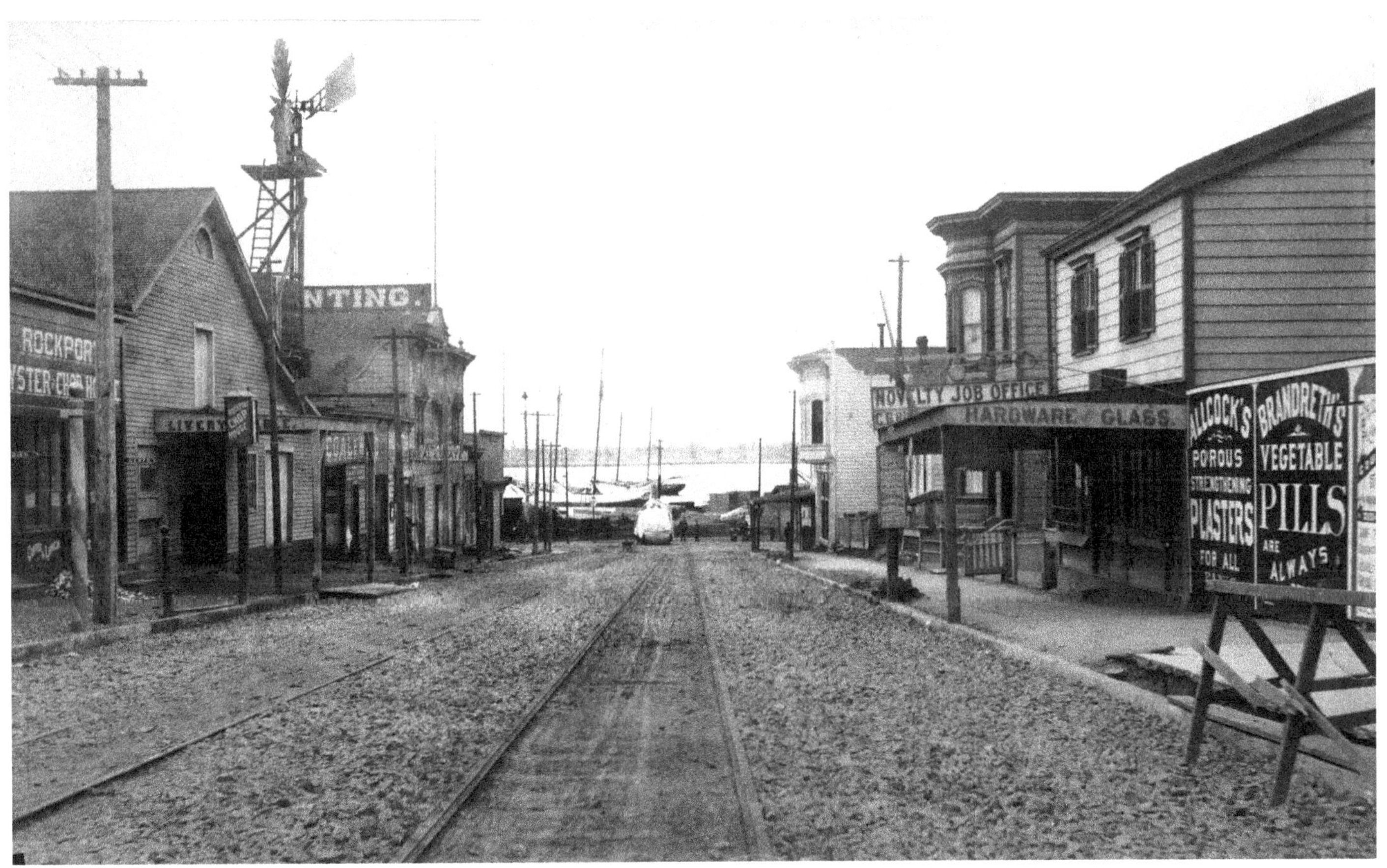

Early settler James Larue, a devout Presbyterian from Michigan, took over existing operations at a wharf in the community of San Antonio used to ship hides from the ranch of the Peralta family. A picturesque commercial strip grew up at the wharf, photographed by Henry Domes in 1885. Domes had a photography studio on this block of 13th Avenue.

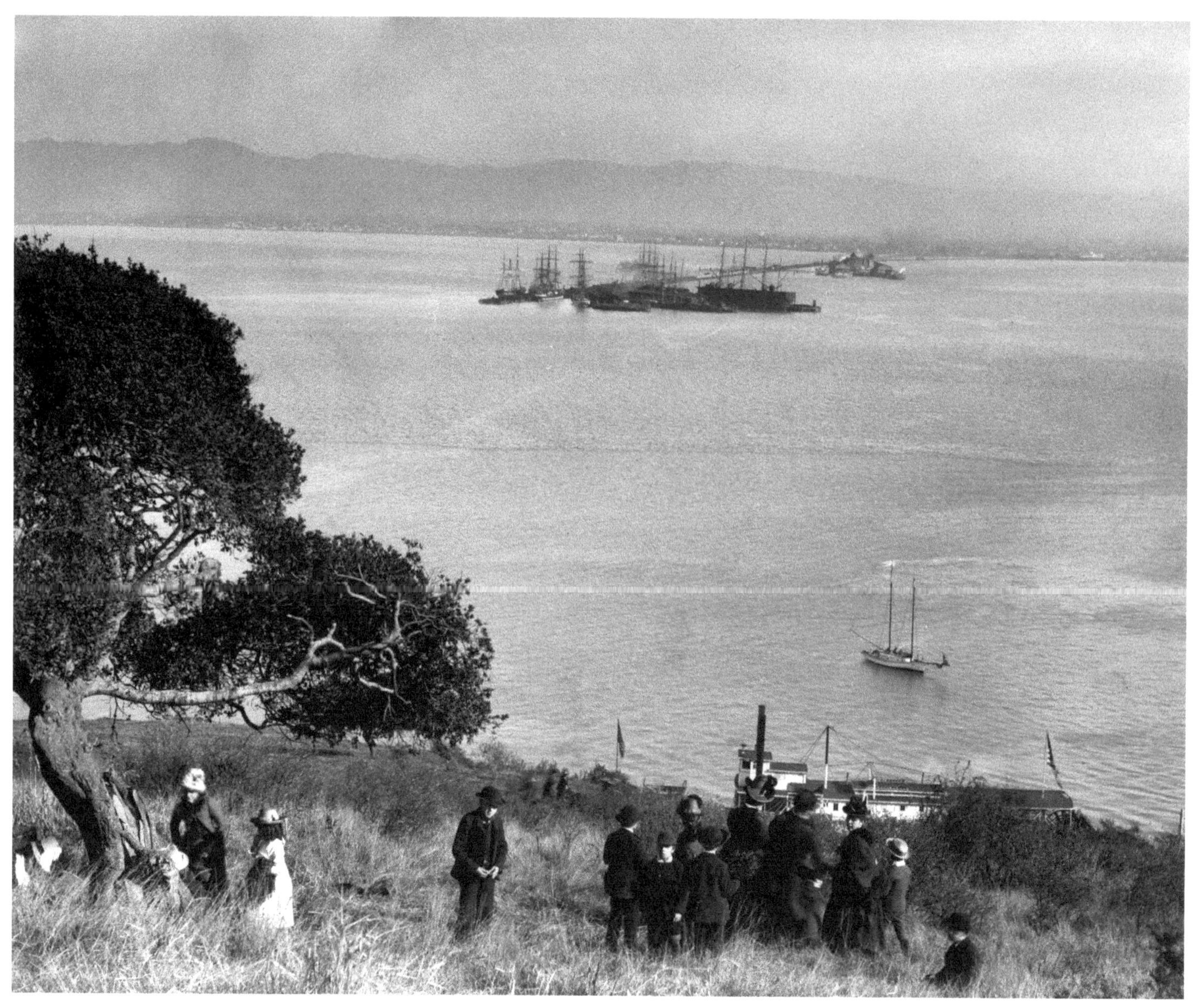

The railroad extended its Oakland wharf to the edge of deep water in San Francisco Bay to allow larger vessels to connect with its overland trains and to shorten the trip by ferry to the opposite shore. It appears as background in a photograph by Frank Rodolph of an outing to Yerba Buena Island around 1890.

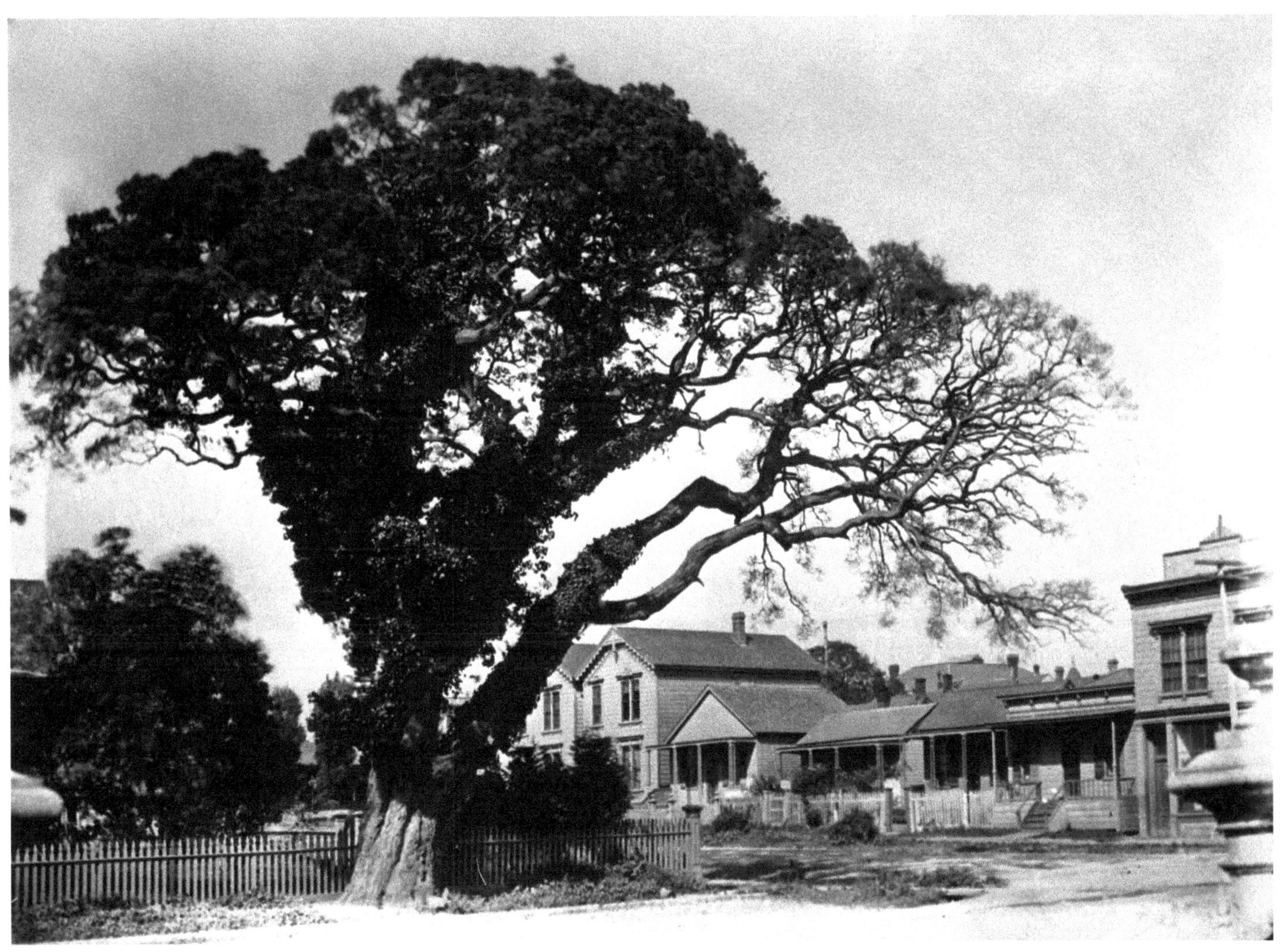

The lore of Oakland's pioneer settlers told how this massive live oak near the home of young author Bret Harte served as the survey landmark used to establish the north-south axes when cartographers established the street grid for the original town site.

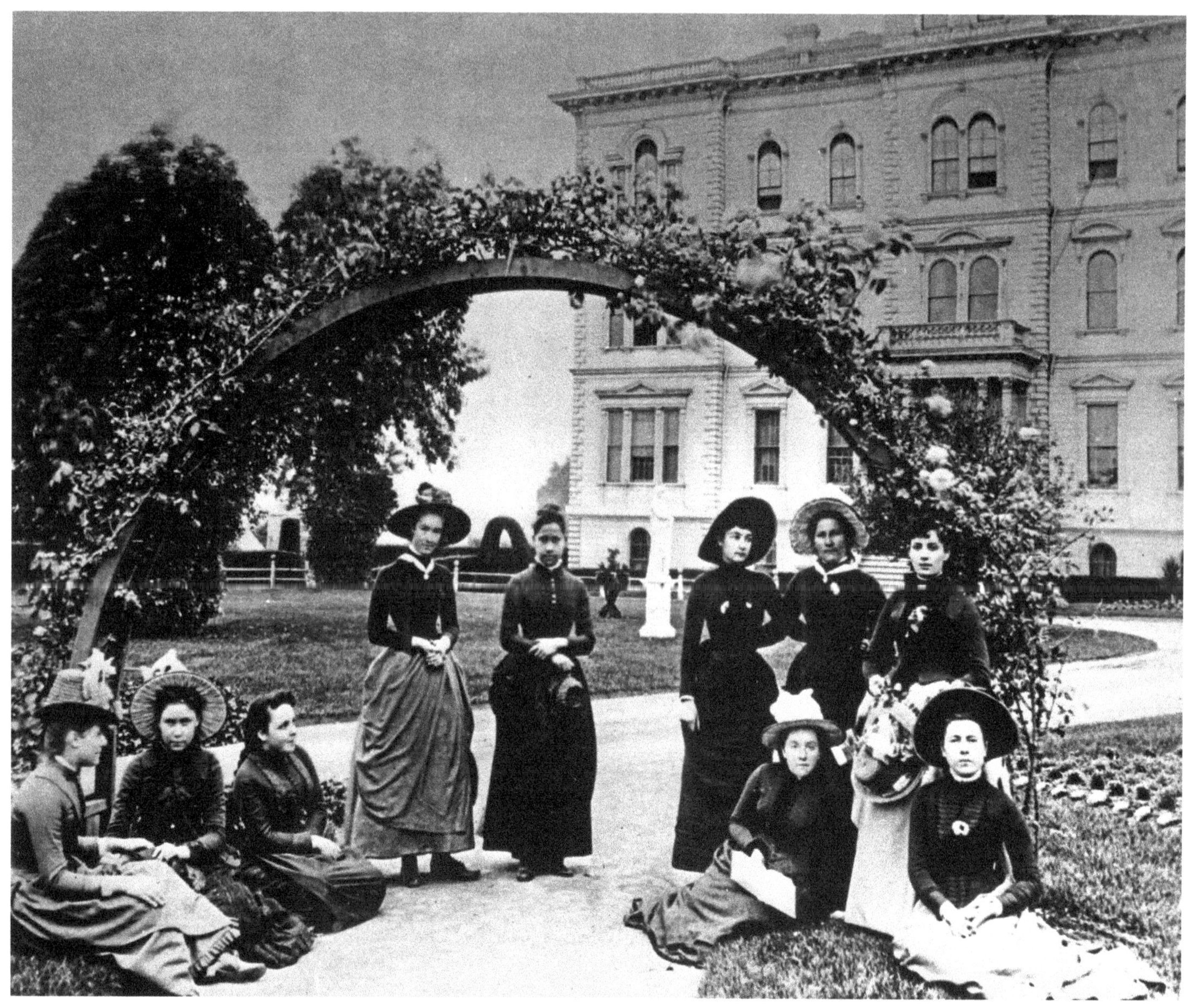

In 1868, a small group of French-Canadian nuns of the Sisters of the Holy Names established an academy for girls on a scenic spot overlooking Lake Merritt. Their Convent of Our Lady of the Sacred Heart grew to become Holy Names University. A group of graduates in the class of 1890 are shown posing on the original site of the school, now occupied by Kaiser Center.

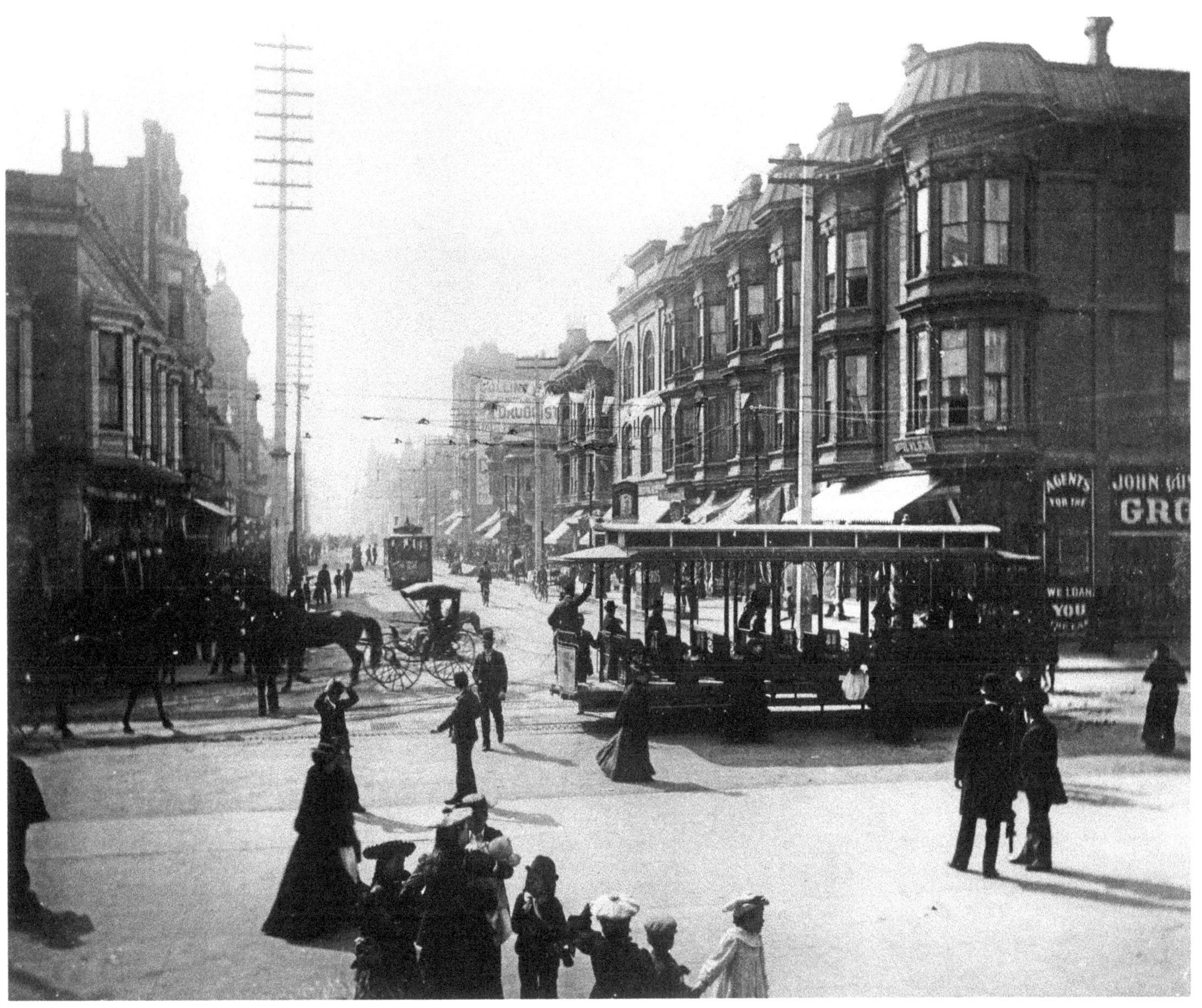

A stretch of Washington Street attracted shoppers from the entire East Bay region, serving as an incubator for some of the leading retail enterprises to emerge from Northern California, such as I. Magnin, Taft & Pennoyer, H. C. Capwell & Company, and the Ghirardelli Chocolate Company. This photograph was made around 1890.

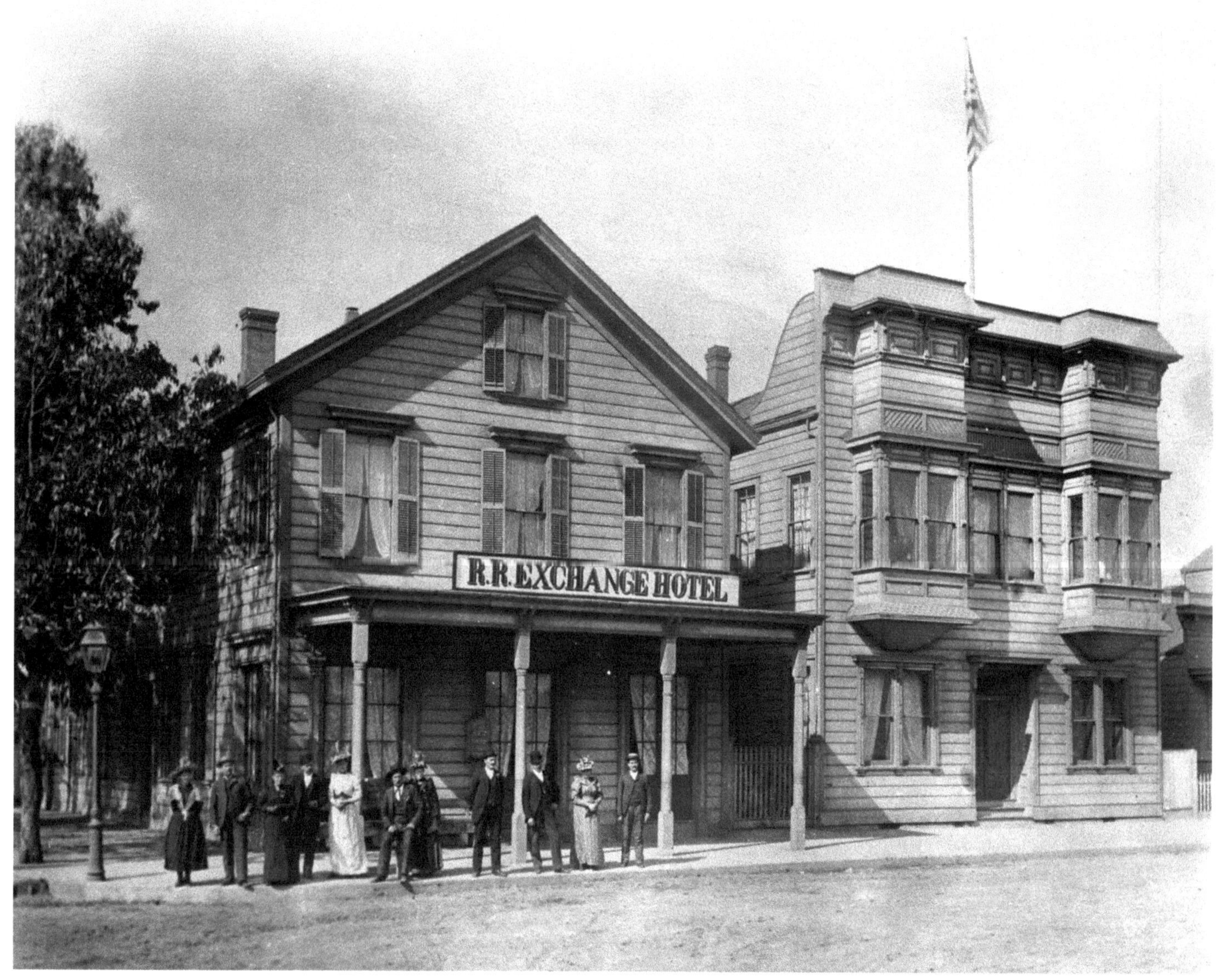

The Oakland Point neighborhood grew up around the terminus of the Southern Pacific Railroad, along Seventh Street where the tracks led to the wharf. Rooms at the Rail Road Exchange Hotel, shown here in 1894, offered lodging closest to ferries to San Francisco and the end of the line of the overland train.

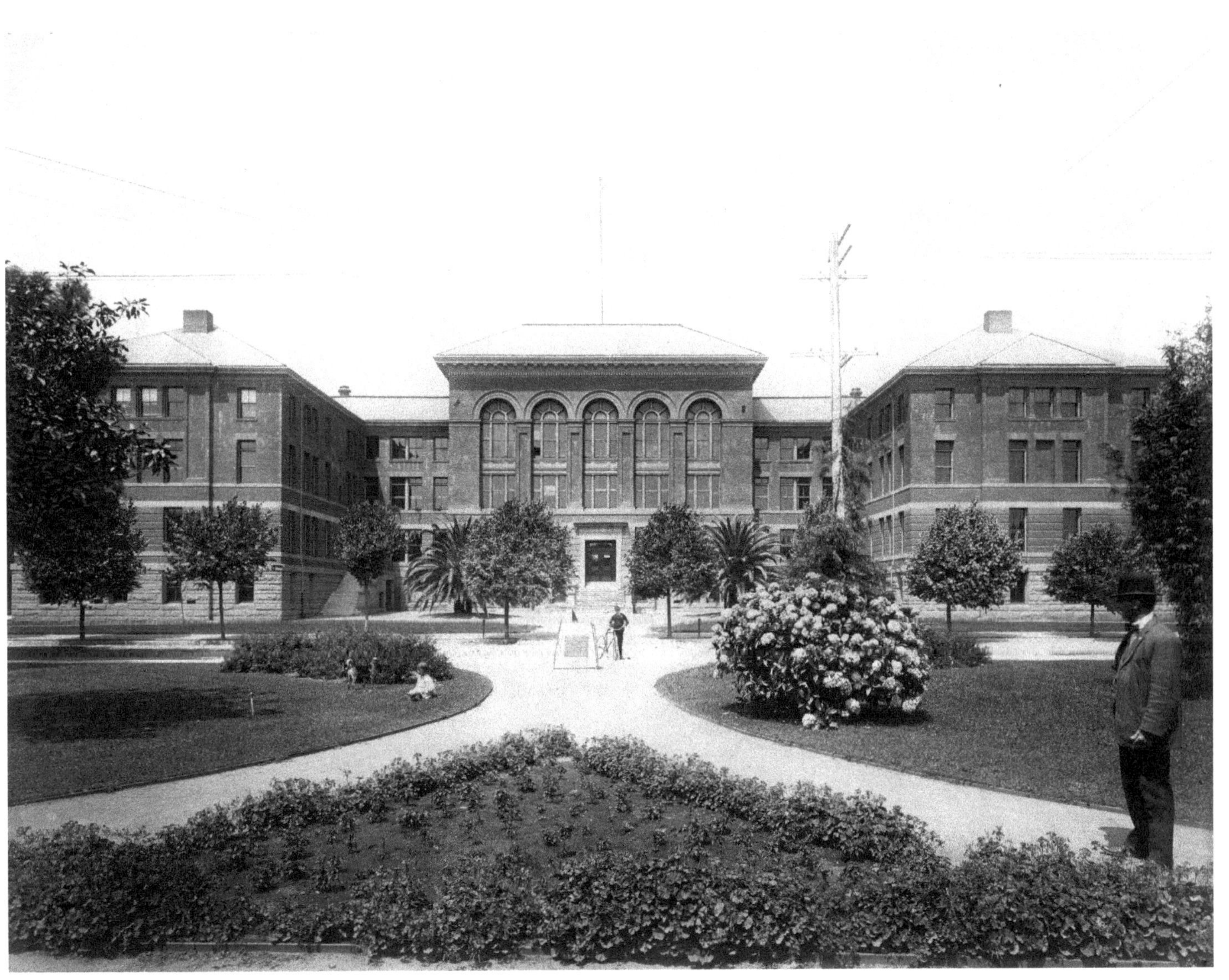

Oakland taxpayers financed the first public high school in California, established in 1871. A new building, shown here, was erected in 1895, occupying an entire city block of prime downtown real estate. Its faculty over the years has included numerous academic luminaries, led by poet Edwin Markham, whose poem "Man with the Hoe" was the most widely read poem of his lifetime after its syndication in the newspapers of William Randolph Hearst.

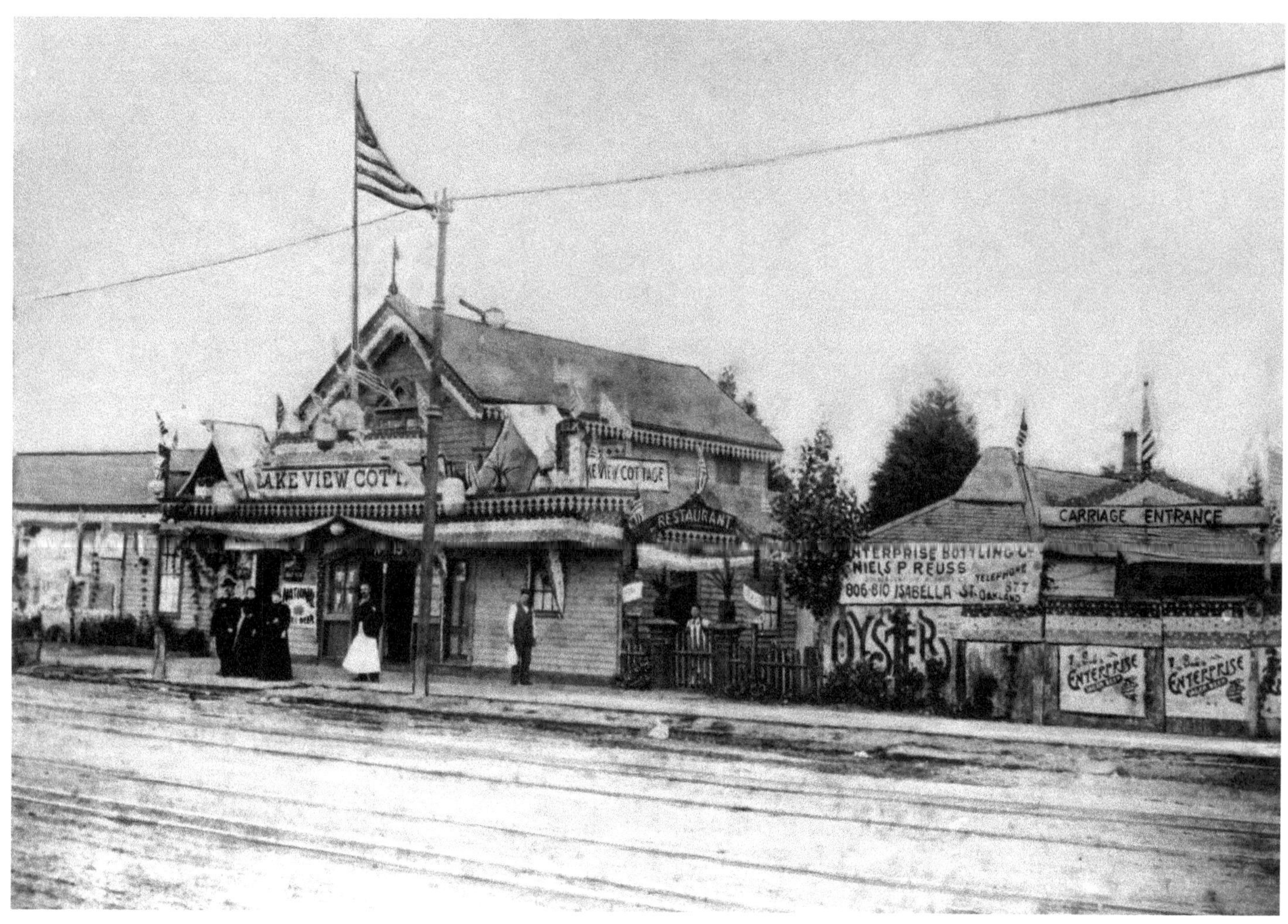

The waters of Lake Merritt became a popular attraction for sportsmen and recreation seekers. Lake View Cottage sat at the western end of the 12th Street Dam, adjacent a popular waterfront restaurant, Bellevue du Rendez-vous de Chasse, known popularly as the "House of Blazes" after its proprietor, Charles Blaise. This photograph, dated July 4, 1895, was touched up prior to publication in the *Oakland Tribune.*

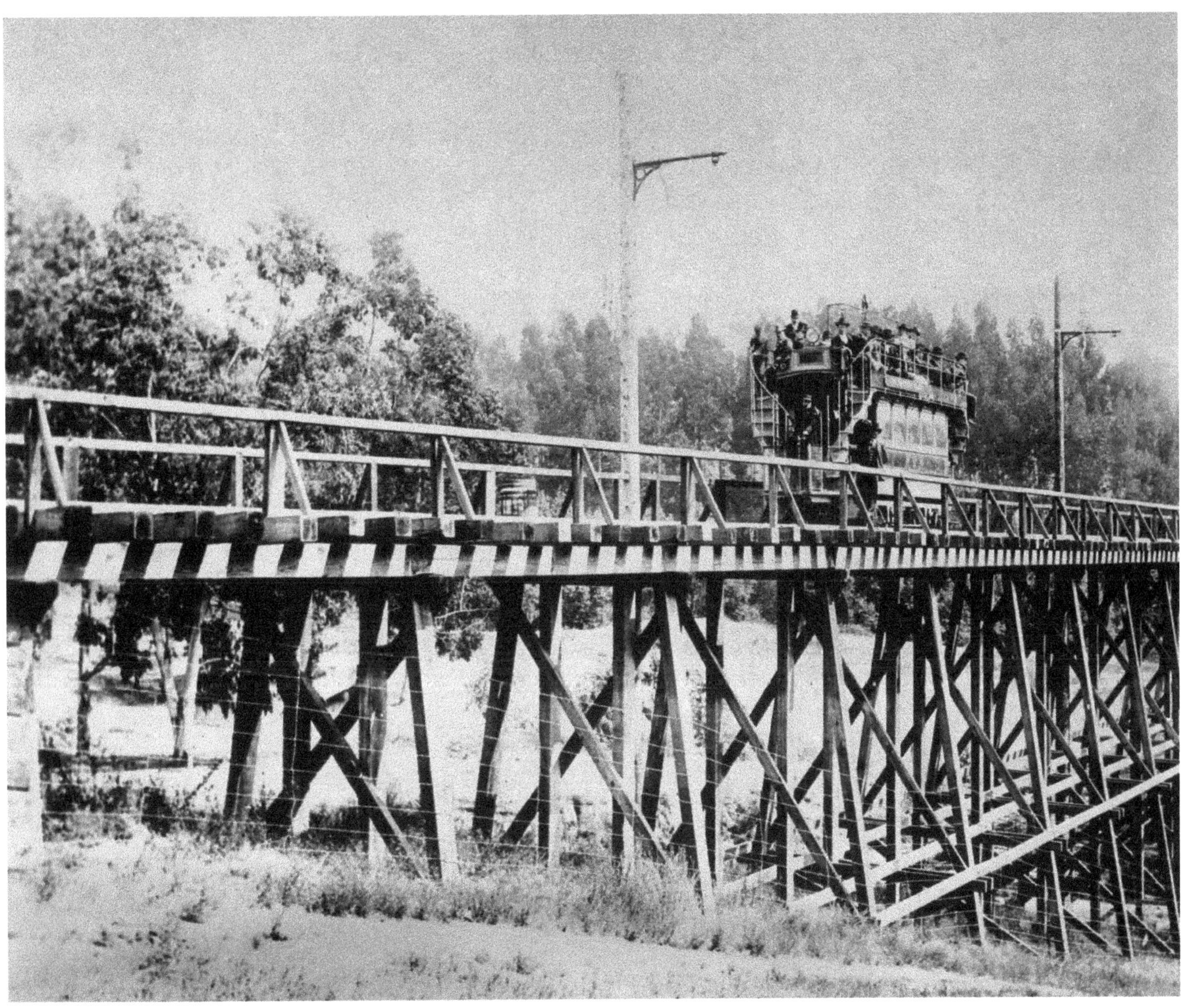

Access to rail service was an essential amenity for home buyers in the nineteenth century. To attract buyers to newly subdivided hillside tracts above Oakland, developers erected a long trestle over Indian Gulch. The neighborhood then became known as Trestle Glen, a reference to the railroad structure.

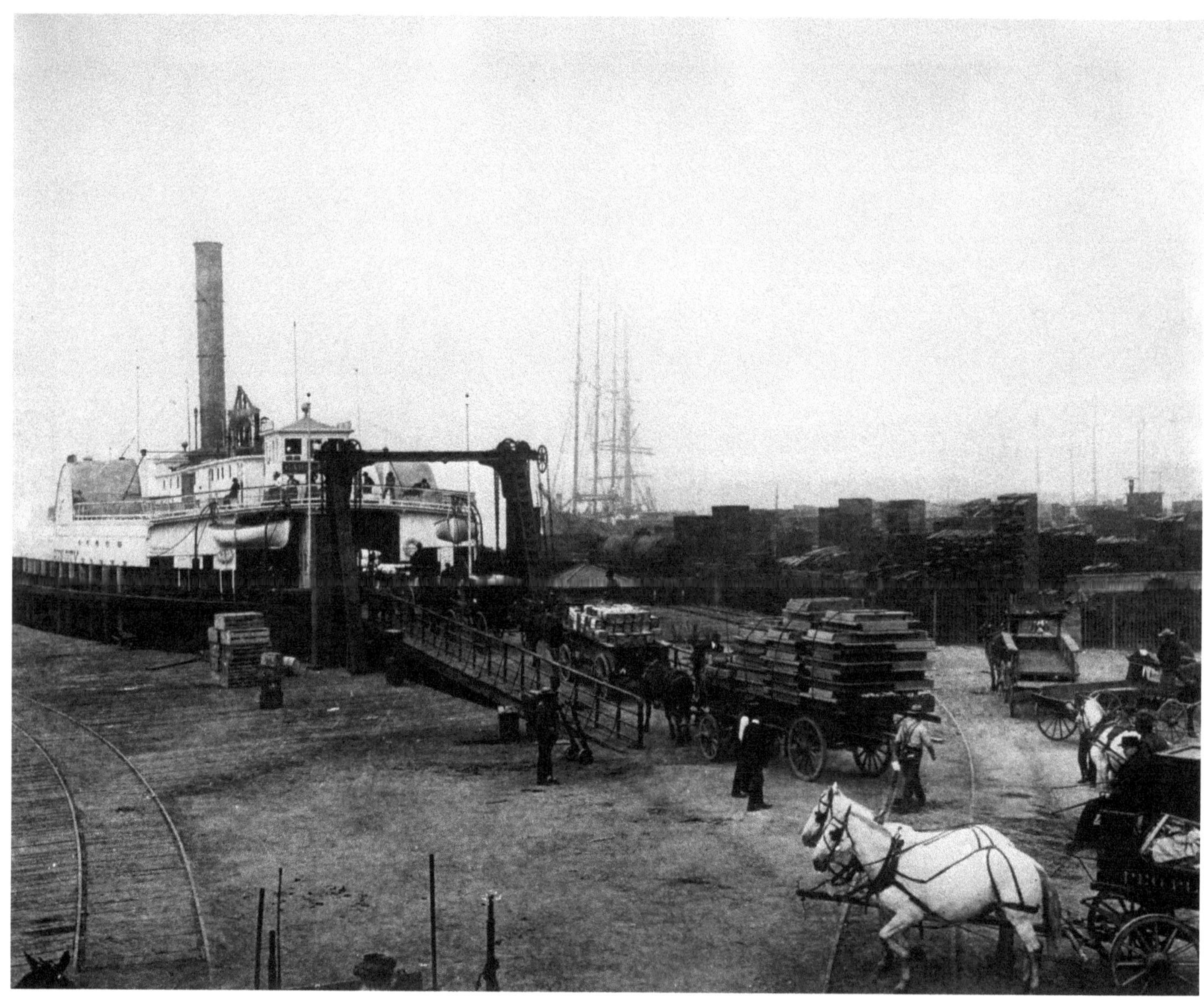

The dock adjacent the Oakland Lumber Company served the "nickel" ferries leaving from the Oakland Municipal Pier, the last remaining piece of the waterfront that remained under public ownership at the time. *The Garden City* is shown loading cargo at the pier, sometime in the 1890s. The nickel ferries could operate at reduced fares by using the municipal pier, avoiding lease fees charged at other docks.

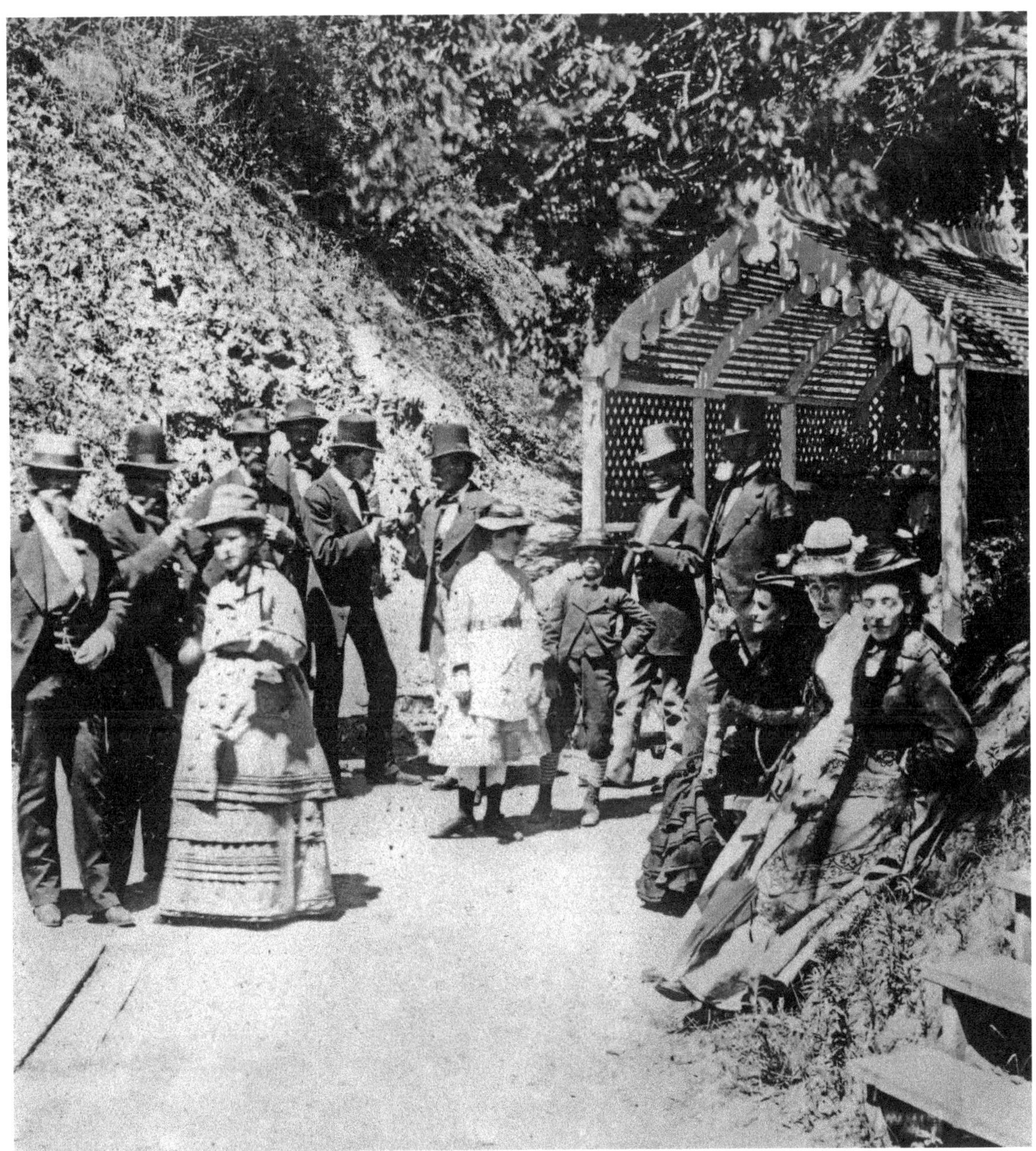

Author Mark Twain once covered the news of the day in the East Bay for a San Francisco newspaper. He returned to the area after his reports on his treks through Europe, published serially in a New York newspaper to become *Innocents Abroad,* made him a well-known young writer. Photographer Eadweard Muybridge took this photograph at the gates of Piedmont Springs, which identifies one of the two men sharing a gourd of spring water as Twain. The authenticity of the identification rests unconfirmed.

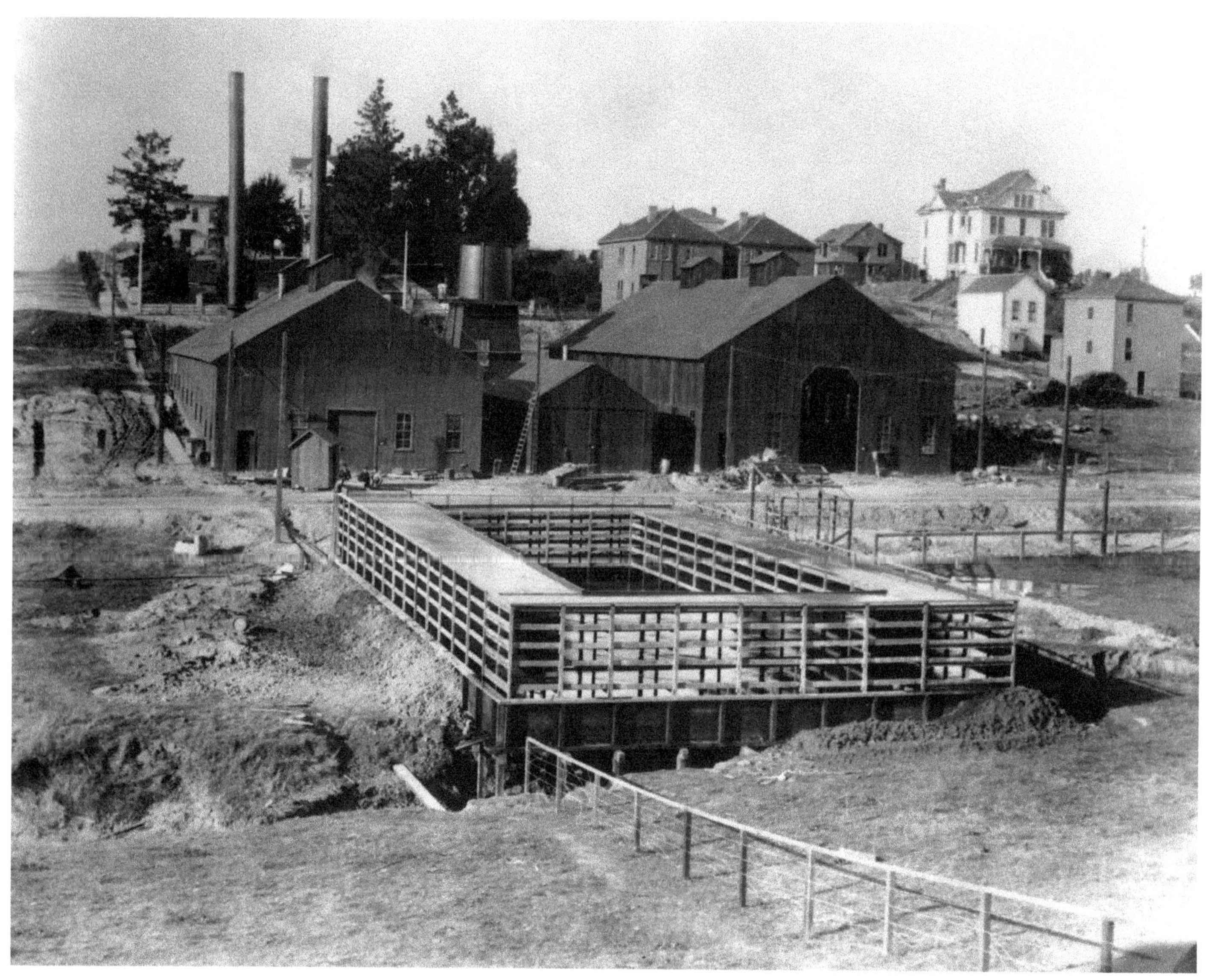

The California Jute Mill Company, shown here in the 1890s, was the only commercial manufacturer of jute products (goods like burlap sacks and twine) in the state. The mills occupied the entire block along Third Avenue between East 11th and East 12th streets in the former town of Clinton just east of Lake Merritt. The Jute Mill workforce included women and children, mostly occupied at looms.

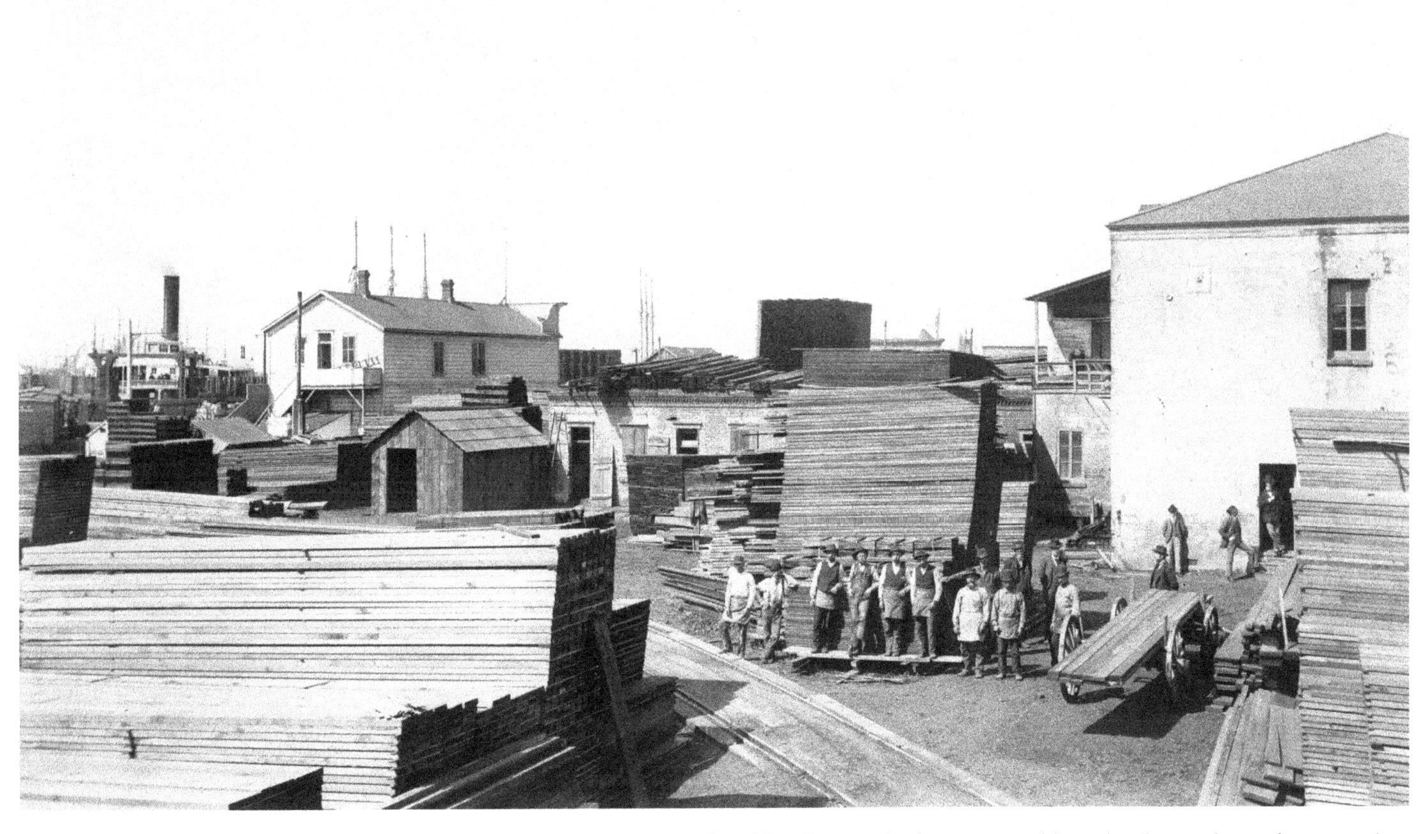

Tall stacks of milled timber from California's ancient forests lined Oakland's inner harbor at several large lumberyards, ready to supply a building boom that carried on relentlessly throughout California. From Oakland, the lumber could be moved by rail or by barge almost anywhere in the state. The Oakland Lumber Company, on the waterfront at the foot of Franklin Street, is seen here in 1894.

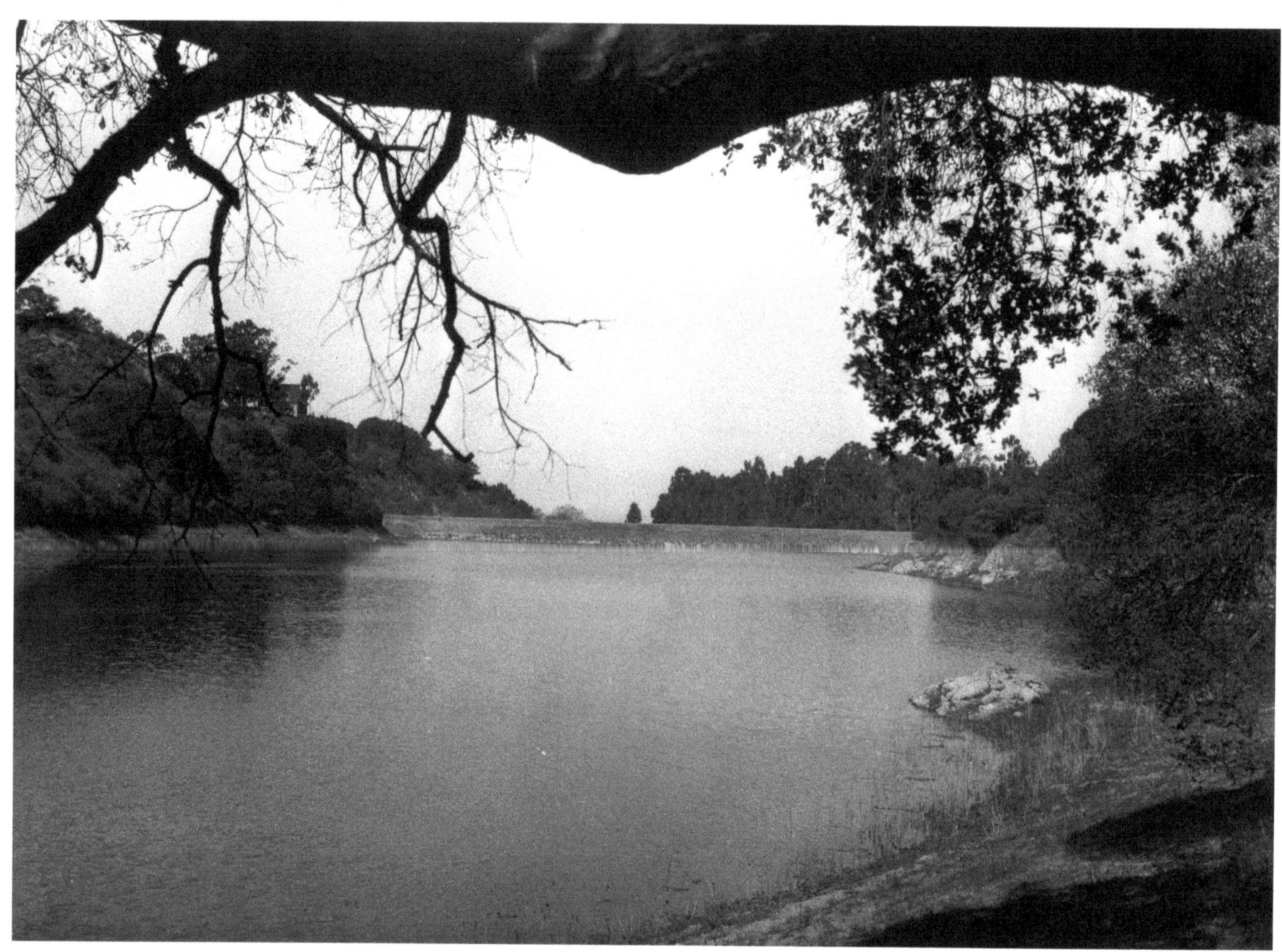

French-Canadian immigrant Anthony Chabot obtained the water he supplied through his Contra Costa Water Company from dams he constructed in the Oakland hills. For construction of his dams, Chabot applied techniques used in hydraulic gold mining, where entire hillsides were washed away, with the gold rinsed out in massive sluices. Temescal Dam, shown here, was the first dam built using Chabot's methods, and the first dam of its kind in California.

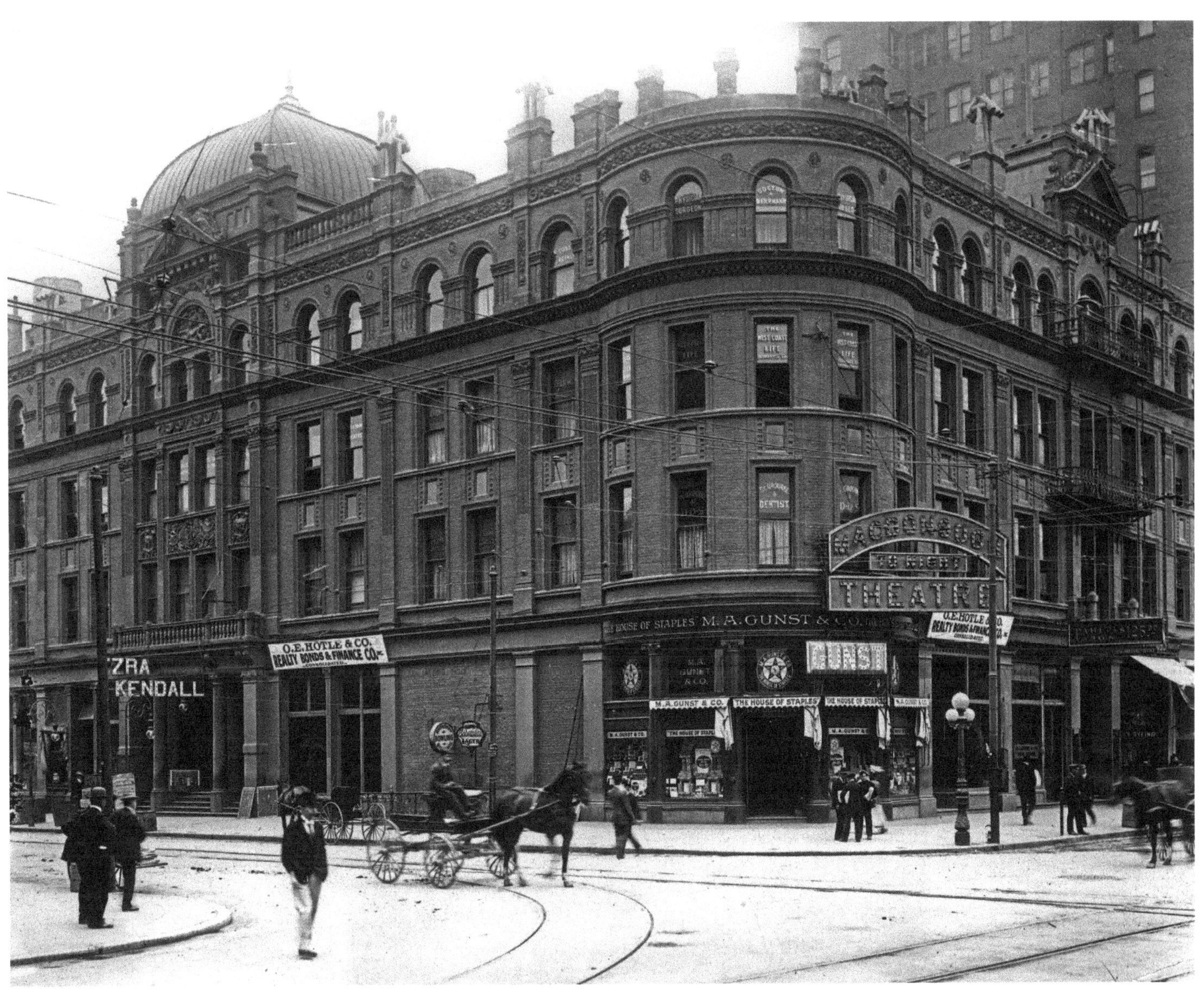

The Macdonough Theatre was the largest of several popular venues in Oakland for live theater. A competitor, Ye Olde Playhouse, introduced the world's first revolving stage as a gimmick to attract an audience. Their attendance as young men at plays in Oakland helped to inspire the careers of two Pulitzer Prize–winning playwrights, Sidney Howard and Thornton Wilder.

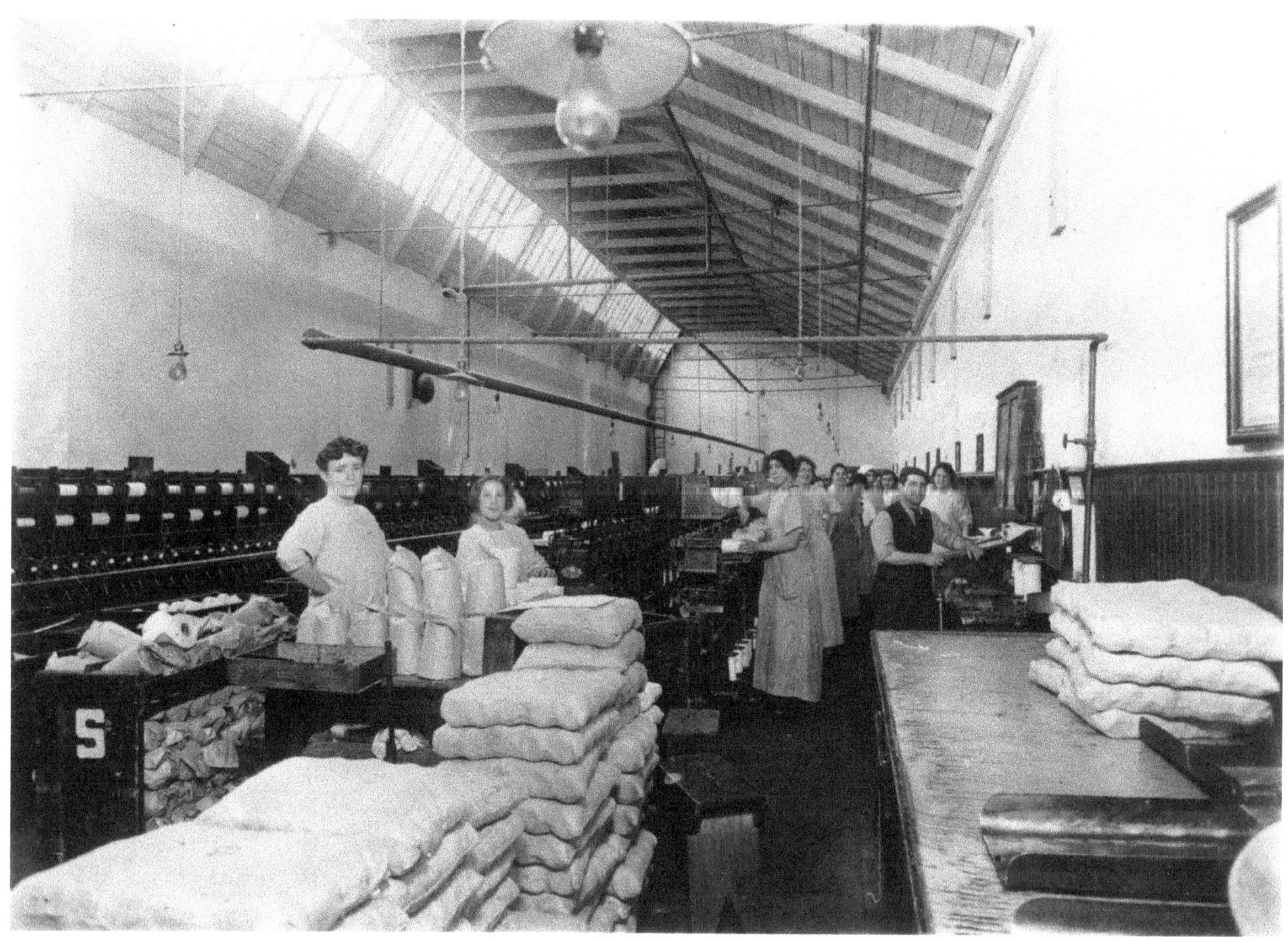

The twine works at California Cotton Mills was part of the largest textile mill on the Pacific Coast. Its workforce consisted largely of Portuguese Americans from the Azores Islands, who insisted their pay be made in silver. The neighborhood earned the name "Jingle Town" after the sound the silver coins made in the workers' pockets every payday.

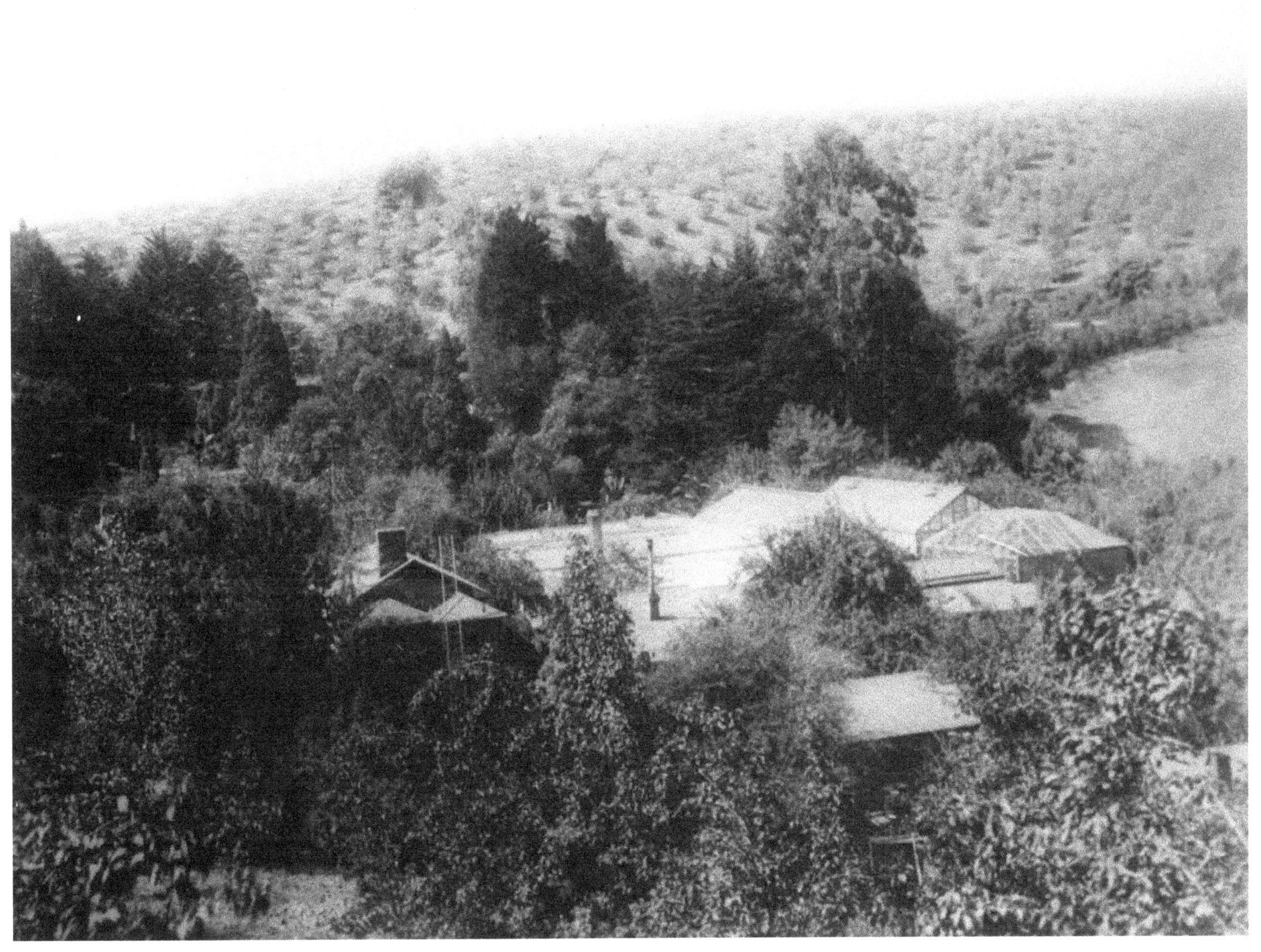

The hills above Oakland in the north provided a bucolic setting for Fernwood, an expansive estate first owned by Colonel Jack Hays, heralded for his exploits as a leader of the Texas Rangers. Hays sold the property to real estate developer William J. Dingee, who built a spacious mansion on the site. It burned in a spectacular fire on October 18, 1899. This photograph shows Dingee's nursery sometime before the fire.

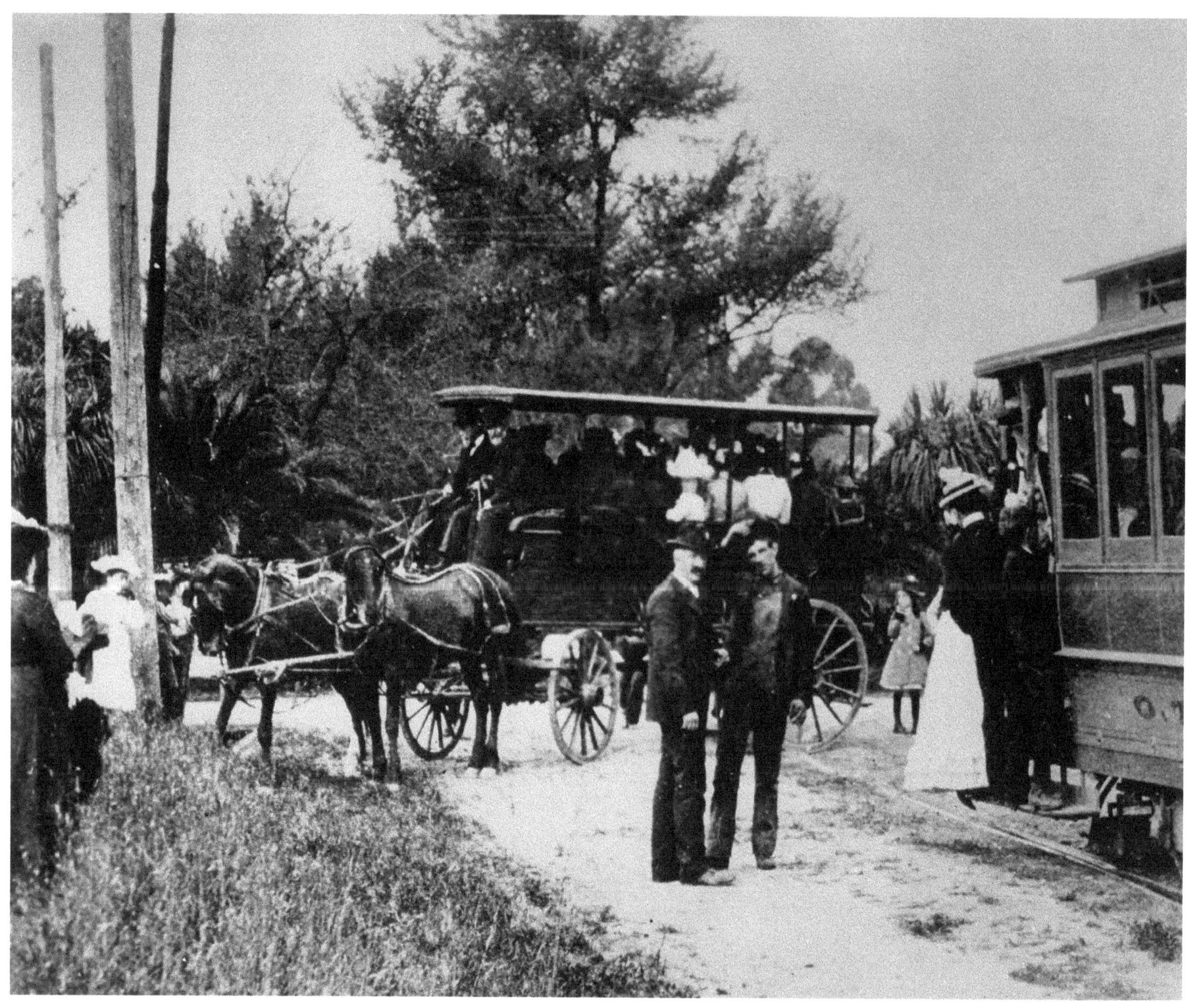

Electric streetcars represented one of the first significant improvements made to urban transit in California, introduced to Oakland in 1898. A photographer captured the inaugural run of that first electric car, operated by the Oakland Traction Company.

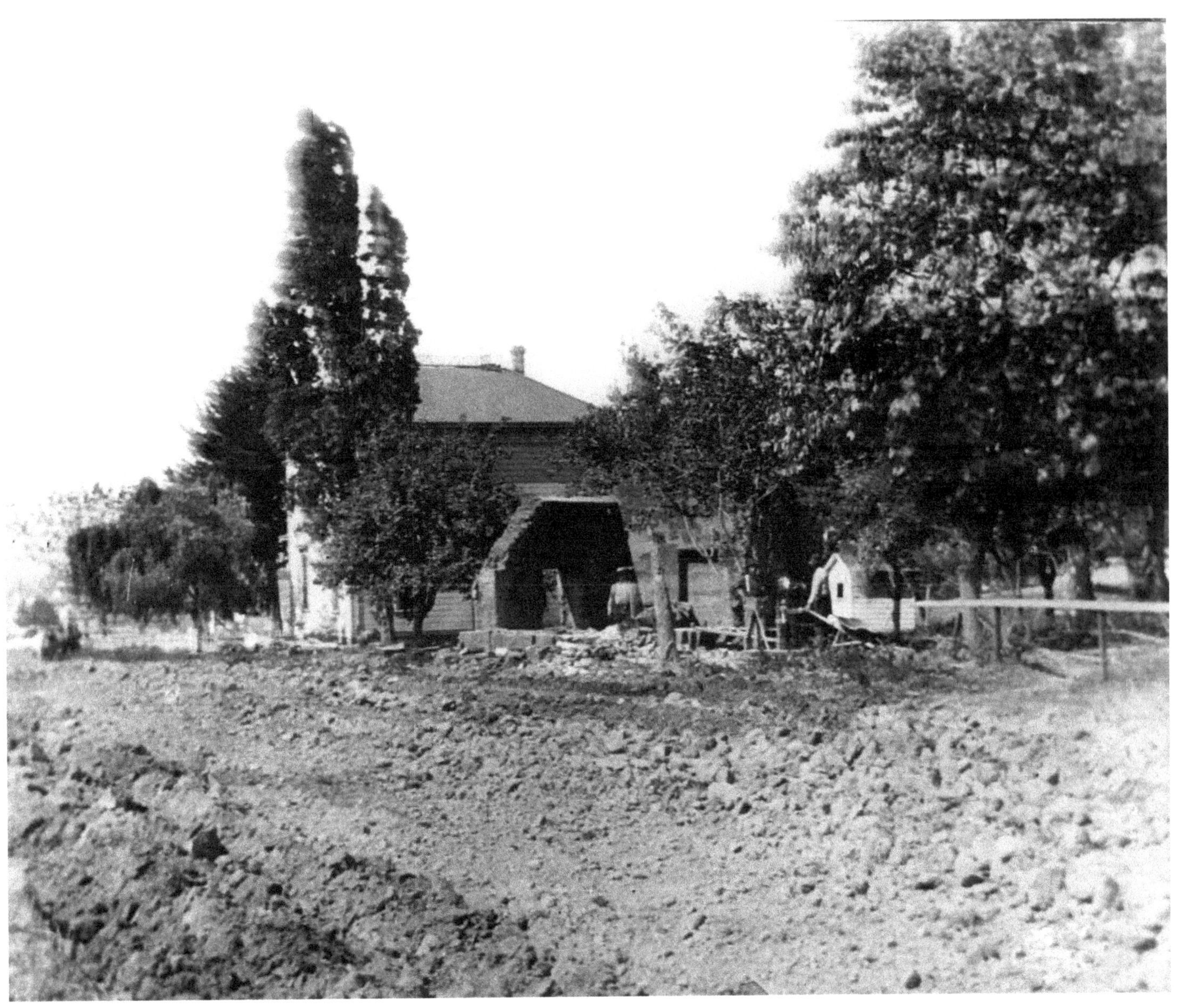

A strong earthquake in 1868 on the main fault that dissects Oakland turned the adobe house built by Antonio Peralta for his family in 1840 into a pile of rubble. The ruins remained after a wooden house was constructed to replace the adobe in 1870. Photographer Charles Dealey photographed the residence in 1899. Between Peralta and his brothers, Vicente, Hermenegildo, Domingo, and Ignacio, a total of 11 adobe buildings were constructed on the former Rancho San Antonio. Earthquakes destroyed them all.

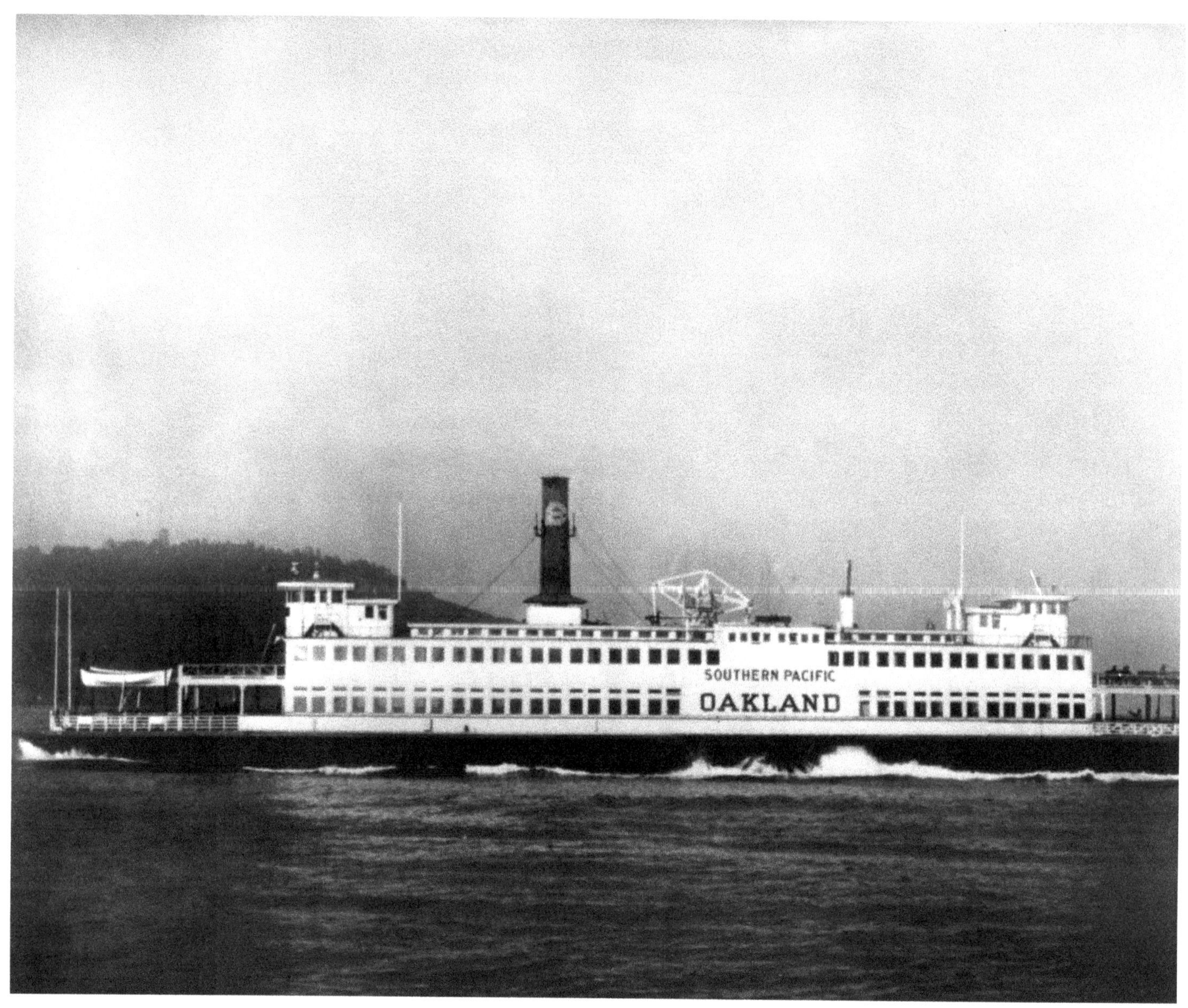

Ferry service expanded greatly in the later decades of the nineteenth century, employing vessels capable of huge loads. The *Oakland,* shown here, was a converted paddle-wheel steamer that originally operated on the Sacramento River. It began service as a ferry on the bay in 1875 and was still making the run in 1940 when it burned. The fire ended a record span of service for the sturdy vessel.

Athens of the West

(1900–1928)

Except for that of its neighbor across the bay, Oakland's population quickly eclipsed that of every other city in California. Newcomers were transported both by sea and on the Transcontinental Railroad, one of the greatest engineering feats in human history up to that time, whose western terminus lay at a wooden pier on the city's western tip.

The influx brought the entire spectrum of American society, from retiring millionaires to penniless refugees, who came as part of the mass migration reaching North America from the nations of Europe. The newcomers, particularly bachelors and young families, hailed from Germany, Italy, France, and Ireland, but also from Greece, Croatia, Slovenia, and the Azores Islands. Irish and Chinese immigrants also settled into Oakland after completing construction of the Transcontinental Railroad, and the city became an early center of African-American culture on the West Coast.

Oakland's own Jack London emerged in the new century as the best-selling writer of his time. The mayor of Oakland, George C. Pardee, won election as governor of California, bringing his staunchly Progressive platform to the state capital. His supporters in the Republican Party solidly controlled local politics, and the work began to prepare the city for the industrial expansion that consumed the attention of public officials and capitalists alike.

Ambitions toward sophistication had been running strong. Across the bay in San Francisco, while city boosters high-handedly proclaimed that city to be "the Paris of the West," Oakland had emerged as "the Athens of the West." As in Athens in antiquity, Oakland of the late nineteenth century was richly cosmopolitan, possessing an abundance of opportunities for learning, athletics, and recreation. Literature and the arts flourished while local residents took on the daunting challenges of infrastructure posed by the new environment. A dam across the San Antonio Creek, best described as a brackish slough, produced a shimmering lake situated at the city's geographic center. An earthen dam in the hills, of a type never before attempted, helped to sustain a supply of drinking water for the rapidly growing city. And the spoils of dredging work turned a turgid tidal estuary into a port that could rival any.

While San Francisco's claims that it could rival Paris drew mostly snickers from the world's travelers, Oakland could quietly defend its Athenian ambitions as the new century got underway.

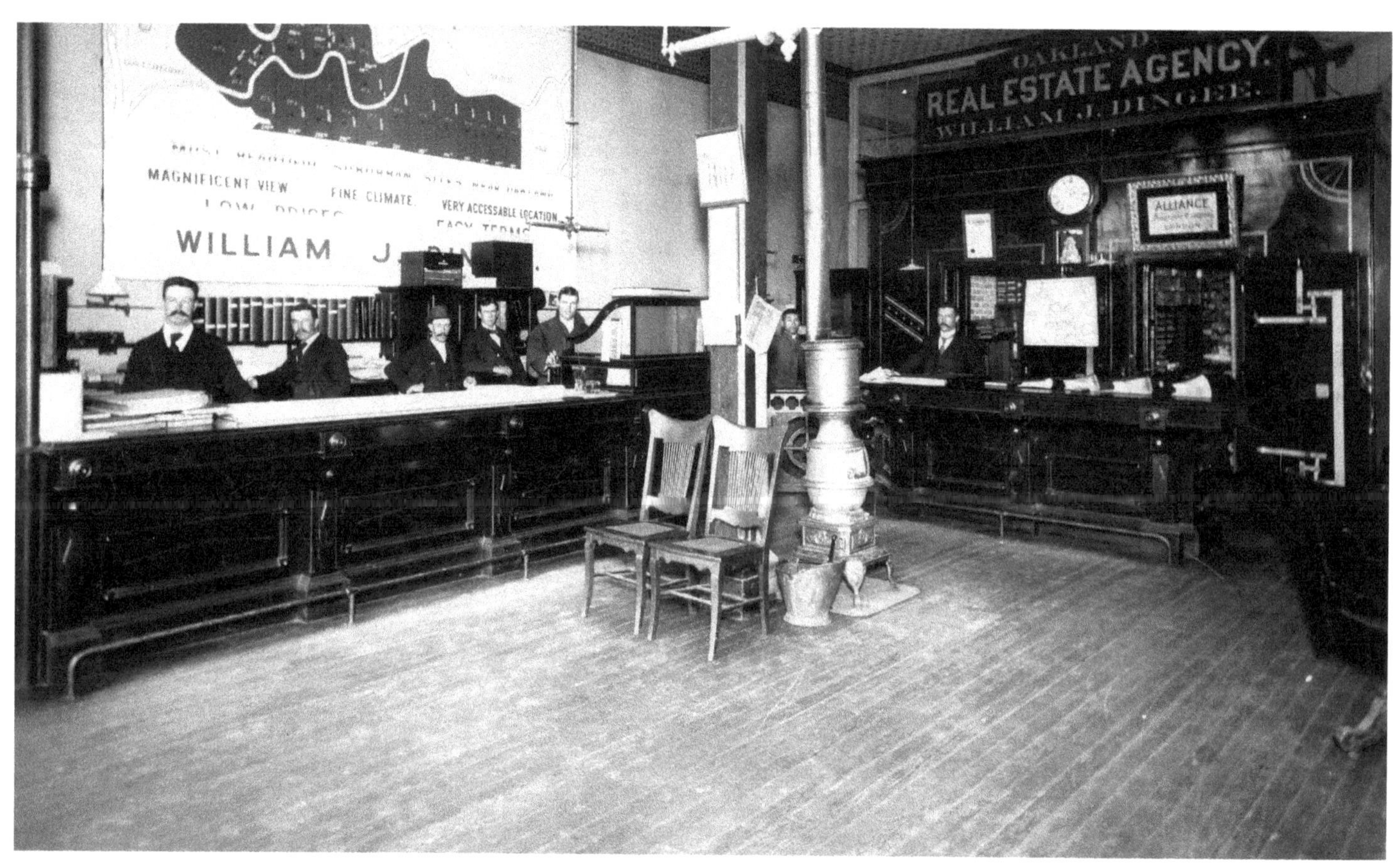

William J. Dingee began as a clerk at the business later named for him and by the beginning of the twentieth century was one of Oakland's wealthiest residents. Besides selling real estate, he provided residential water services from wells he operated in the hills behind Montclair and in East Oakland. By 1921, he was bankrupt, in debt for more than $800,000.

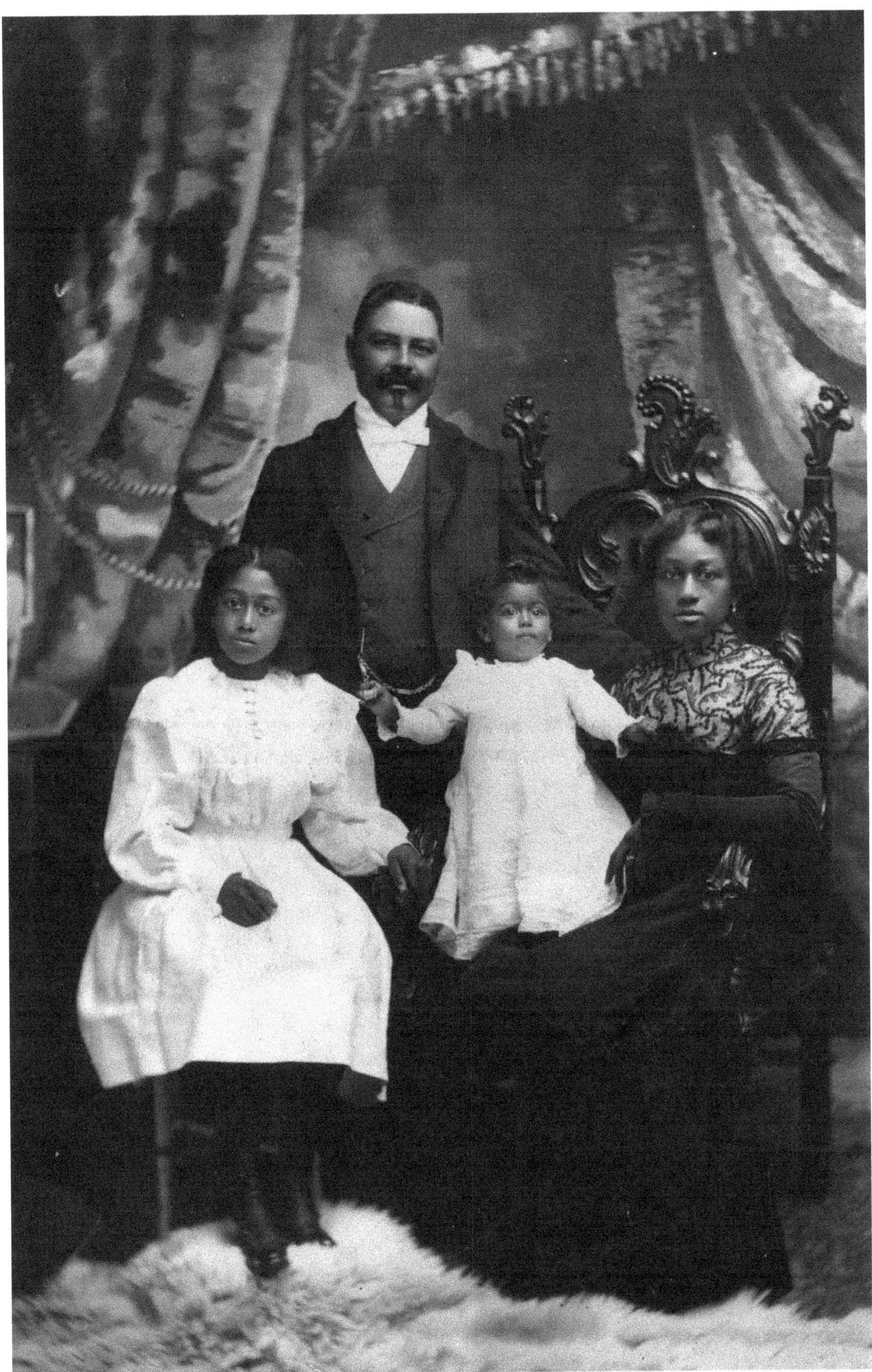

William T. Shorey, the first African-American sea captain, raised his family in a picturesque bayside setting along Oakland's western shore. He poses with his family for this photograph in 1900.

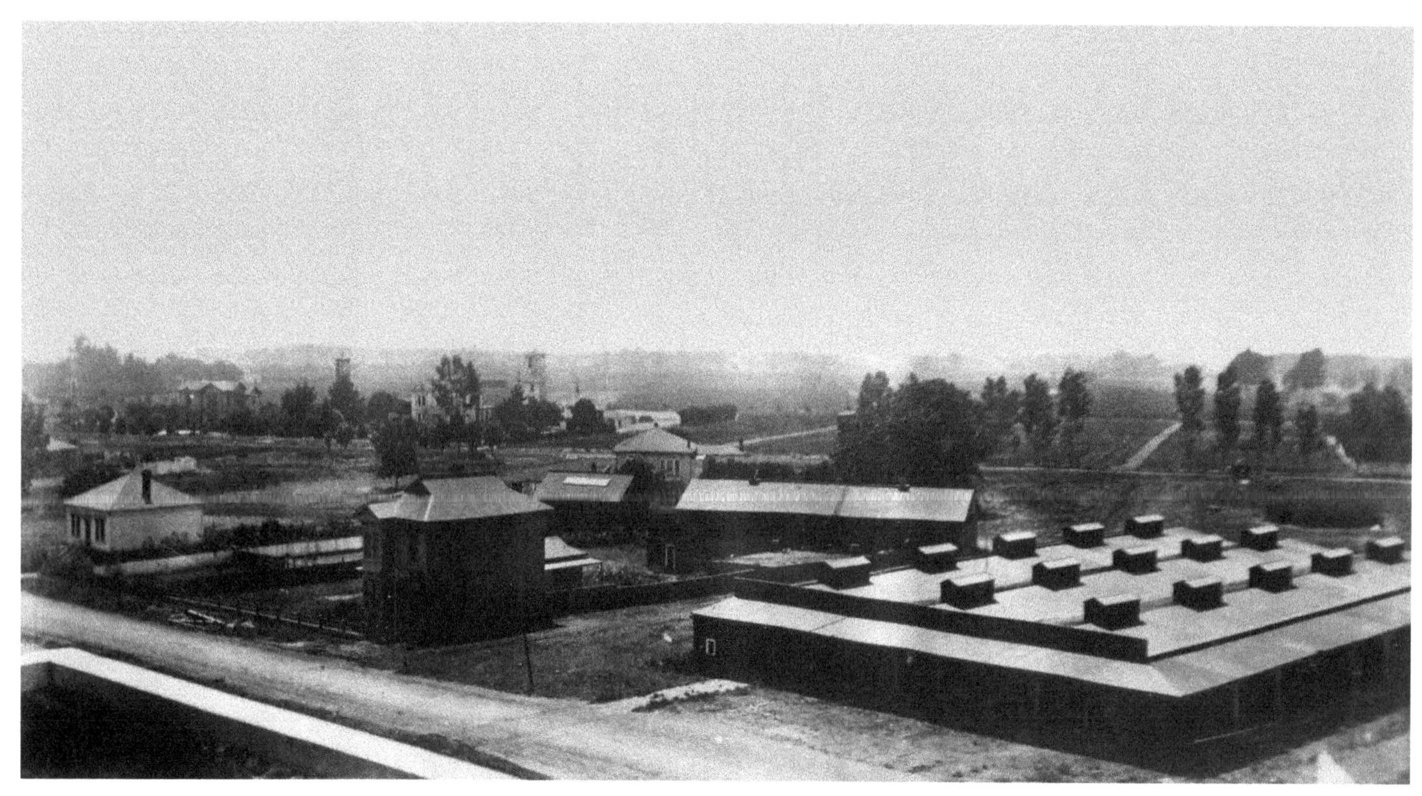

Packing and processing food grew into a large and lucrative industry in Oakland very early on. The Lusk Canning Company in Temescal, now a district in North Oakland, packed some of the first California-grown fruits and vegetables sold on the East Coast.

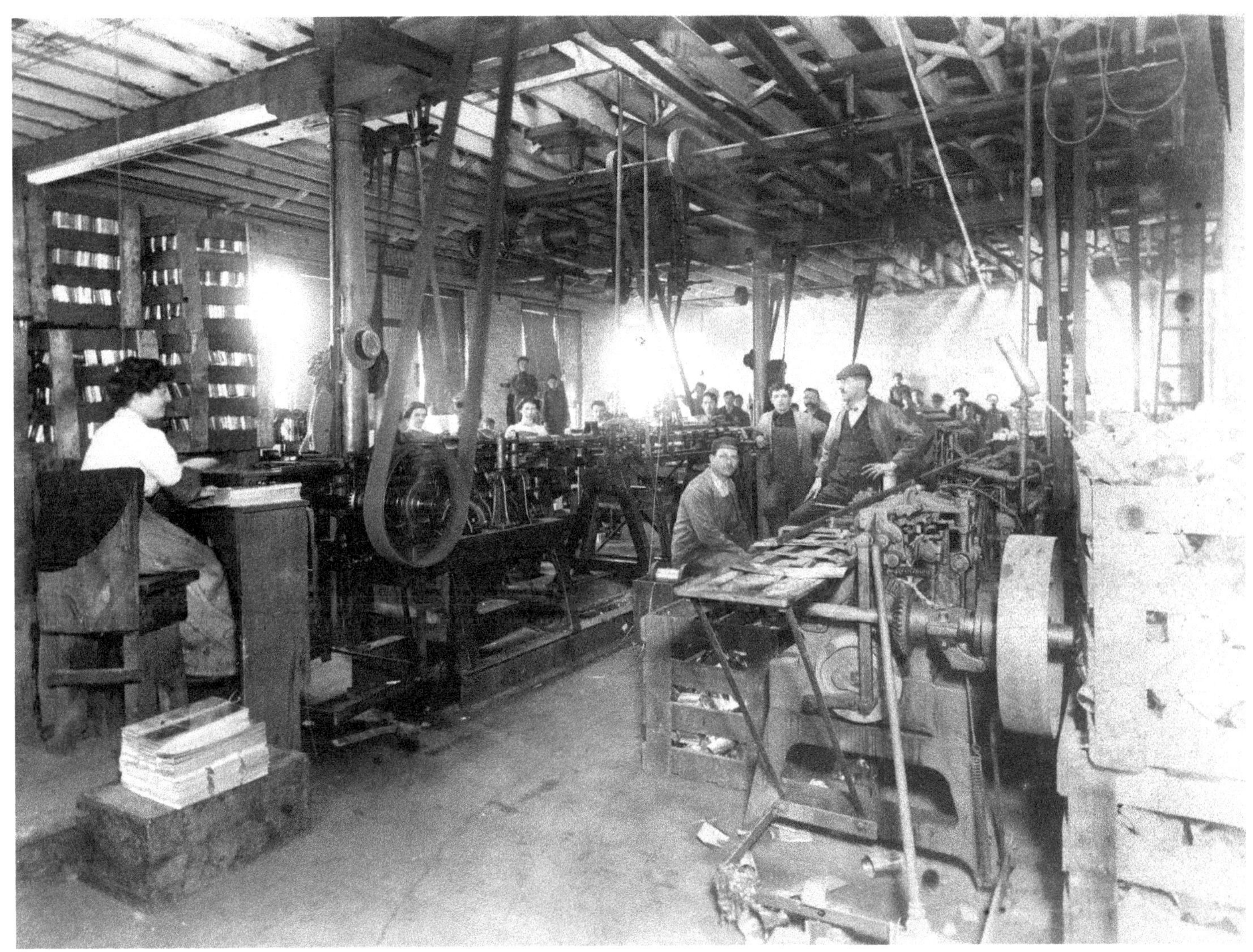

New technology greatly enhanced conditions in the canning industry, where women worked side-by-side with men. A camera recorded an early stage of cannery automation at the Hickmott Asparagus Canning Company on April 15, 1902.

Following Spread: By the first decade of the twentieth century, downtown Oakland was the commercial, social, and cultural center of California's second-most-populous county, following only San Francisco.

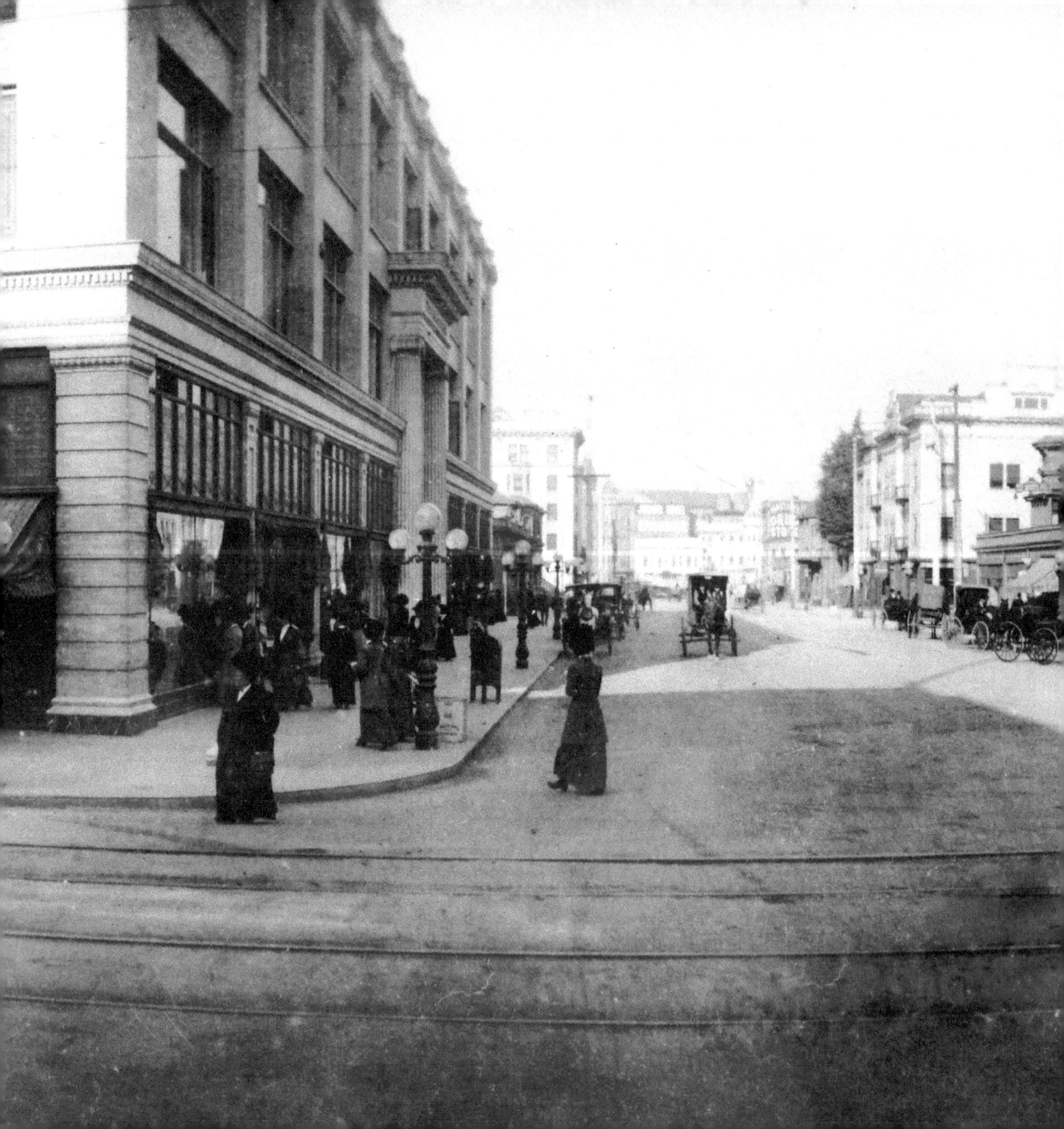

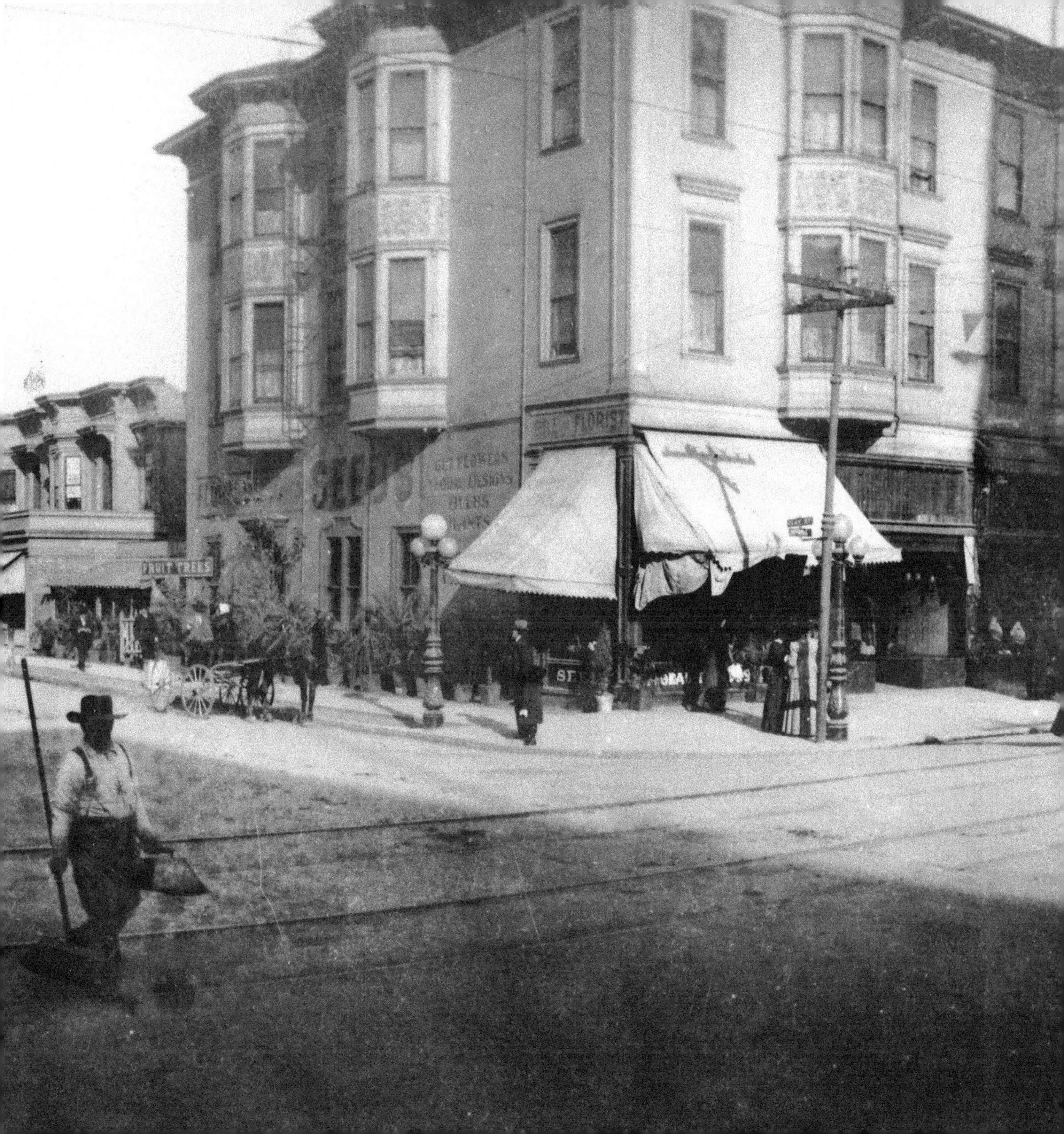
FRUIT TREES
FLORIST
BULBS

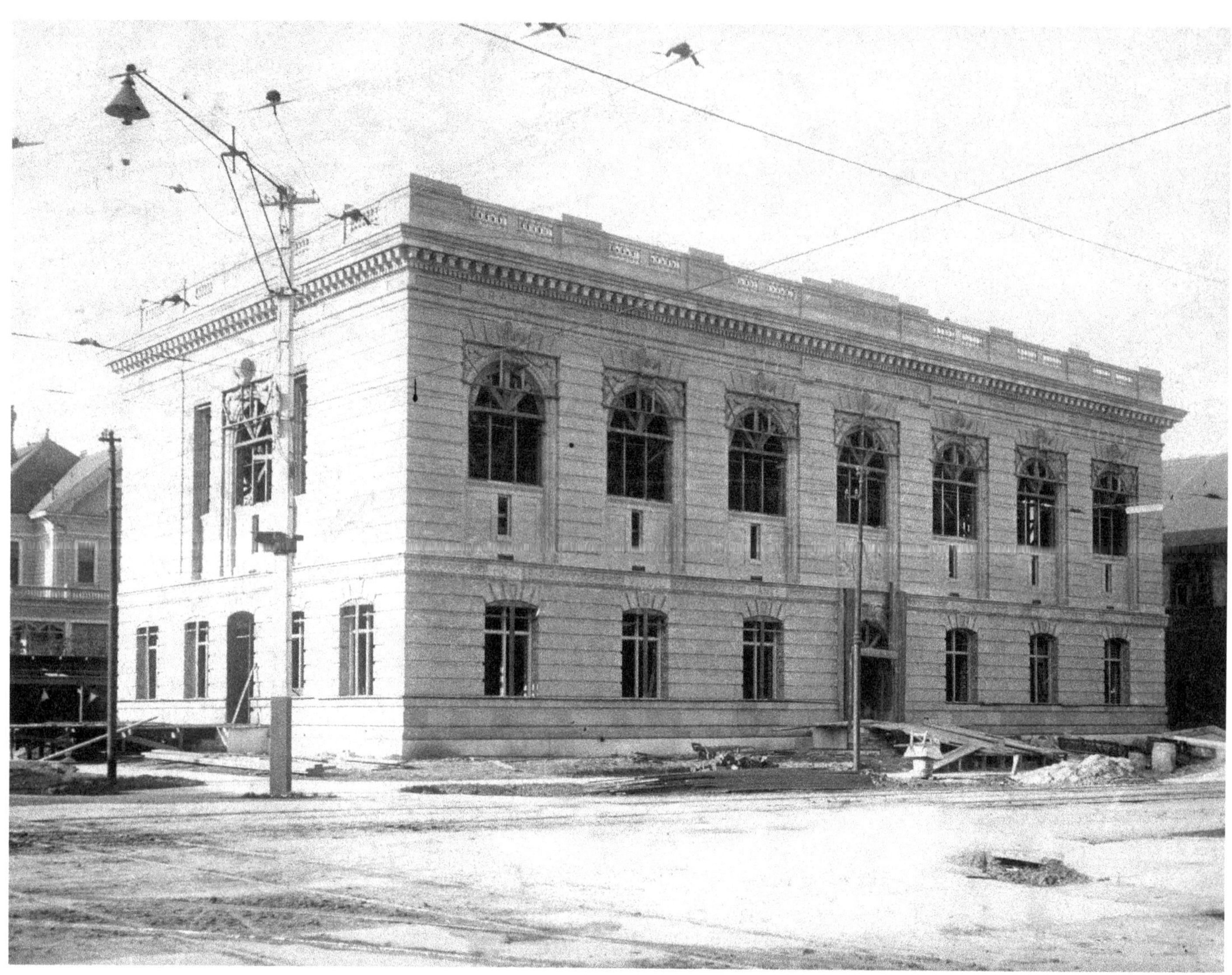

A brand-new main library, financed with the help of Pittsburgh industrialist Andrew Carnegie, helped to elevate Oakland's status as a center of learning and literature when it opened in 1902. Fully restored after sustaining severe damage in the earthquake of 1989, the building today houses the African-American Museum and Library of Oakland.

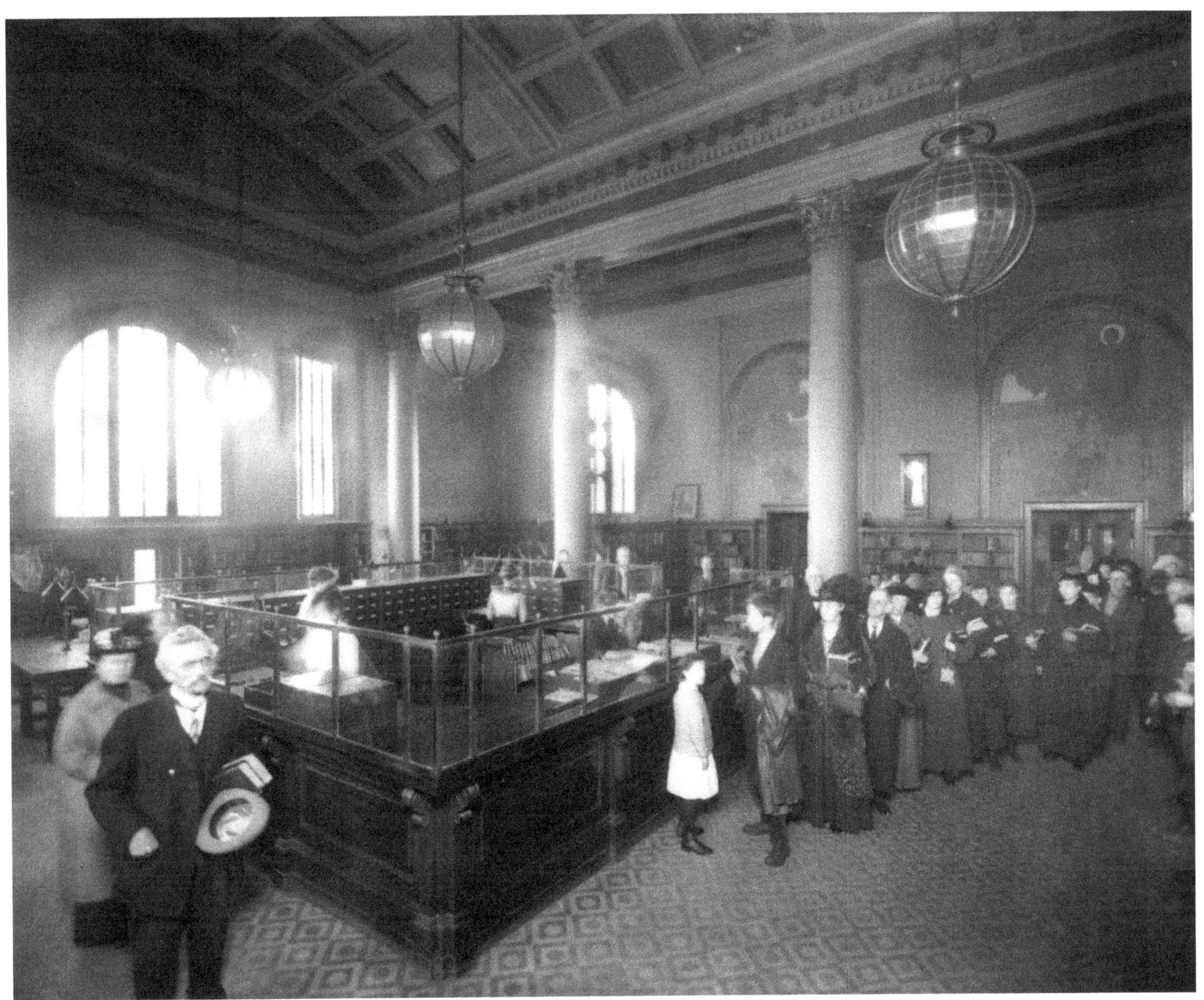

The Carnegie building represented a unique creative collaboration between two brothers, William and Arthur Mathews, sons of one of Oakland's first architects. William was also an architect and designed the structural portions of the building. His brother, Arthur, a painter, contributed a series of murals and worked with his wife, Lucia, on other interior features.

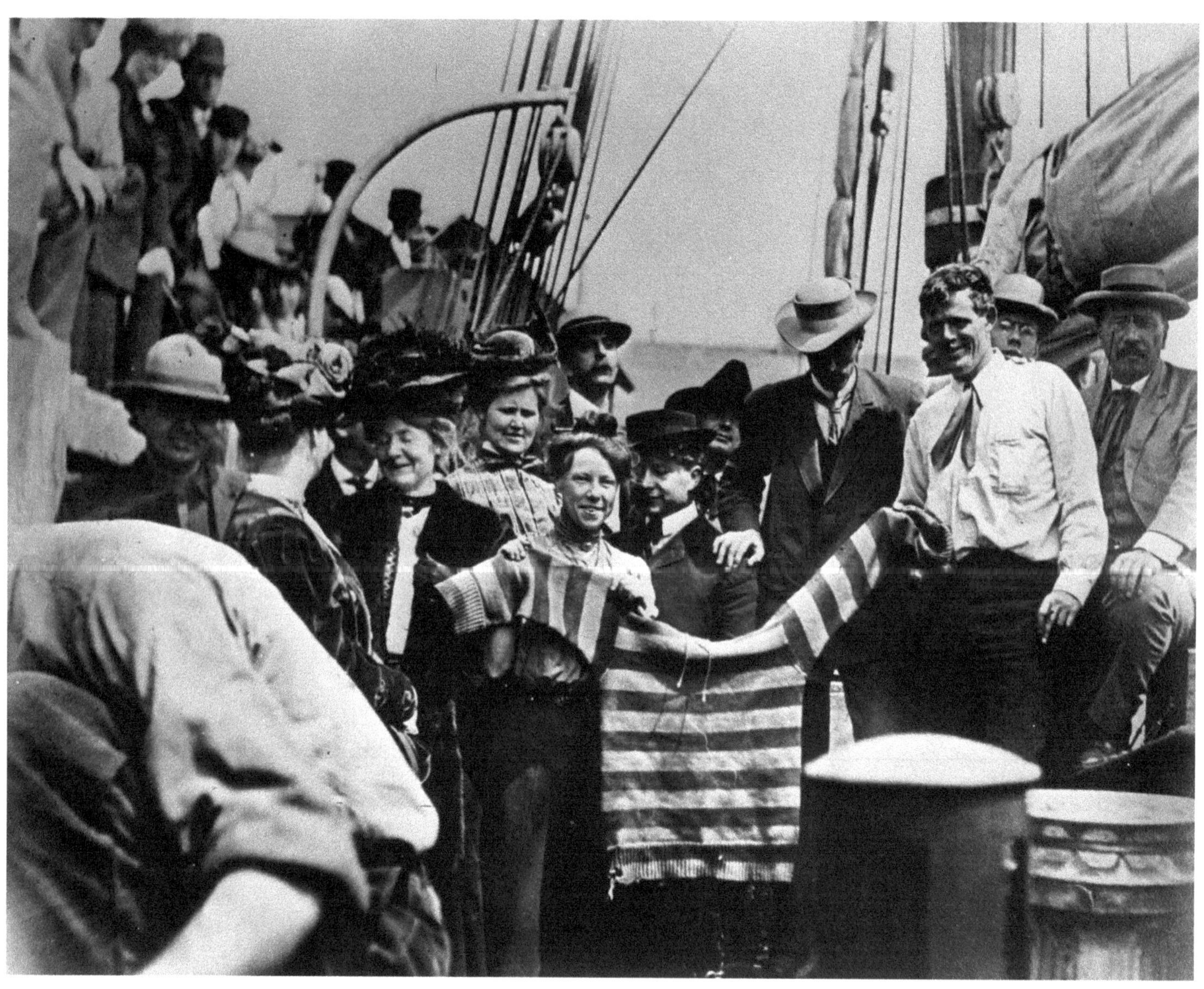

Jack London would become a best-selling and widely photographed author during his lifetime. Here he appears with his wife, Charmian, and a group of well-wishers at the start of the couple's aborted attempt at a trip around the world aboard their custom yacht, *The Snark.* The trip ended in the South Seas when London realized he was not adequately trained to navigate using the southern skies.

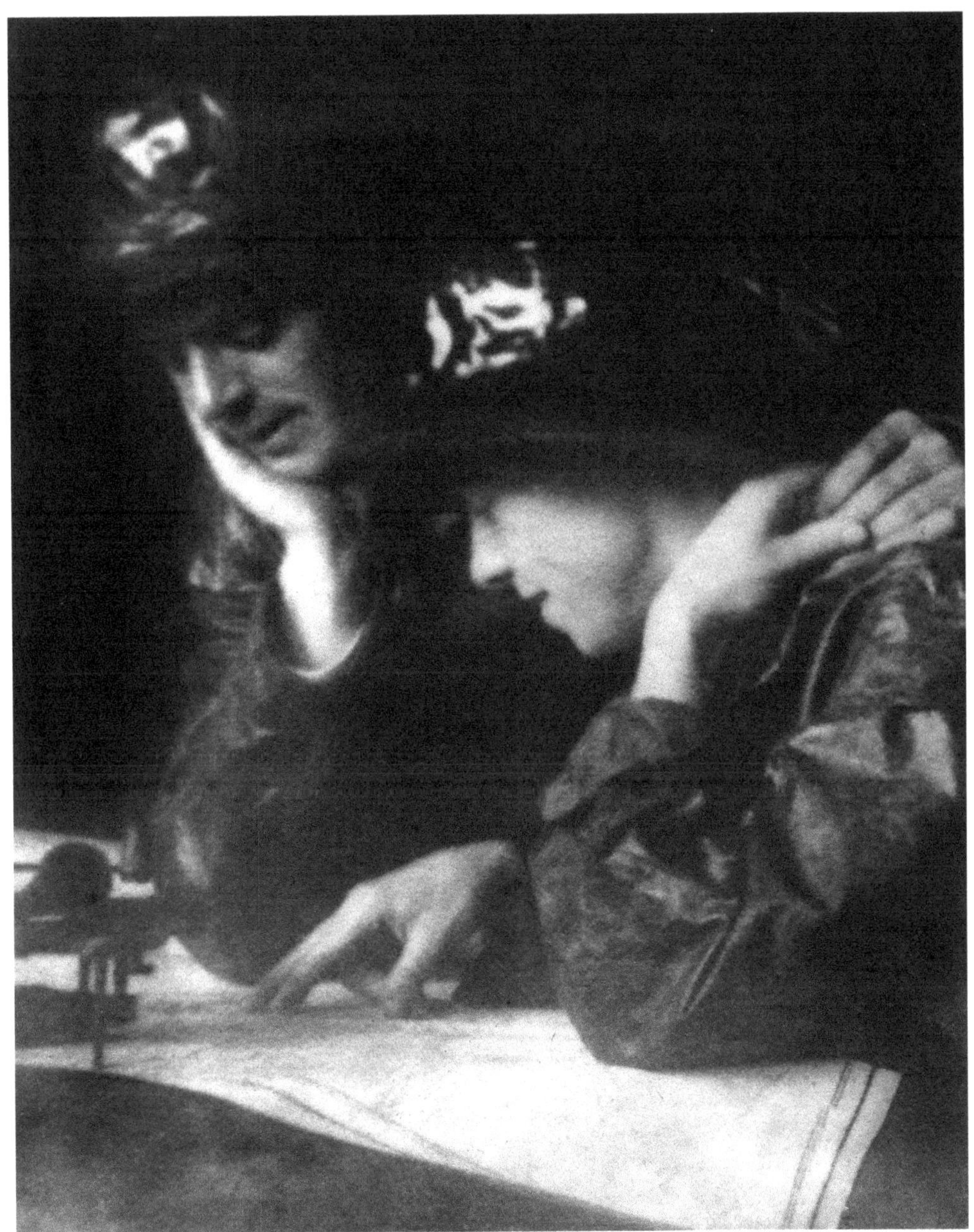

Author Jack London, who achieved great fame almost overnight after the publication of his adventure classic *The Call of the Wild,* attributed much of his success to the relationship he had as a child with the first director of the Oakland Public Library, poet Ina Coolbrith. Another close friend, photographer Anne Brigman, took this picture of London with his wife Charmian.

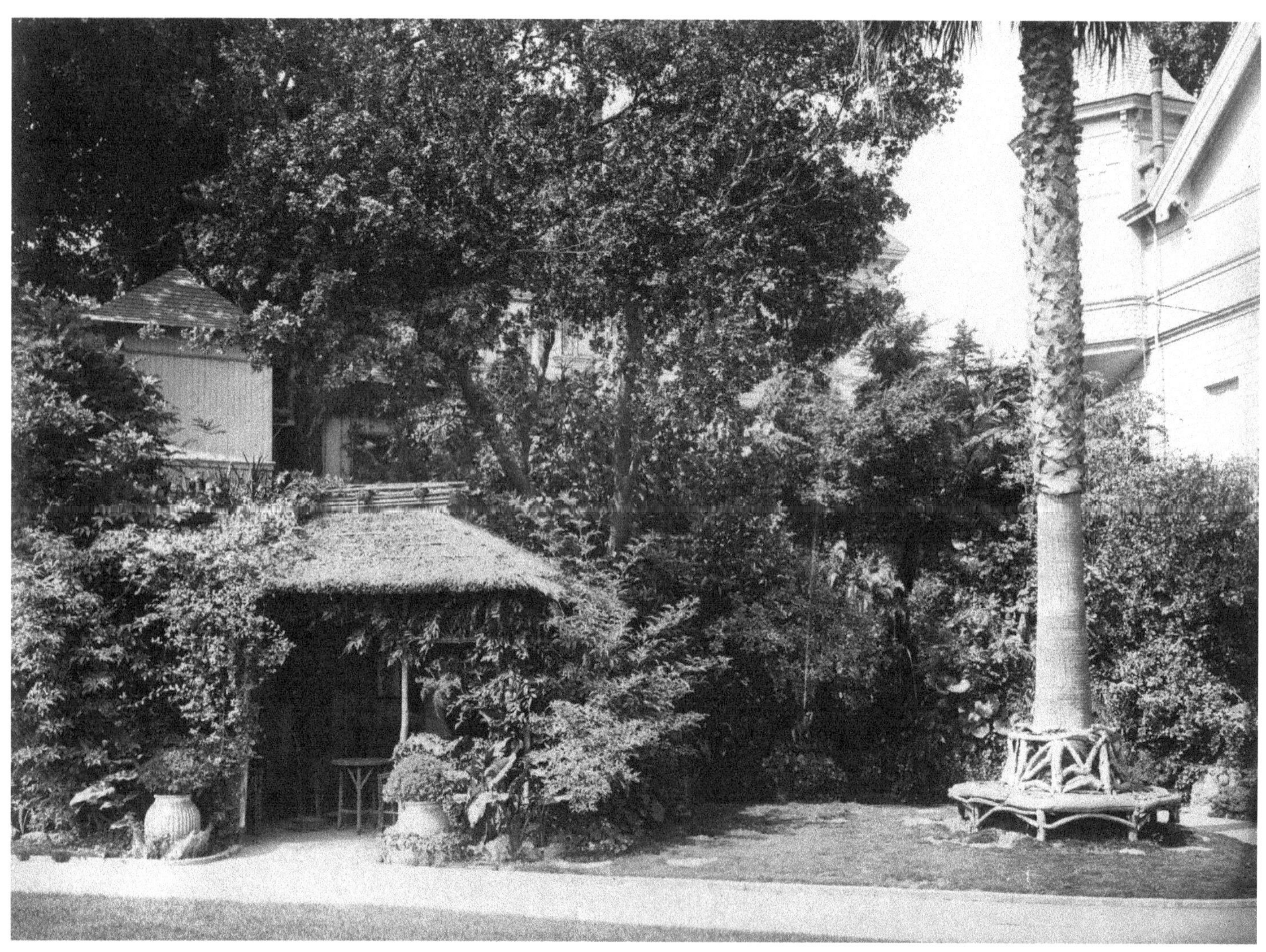

The South Seas captivated prominent Oaklander August Schilling, who made his fortune in the spice trade. He exploited Oakland's exceptional weather for a garden on the shores of Lake Merritt filled with exotic plants, many recovered on his frequent trips to the East Indies. Schilling opened his gardens to the public.

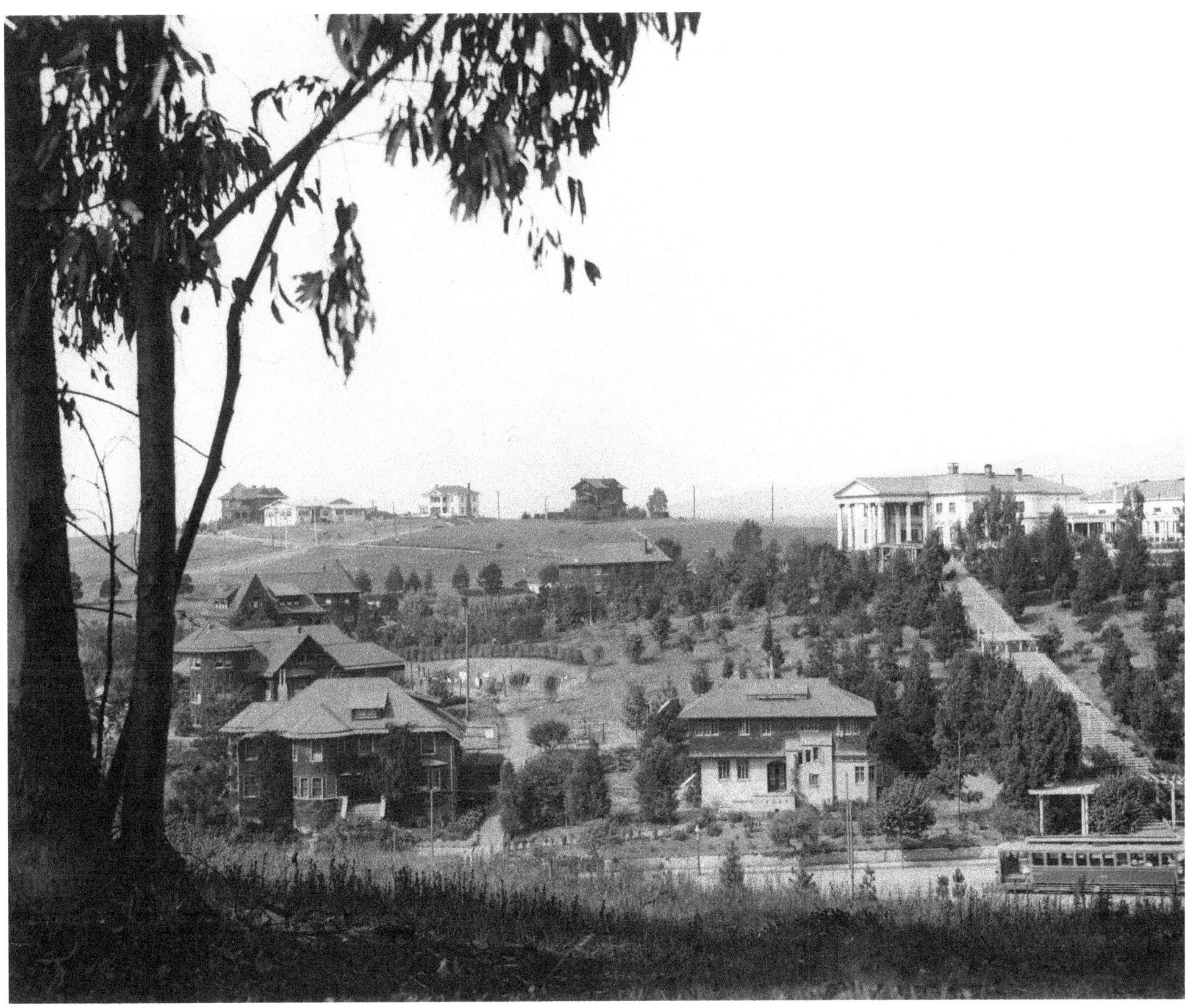

Across Lake Merritt, wealthy capitalist Francis Marion Smith opened his expansive estate, Arbor Villa, to help needy children and local immigrants. In memory of his late wife, Smith built a group of cottages to house orphan girls. On a hilltop, he built the Home Club to help local German immigrants preserve their heritage during a time of anti-German sentiment.

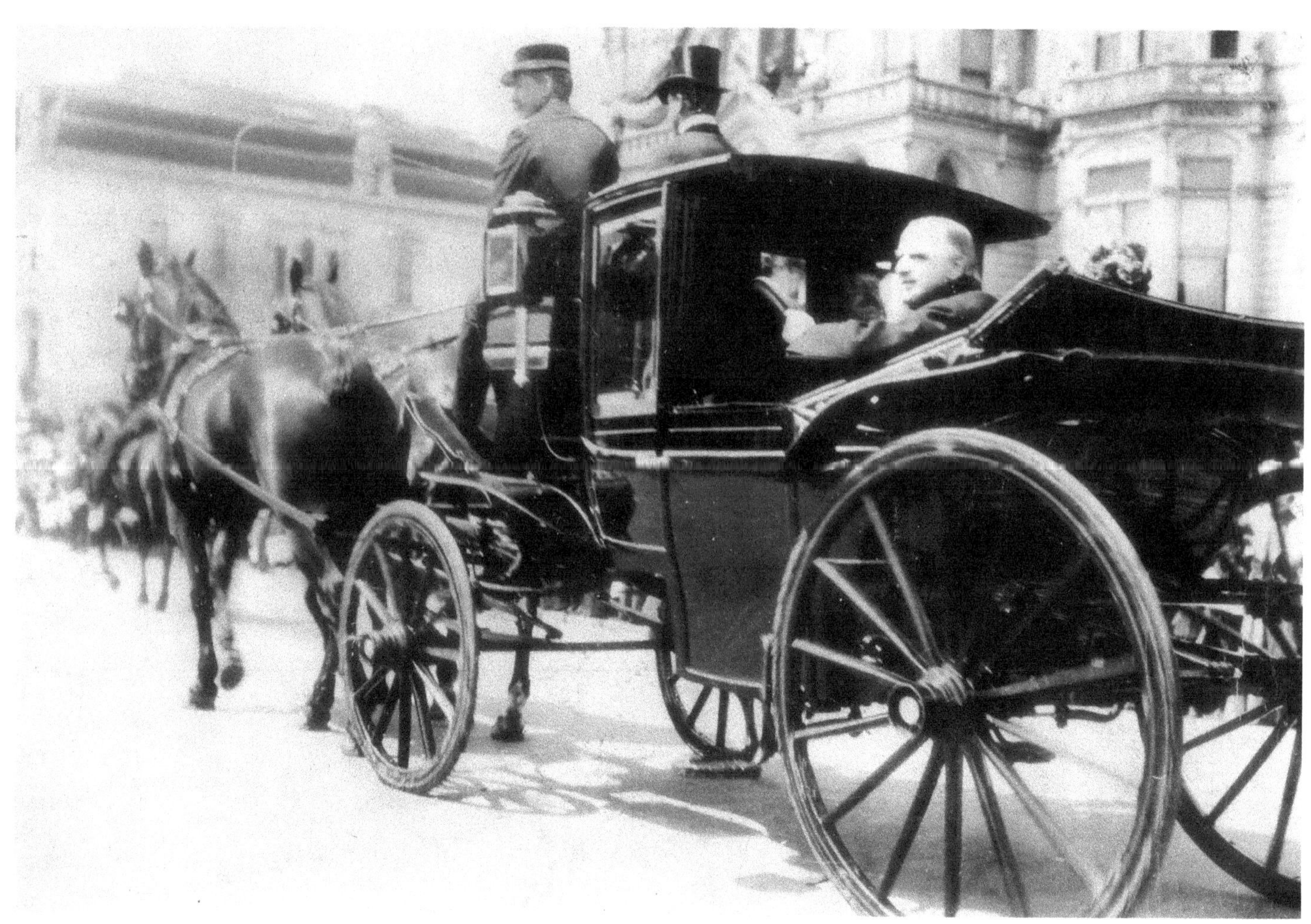

President William McKinley rewarded the support of Oakland's powerful and progressive Republican Party establishment with a visit in May 1901. He toured the city in the back of a carriage, riding with the mayor, Anson Barstow, and Edson Adams, Jr., the son of one of the city's founders.

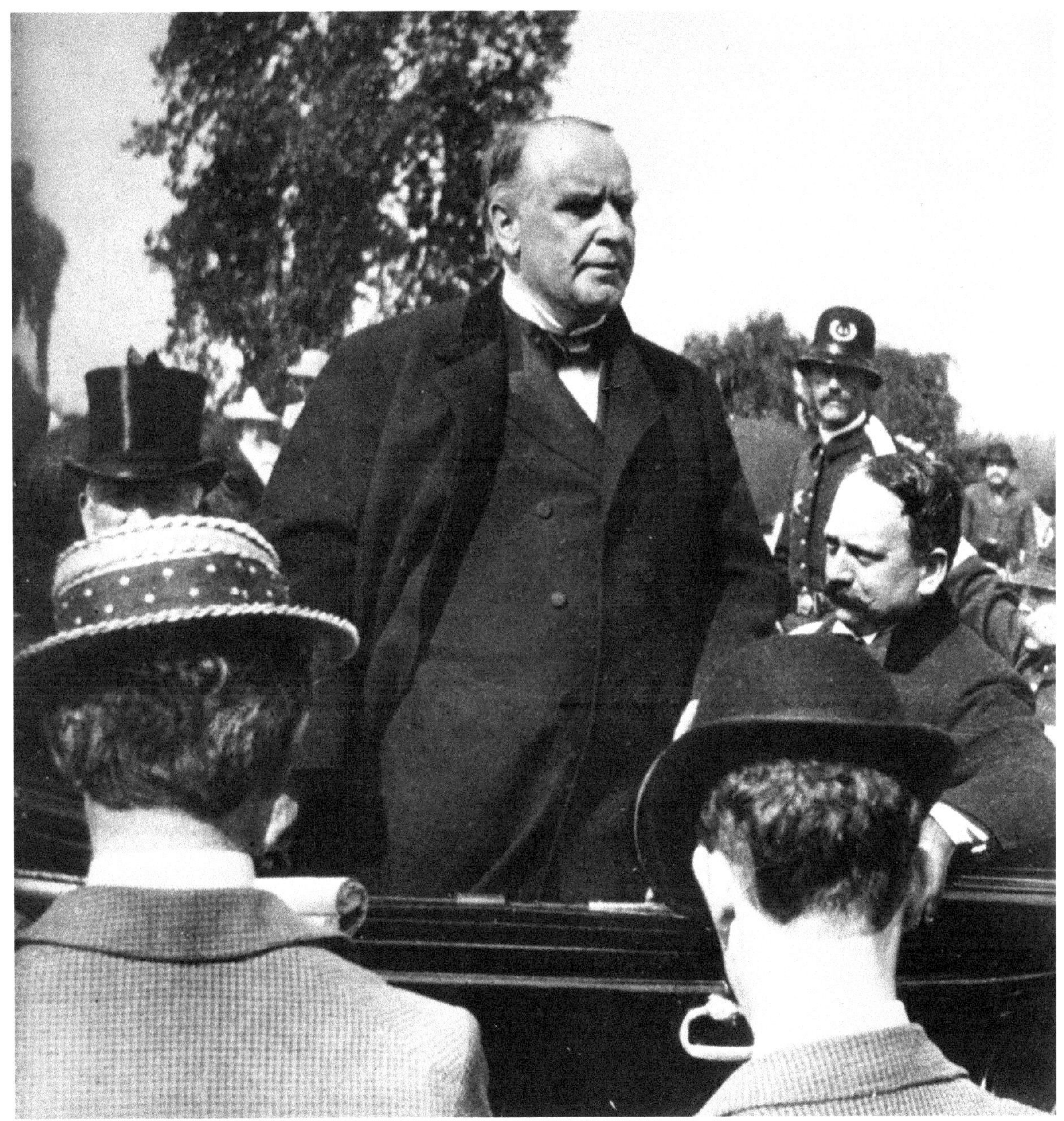

McKinley delivers a speech while standing in the backseat of a carriage, with Edson Adams, Jr., looking on. The president would be assassinated by anarchist Leon Czolgosz in September while attending the Pan-American Exposition in Buffalo, New York.

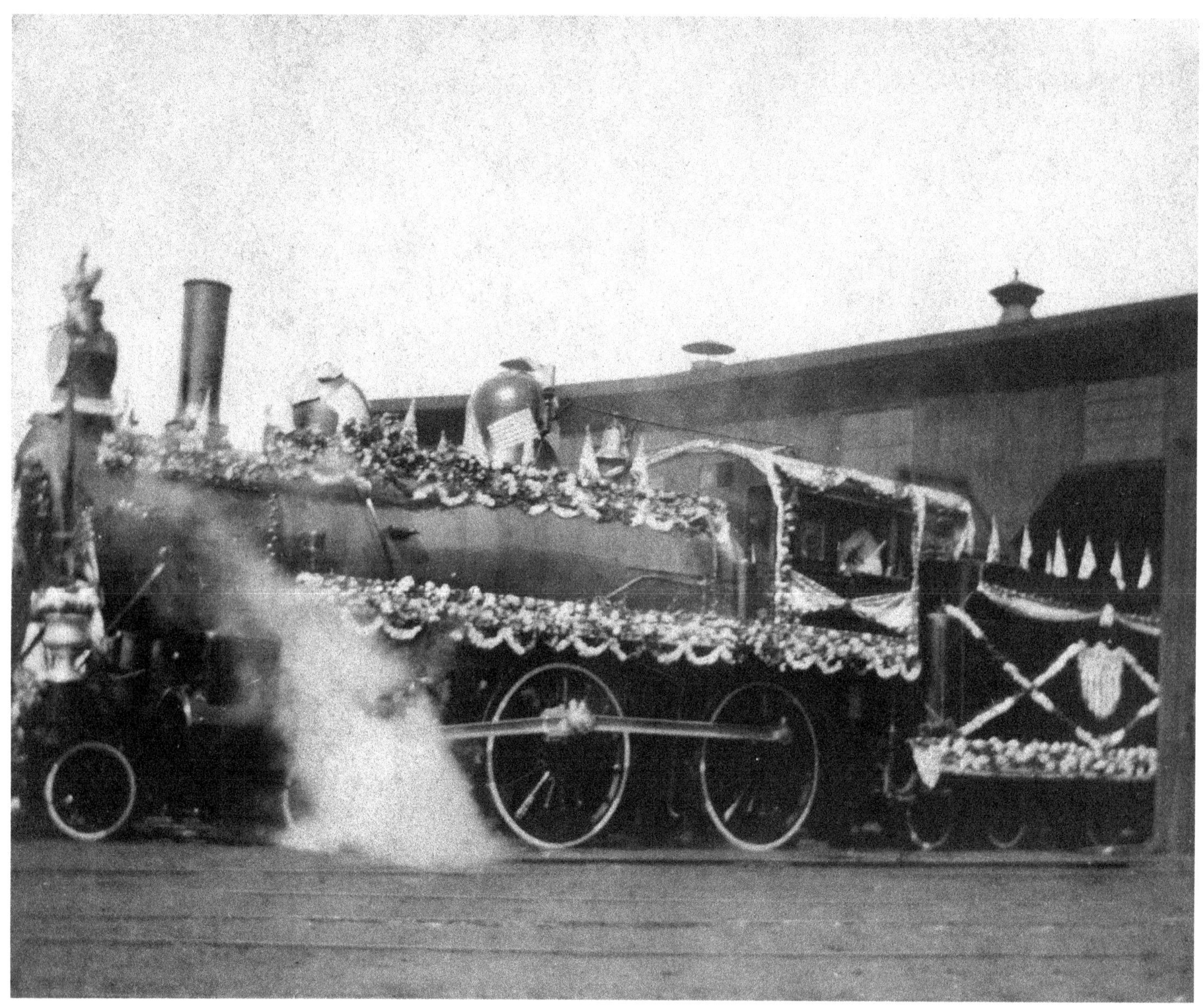

The highest levels of security were in place when McKinley's successor, Theodore Roosevelt, passed through Oakland on his way to a speech in Berkeley. The host committee leased a locomotive and caboose from the Southern Pacific Railroad and filled it with soldiers and armed veterans, who served as guards to escort the president on his travels. The visit included a camping trip in Yosemite with John Muir.

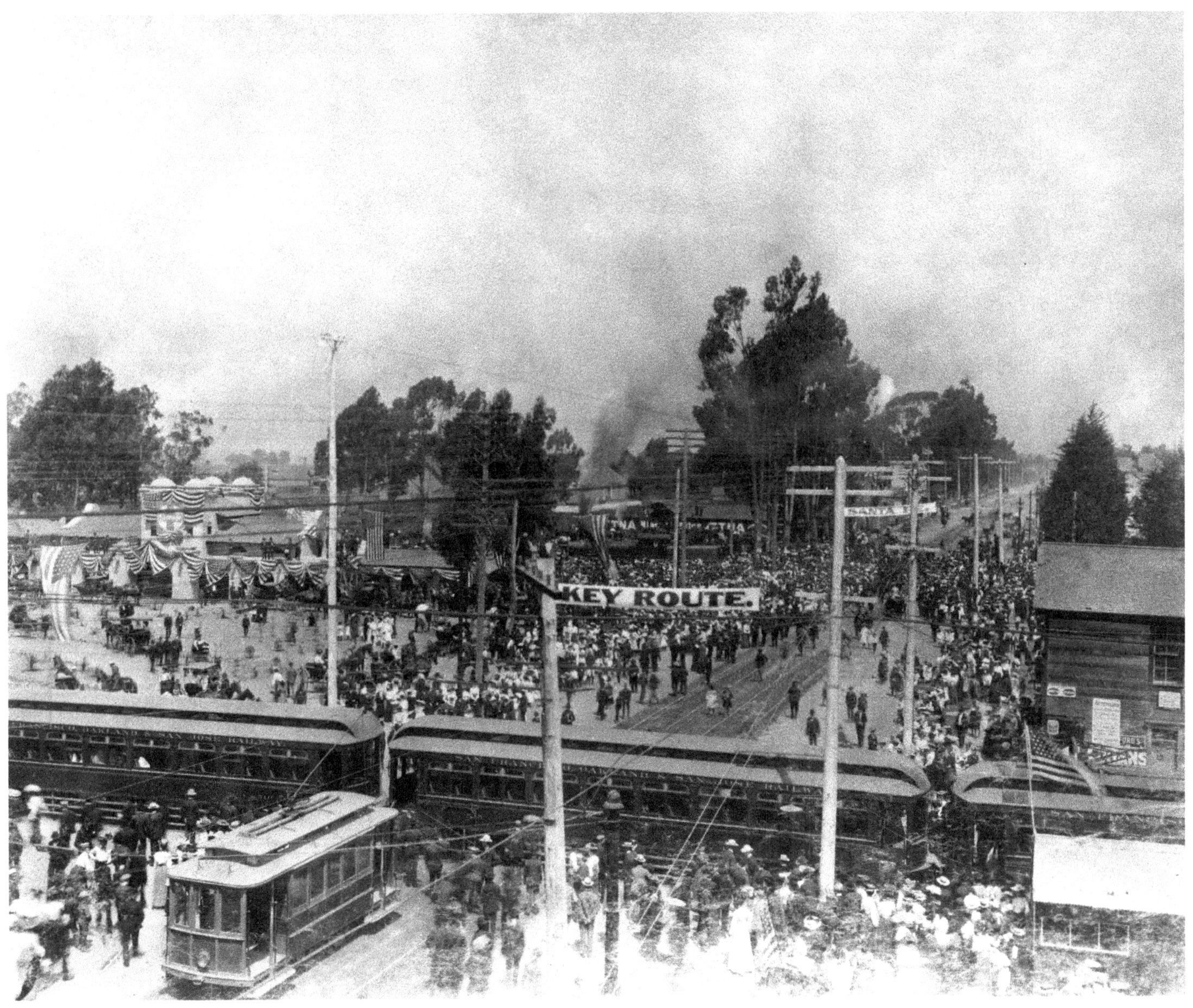

The streets of Emeryville were filled with well-wishers for the arrival of the Atcheson, Topeka and Santa Fe Railroad in 1904 to challenge the monopoly grip held by the Southern Pacific on Oakland's waterfront. That Santa Fe train is seen here passing through Emeryville at San Pablo and Yerba Buena avenues to its new Oakland wharf, made possible through the acquisition of a bankrupt company with franchise rights to the waterfront.

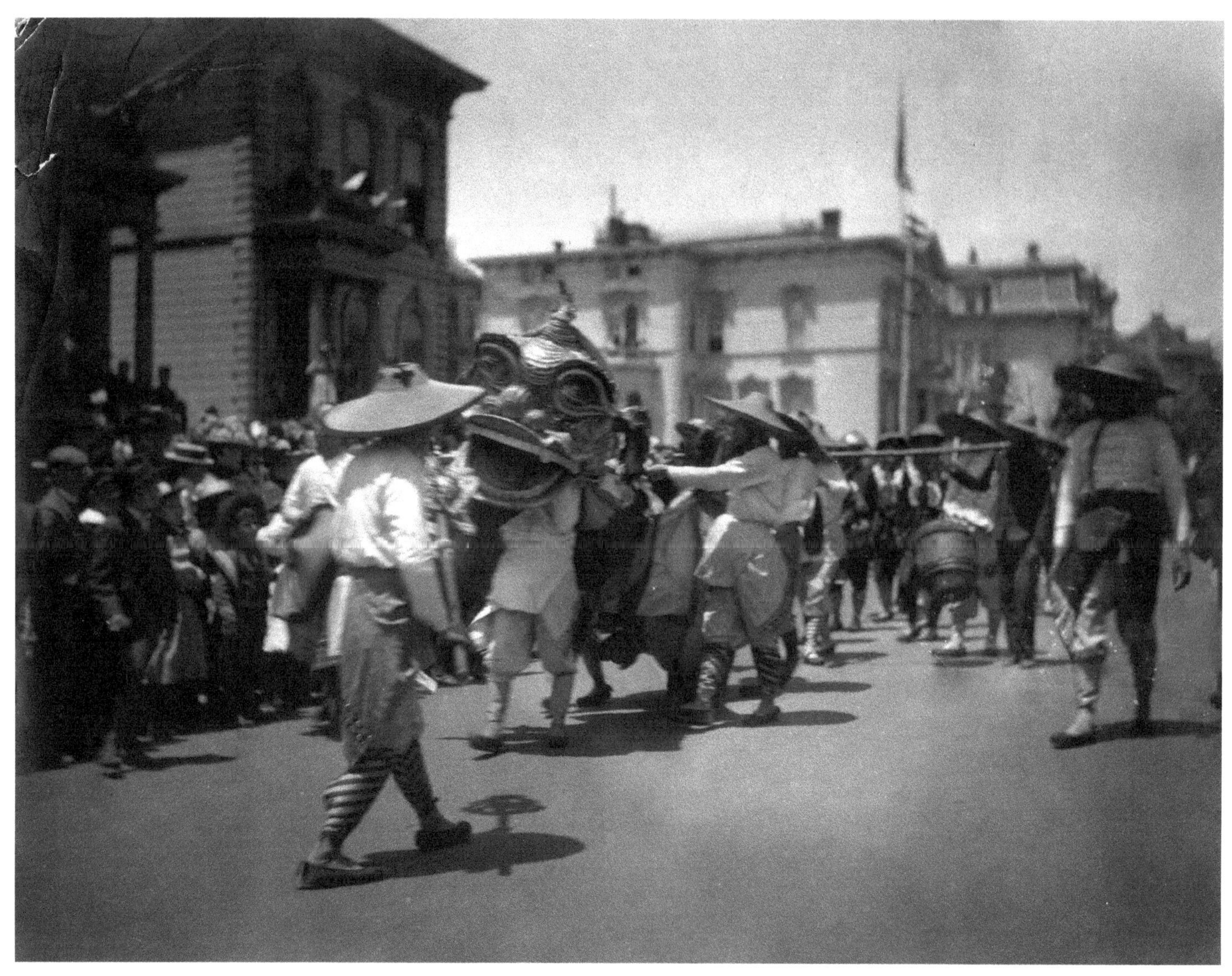

Members of Oakland's Chinese-American community, the earliest ethnic community to form in the city, assemble into a dragon for a parade sometime before the earthquake of 1906.

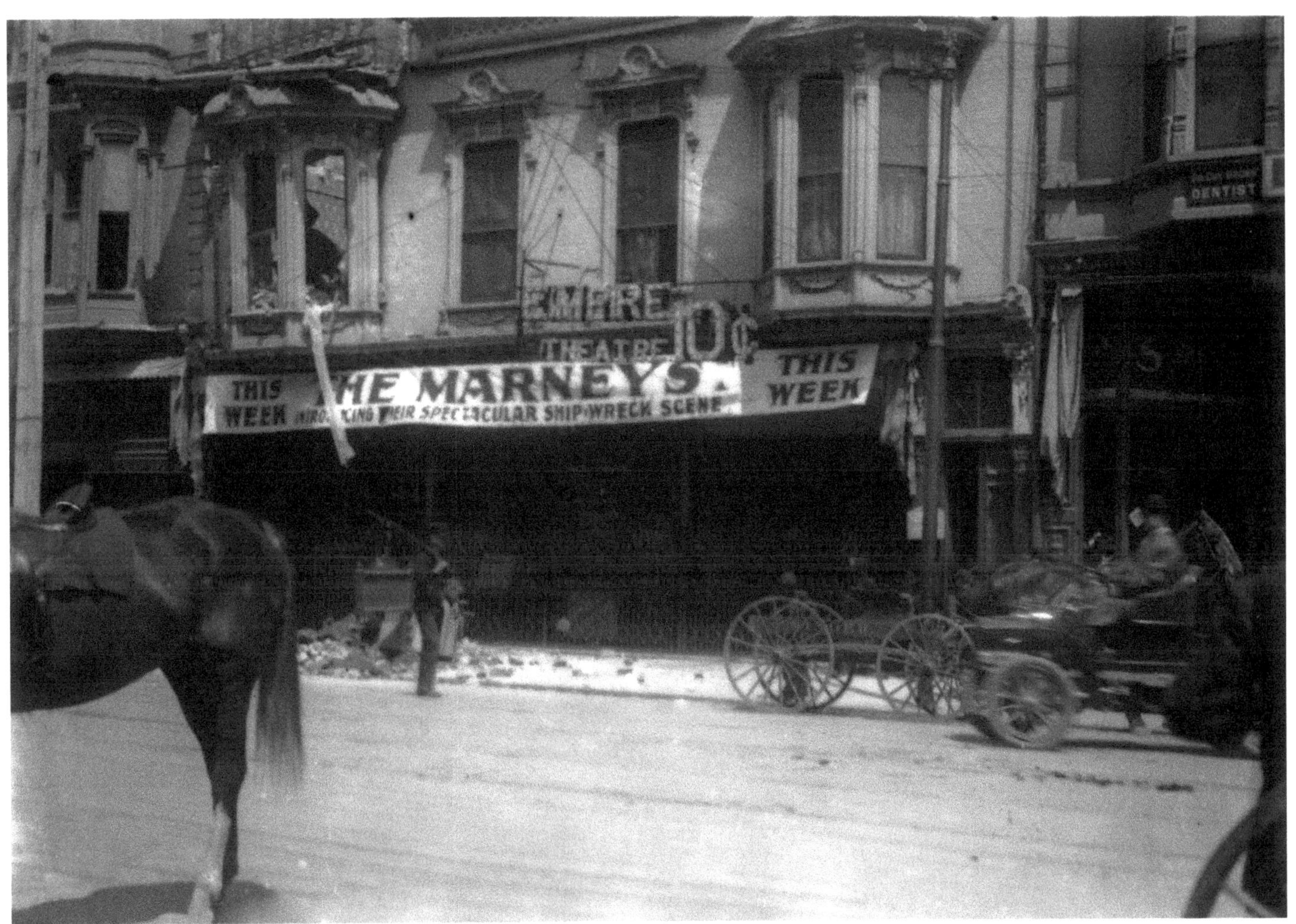

Near dawn on April 18, 1906, one of the most powerful earthquakes ever recorded in North America struck along the San Andreas Fault, two miles offshore from San Francisco. The event would bring near complete devastation to that city. In Oakland, only moderate damage was reported, beyond the tragedy at the Empire Theatre, where the roof collapsed killing five members of the burlesque troupe performing there who were asleep in rooms upstairs. The banner advertising the troupe proclaimed, but now laments, "The Marneys: Introducing Their Spectacular Ship-wreck Scene."

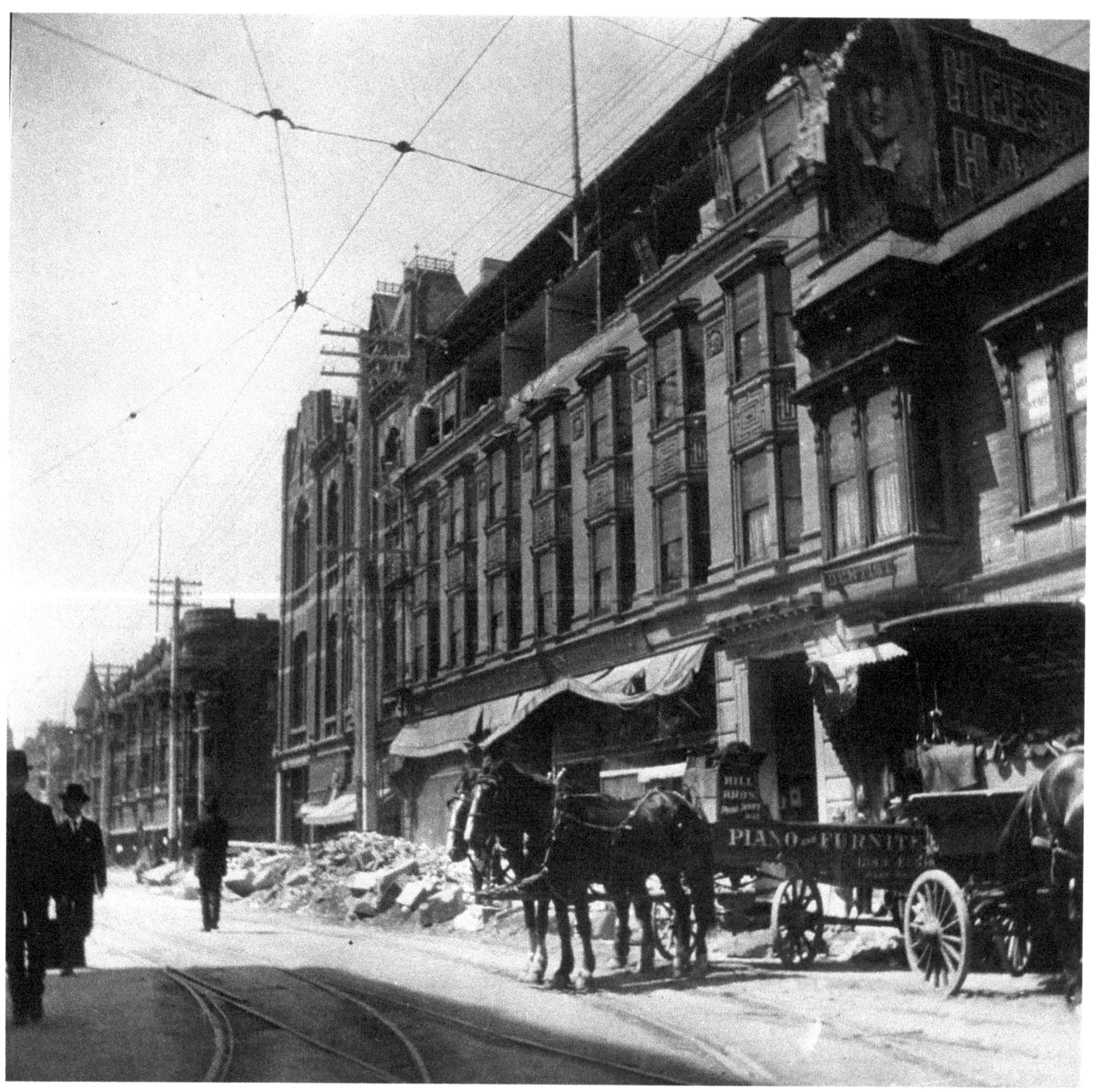

Bricks and stone fell from the facades of buildings along Washington Street in the earthquake.

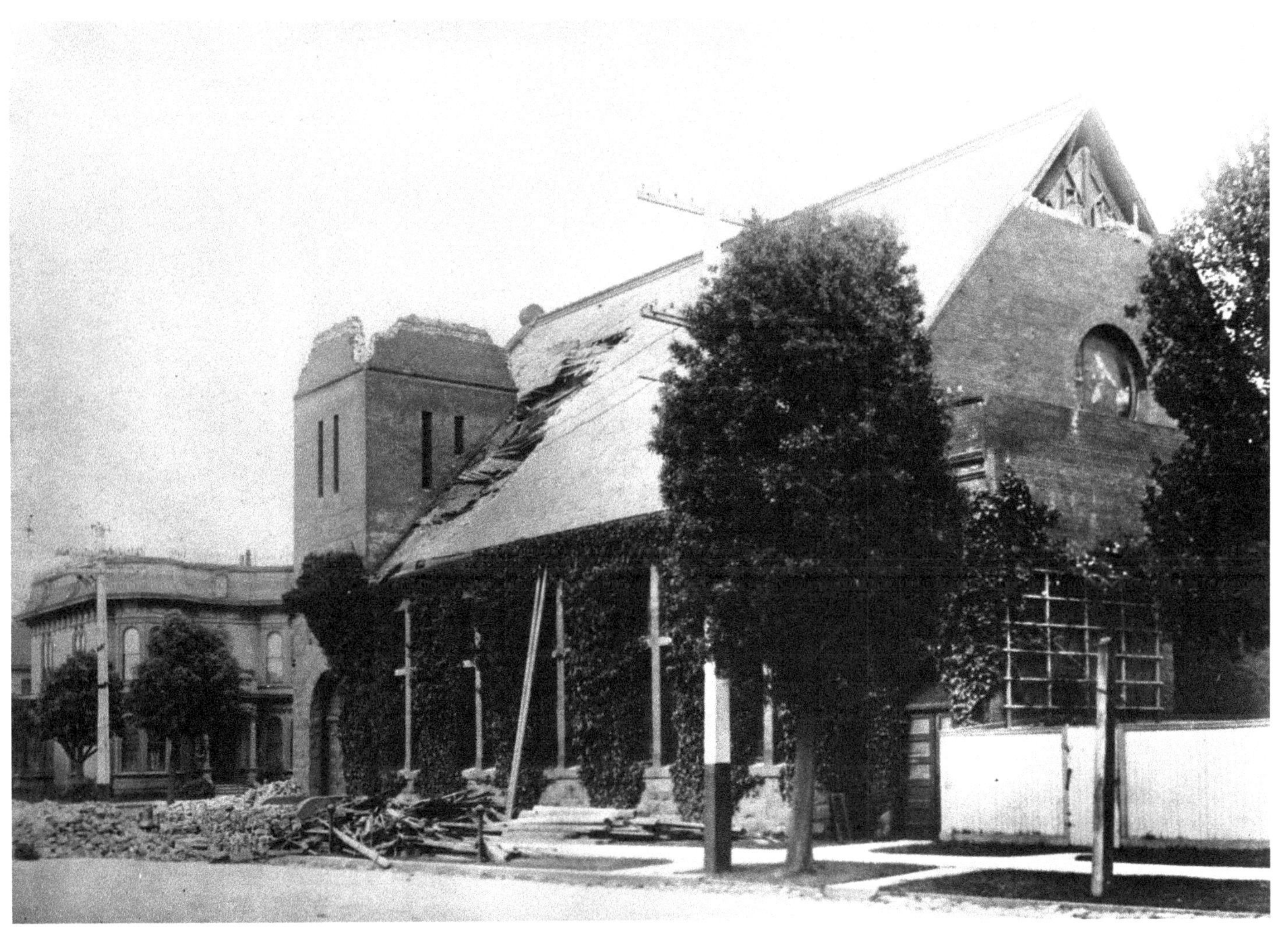

The earthquake took down the steeple of Oakland's First Unitarian Church, housing a congregation that included many of the city's most politically active residents. Similar damage occurred to the structure in the earthquake of 1989.

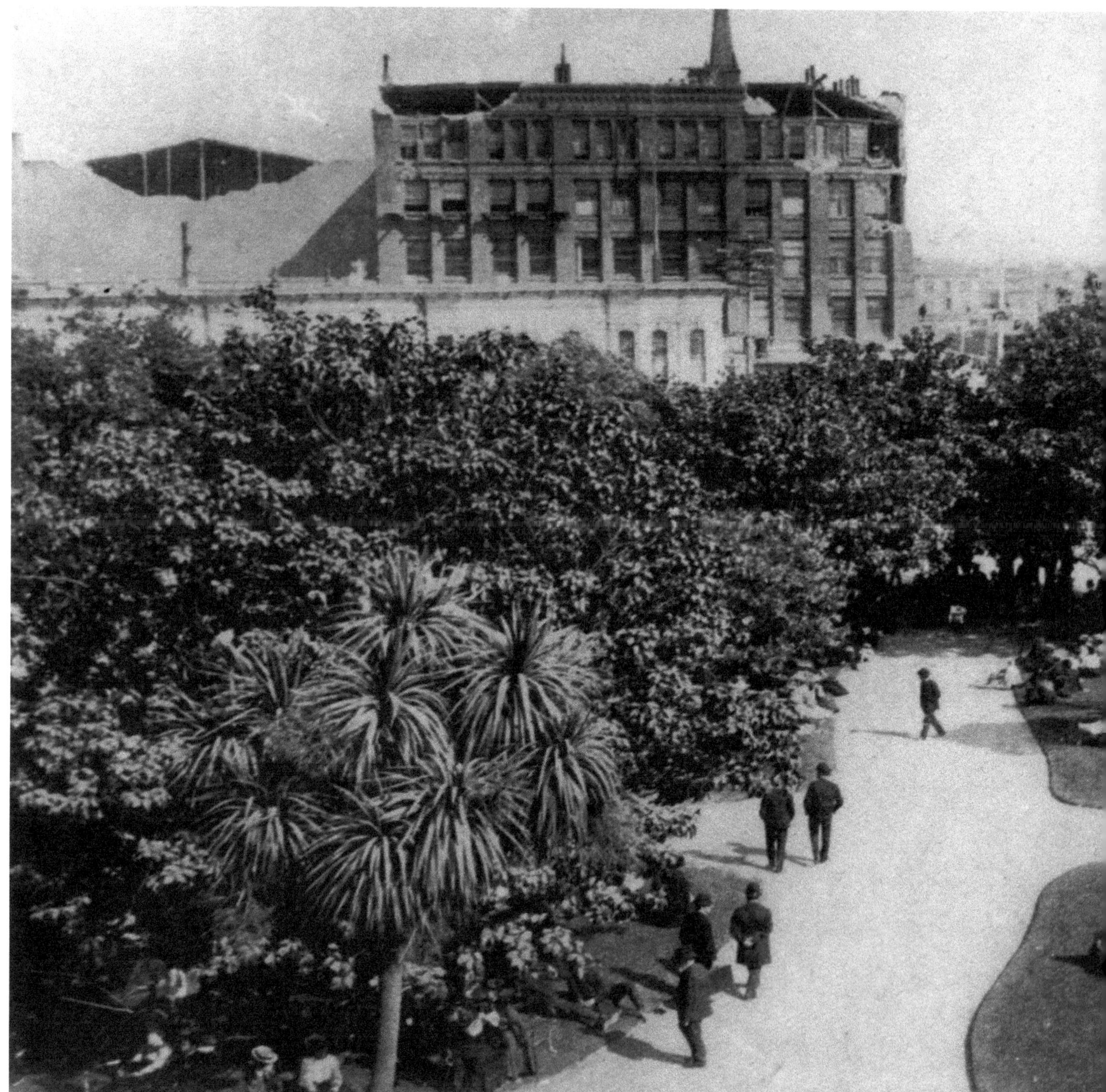

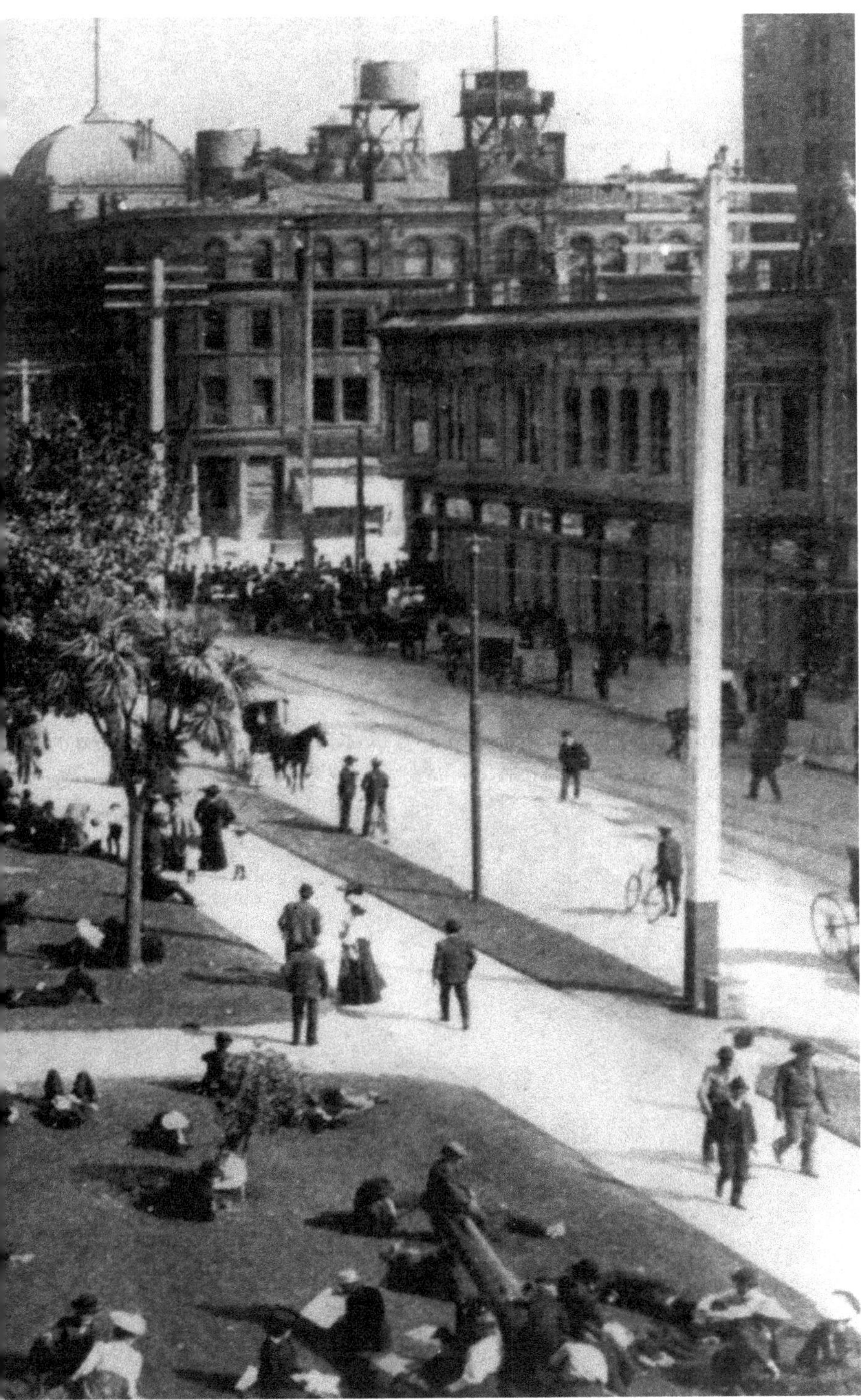

Stunned residents gather at City Hall Plaza on the morning of April 18, 1906, surveying the damaged skyline and preparing for the arrival of thousands of displaced San Franciscans who were boarding the ferries to flee the wreckage of their city.

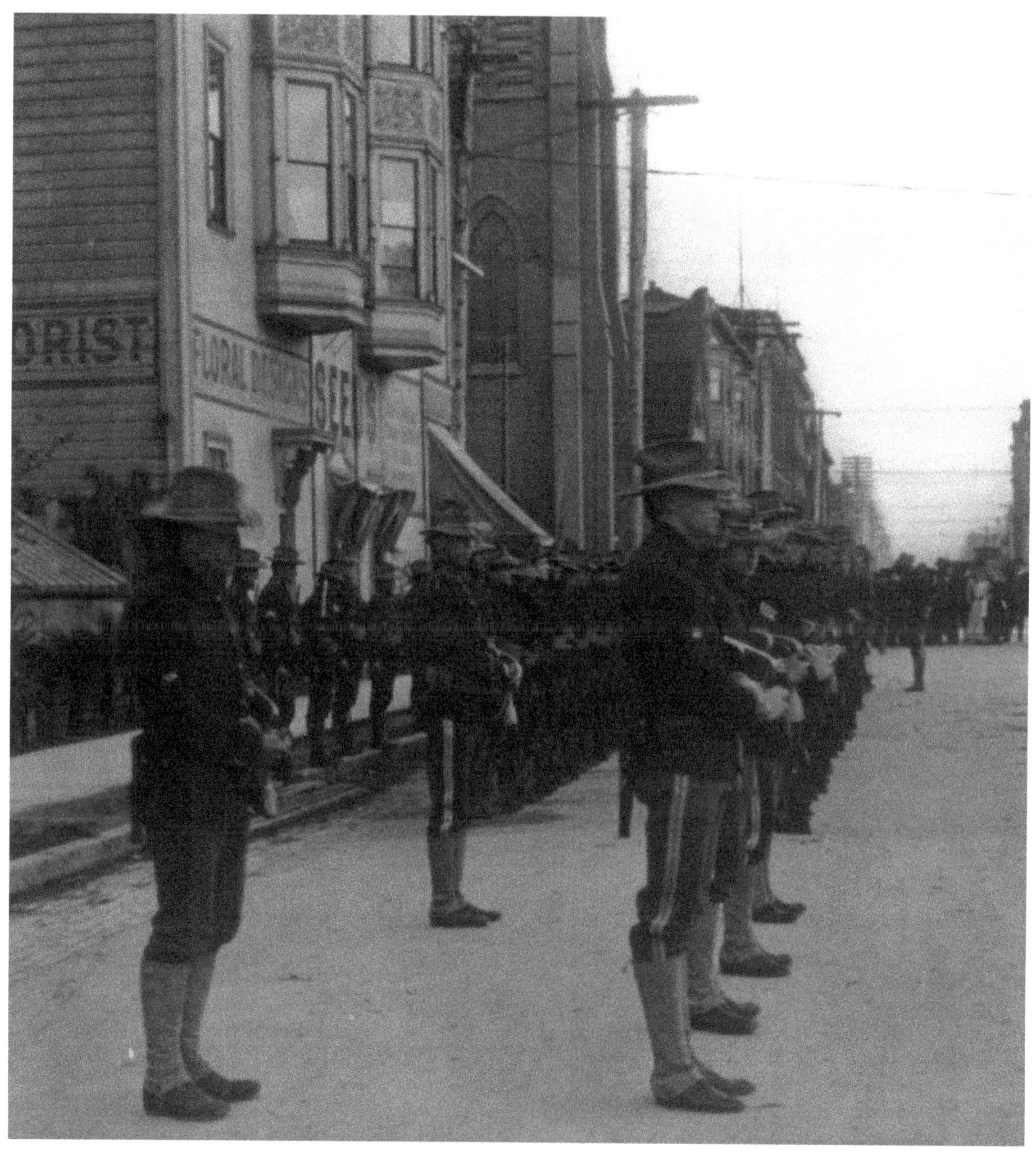

Oakland took great pride in the response by its residents in the relief efforts following the earthquake of 1906. Governor George C. Pardee, a former mayor of Oakland, made the city the base of the state's emergency and militia response. He was in Oakland on May 10, 1906, for the drills of Company A and Company G of the Fifth Regiment of the National Guard shown here.

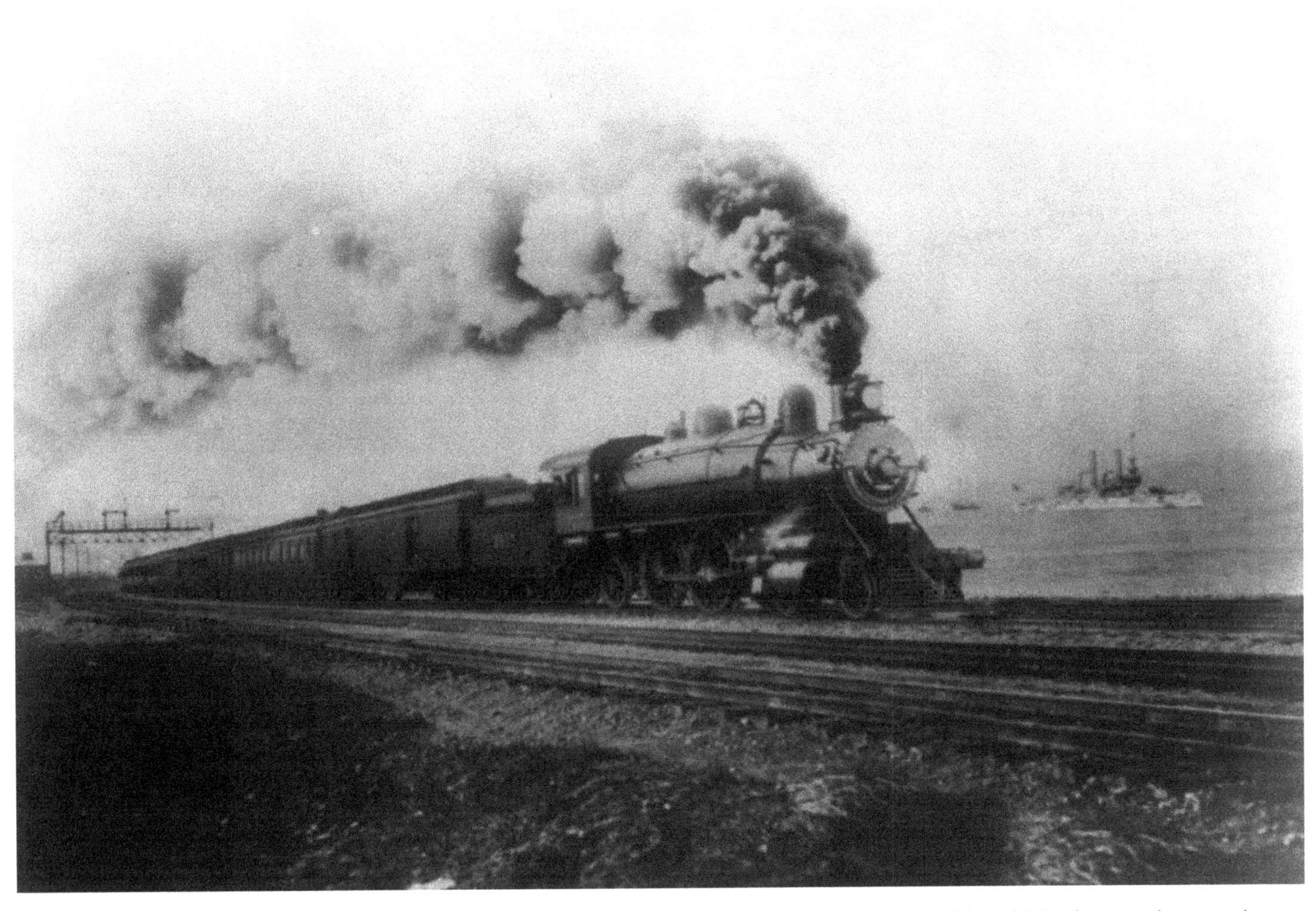

Throughout the crisis, the overland railroad steamed on. Here a train heads north from a station at 16th and Wood streets that served the trains heading over the Sierra Nevada by way of Sacramento and the coastal route between Los Angeles and Seattle.

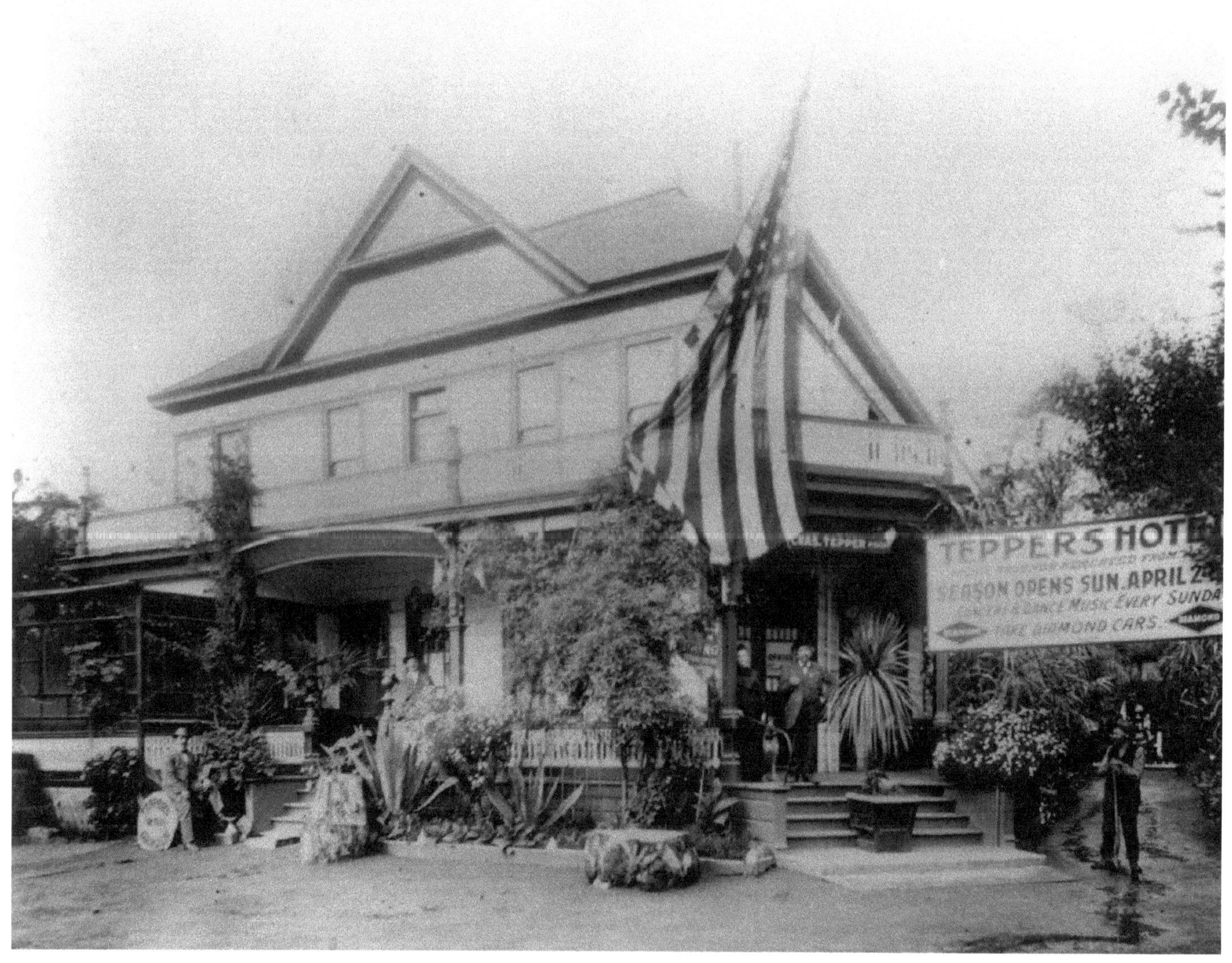

Just beyond the city limits to the east, Charles Tepper opened a resort offering beer and polka to his guests in an outdoor setting. Tepper had arrived with large numbers of German immigrants to Oakland beginning in the 1880s, many of whom settled on small farms and dairies on the city's eastern outskirts.

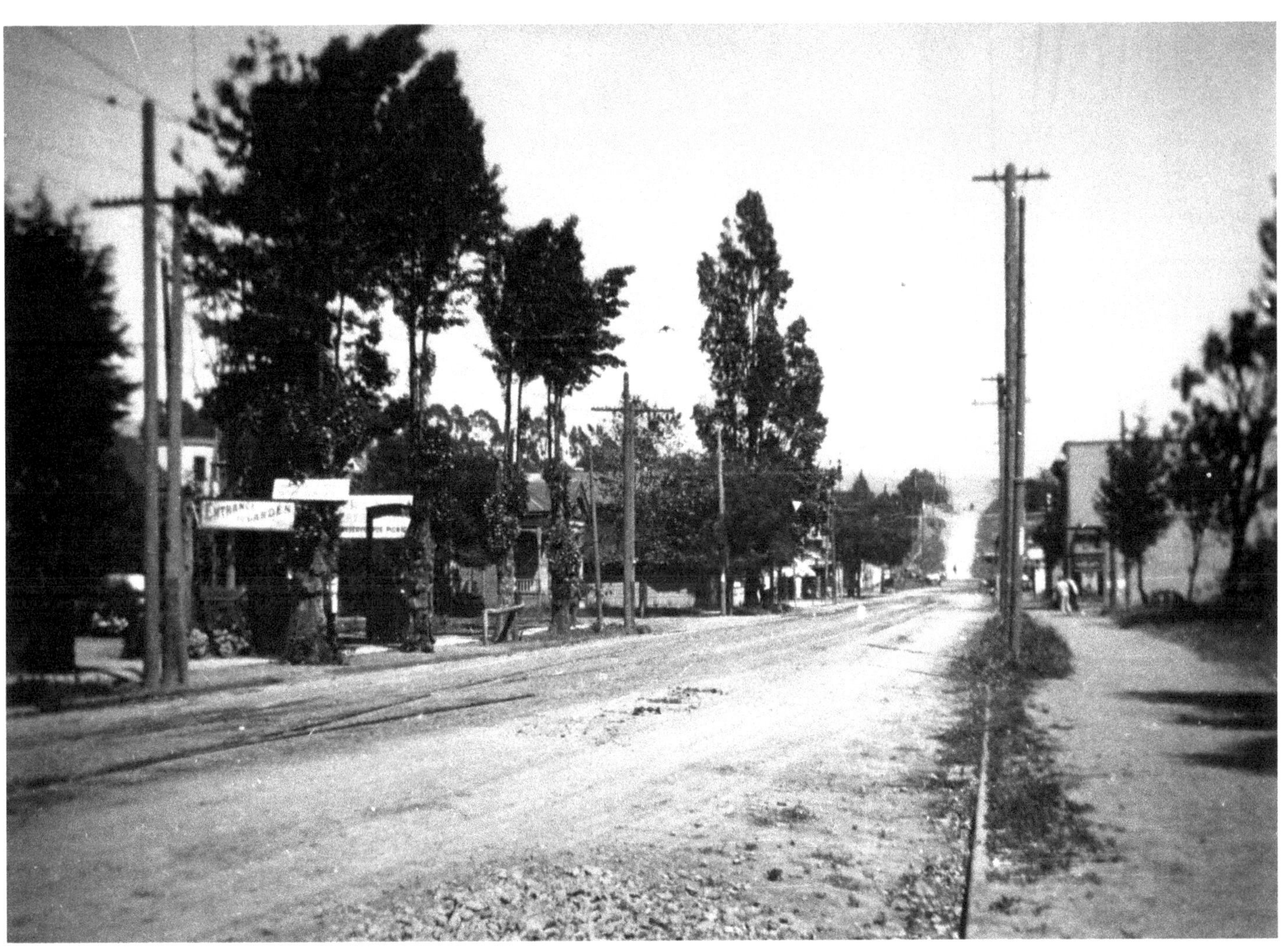

The stretch of Hopkins Street that passed Tepper's resort, visible here on the left, would become a main thoroughfare, renamed for General Douglas MacArthur after World War II, that linked Oakland to the rapidly growing southern and eastern suburbs. By the 1950s, a freeway running parallel to MacArthur Boulevard was required to undo traffic congestion.

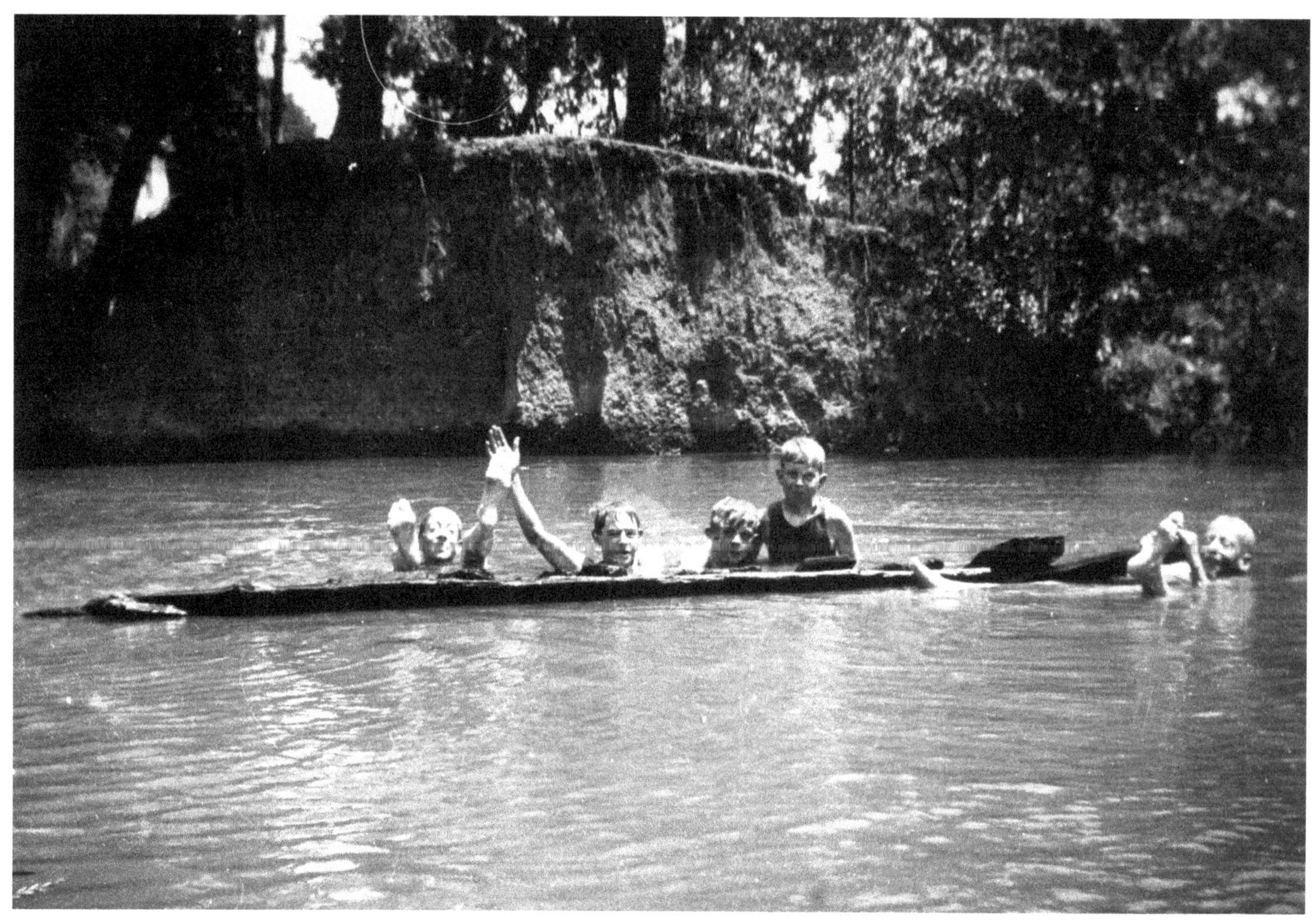

Not far from Tepper's resort on property once owned by horticulturalist Henderson Luelling, a dam across Sausal Creek created a popular plunge for neighborhood children, shown here in 1908. Along this creek in the 1850s, Luelling propagated the first cherries and apples grown commercially in California. He named his estate "Fruit Vale," from which the district got its name.

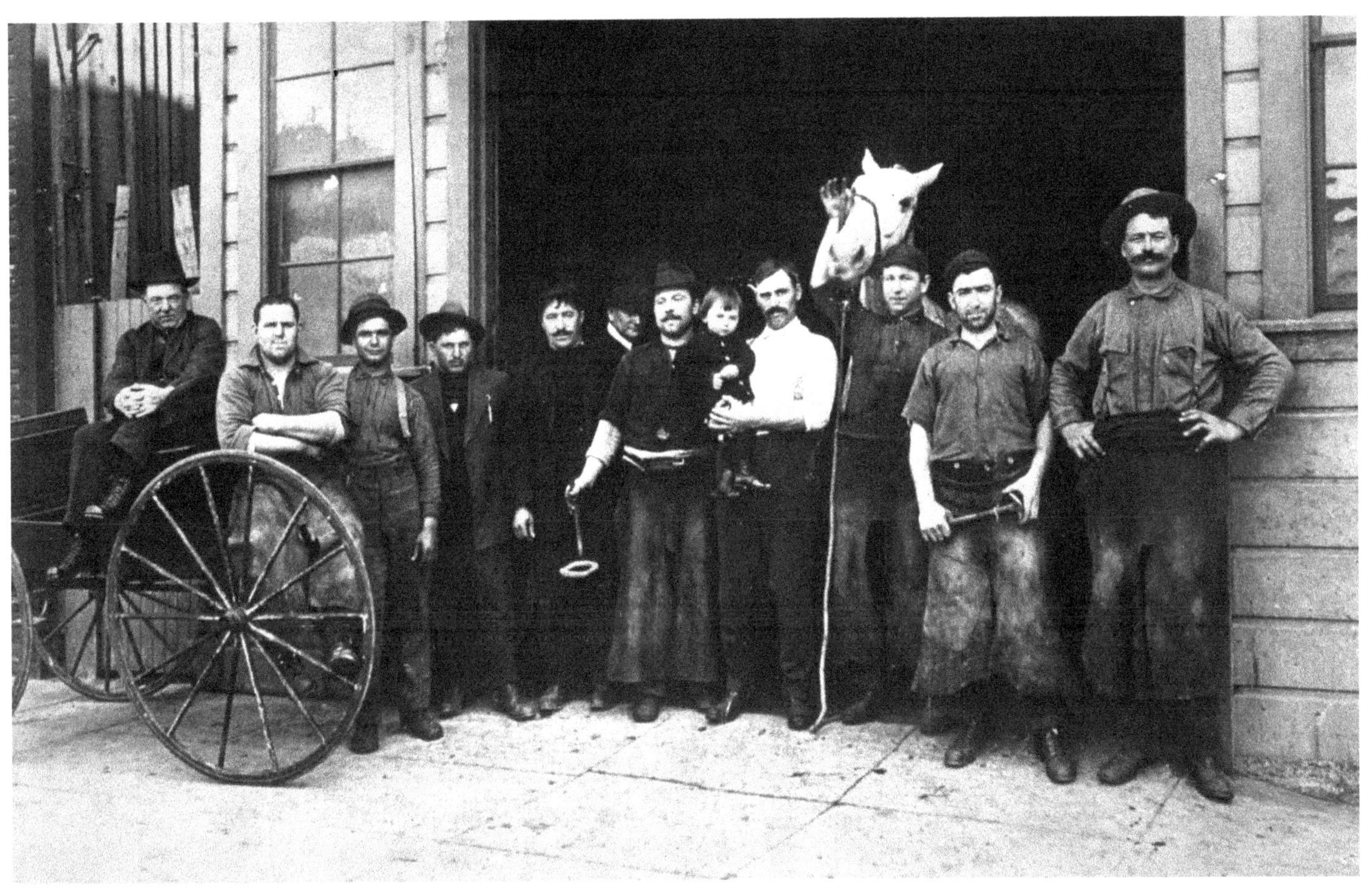

While some Oaklanders pursued the latest advances in vehicular technology, the blacksmiths at Oakland Horseshoe Shop made their livelihood supplying a much older method of transportation. Photographer Louis J. Teslo made his living from a shop in the Temescal district taking pictures of his fellow Americans, those of Italian descent like the men employed at the shop shown here.

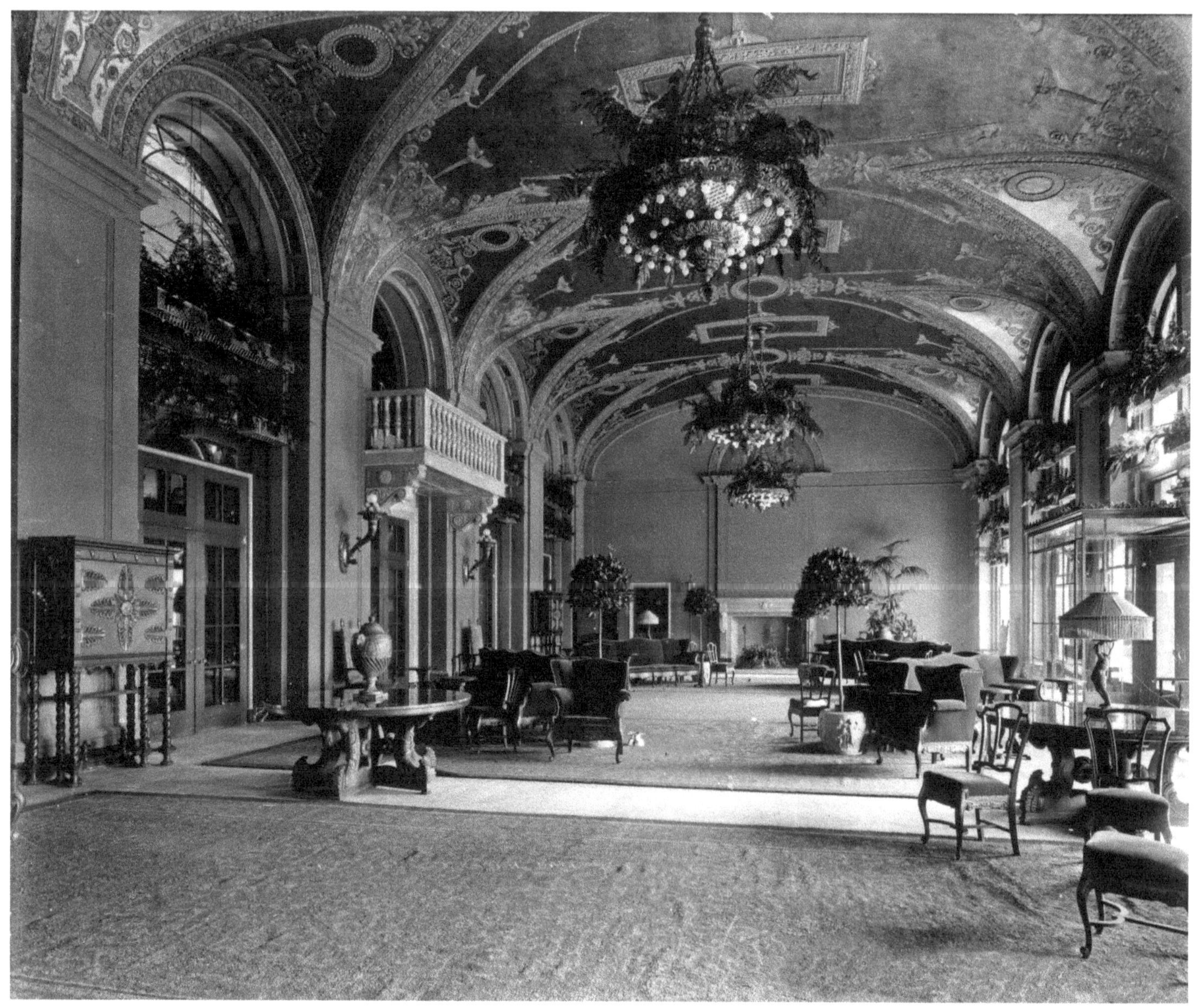

Hotel Oakland provided luxurious lodgings only a few short blocks from the auditorium and Lake Merritt. The hotel included a palatial lounging room, shown here, a large banquet room serving gourmet food, and plush penthouse suites. The Oakland served as the official West Coast hostelry of the Lincoln Highway, the nation's first cross-country roadway, which passed by its front doors.

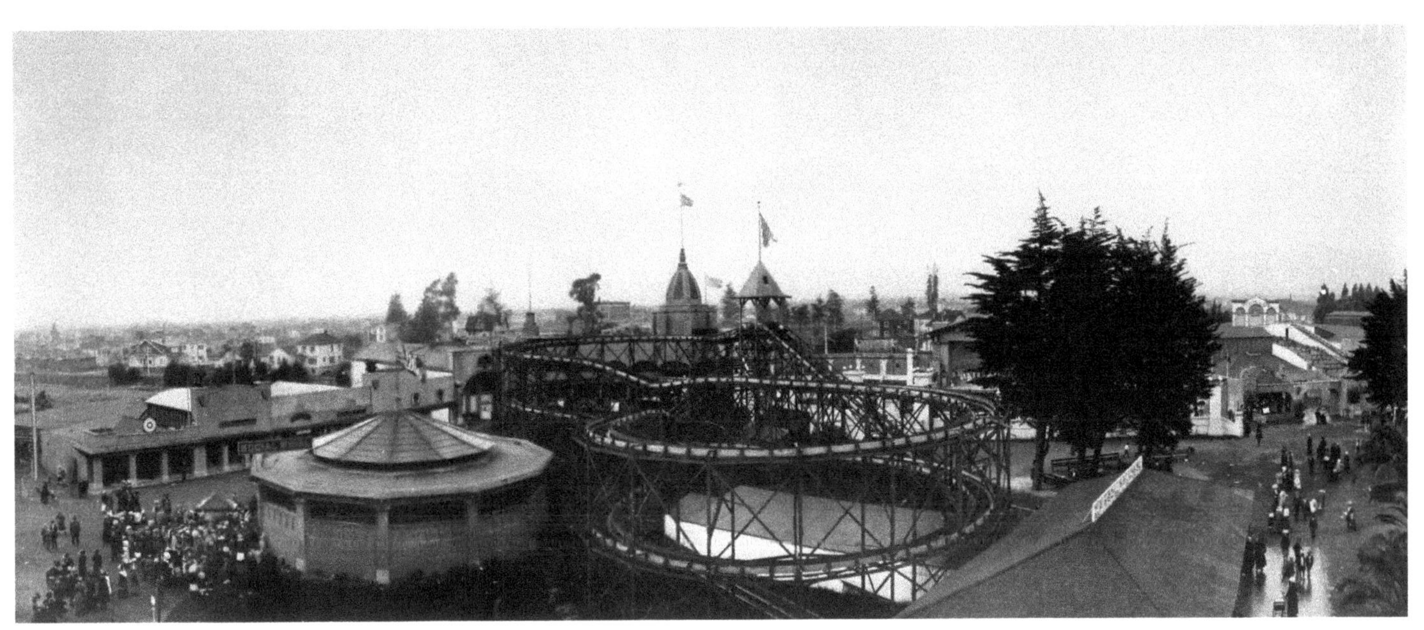

Idora Park in North Oakland had something for everyone: a gargantuan roller coaster and numerous other rides, picnic grounds, photo booths, and an arena with the first outdoor public address system in the nation, created by Oakland's Magnavox Company. Hobart Bosworth began his acting career in plays performed in the arena, and Fatty Arbuckle starred in films shot on location in the park. Idora Park was demolished in 1929 for a housing development.

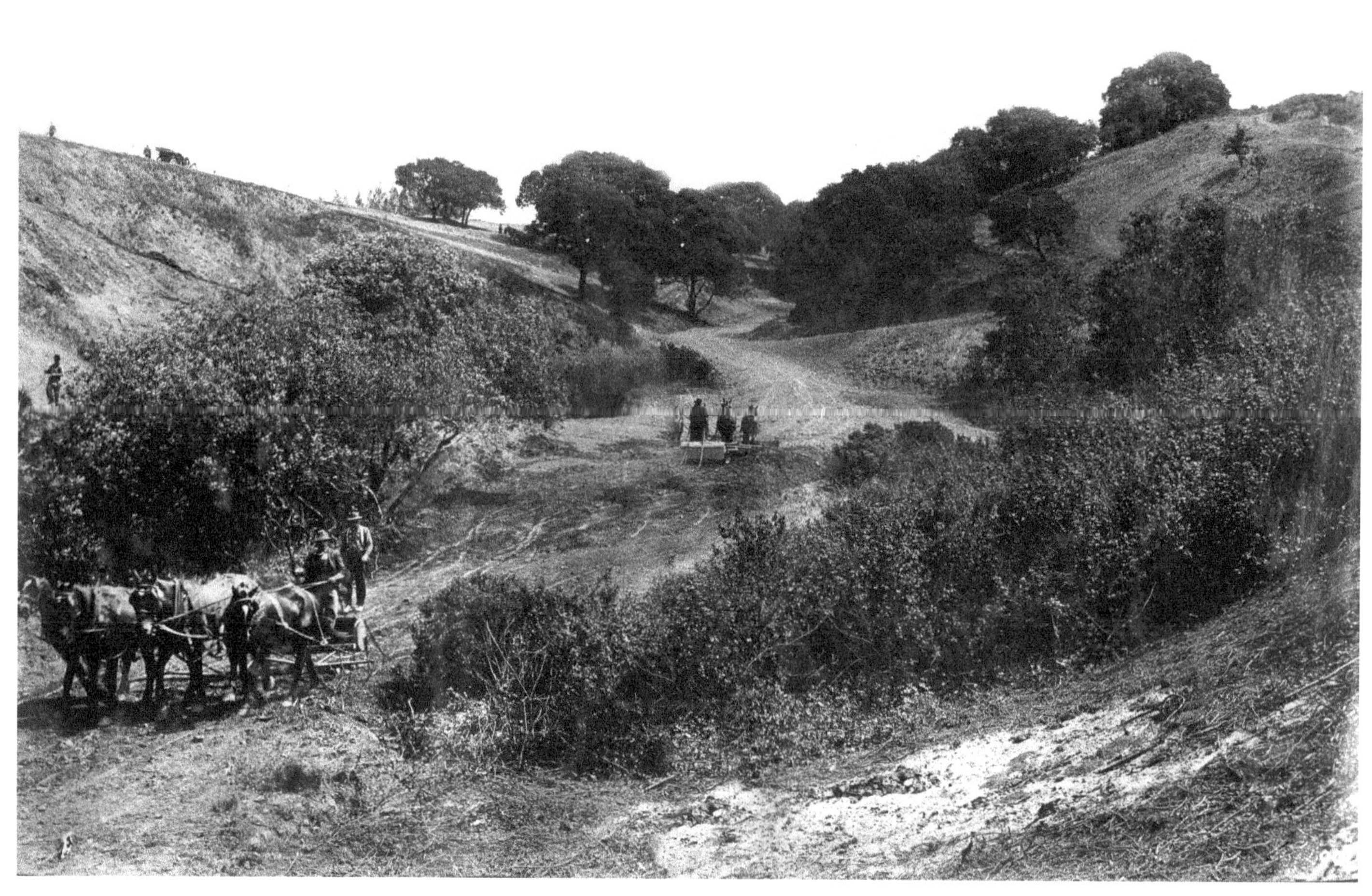

Oakland's surging growth at the start of the twentieth century slowly pushed its residential neighborhoods upslope, keeping road crews busy extending city streets into the hills. Like so many other cities in the country, the upland lots attracted far higher prices than home sites on the flatlands.

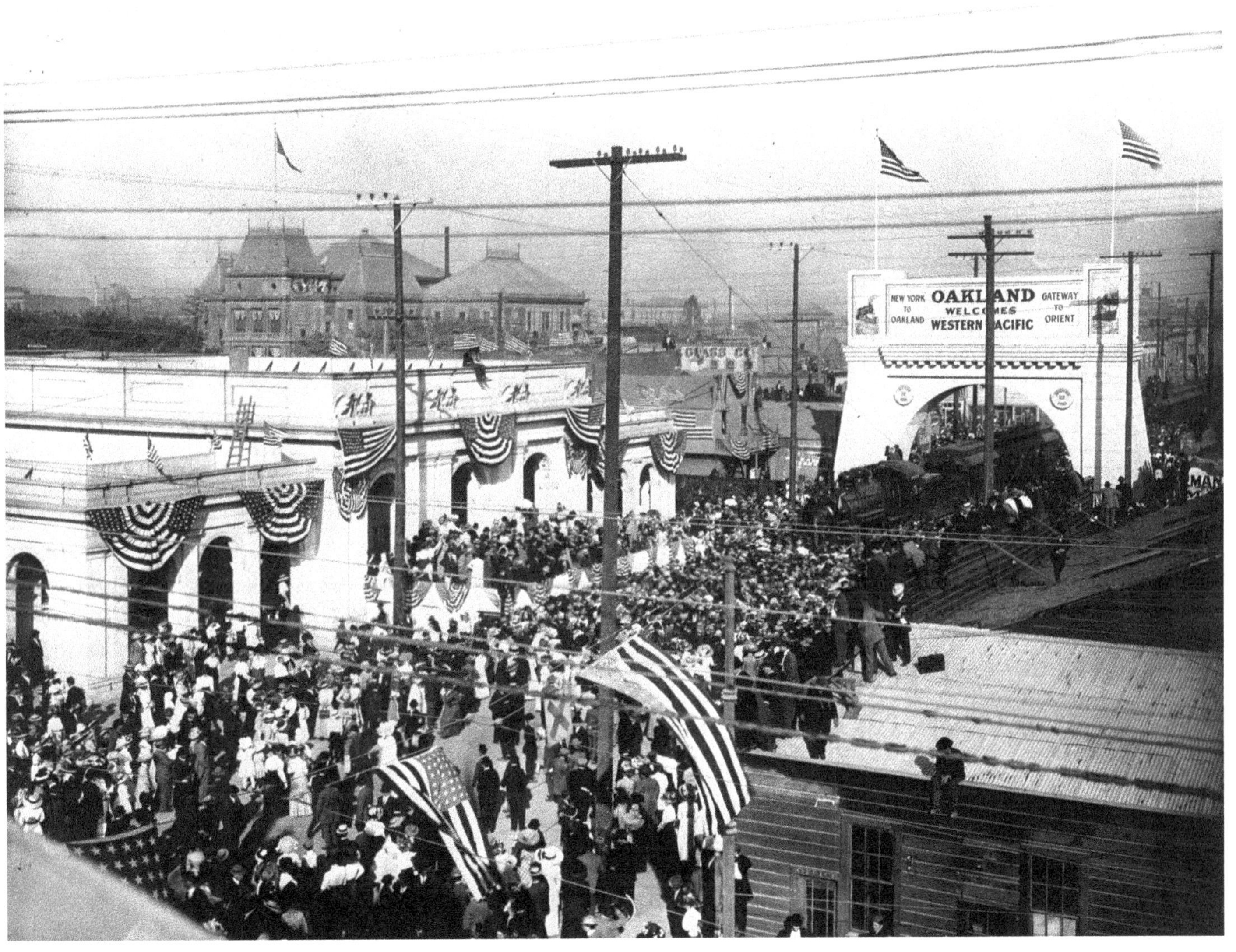

The arrival of the first train of the Western Pacific Railroad represented a great triumph after decades of litigation against the Southern Pacific Railroad. A photographer captured the arrival of the first cars of Oakland's newest rail carrier, bringing an end to the Southern Pacific's monopoly, which had choked progress on the city's waterfront for so long.

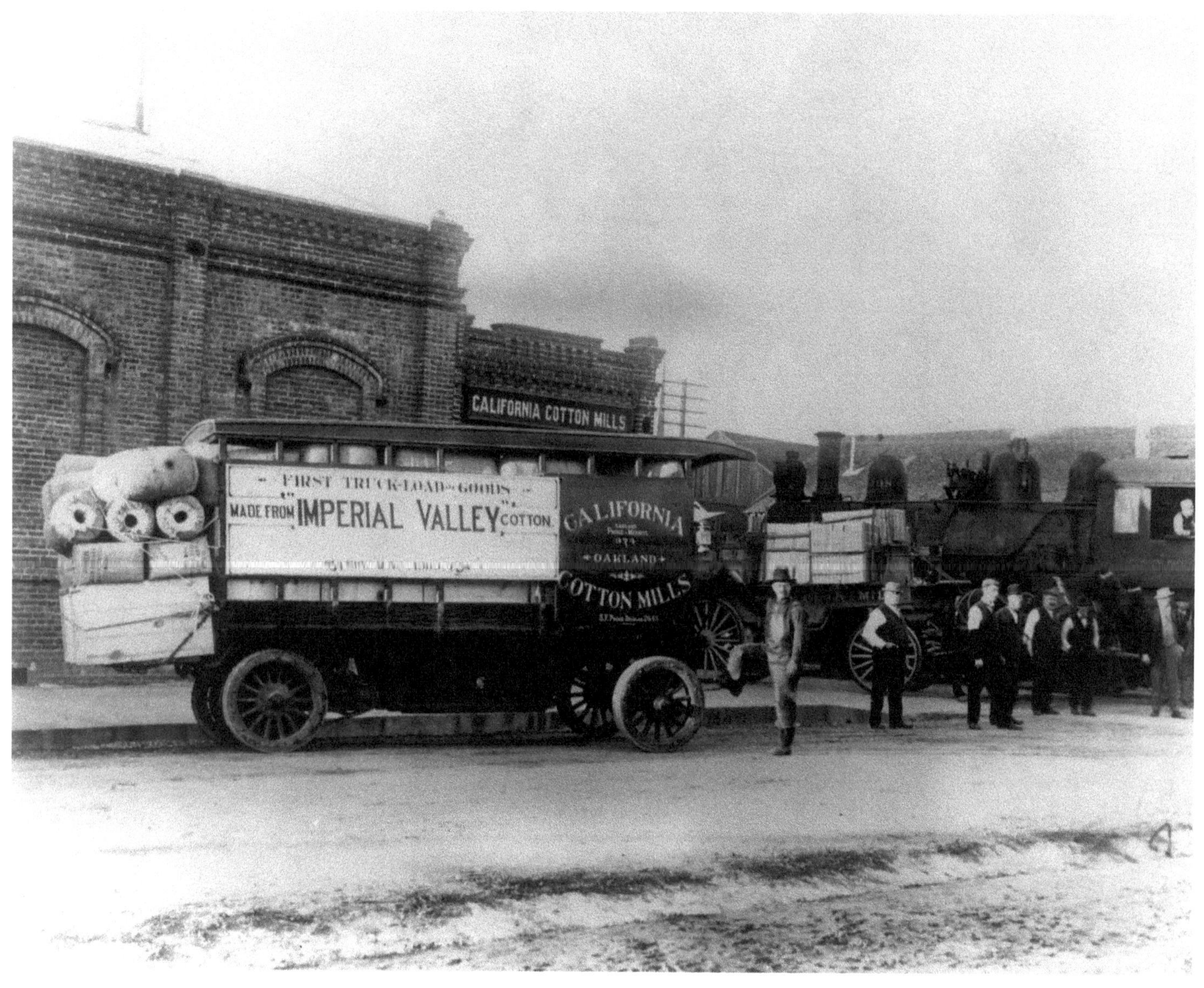

In 1909, the California Cotton Mills would spin the first skeins of thread from cotton grown in the distant Imperial Valley. A costly canal carrying water from the Colorado River had been completed to irrigate the arid deserts, making cotton farming in the valley feasible.

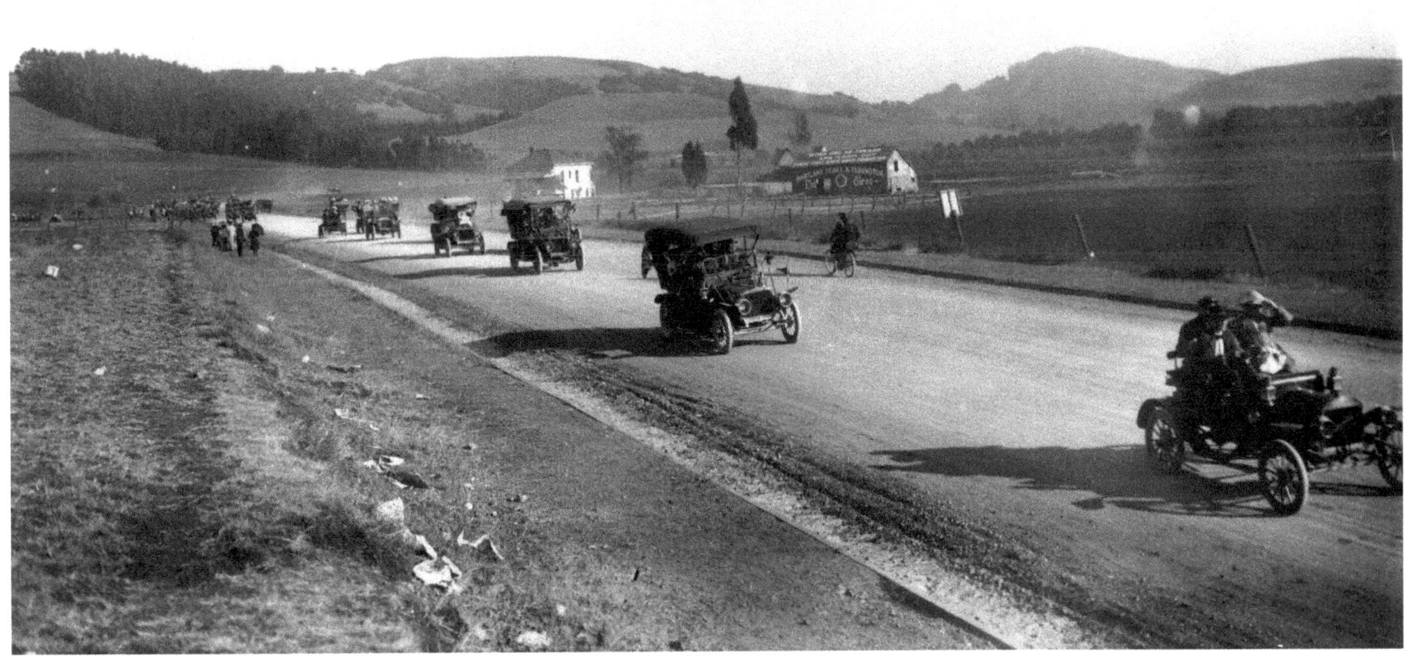

The 250th anniversary of the first European exploration of San Francisco Bay by Gaspar de Portola was cause for celebration and reason for a festival to show off the progress of San Francisco's recovery from the 1906 earthquake. Included in the 1909 Portola Festival was California's first major car race. Photographer Jack Frost caught the race on its way through East Oakland along Foothill Boulevard. In the distance, the Maryland Peart and Elkington tire company advertises by barn, "When our re-treads are worn out, their cost have been forgotten."

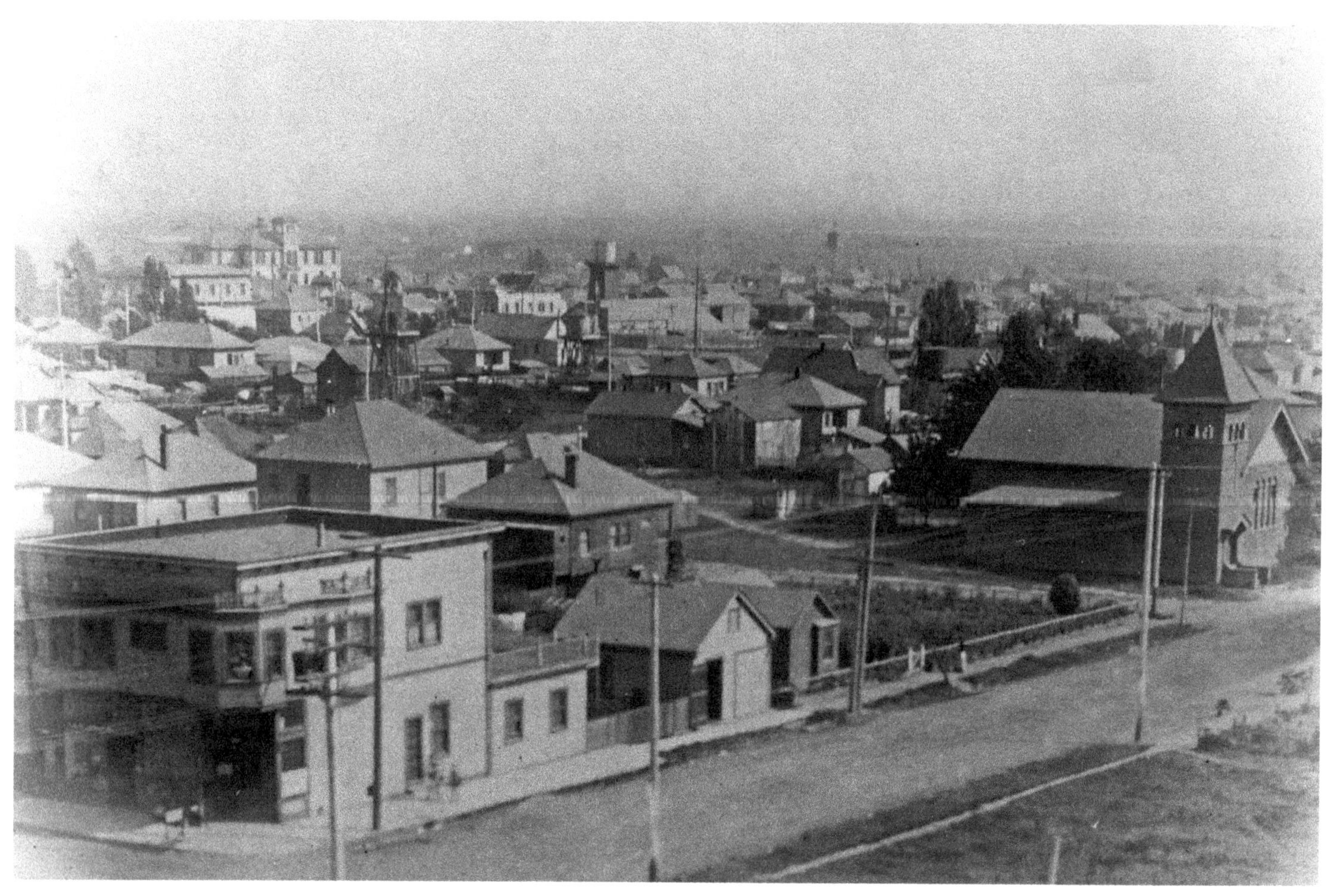

The unincorporated town of Melrose, with its post office and rail stop, along with neighboring communities Fruitvale and Elmhurst, came into the city limits in the historic annexation of 1909. It would soon be transformed into Oakland's industrial heartland.

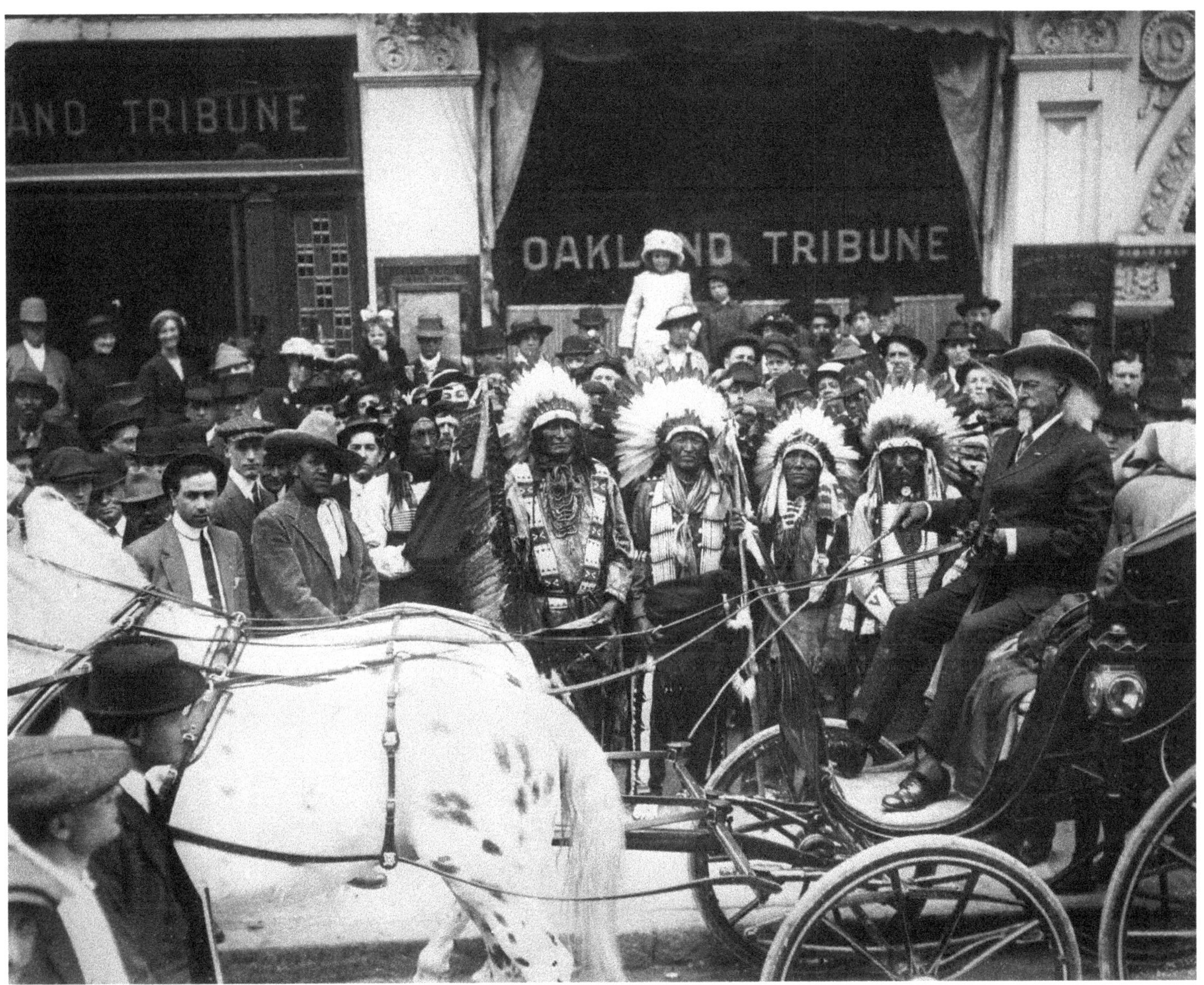

"Buffalo Bill's Wild West and Congress of Rough Riders of the World," William F. Cody's spectacular arena exhibition displaying the experience of the early American West, did as much to shape perceptions of that era as did eyewitness reports. While in Oakland during travels billed as the final tour, Cody poses with members of his cast for a publicity shot on October 1, 1910.

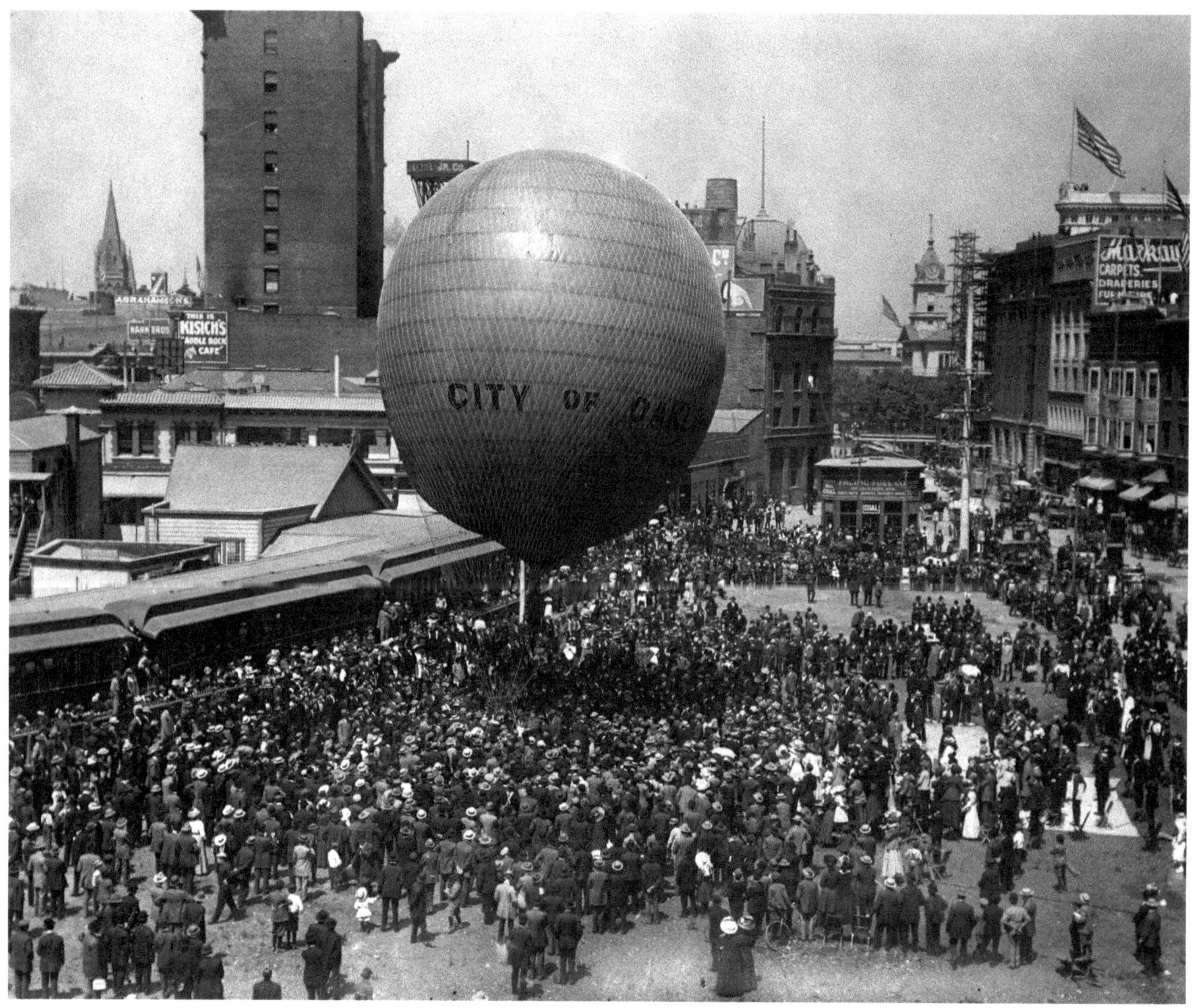

In August 1910, members of the Oakland Aero Club raised *The City of Oakland* on its maiden flight from the central streetcar station downtown. The hot-air balloon was lifted out over the hills and beyond Pleasanton, where a botched descent dragged its riders over a rocky field for more than 2,000 feet before the landing was accomplished. This rooftop view of the impending lift-off wasn't shared by many. Two youngsters, at lower right, have requisitioned the upper reaches of a wheelbarrow to improve their angle on the spectacle.

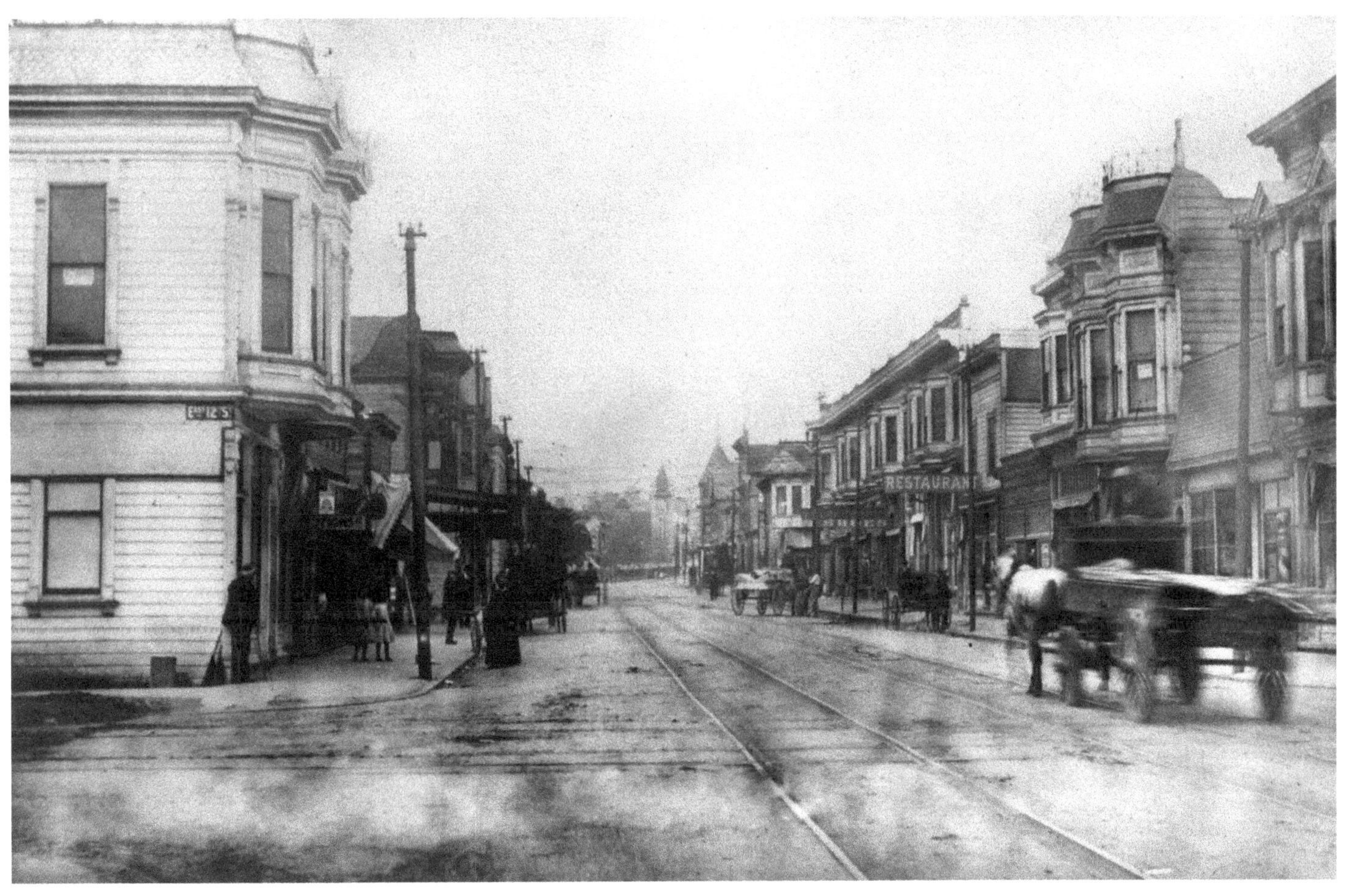

Following annexation of extensive tracts of land in 1909, the neighborhood commercial strip along 23rd Avenue no longer sat on the edge of town. Photographer Hugo Weitz, with a studio nearby, photographed the scene there around 1910.

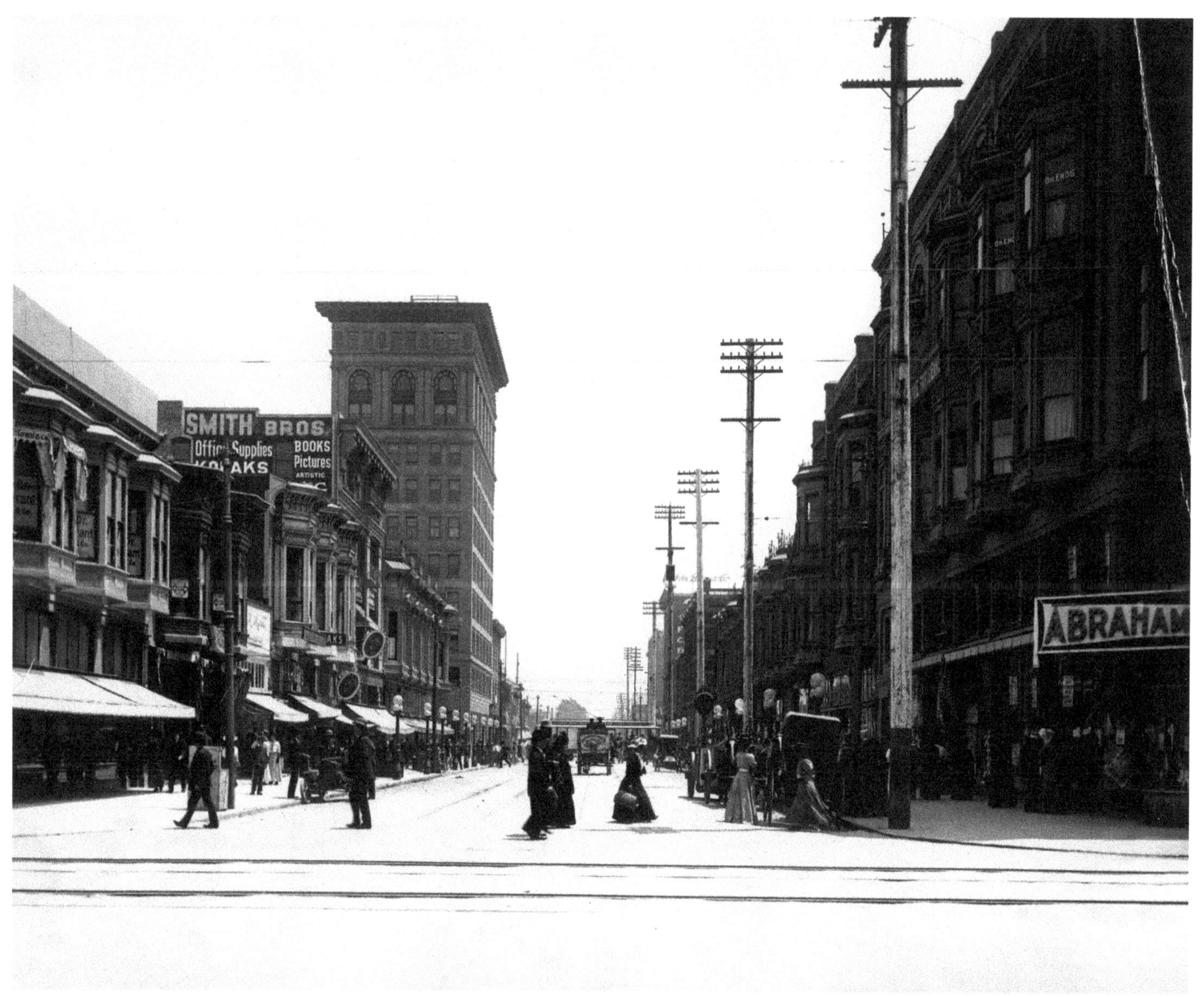

Clear signs of transition from wagons to automobiles are preserved in a view down Broadway around 1910. A high-rise building housing the Oakland Bank of Savings appears on one corner, and in the foreground a shiny new Ford has parked along the street.

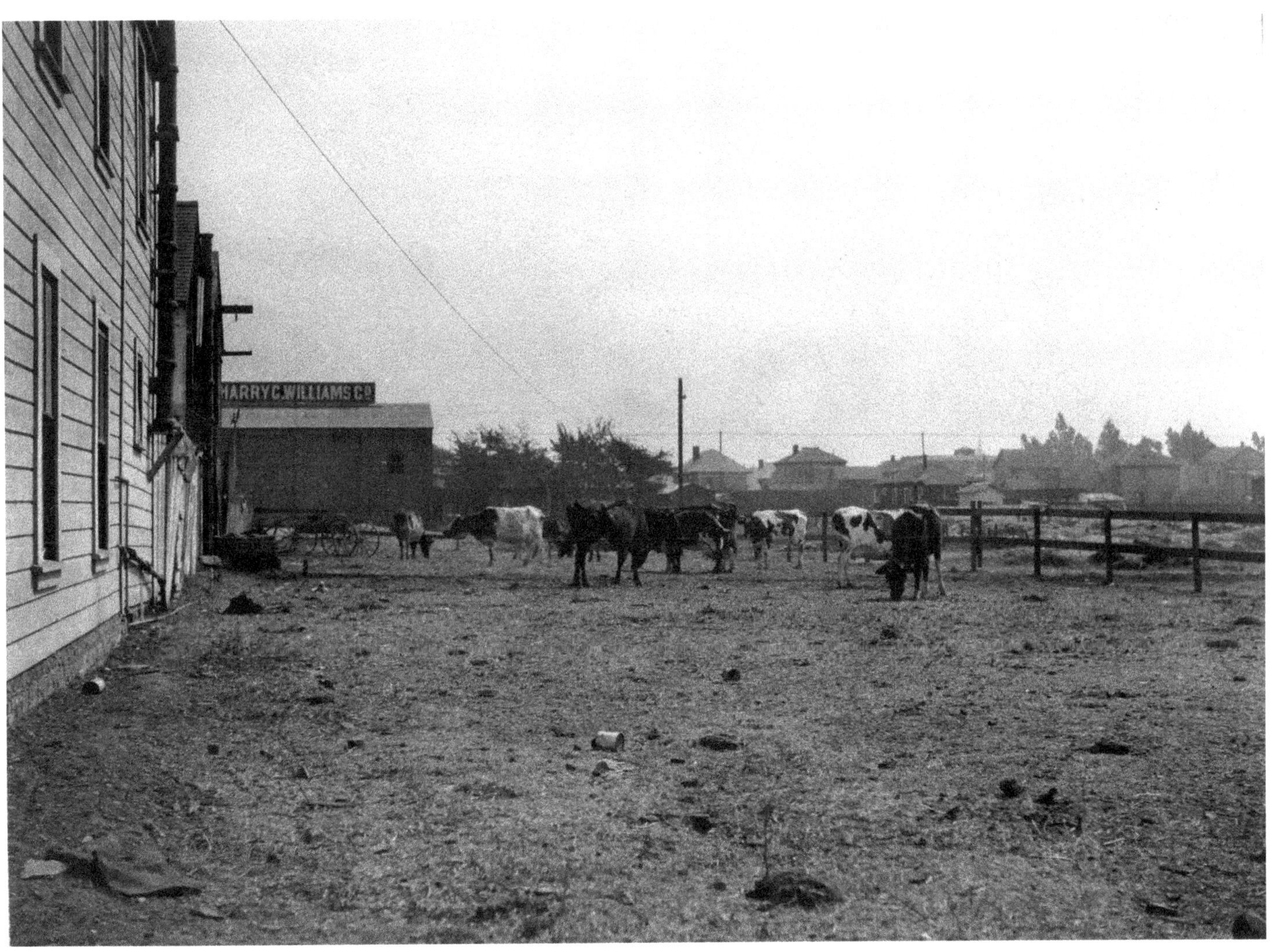

As industry began to create most of the new jobs, cattle remained a significant component of Oakland's economy. A section of neighboring Emeryville was known as "Butchertown" for its extensive stockyards and slaughterhouses. Dutch immigrant Felix Vandershoot, a carpenter with the railroad, supplemented his income with milk from cows raised at his home on Union Street in West Oakland, shown here in 1913.

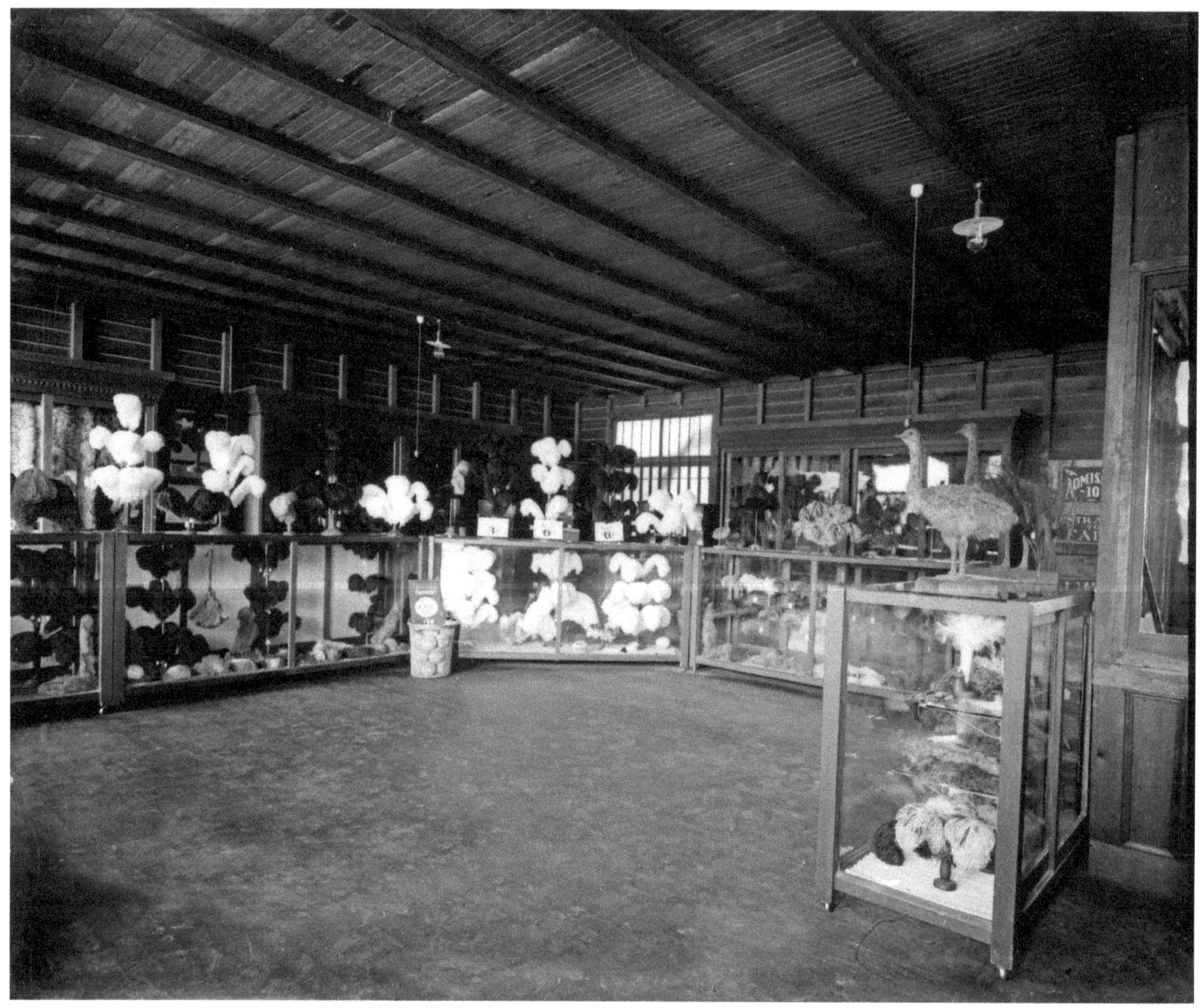

The hottest trend in fashion provided one East Oakland business with a lucrative commodity: ostrich feathers for the millinery trade. The Golden State Ostrich Farm raised the birds, shipped feathers internationally, and sold samples from its showroom on East 14th Street, shown here in 1910.

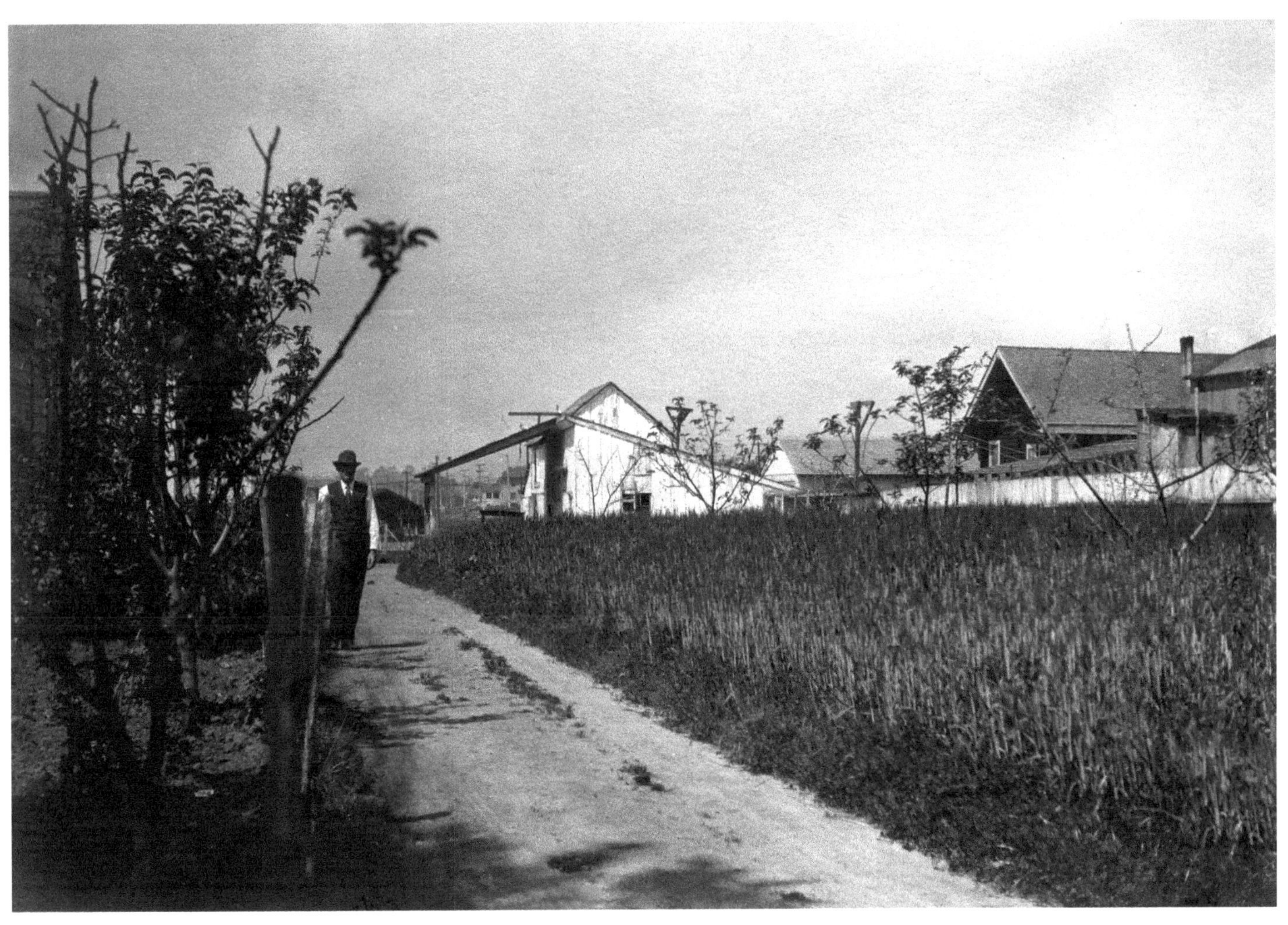

Chris Klein continued his ranching operations in Melrose as factories and houses were under construction throughout East Oakland. He appears strolling the grounds of his ranch in this snapshot from 1913.

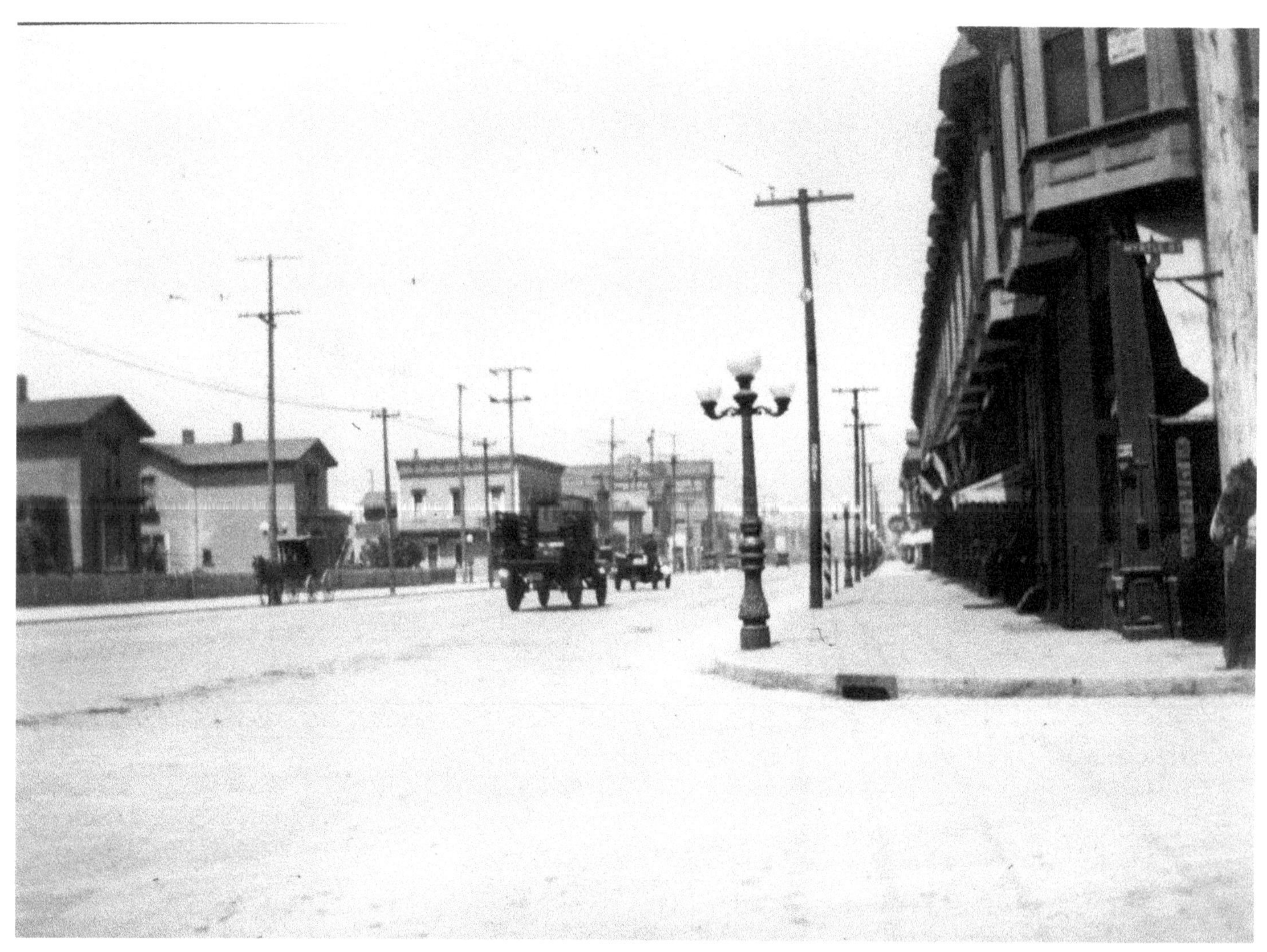

The automobile caught on quickly in Oakland, and Seventh Street, the main thoroughfare between downtown Oakland and the ferries, marine terminals, and rail yards of the Southern Pacific, would soon be clogged with traffic. Horace E. Smith captured the scene at Seventh and Myrtle streets with his Kodak Brownie camera in the summer of 1913.

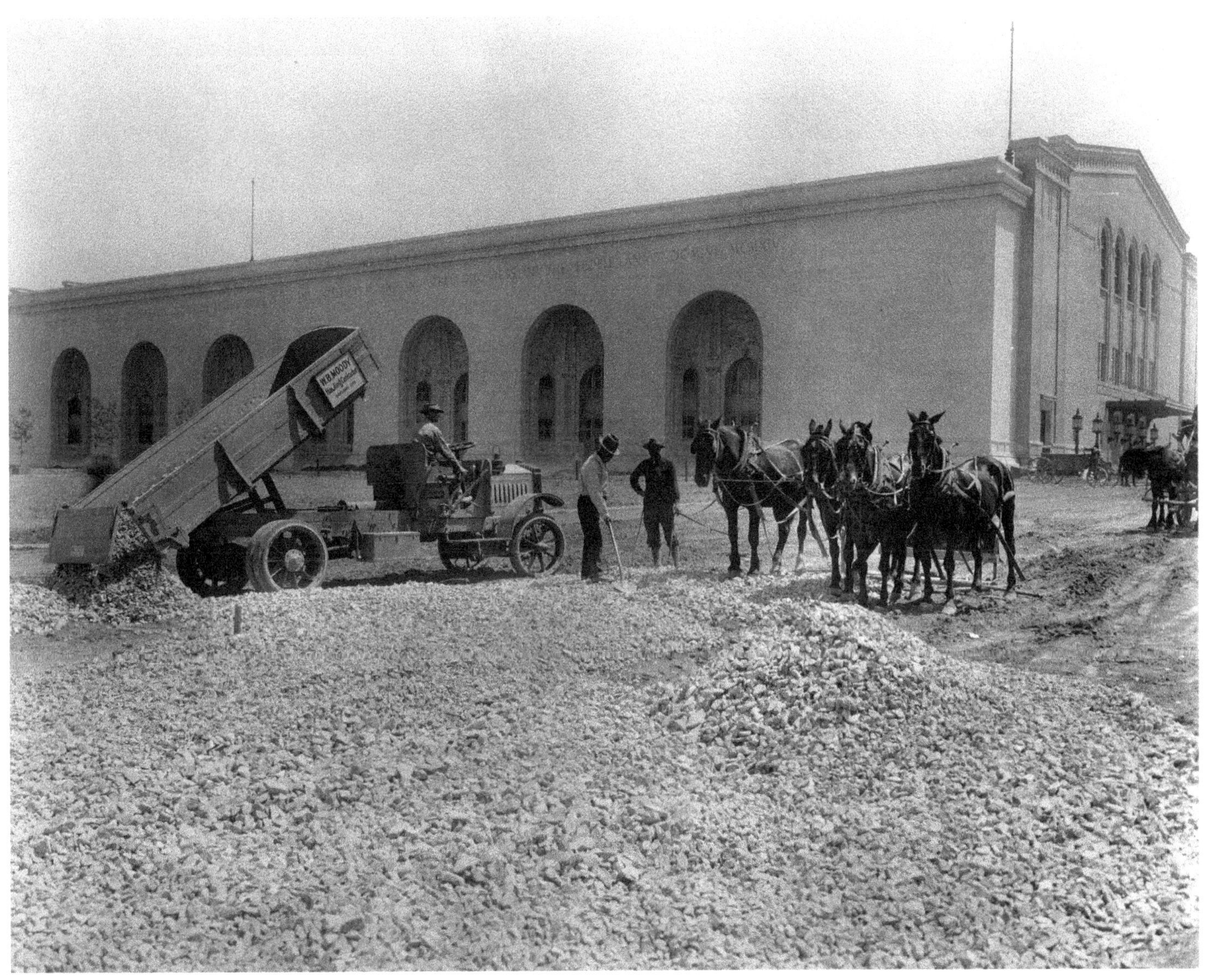

A large public assembly facility was central to the vision of Mayor Frank K. Mott in his ambitious plan for civic improvement. Under his leadership, a bond measure passed to finance those improvements, including construction of the Oakland Municipal Auditorium designed by leading architects Harry Hornbostel and John Joseph Donovan. A photographer captured city workers laying gravel for a grand promenade in front of the building.

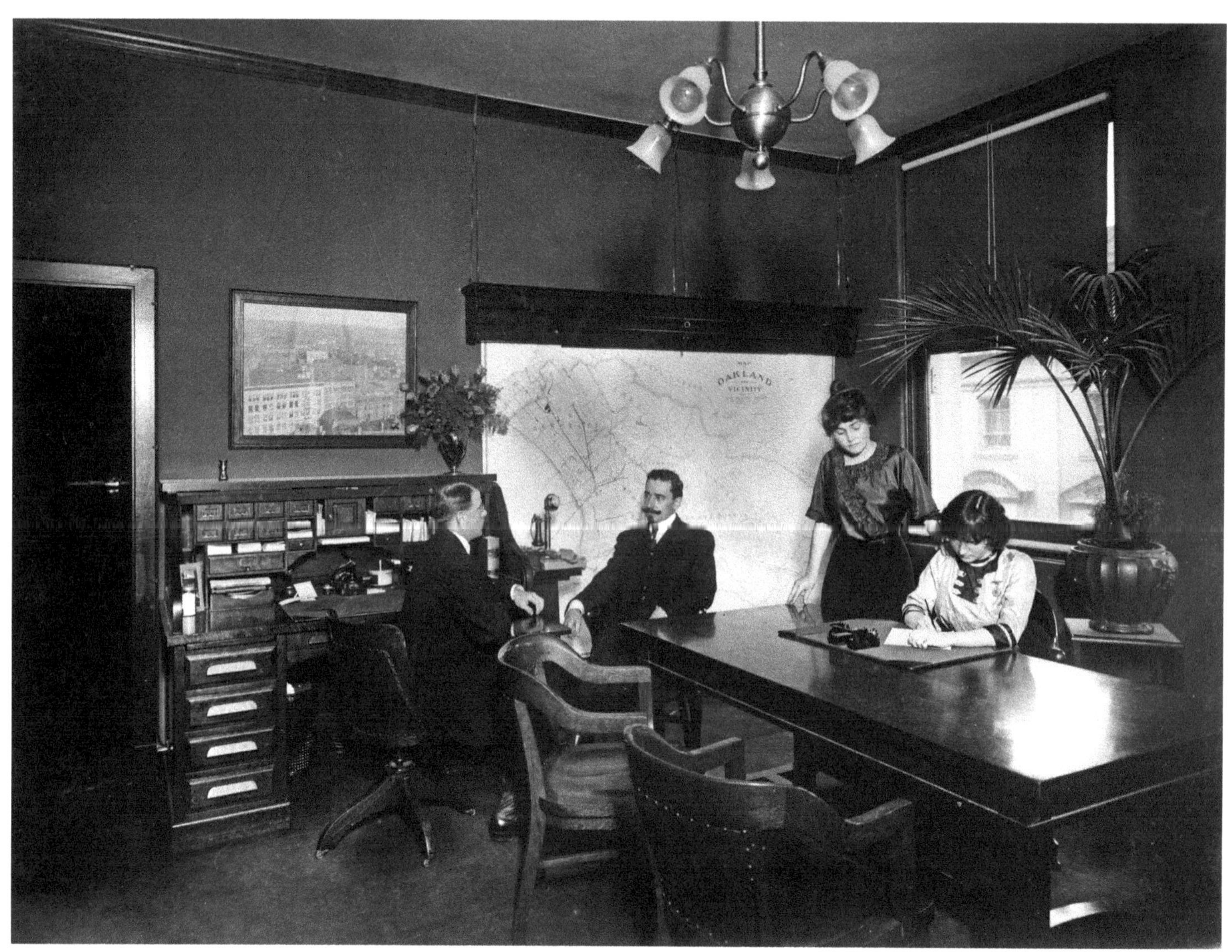

The office of the Realty Union formed to carry on the activities of a predecessor company, the Realty Syndicate. Together, these firms developed nearly half the city's residential properties, along with large tracts in the neighboring cities of Piedmont, Berkeley, Alameda, and Hayward. Staff poses here in the office of the Realty Union in 1912.

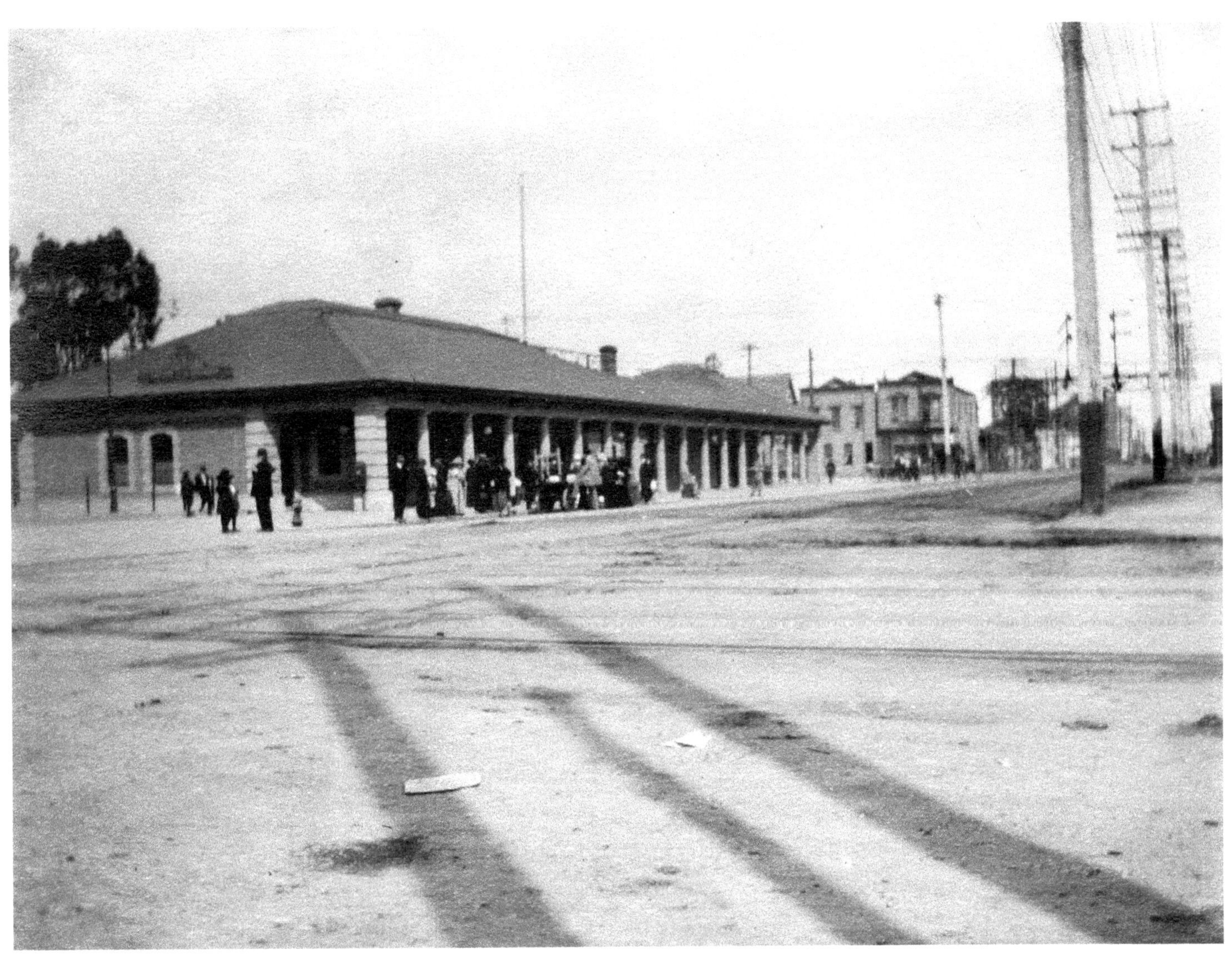

Before beginning his career in local politics, Mayor Frank Mott, in partnership with Edward A. Howard, was well known to local builders as a large supplier of building materials at the corner of First Street and Broadway. His partner was a member of one of the three Howard families prominent in Oakland. The Southern Pacific Railroad acquired the site for a passenger station, pictured here in 1913.

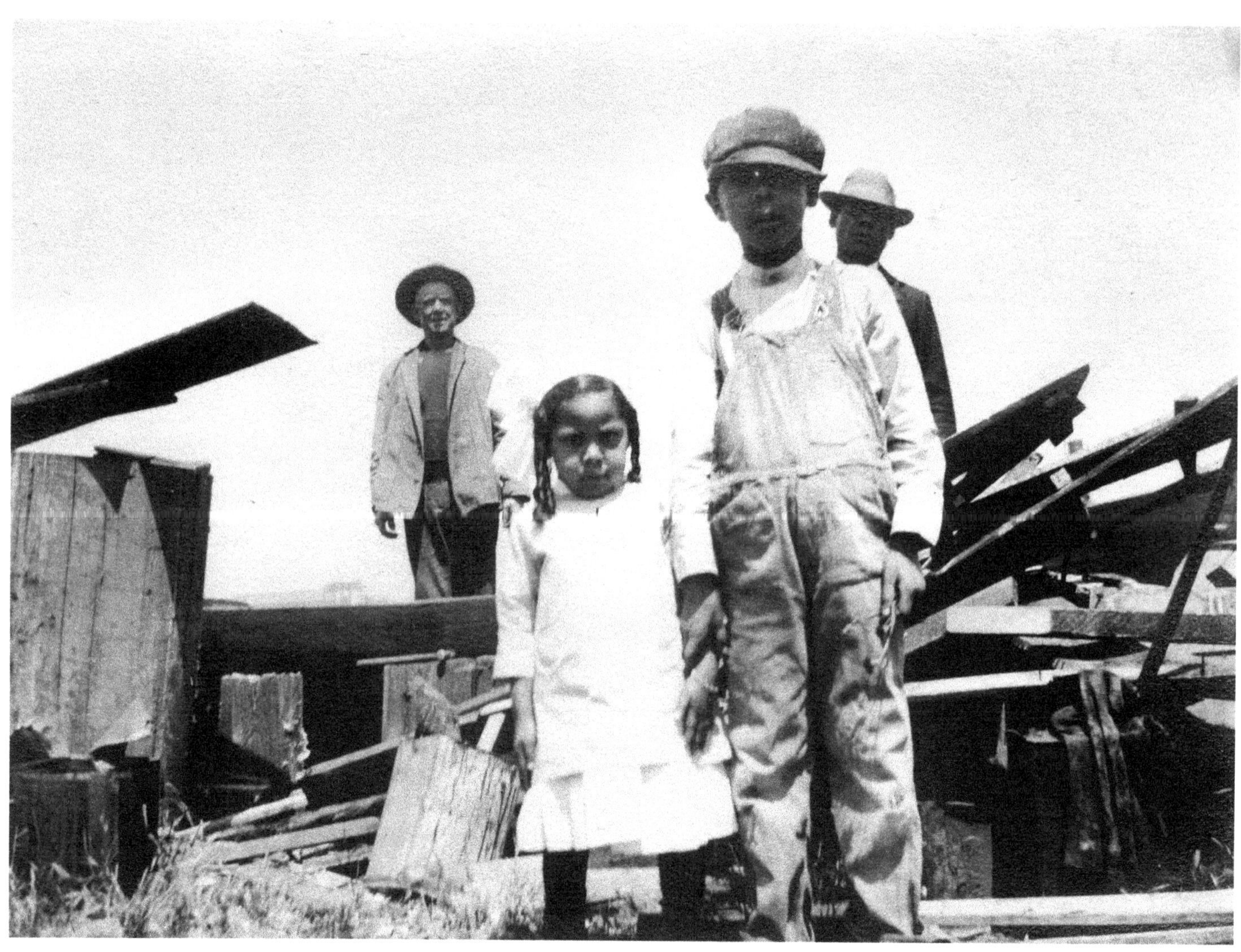

This snapshot, taken in July 1913 somewhere along the Oakland waterfront, bears the inscription, "A quartet: a boatbuilder's companions."

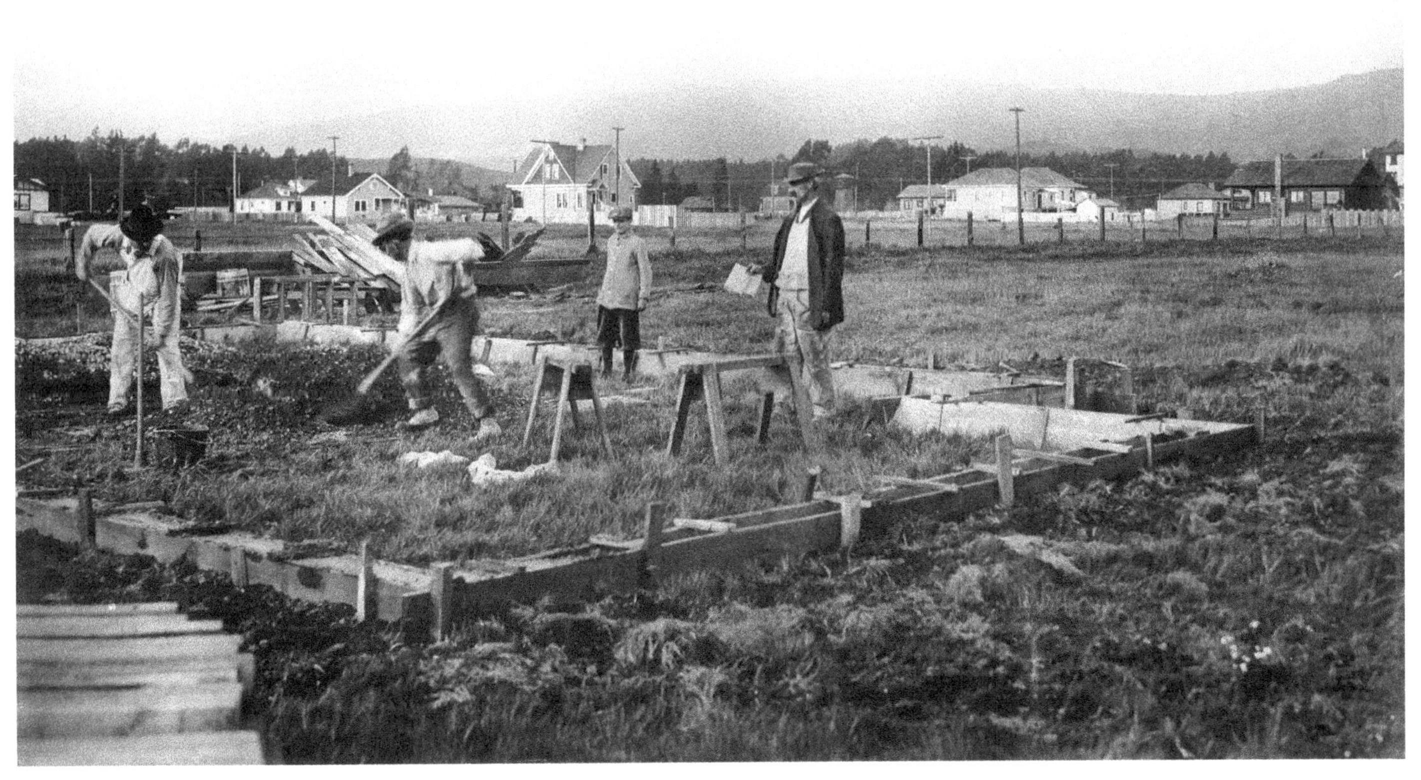

Scenes like this one in the Elmhurst district in 1914 would become ubiquitous during World War I. A mass migration of workers bound for new jobs in manufacturing boosted the need for home construction. One realtor during the era boasted that a new home sold in Oakland every seven minutes.

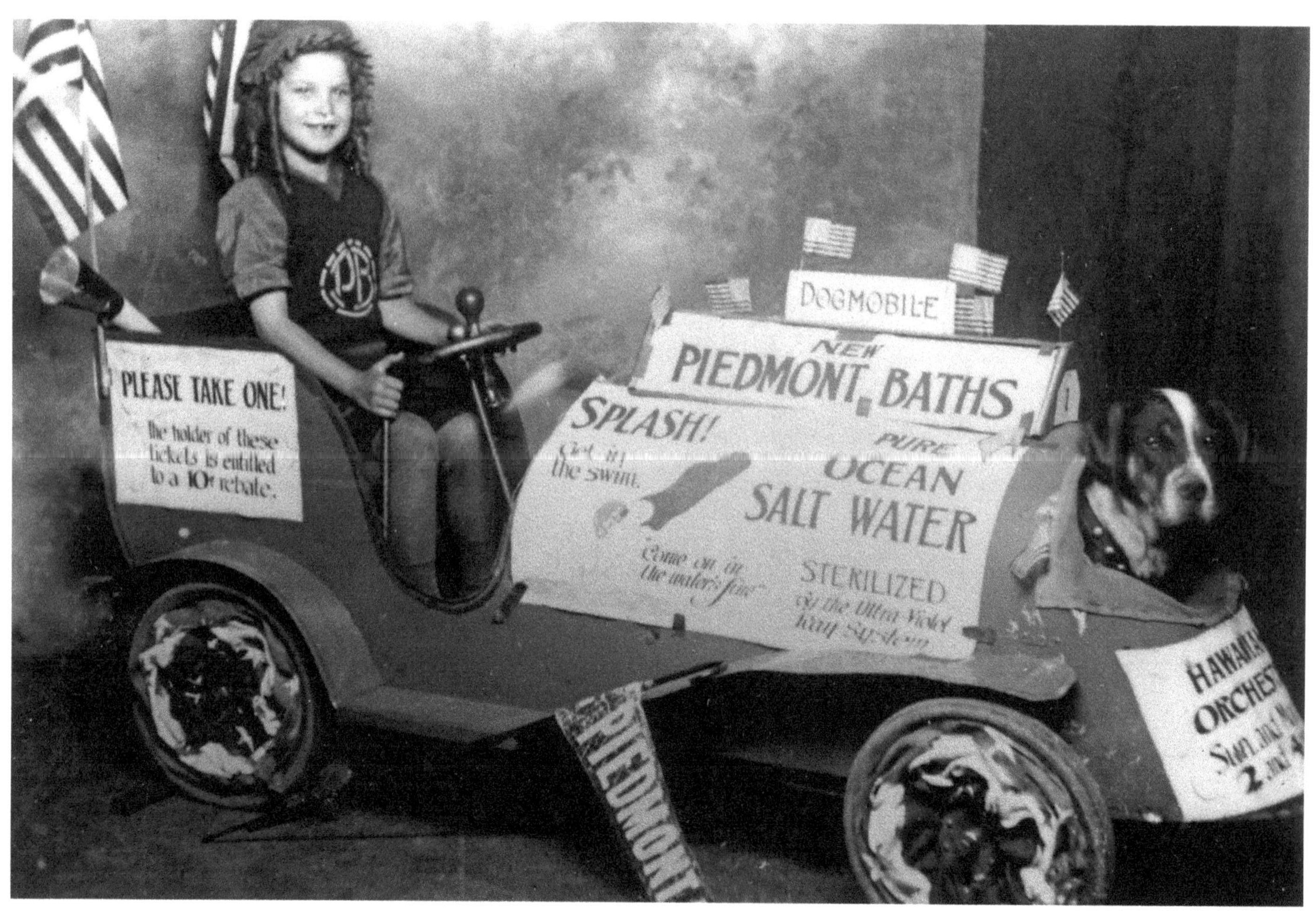

Stella Aydlott earned pocket money with her dog Jack providing the propulsion for their "Dogmobile." The vehicle toured the city to promote the Piedmont Baths, a popular resort near the north shores of Lake Merritt with swimming pools and a baseball park. The pools were heated with steam generated by the engine that ran the Consolidated Piedmont cable car.

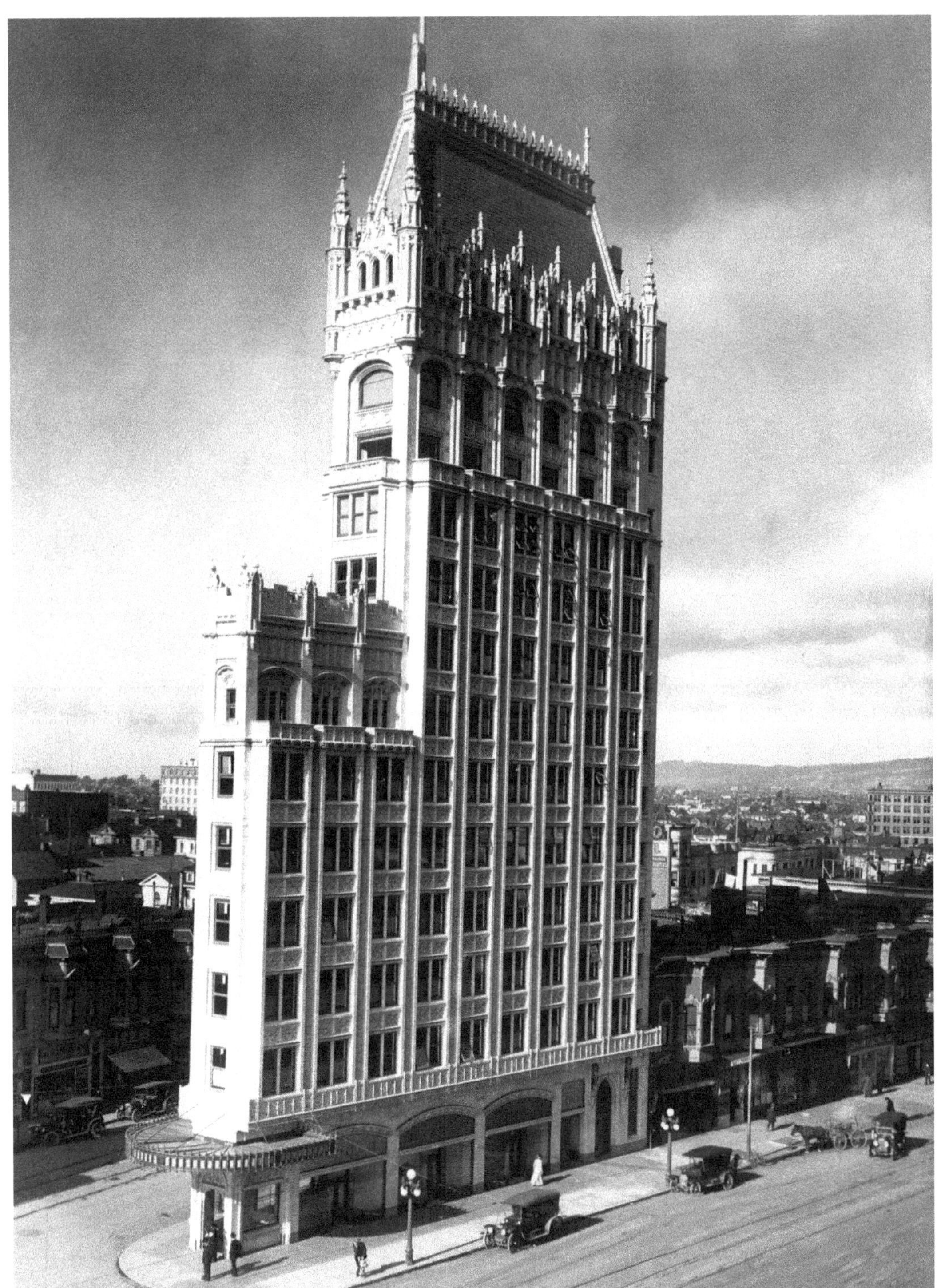

The bold Beaux-Arts design of the Federal Realty Company's headquarters, completed in 1914, further established Oakland's reputation as a leading center of architectural achievement. The building continues to anchor the area where Telegraph Avenue, Broadway, and 16th Street converge.

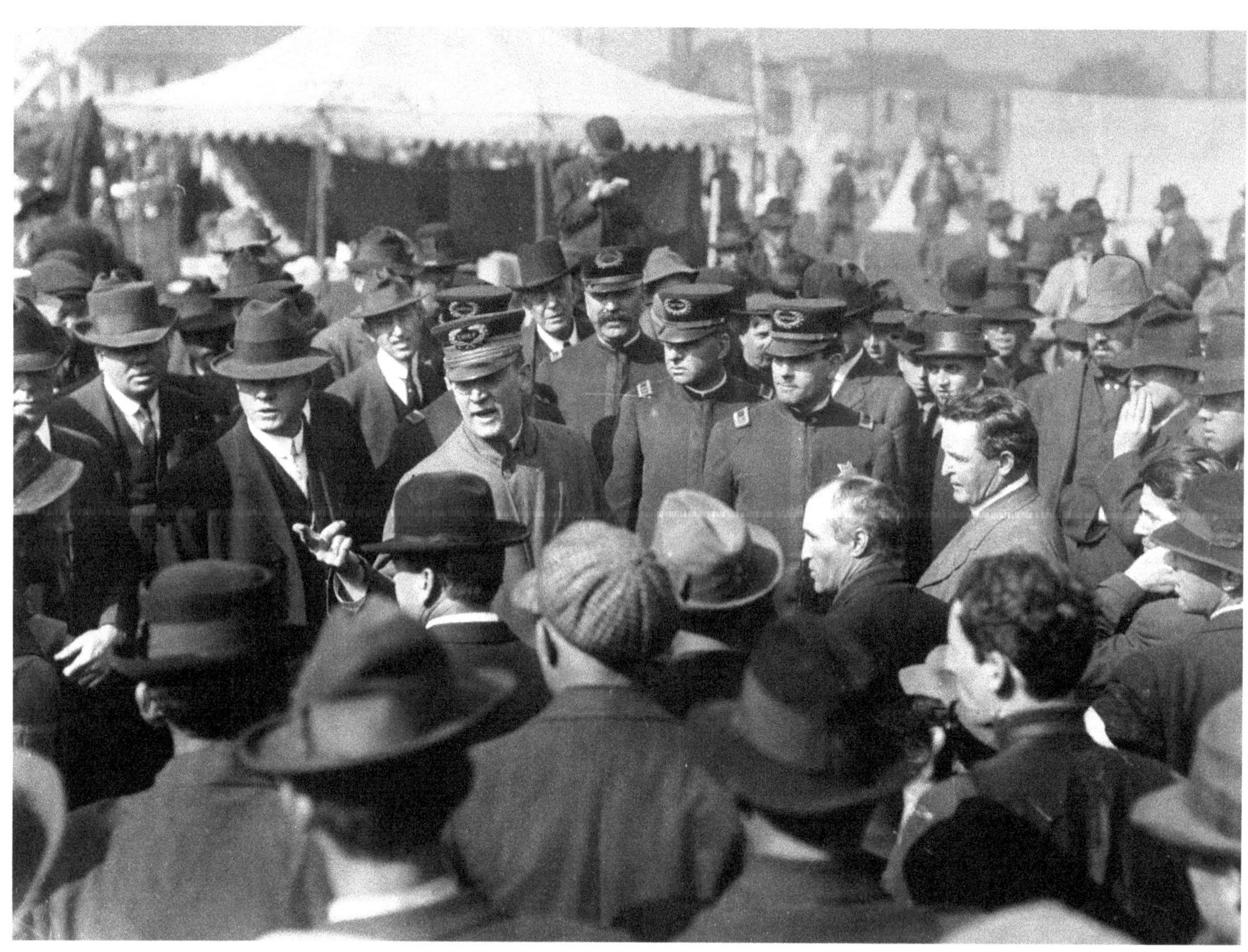

A delegation of unemployed men heading east on the second nationwide march on the nation's capital called by Jacob Coxey in 1914 was greeted upon arrival in Oakland by Walter J. Peterson, the city's chief of police, along with his counterparts from other local agencies. Peterson is shown delivering quit orders to Charles Kelly, who led the marchers from San Francisco. Author Jack London was along on the first such march in 1894.

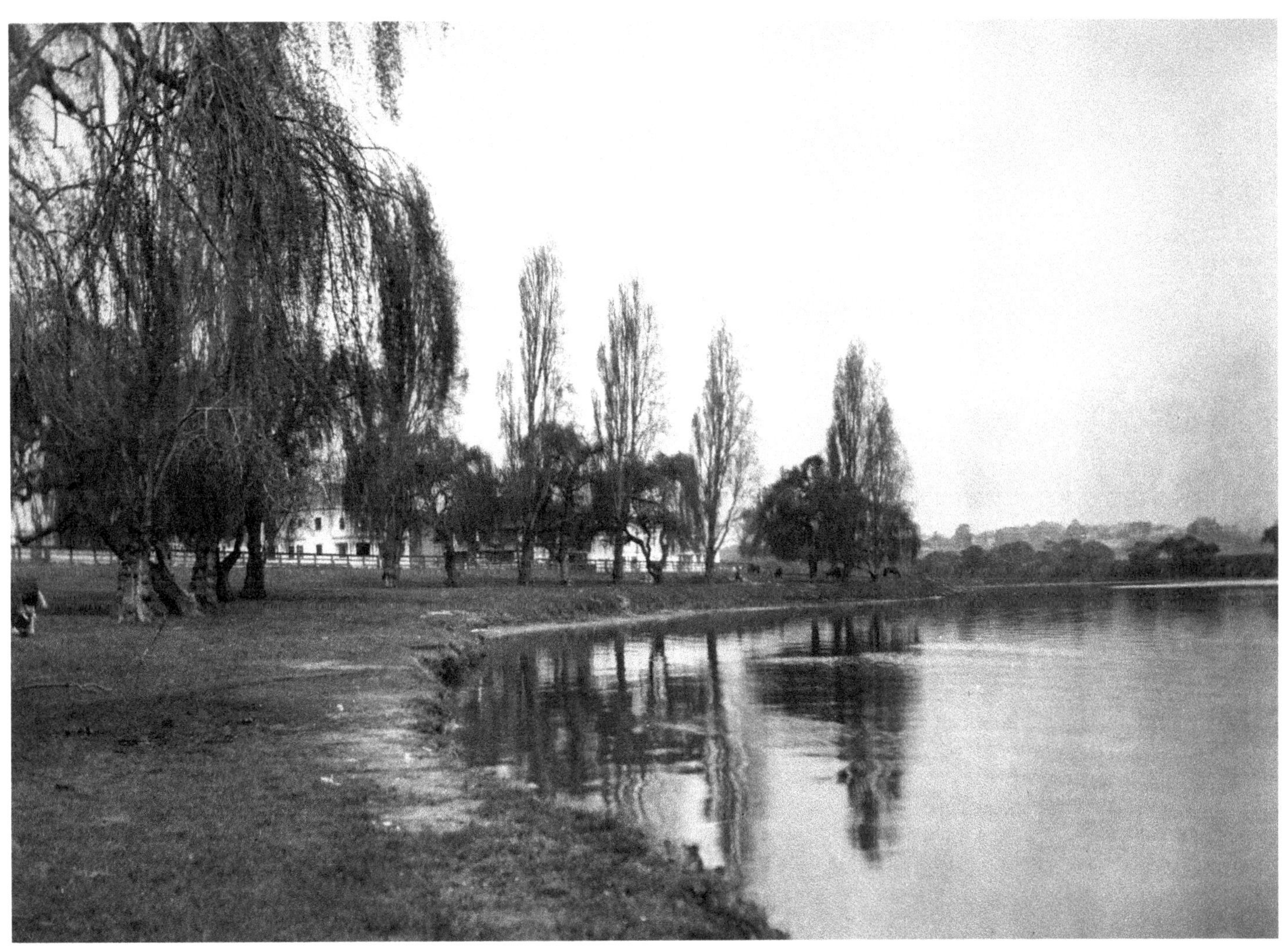

By 1915, when Edward H. Mitchell captured this image for publication as a picture postcard, Lake Merritt was surrounded by public parks, the result of Mayor Mott's successful campaign to enhance his city's beauty.

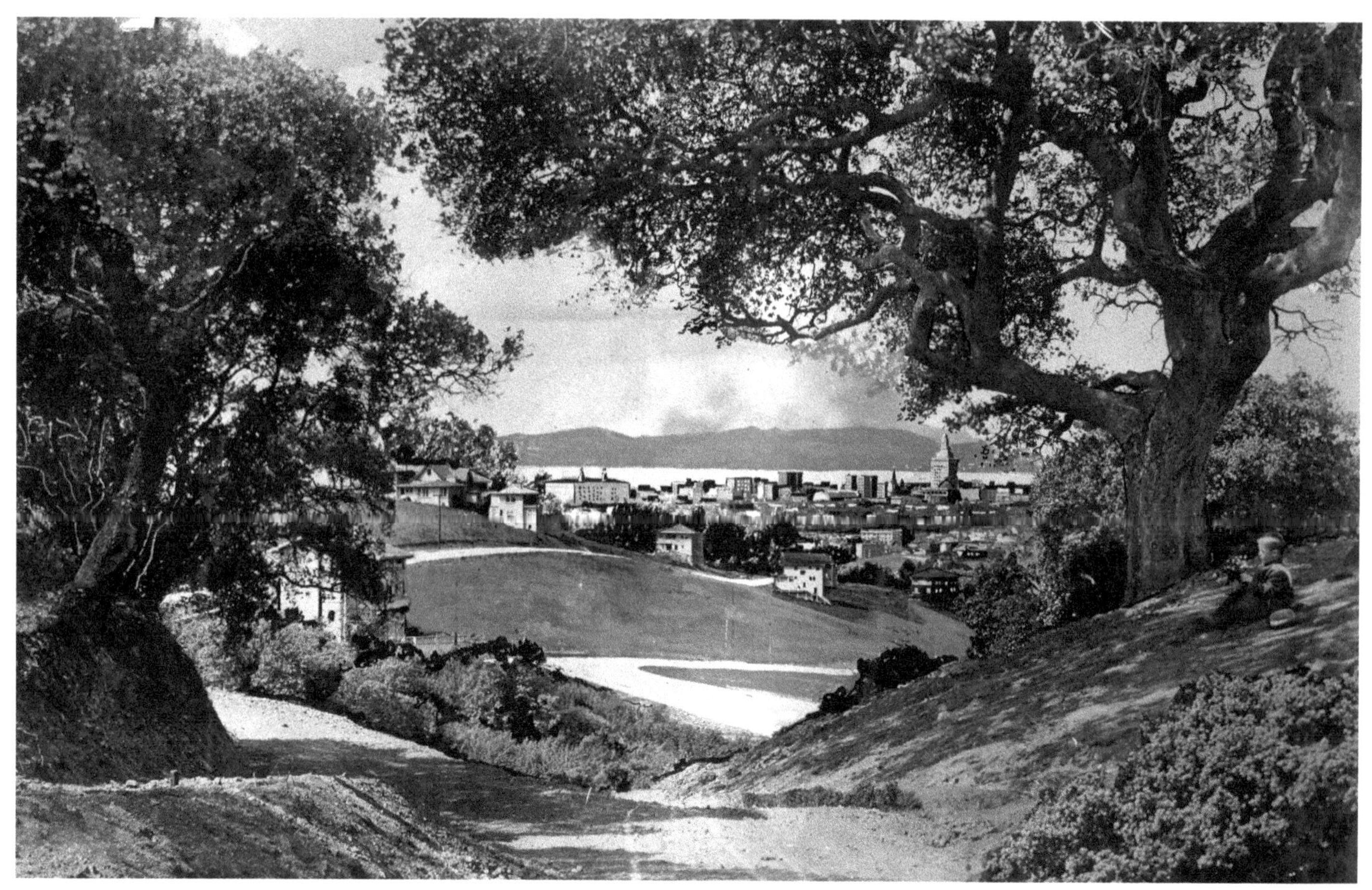

This scene looking south from the foothills was used by realtor Wickham Havens to illustrate the views available from the home sites he had available for purchase around 1915.

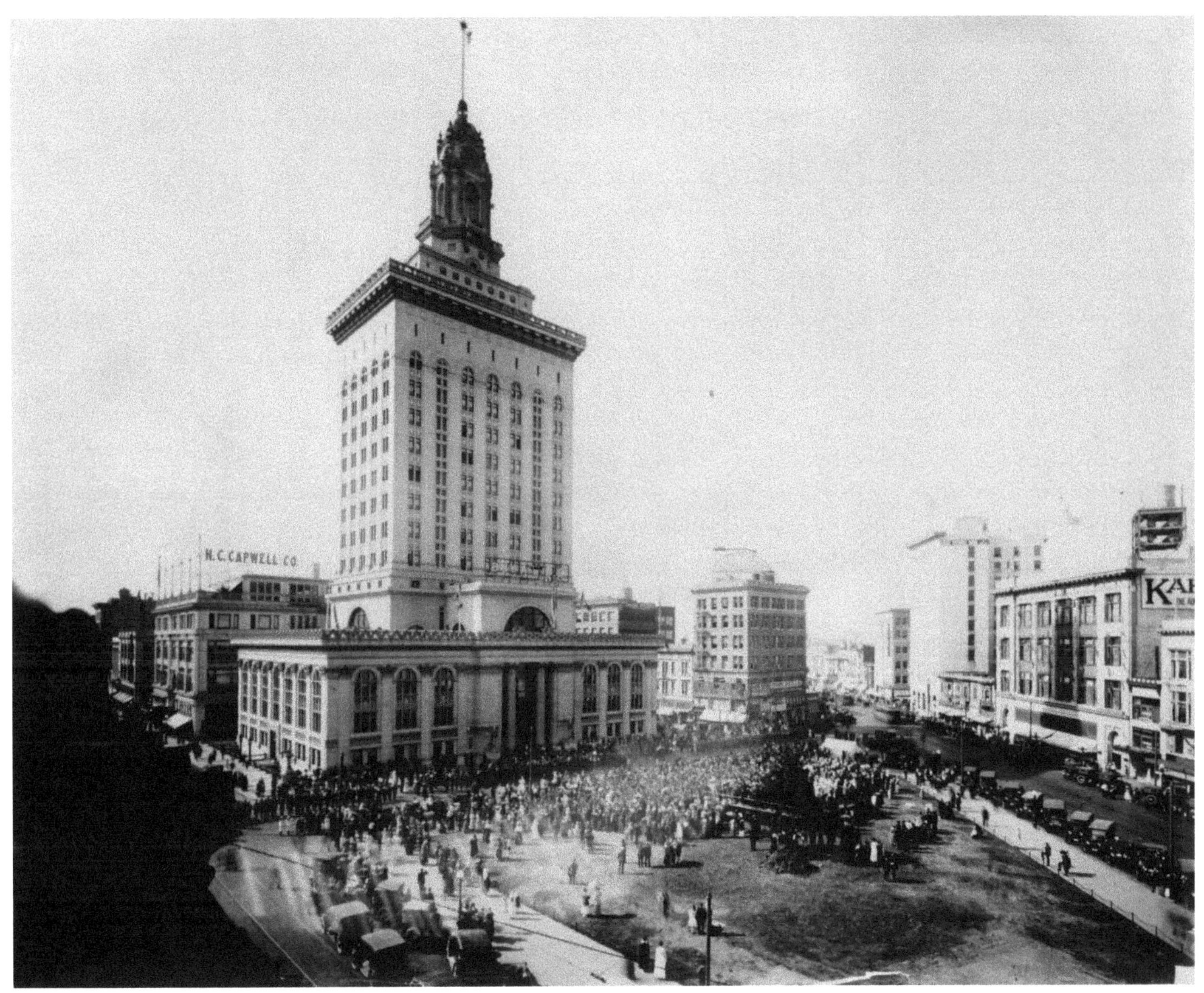

A new City Hall anchored Mayor Mott's extensive Progressive-era municipal construction program. President William Howard Taft laid its cornerstone in 1911. When completed, Oakland City Hall stood as the tallest building west of the Mississippi River. This photograph shows the new building and the large crowd gathered for its dedication in 1914.

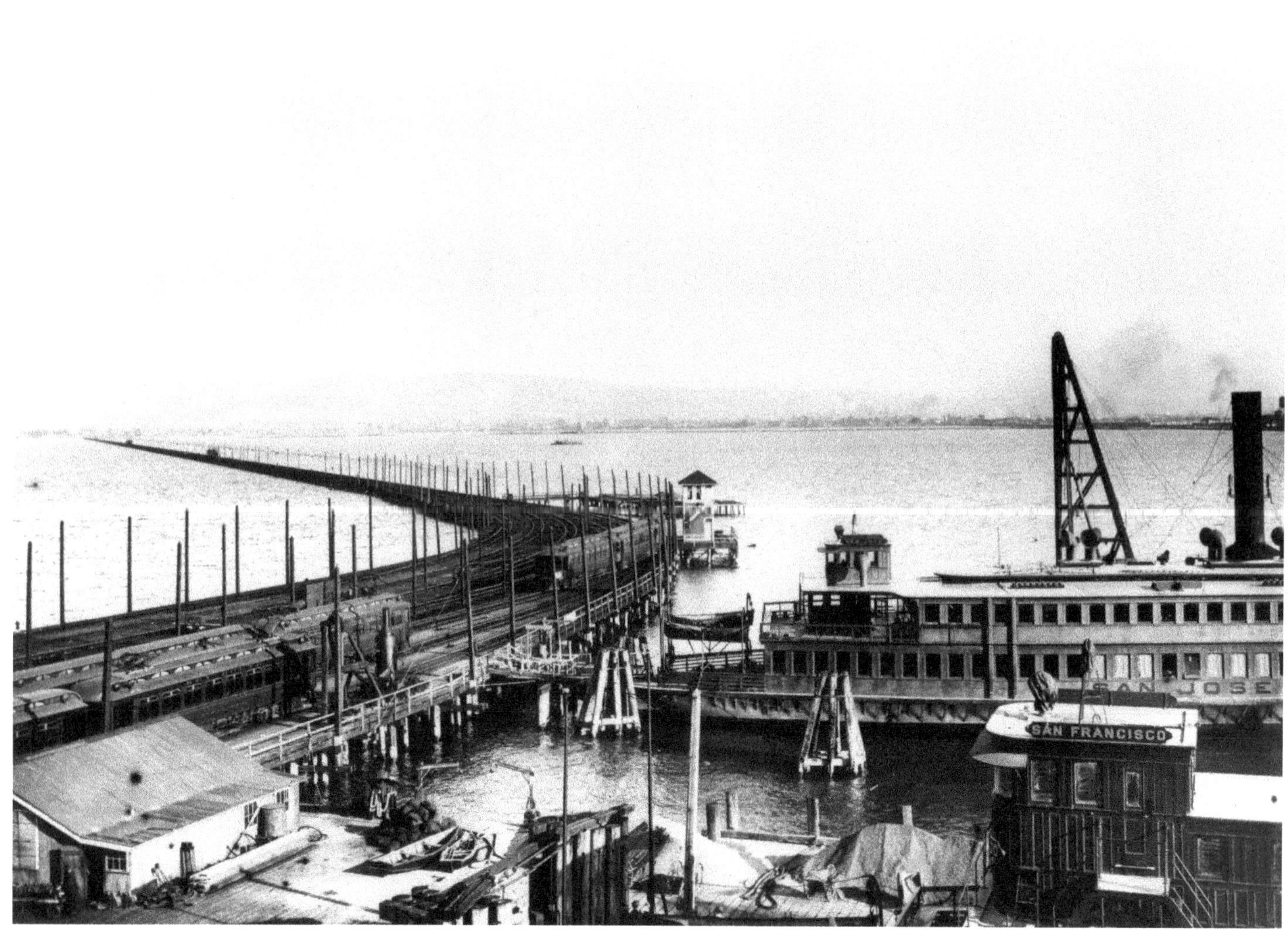

Along the city's northern waterfront, a second long wharf was built to serve the transit ferries, operated by the Key System. The private firm's streetcars ran to the end of the pier where passengers could board the waiting ferries for the trip to San Francisco.

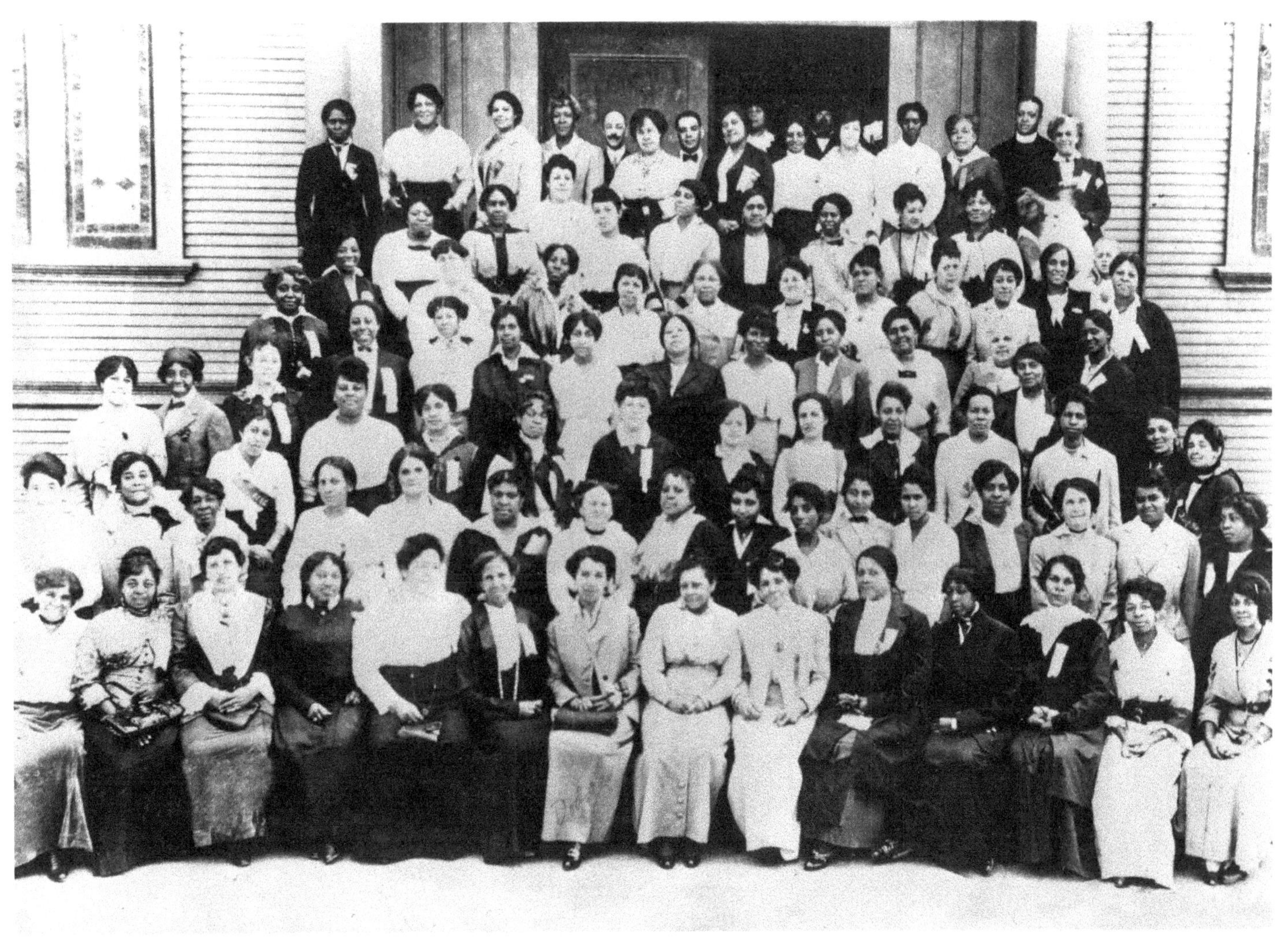

Oakland was selected as the host city in 1915 for the annual convention of the California State Federation of Colored Women's Clubs. One of the state's most active clubwomen, Oakland's Delilah L. Beasley would become the first African-American woman to write regularly for a general interest daily newspaper when the *Oakland Tribune* began running her column, "Activities Among Negroes," in 1923.

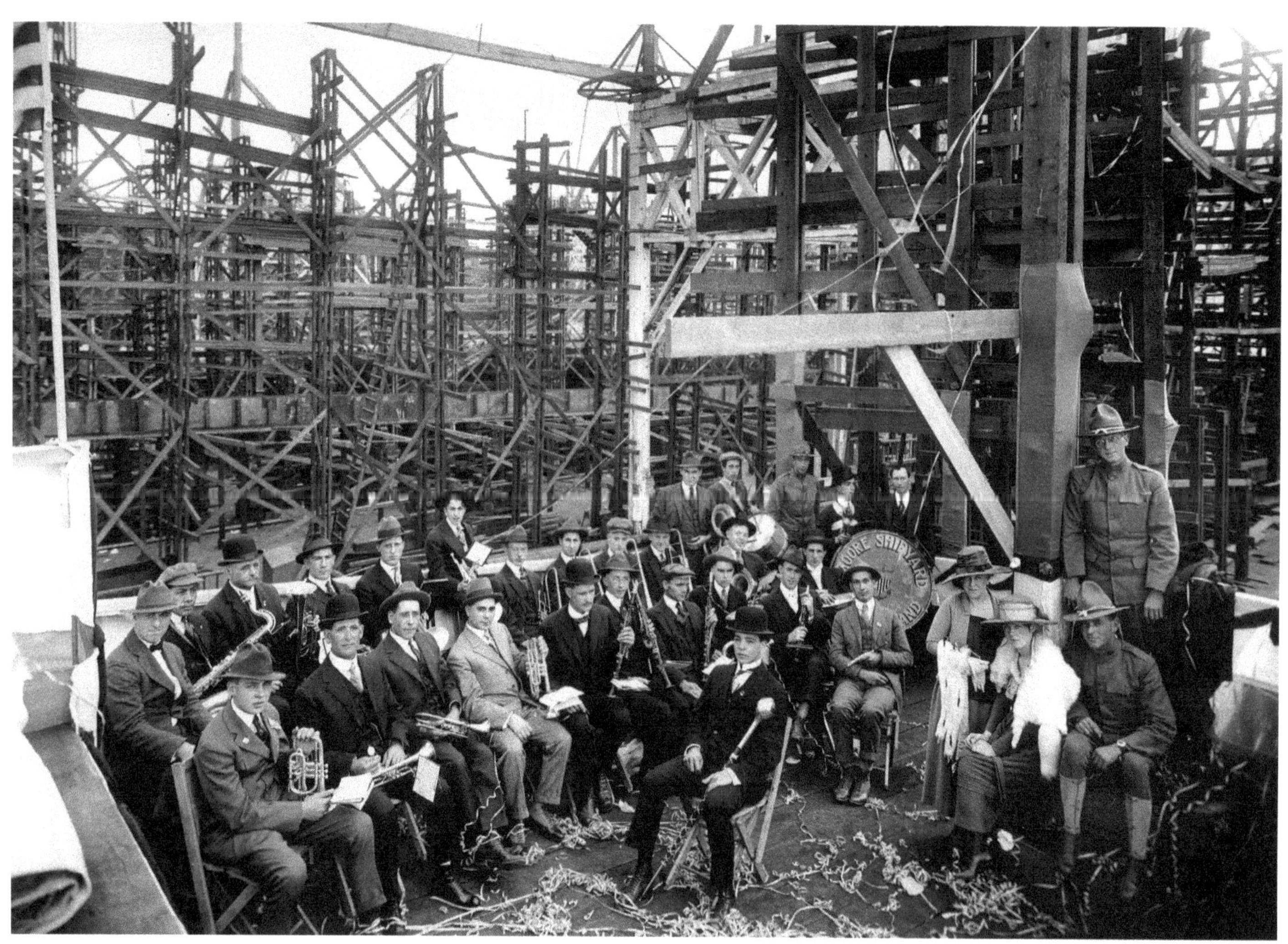

The need for ships to supply a large build-up in naval fighting power during World War I brought a boom of activity—and jobs—to the Moore Shipbuilding Company on Oakland's waterfront. The company's band came together on September 22, 1918, for the christening of the SS *Kamesit,* a freighter of 6,204 gross tons.

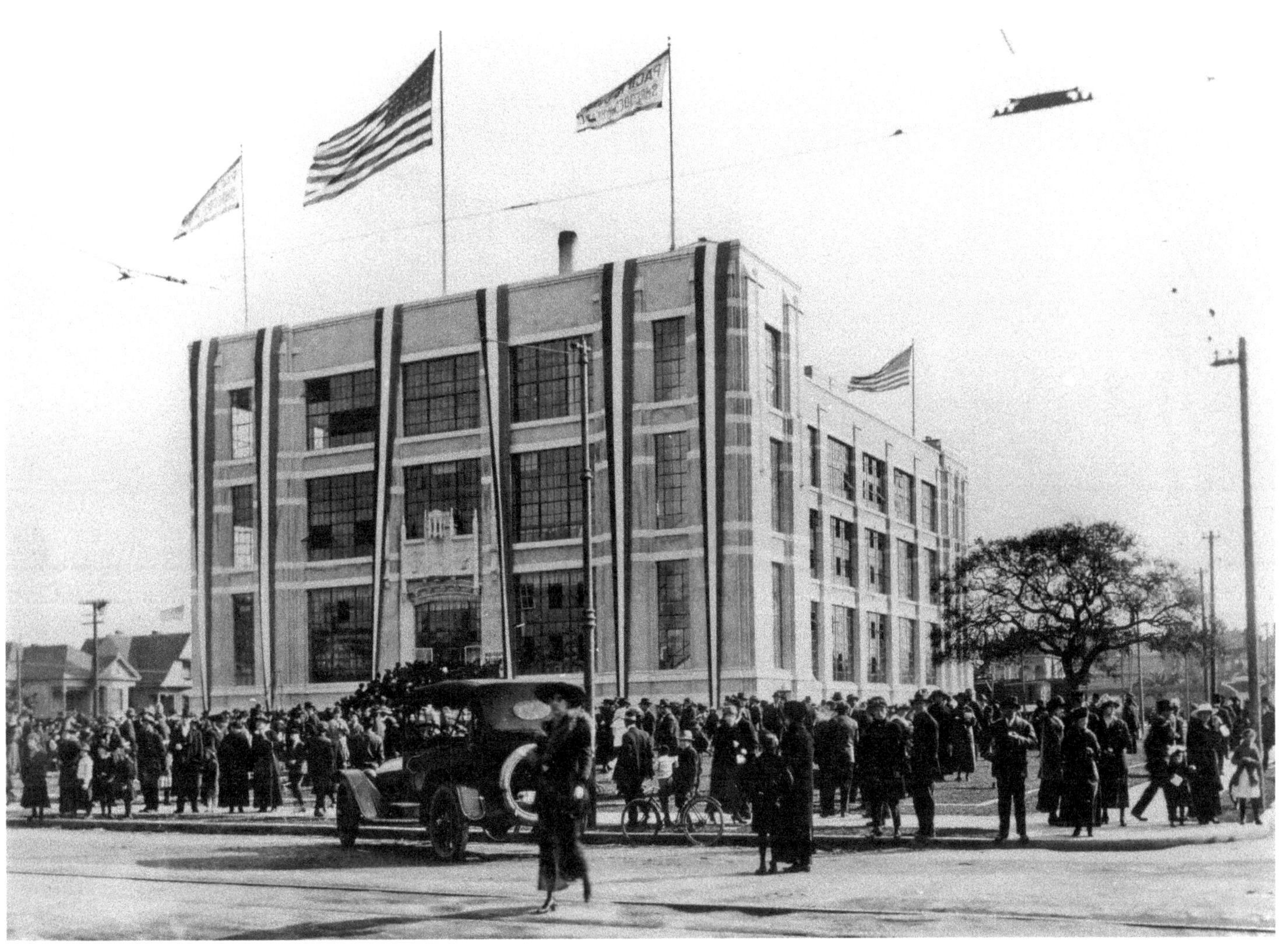

Other industries expanded in the war years, too. Shredded Wheat chose Oakland for production of its popular breakfast cereal for distribution in the western states. The company and the Oakland Chamber of Commerce hosted a neighborhood celebration for the grand opening of its factory, occupying an entire city block at 14th and Union streets, on March 15, 1917.

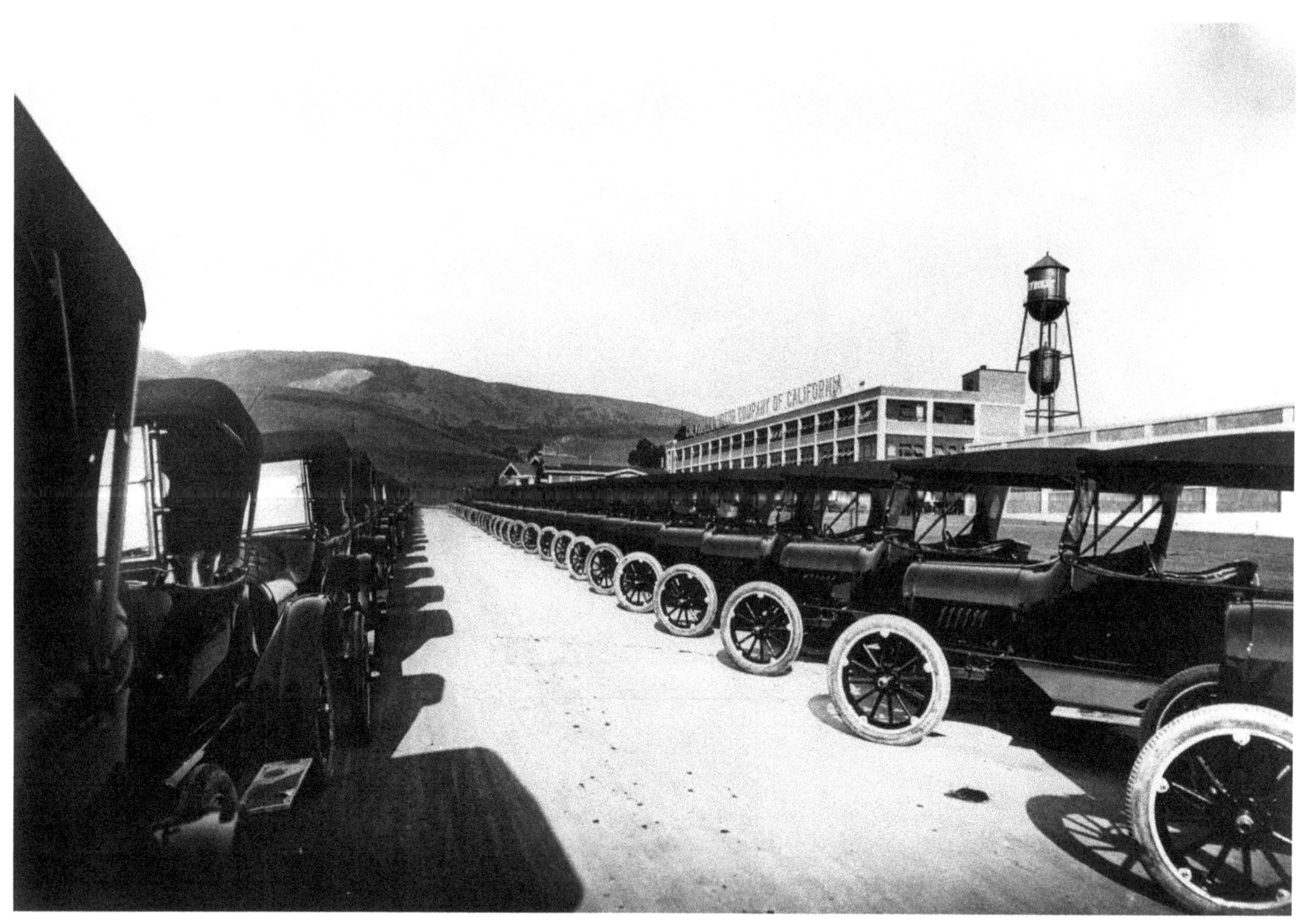

In 1916, the General Motors Company selected Oakland as the site of an assembly plant for its new West Coast subsidiary, the Chevrolet Company of California. After production began, promoters set up this shot, claiming that it showed a single day's output at the new factory. More than a million Chevies were made at the Eastmont district plant before production was moved south to Fremont in 1963.

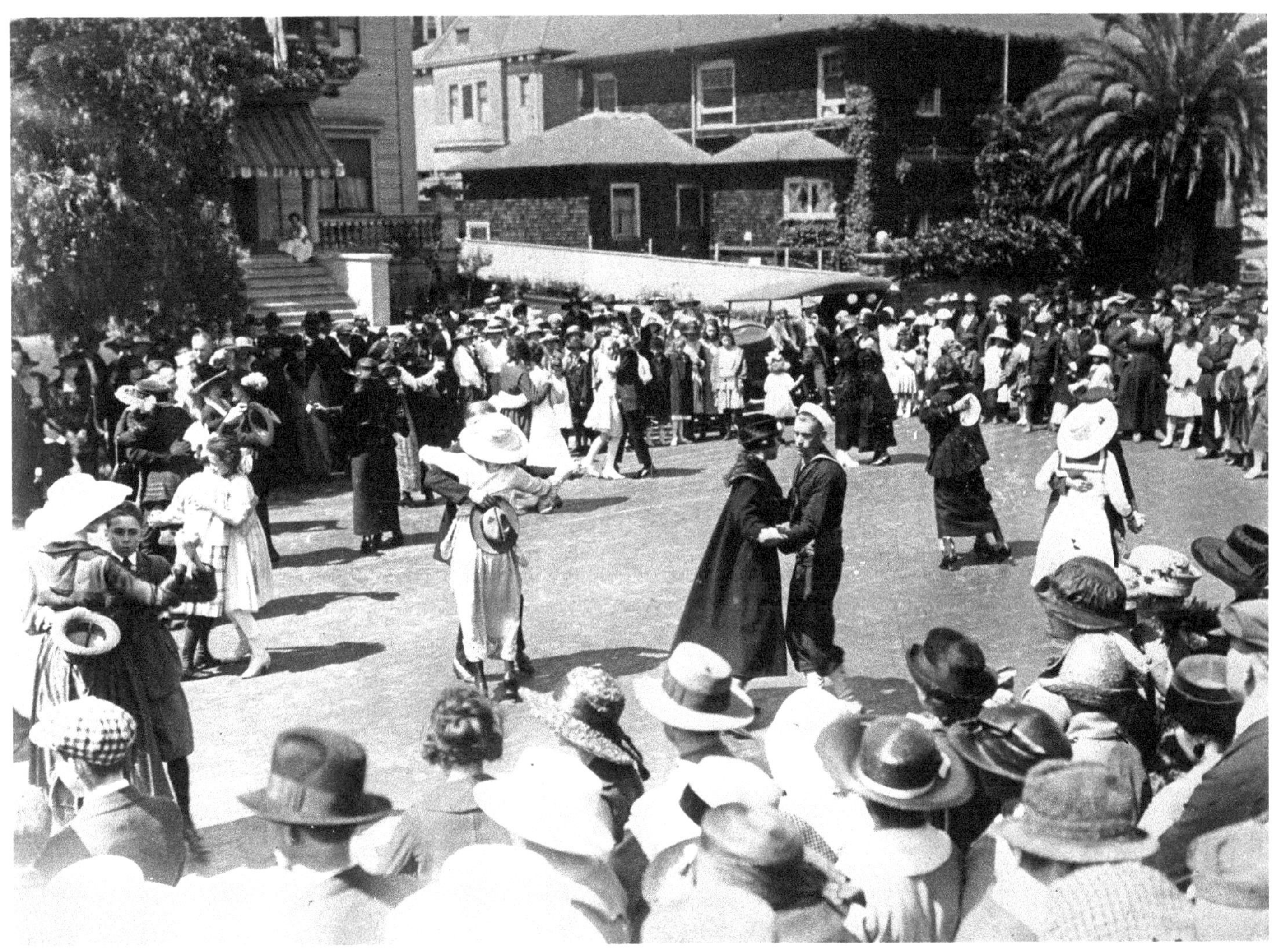

Young women were recruited by the Merchants' Exchange in the summer of 1918 to host a street dance for the fighting men of World War I. Photographer Doc Rogers of the *Oakland Tribune* caught a glimpse of the party for the next day's paper.

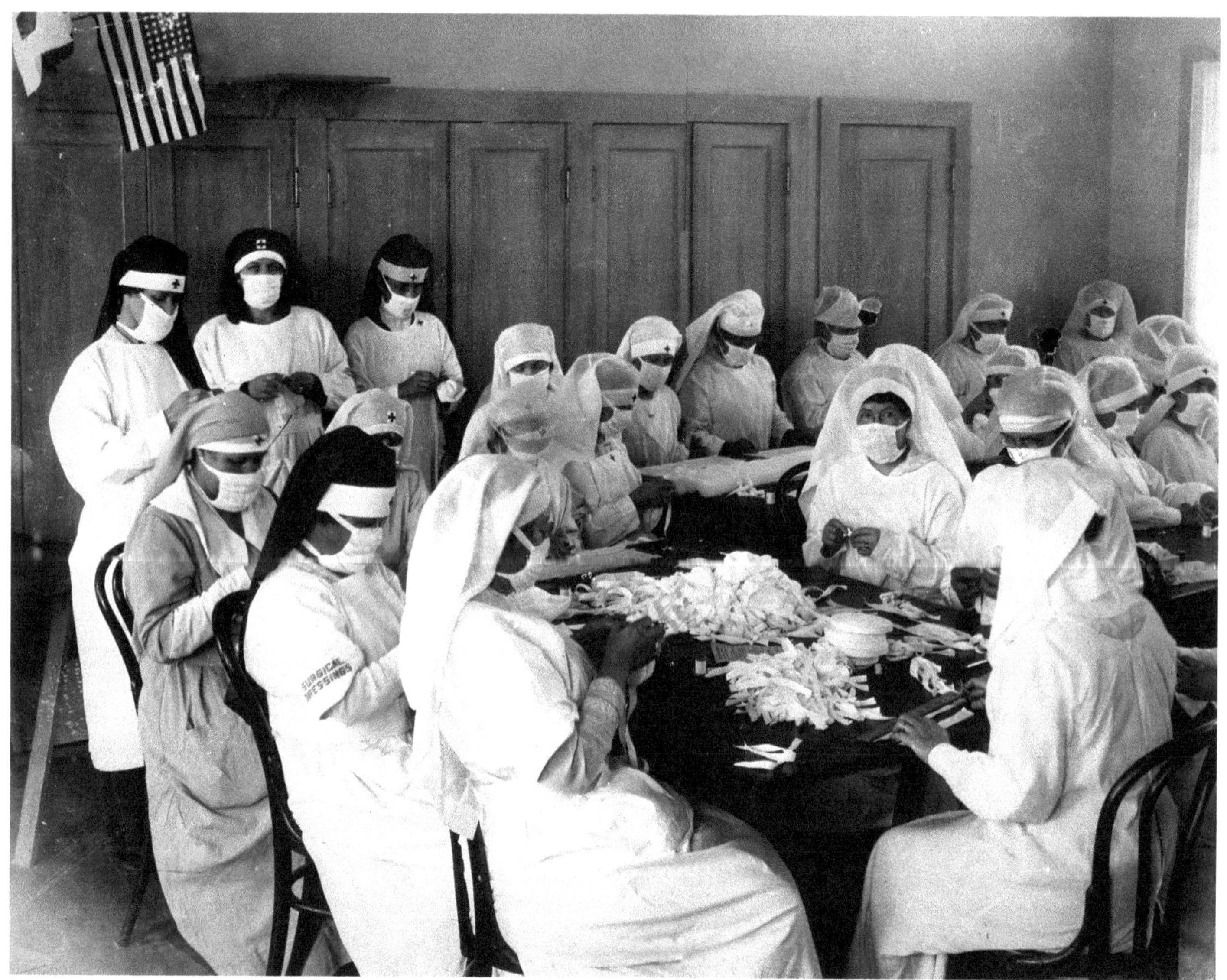

At the height of World War I, a deadly strain of influenza entered Europe from the east, triggering a worldwide pandemic, the deadliest outbreak of disease in history. Nurses for the Red Cross wore masks to prevent the contagion from infecting the surgical dressings destined for the treatment of wounded soldiers overseas.

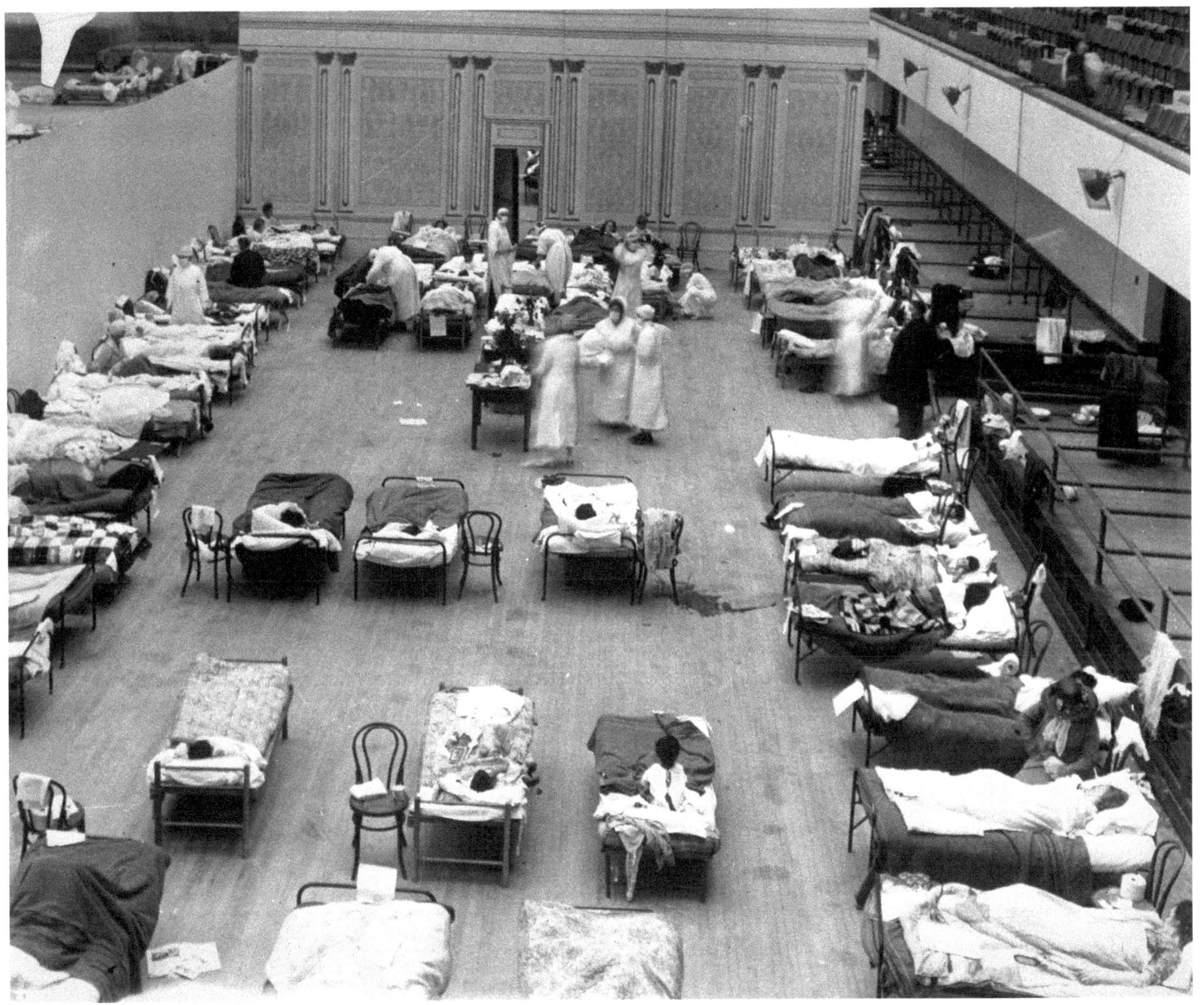

The flu overwhelmed the local hospitals in 1918, and the concert hall of the Oakland Auditorium became a treatment center for victims of the pandemic. Up to 40 million people would die worldwide before the virus ran its course.

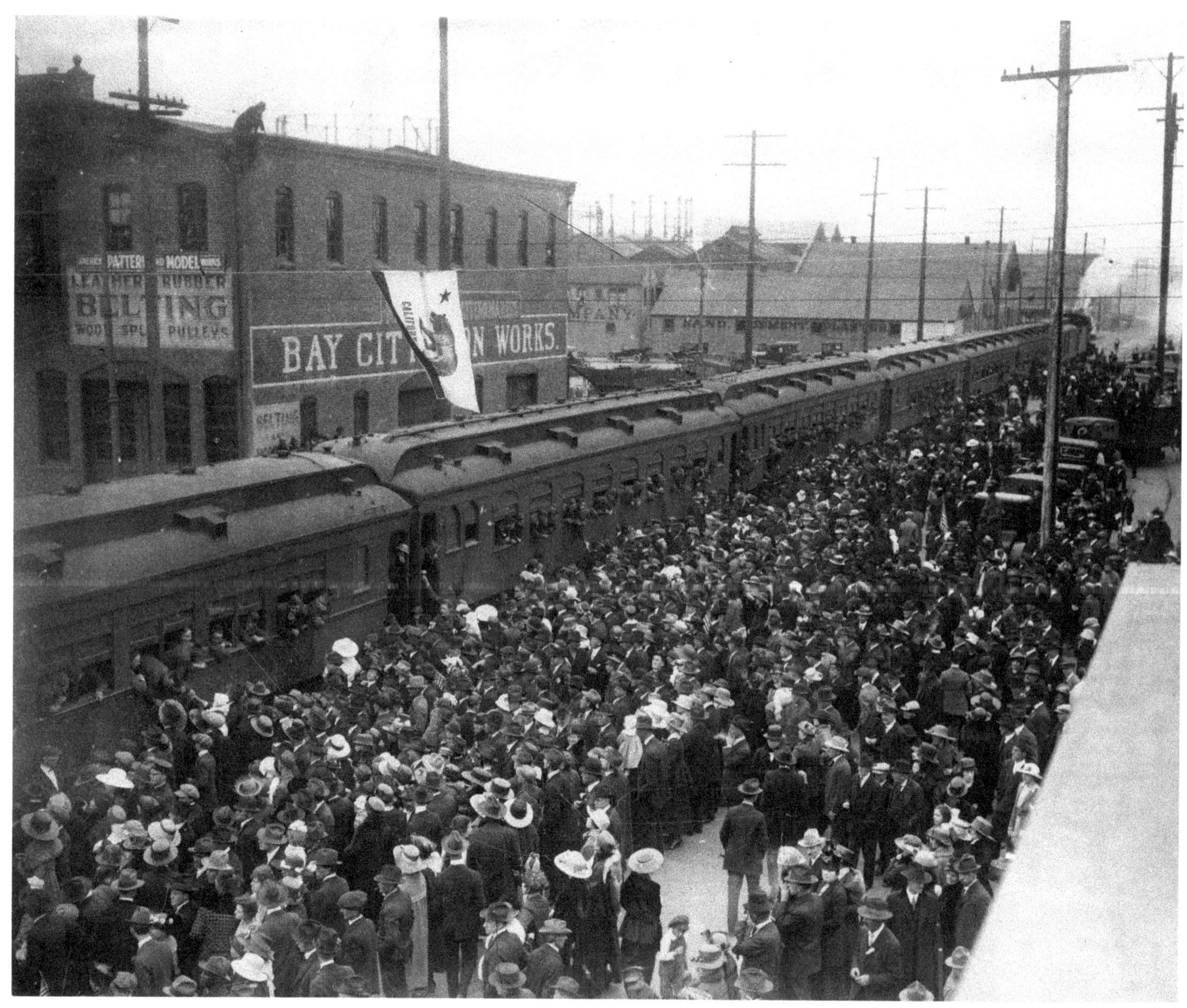

A huge crowd gathered with each new arrival of servicemen returning from combat in World War I. The troops of the 159th Infantry received heroes' welcomes when their train arrived at the First Street station in 1919.

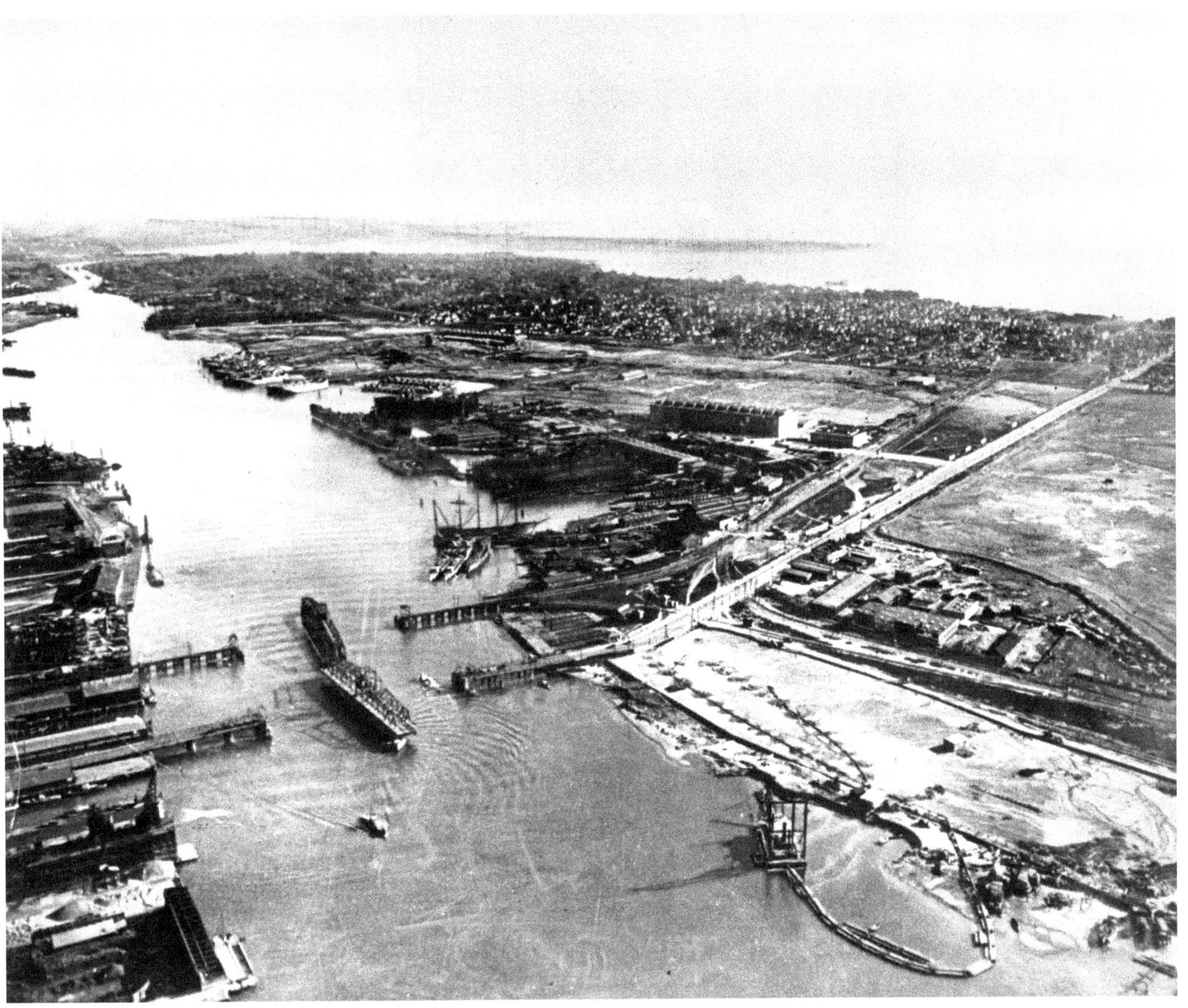

Expansion of its shipbuilding capacity brought extensive development to Oakland's Inner Harbor. An Army cameraman aboard an Air Corps plane documented the progress in this photograph, made sometime in 1919, looking southeast over Alameda. Two swing bridges, one for trains and one at Webster Street for cars and trucks, have opened to make way for a tug. The Posey Tube would replace the Webster Street Bridge in 1928.

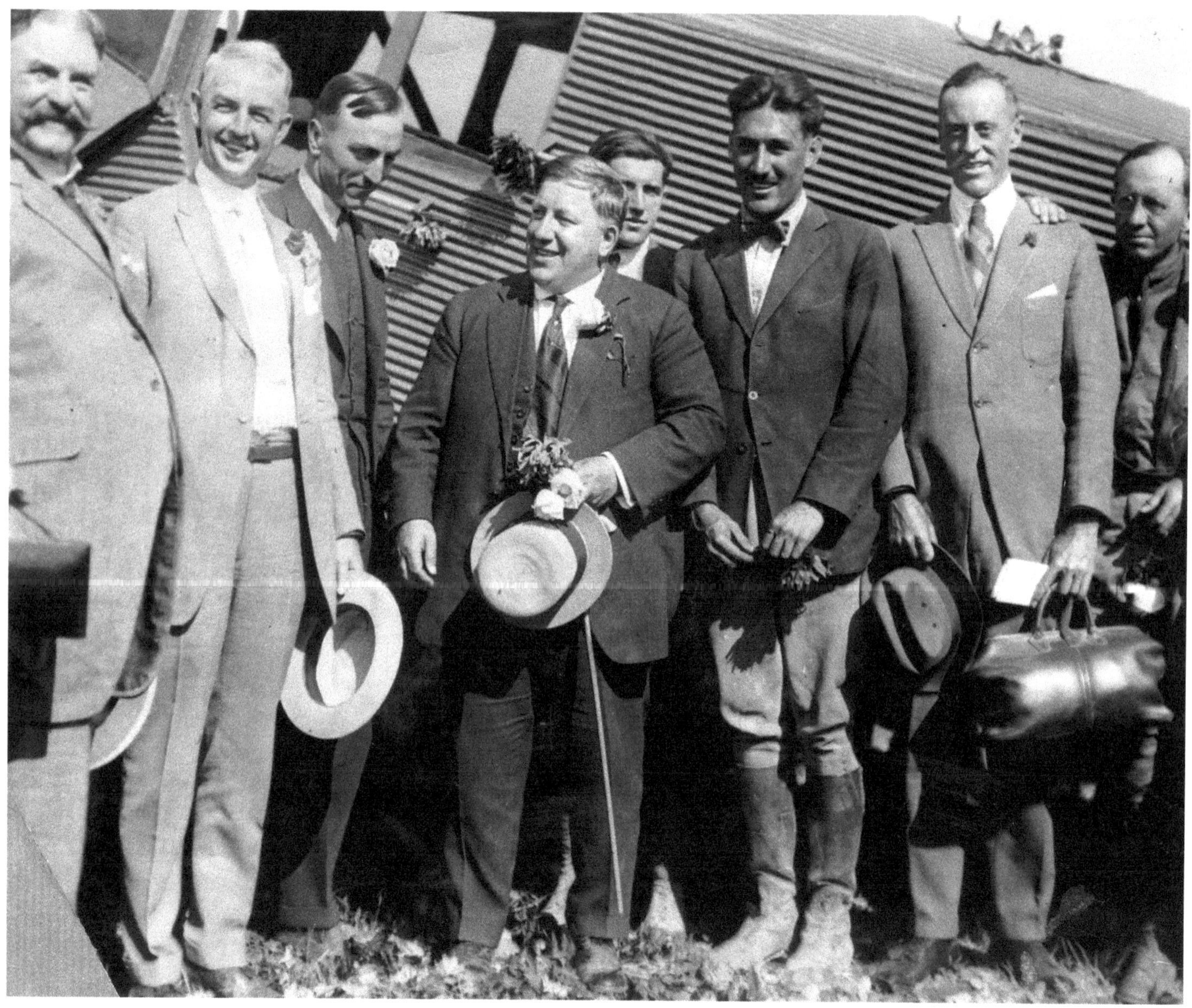

Cliff Durant, whose father founded General Motors, established Oakland's first airport near the future site of the family's automobile venture. Photographer Jack Frost was at Durant Field with his camera for the arrival of the first bags of mail flown cross-country in an all-metal plane. Pilot Eddie Rickenbacker made the delivery and is greeted by Mayor John L. Davie and others on August 8, 1920.

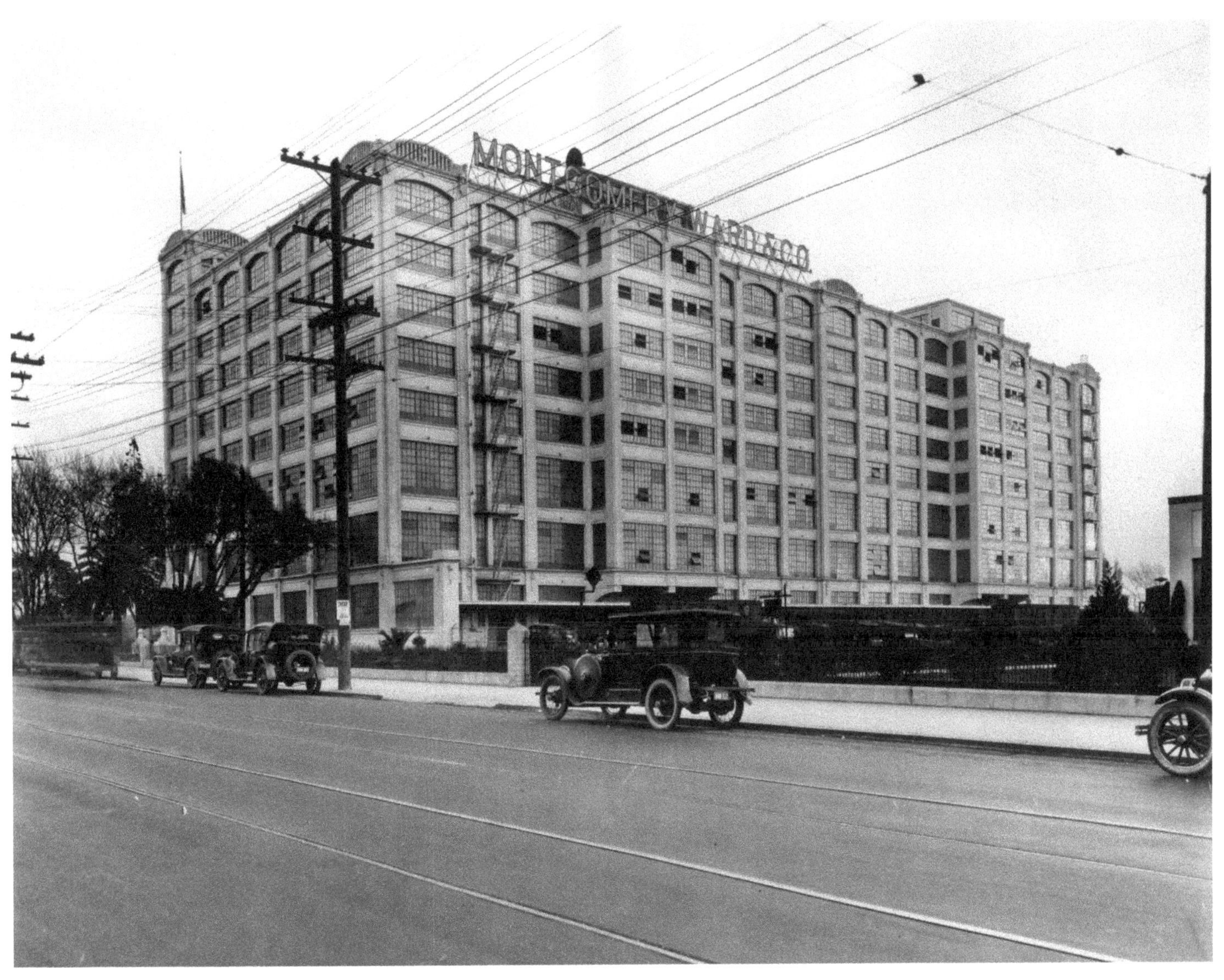

Midwestern retailer Montgomery Ward and Company chose a site in Oakland's Fruitvale district for its West Coast distribution center. Its facility included nearly a million square feet of office, warehouse, and storage space and filled orders from the company's catalog to customers and stores across the west.

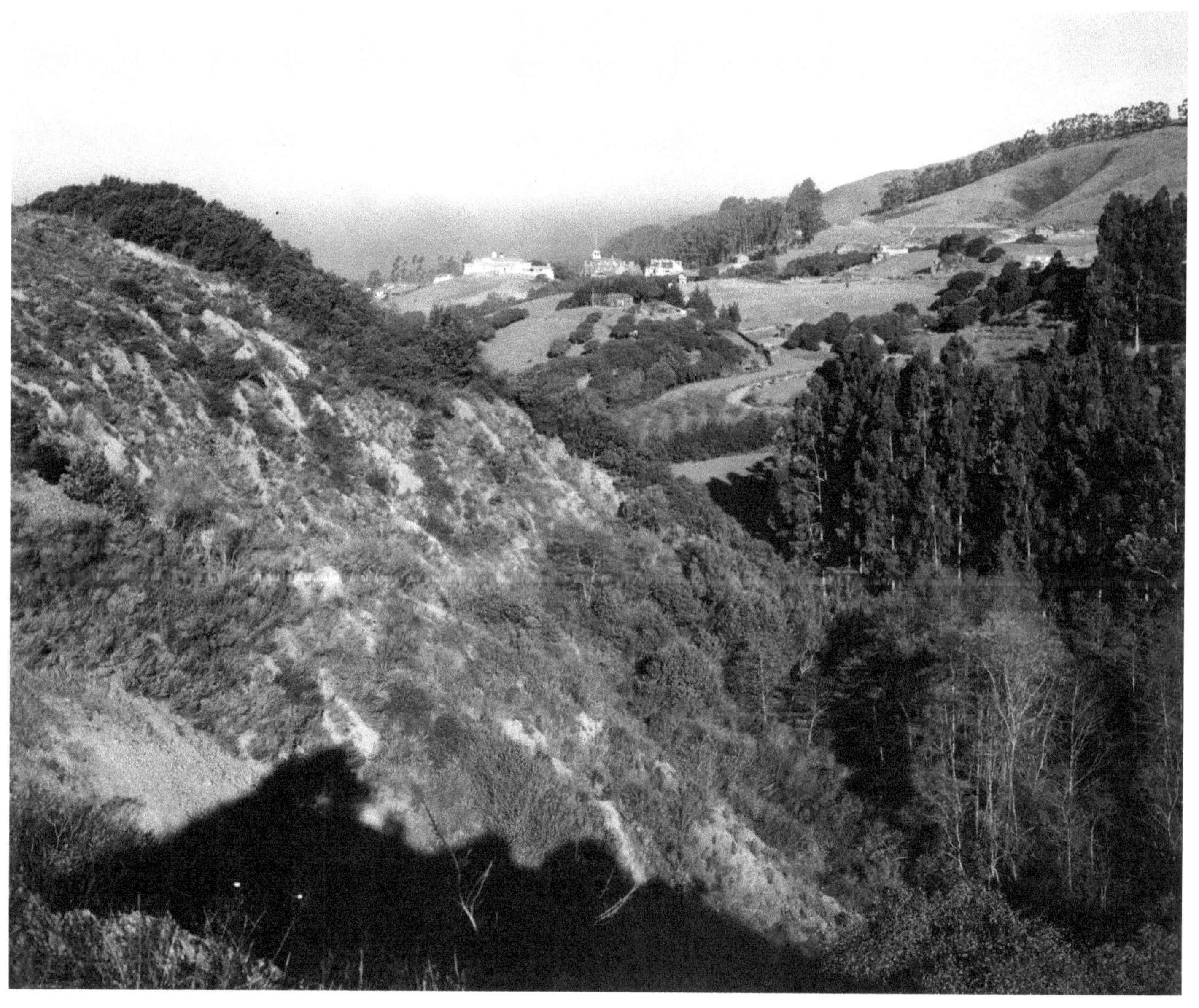

Rapid urbanization failed to diminish the beauty of Oakland's natural surroundings. Photographer Gabriel Moulin chose a view overlooking the canyon carved by Temescal Creek for this image published in a souvenir package by the Pacific Novelty Company.

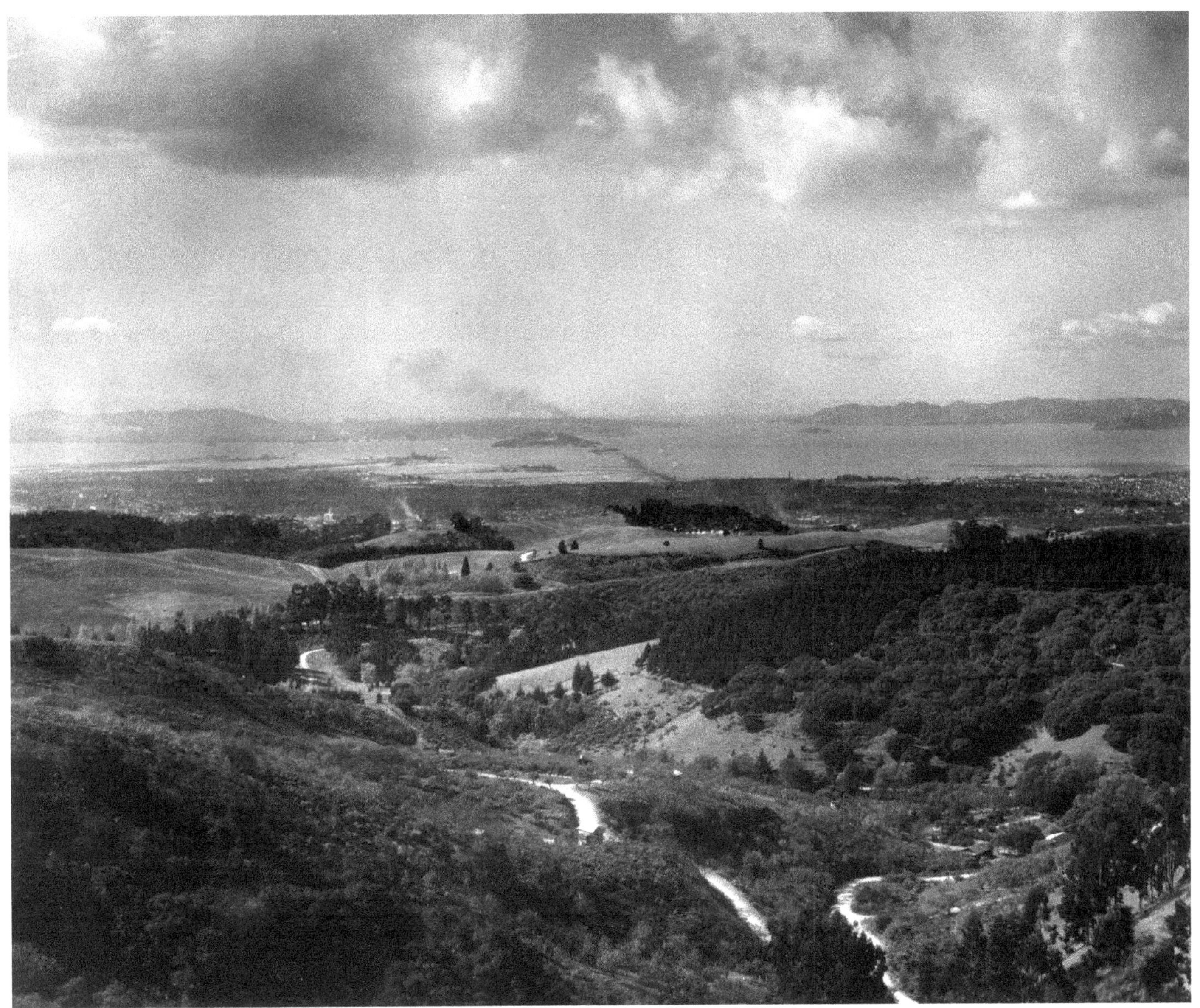

On assignment for a postcard publisher competing with the Pacific Novelty Company, Moulin photographed this view looking west toward the Golden Gate from near the summit of the Oakland hills.

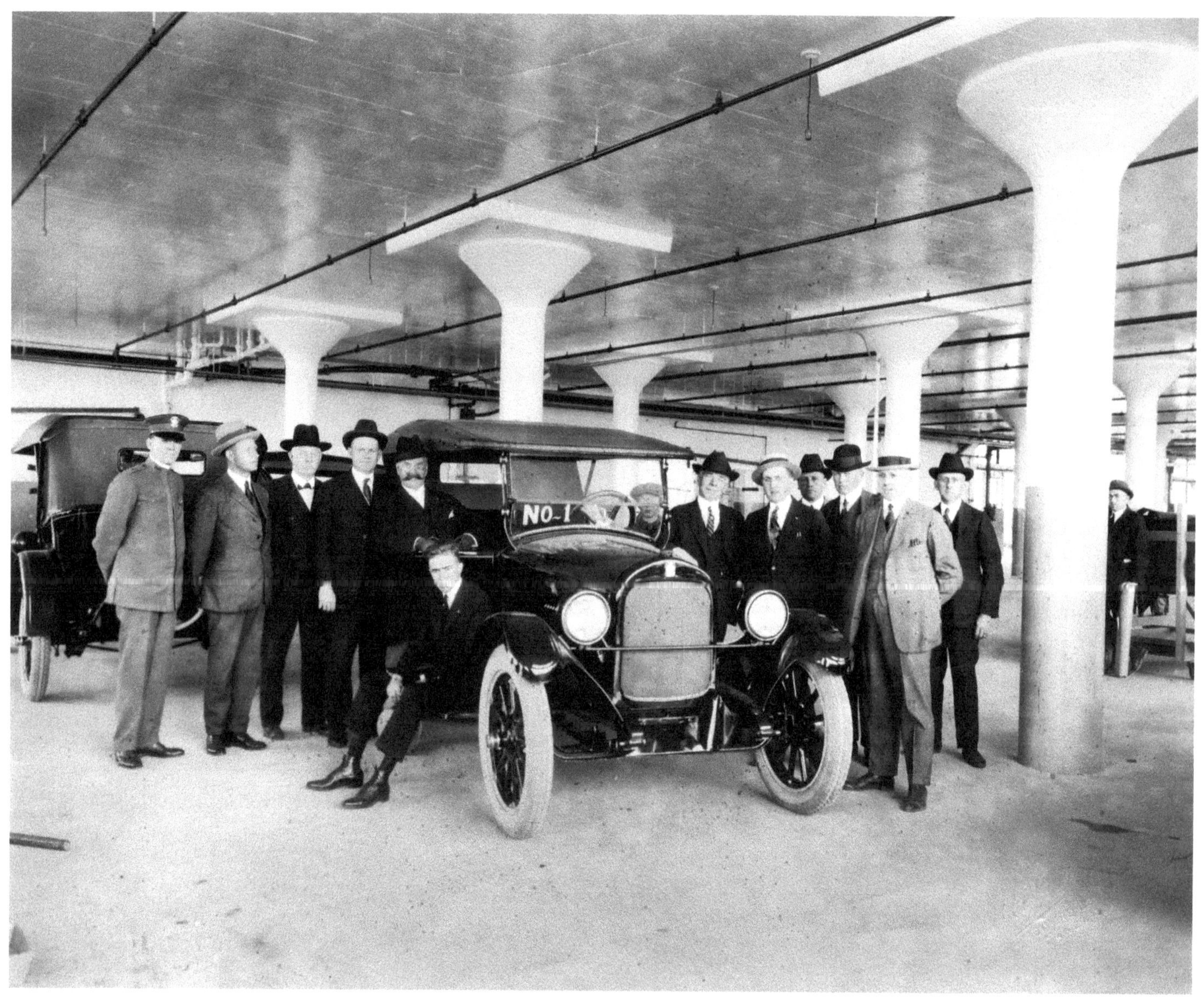

When William A. Durant, a founding executive of General Motors, decided to launch a rival automaker, he converted a small truck assembly plant at 107th Avenue to produce a car he named for himself. Mayor John L. Davie, with moustache, poses in 1922 with Durant and his son Cliff and others next to the first car out of the factory.

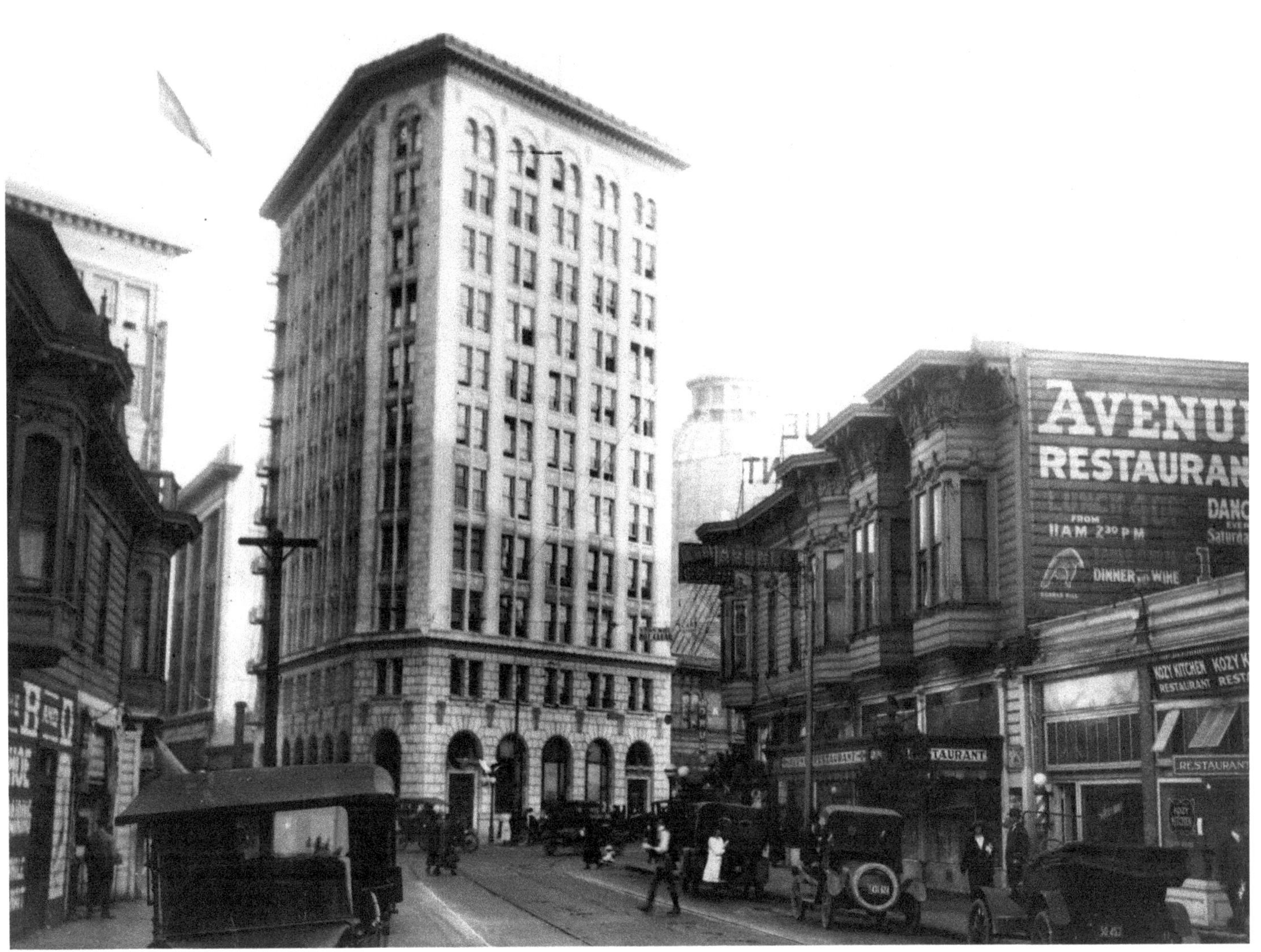

The offices of the First Trust and Savings Bank would not last long as the prominent feature in a view toward the foot of San Pablo Avenue, seen here in the early 1920s. By then, the publishers of the *Oakland Tribune* had big plans in store for the Oakland skyline.

The site selected for the Tribune Tower placed it directly in the front windshield of any vehicle traveling toward it on either of the two main arteries serving downtown Oakland, San Pablo Avenue or East 14th Street. Publisher Joseph R. Knowland commissioned architect Edward Foulkes to create the design. The tower was dedicated in 1923 and dominated the city's skyline for more than three decades.

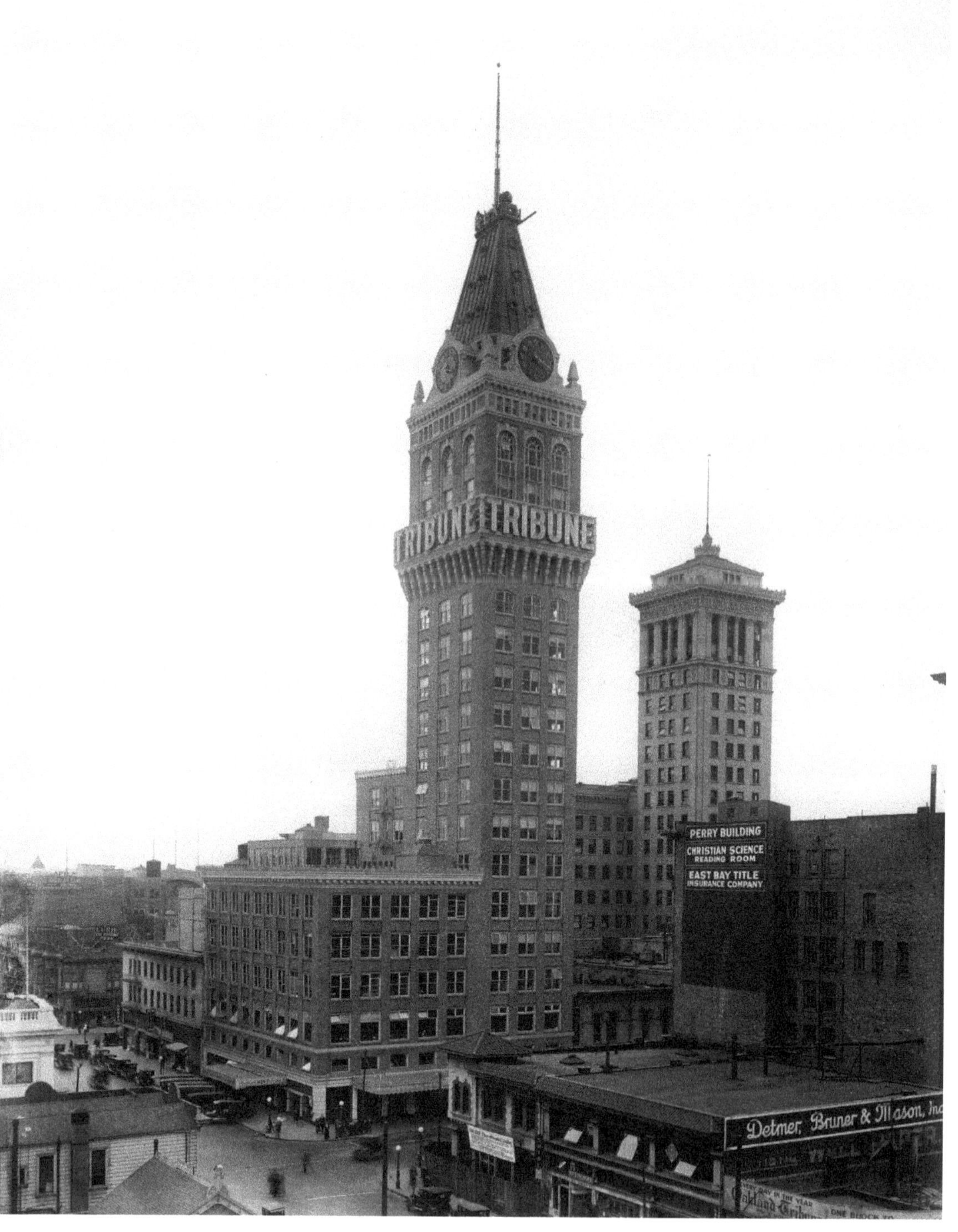

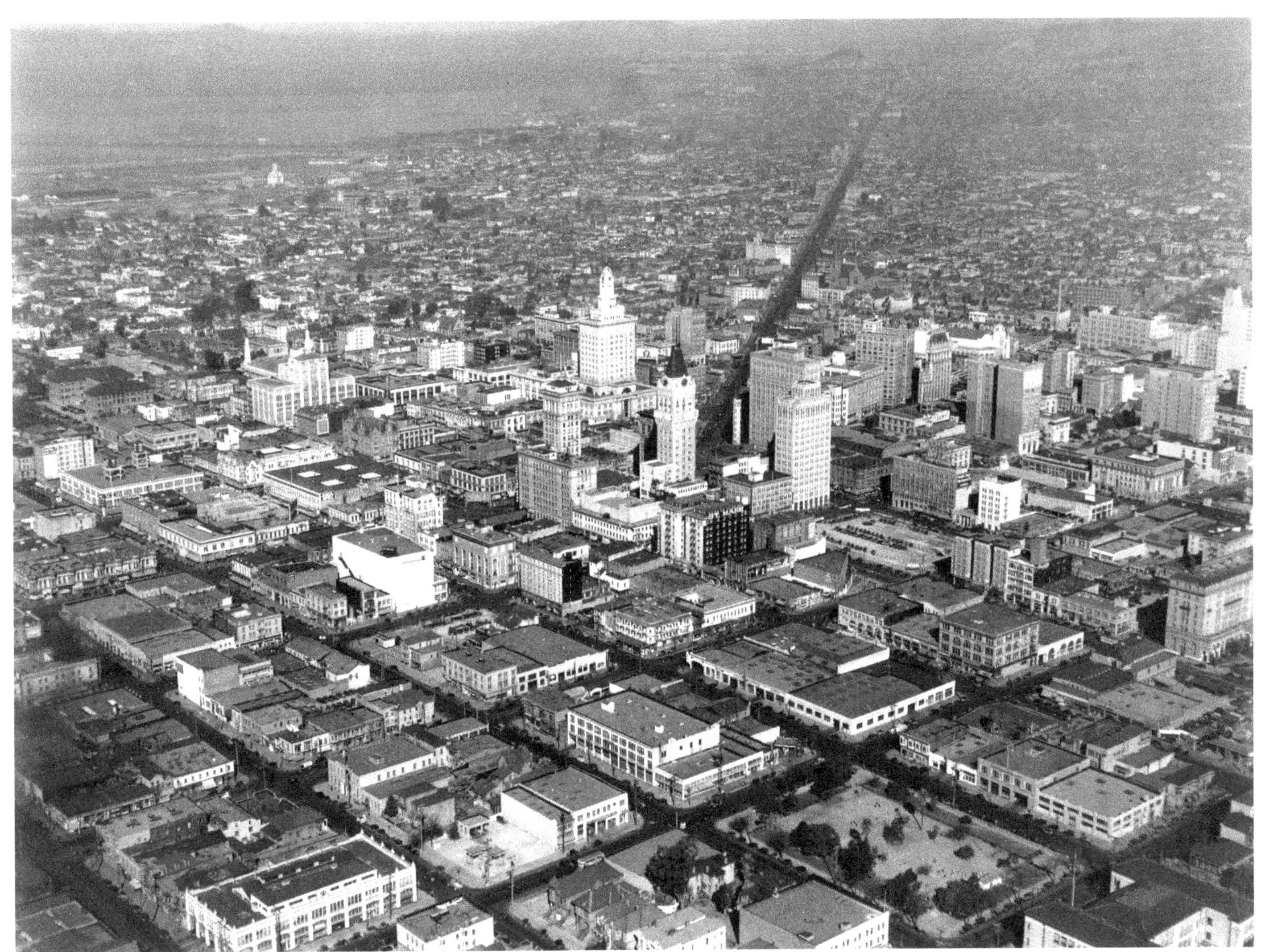

This aerial view illustrates the prominence of the Tribune Tower, just past the foot of San Pablo Avenue, the traffic-choked main thoroughfare headed north through Berkeley, Richmond, and on across the Carquinez Strait to the state capital in Sacramento.

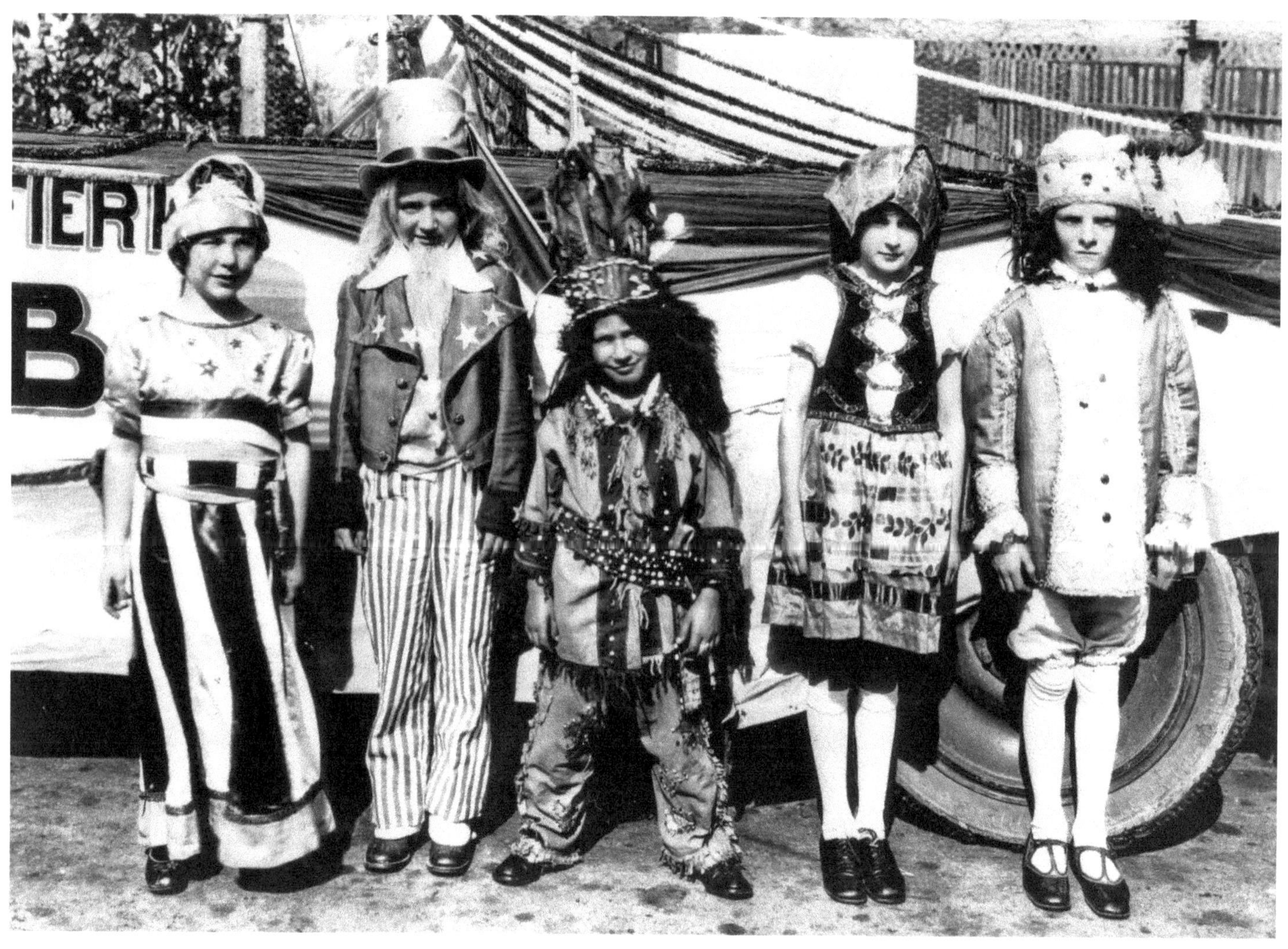

The city's large Italian-American community welcomed the official designation of Columbus Day by making it one of Oakland's most festive holidays—with a parade and reenactment of the explorer's landing on Hispaniola. A group of young participants in the festivities of 1925 pose beside their float to show off their costumes.

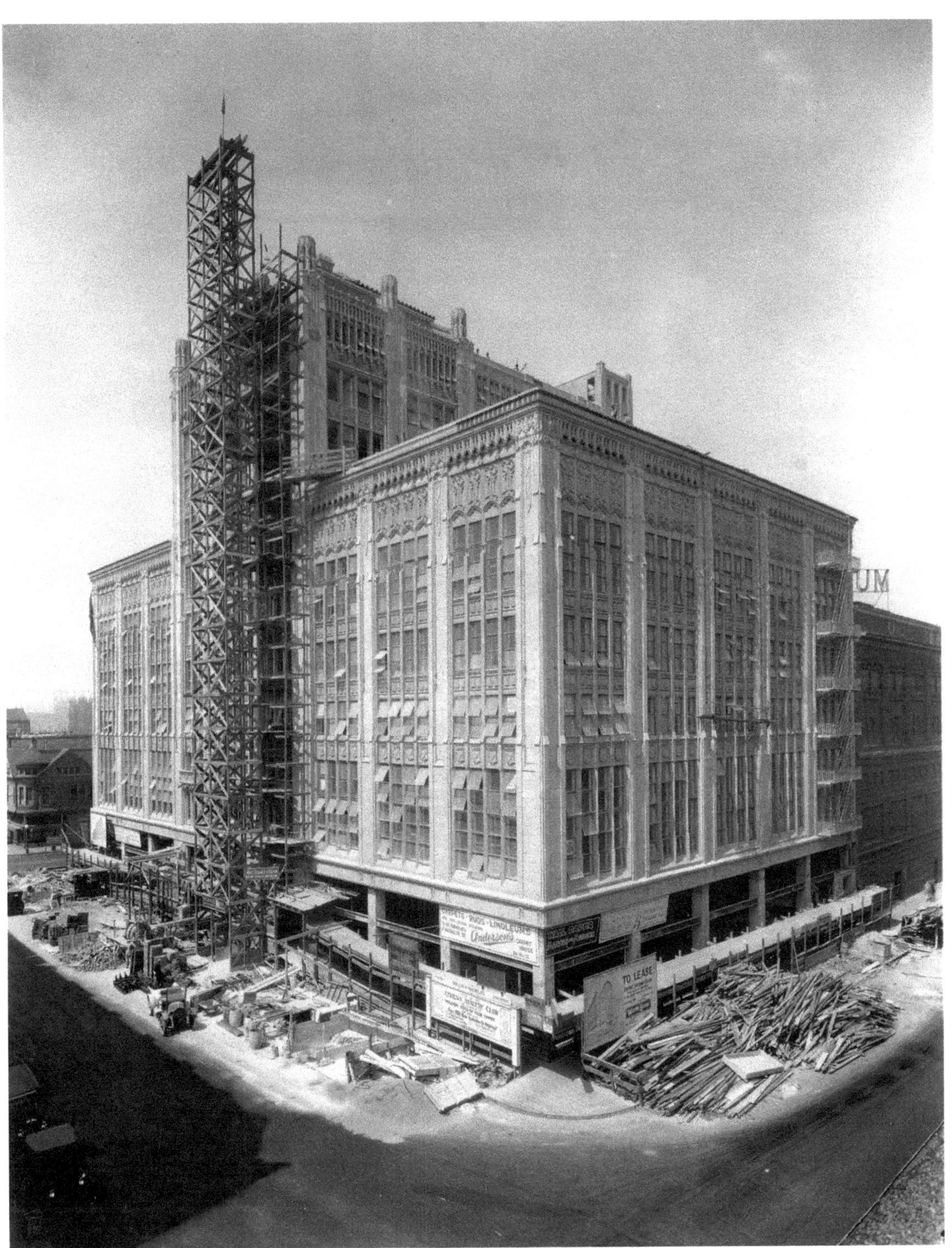

The Athens Athletic Club's expansive Beaux-Arts facility is nearing completion here in 1925. In the 1960s it would succumb to urban renewal, and 20 more years would elapse before construction began on the site cleared by its demolition.

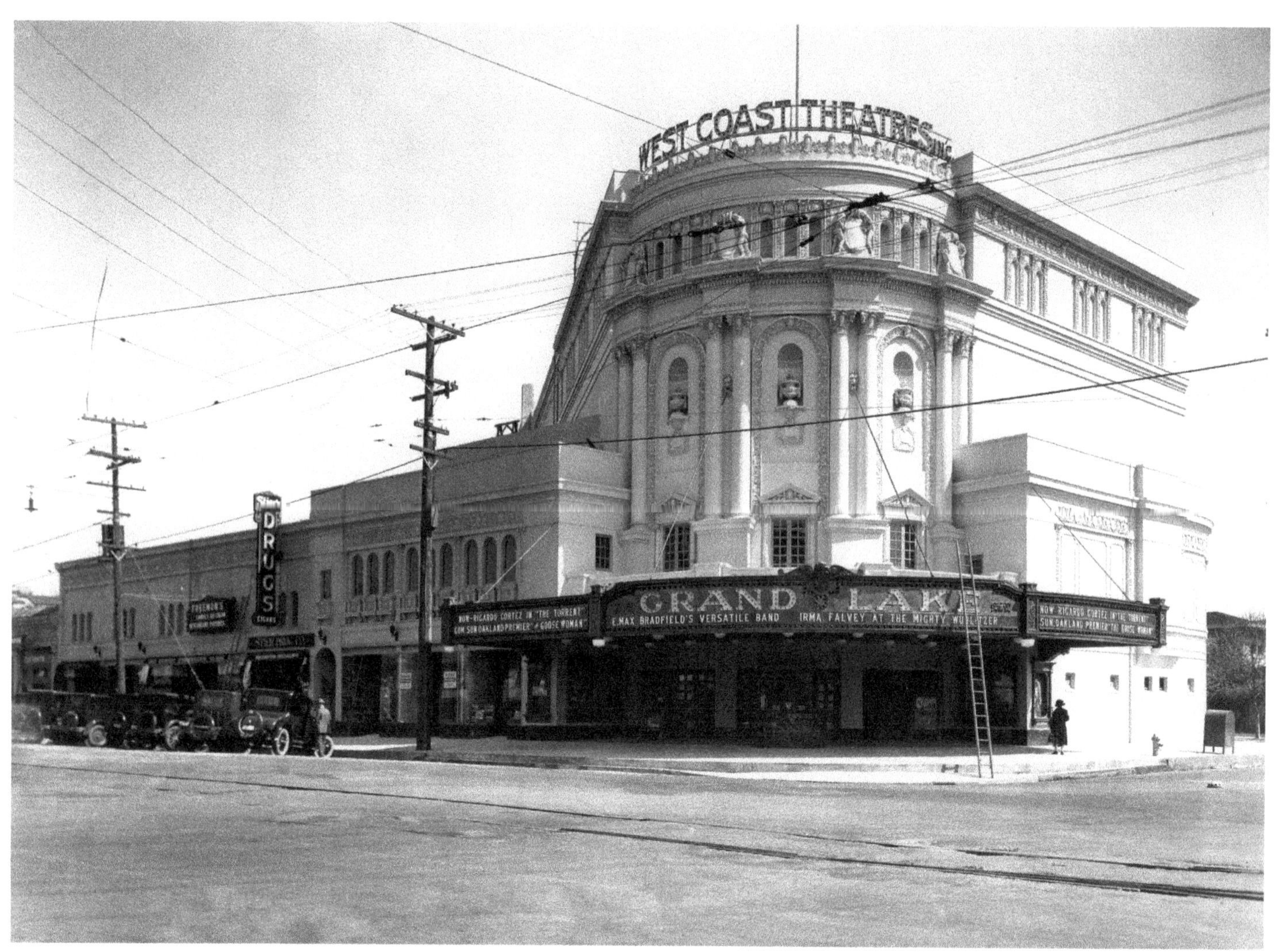

The success of Hollywood led to construction of theaters of all sizes throughout the city. The Grand Lake Theatre on the north end of Lake Merritt was the earliest of the grand movie palaces built in Oakland. It continues to screen first-run films under independent ownership. Showing at the theater around 1925 is *The Torrent,* with Irma Falvey at the "Mighty Wurlitzer" organ.

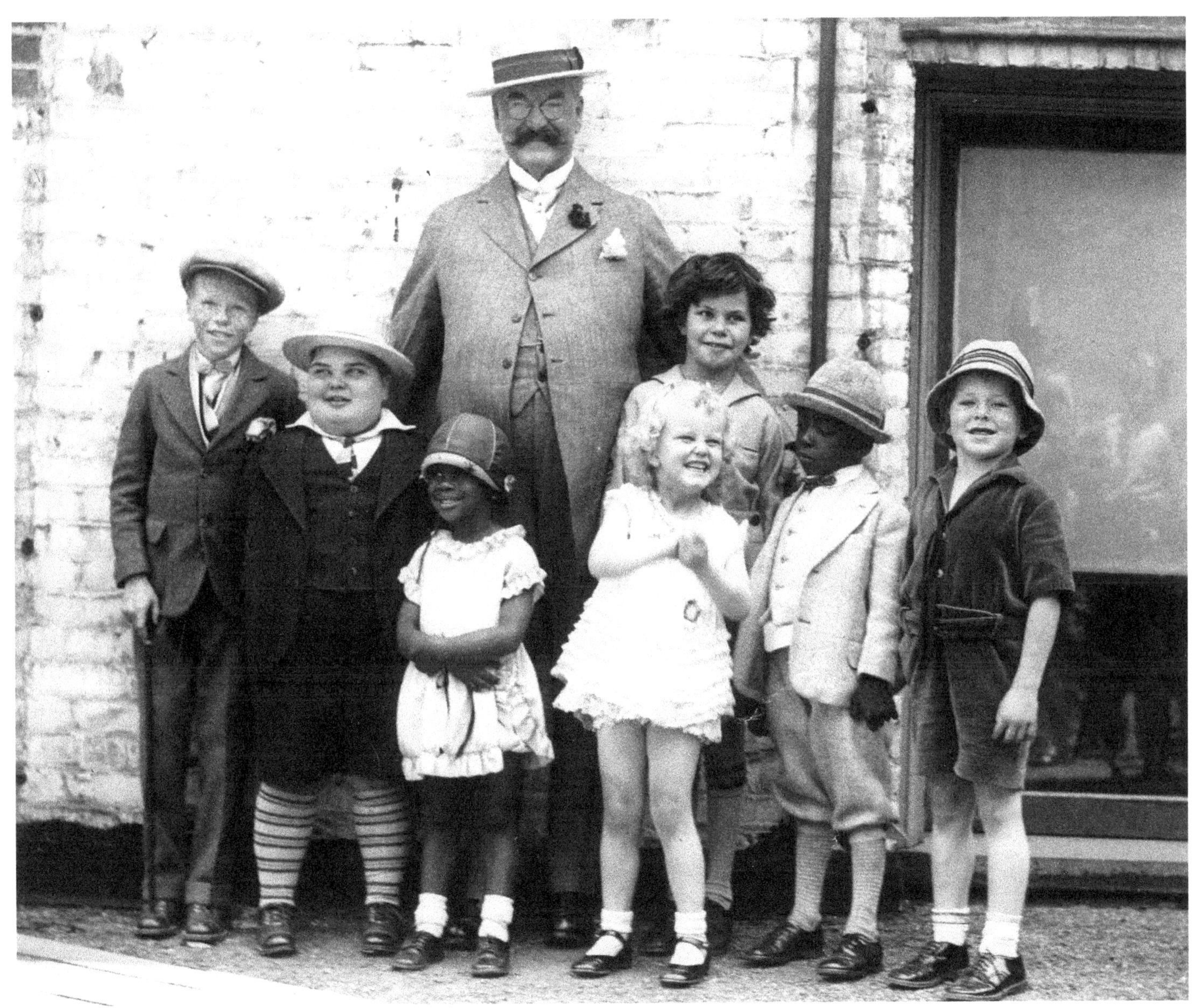

The stars of the "Our Gang" movie comedies came to town in 1927 for a newspaper promotion, posing here with Oakland's mayor John L. Davie outside the Orpheum Theatre. Allen Hoskins, second from the right, retired from the movie business at age 16 and later settled in Oakland, acting in productions in San Francisco.

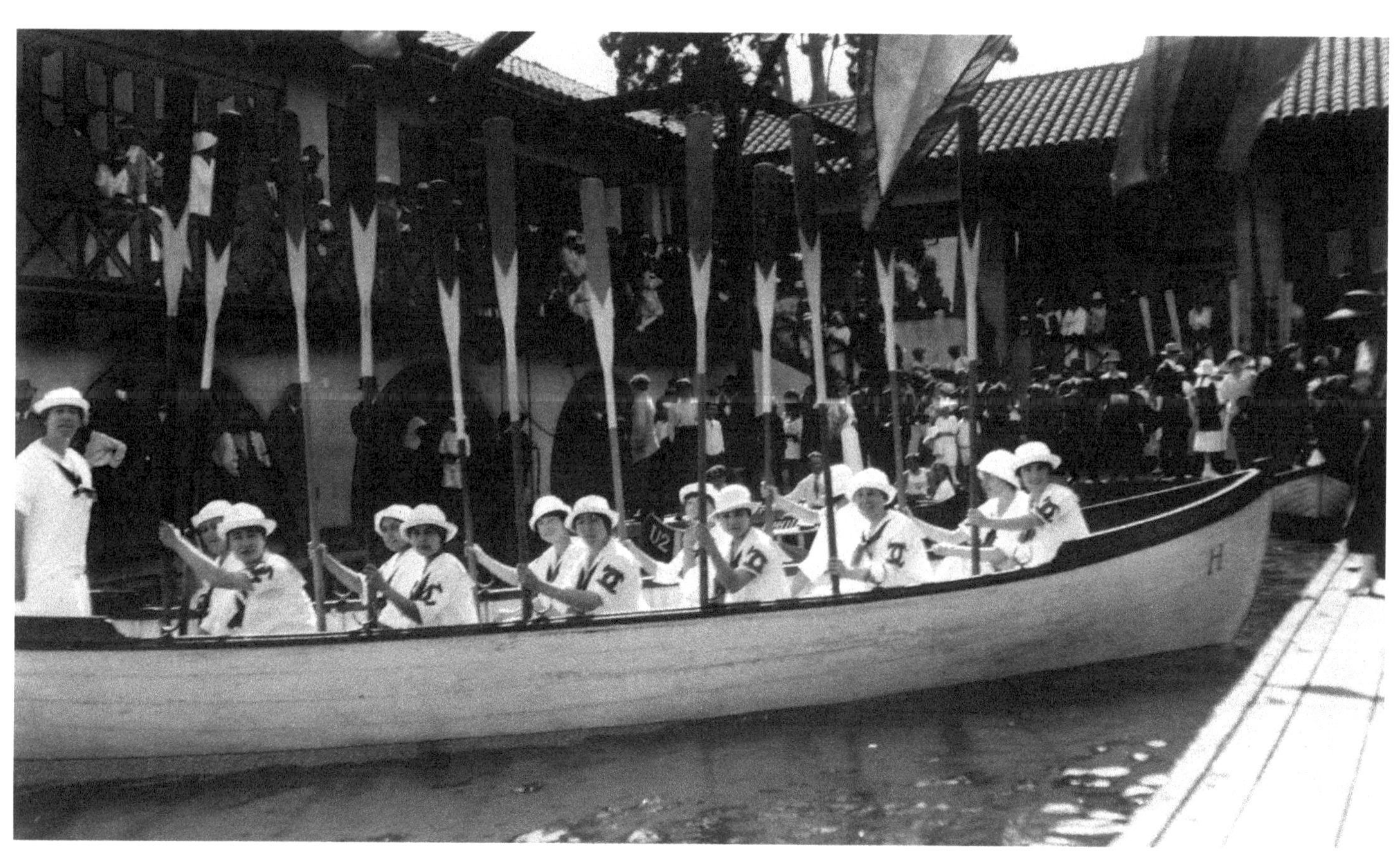

Crews of the Oakland Women's Rowing Club have been training on Lake Merritt since 1916. This club team is ready to race outside the Municipal Boathouse in the 1920s.

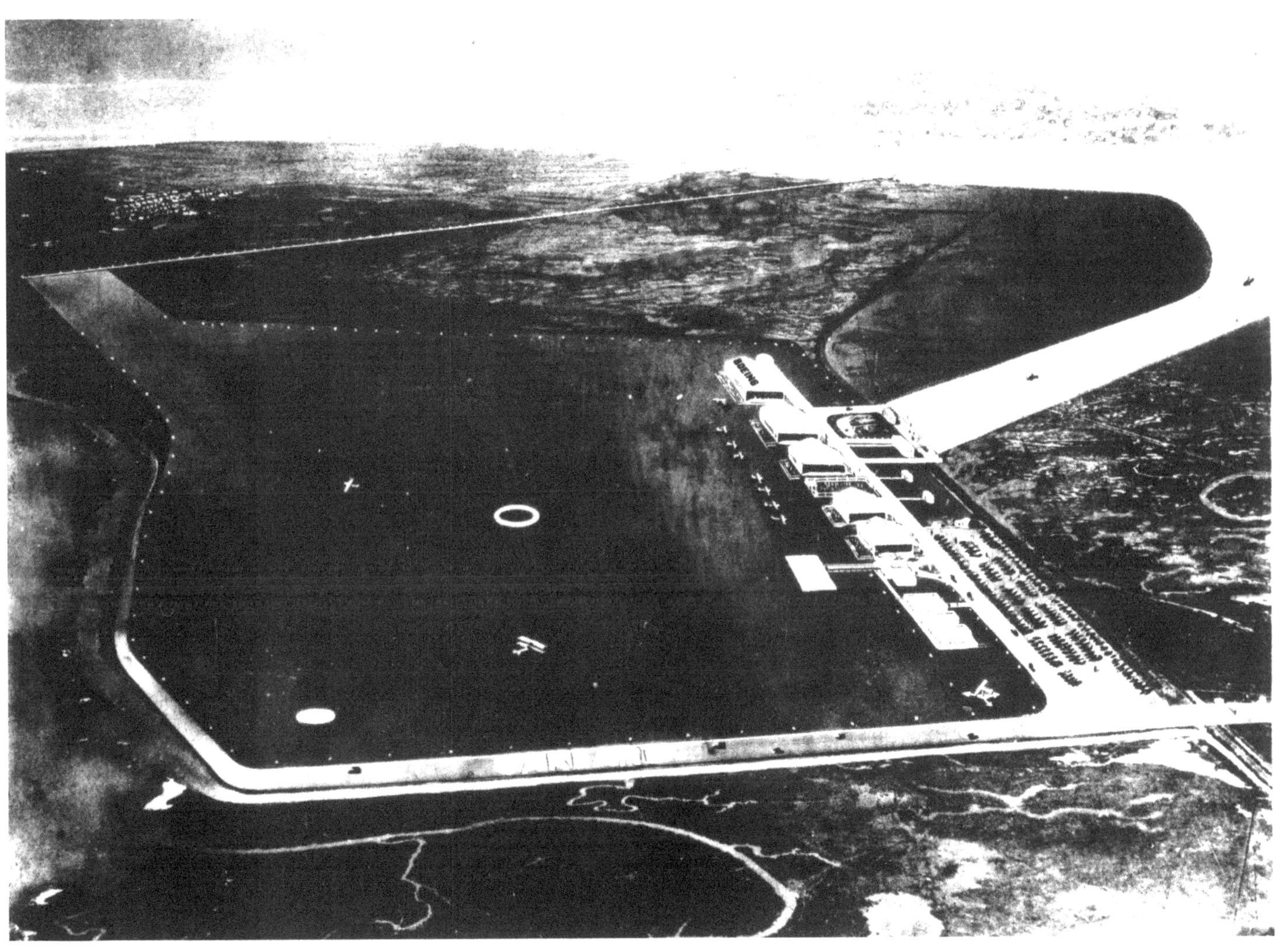

Bay Farm Island, a low-lying swale rising out of the bay shallows, invited use as an airfield and just so happened to lie immediately under the logical flyway of coast-to-coast commercial aviation. Its conversion to the Oakland Municipal Airport required little more than the erection of a few sheds and the grading of the surface.

The thrills of flying too often overshadow its potential for tragic consequences, and the risks were ignored when James A. Dole offered $35,000 in prize money to any pilot who could fly a plane from the mainland to his pineapple plantations in Hawaii. A race ensued, with fliers taking off from Oakland on August 16, 1927. Two planes reached Honolulu. Many others crashed, with ten lives lost.

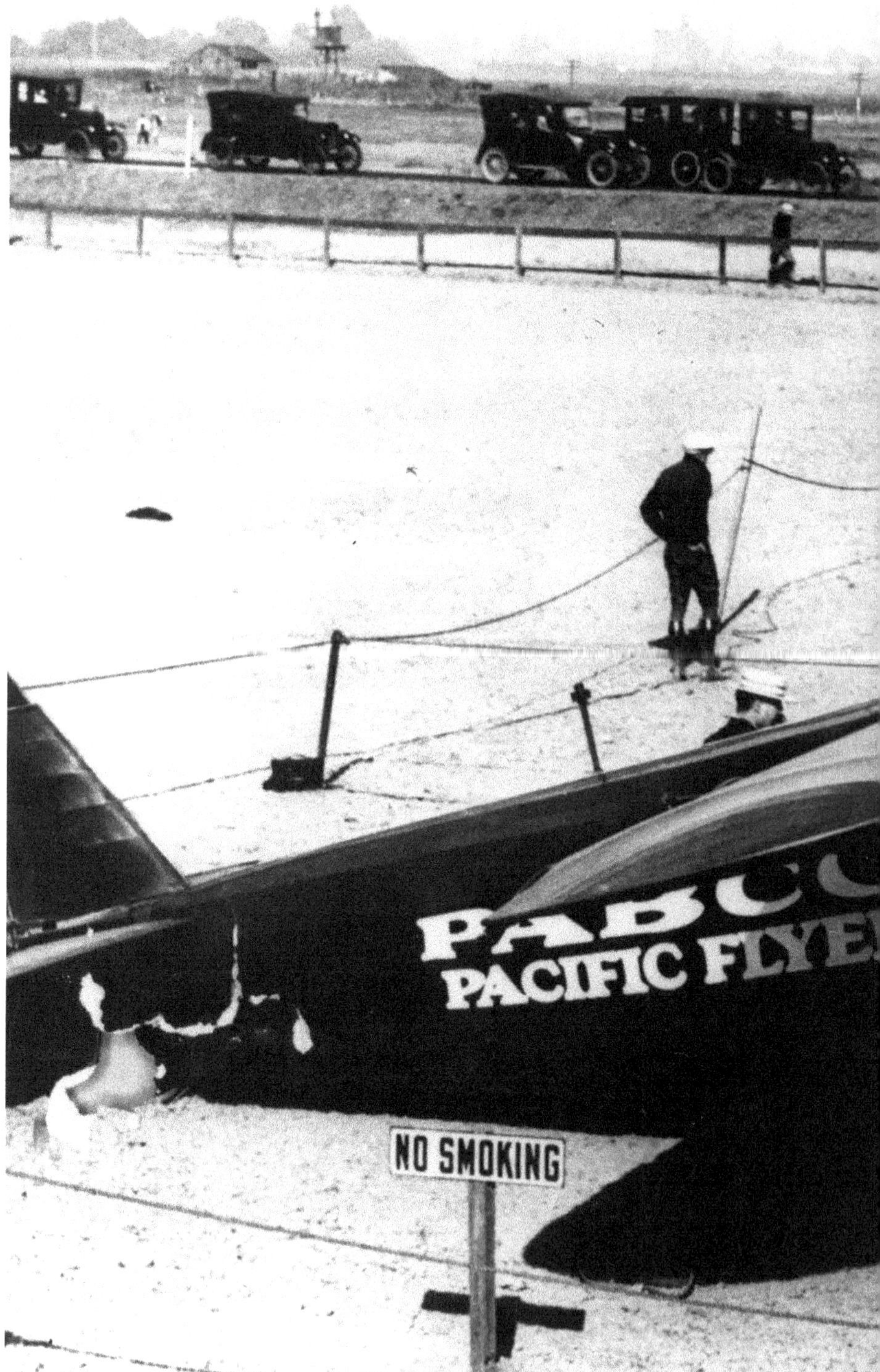

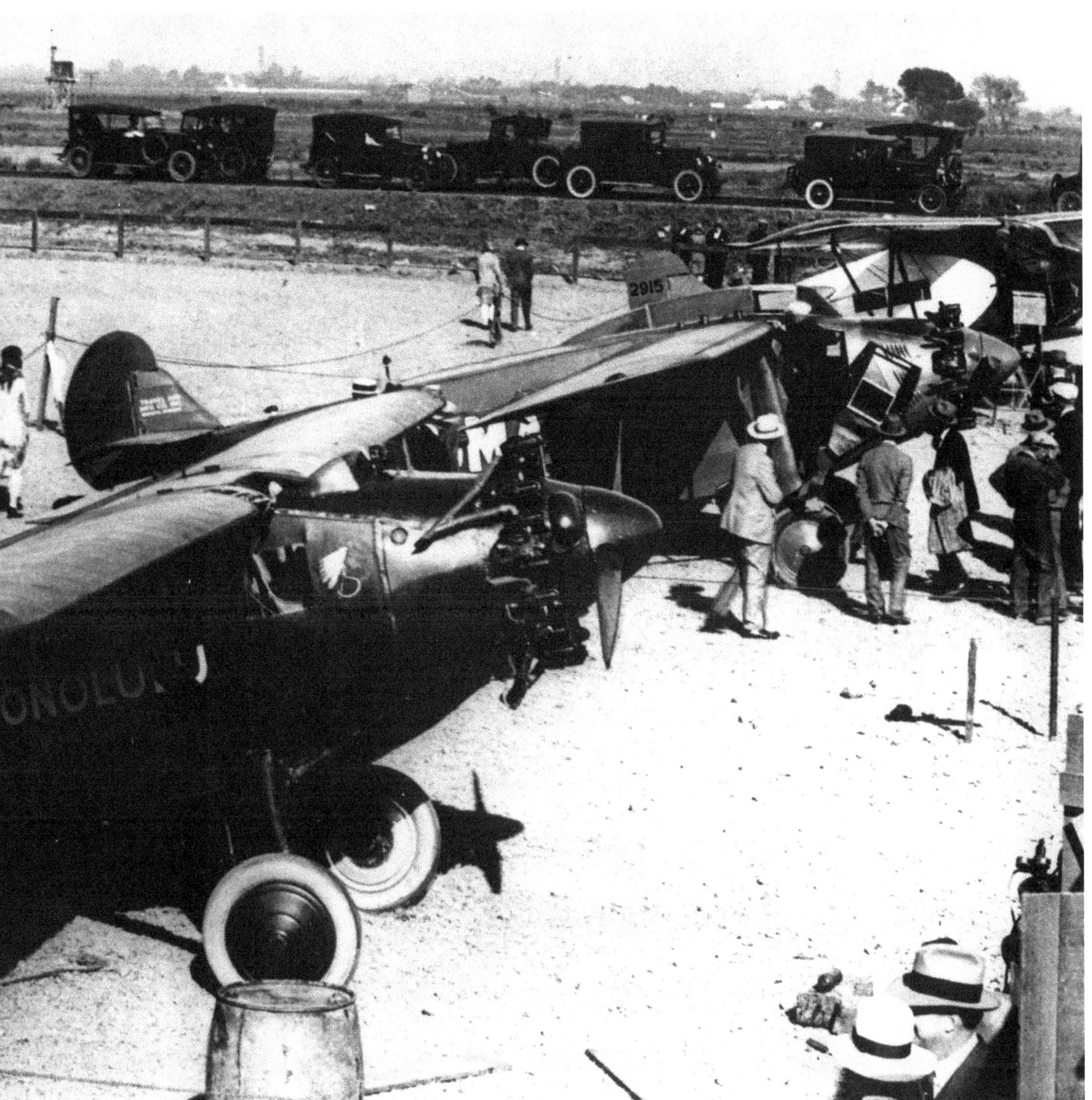
2915
ONOLU

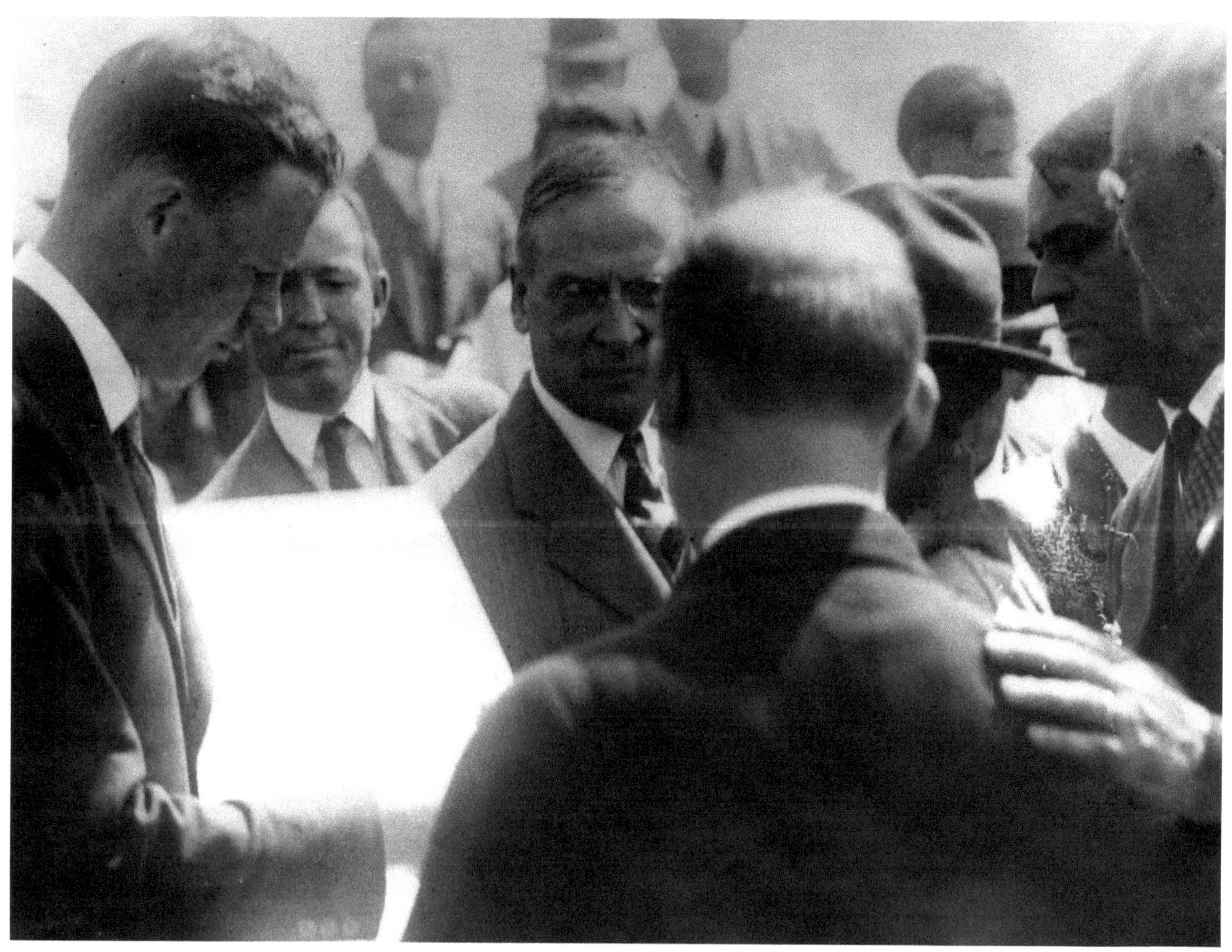

Aviation's biggest celebrity, Colonel Charles A. Lindbergh, paid a visit to Oakland to dedicate the municipal airport on September 17, 1927. A photographer for the *Oakland Tribune* was there to record his arrival. Shown at left, Lindbergh signs the airport's register while *Tribune* publisher Joseph R. Knowland and others look on.

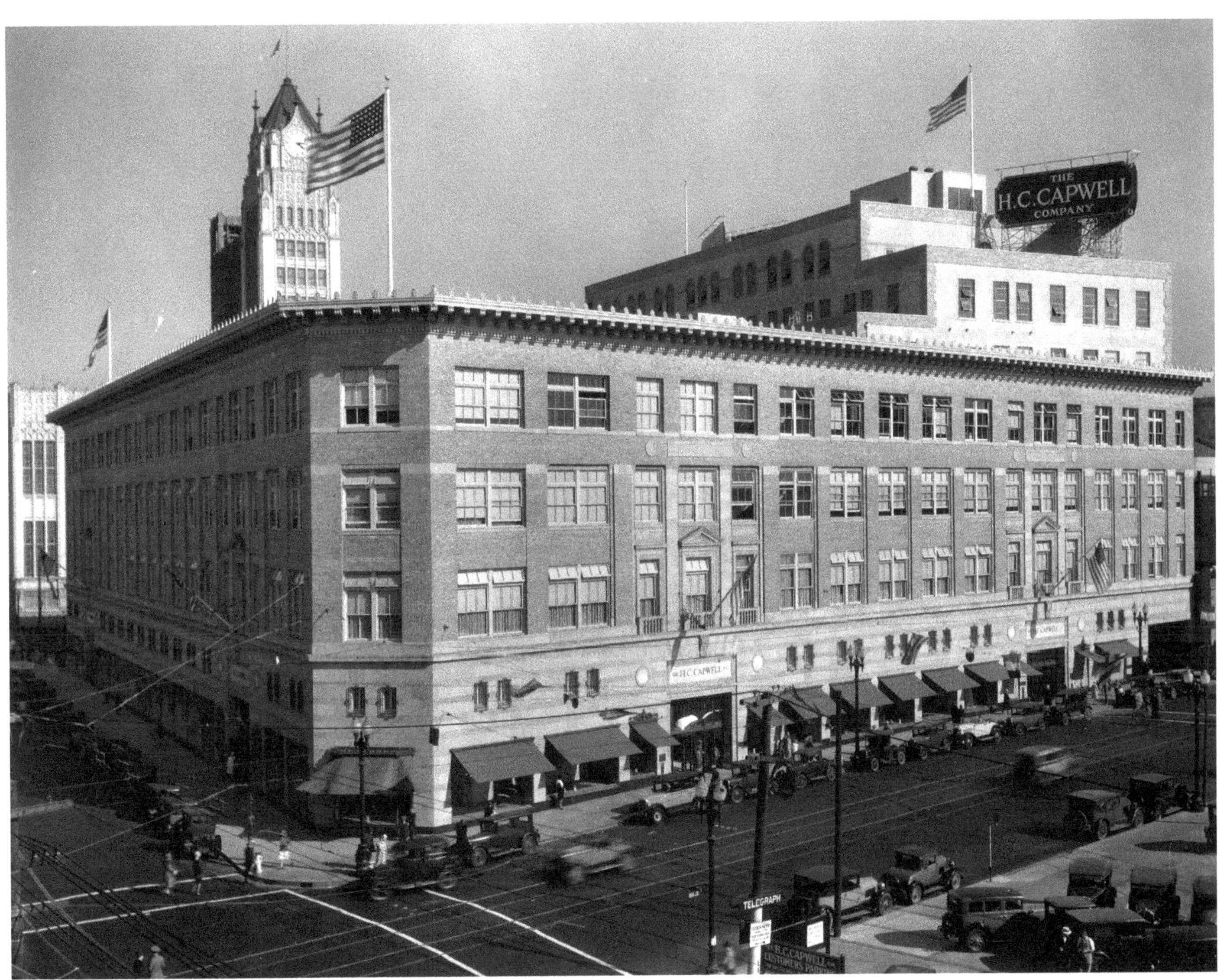

Oakland's ceaseless growth brought great success to the merchants in its retail sector. The merger between San Francisco's Emporium department store and Oakland's H. C. Capwell Company resulted in the construction of a mammoth new department store at 20th Street and Broadway in 1928. The store became a familiar name after branches were established in shopping centers throughout the East Bay following World War II.

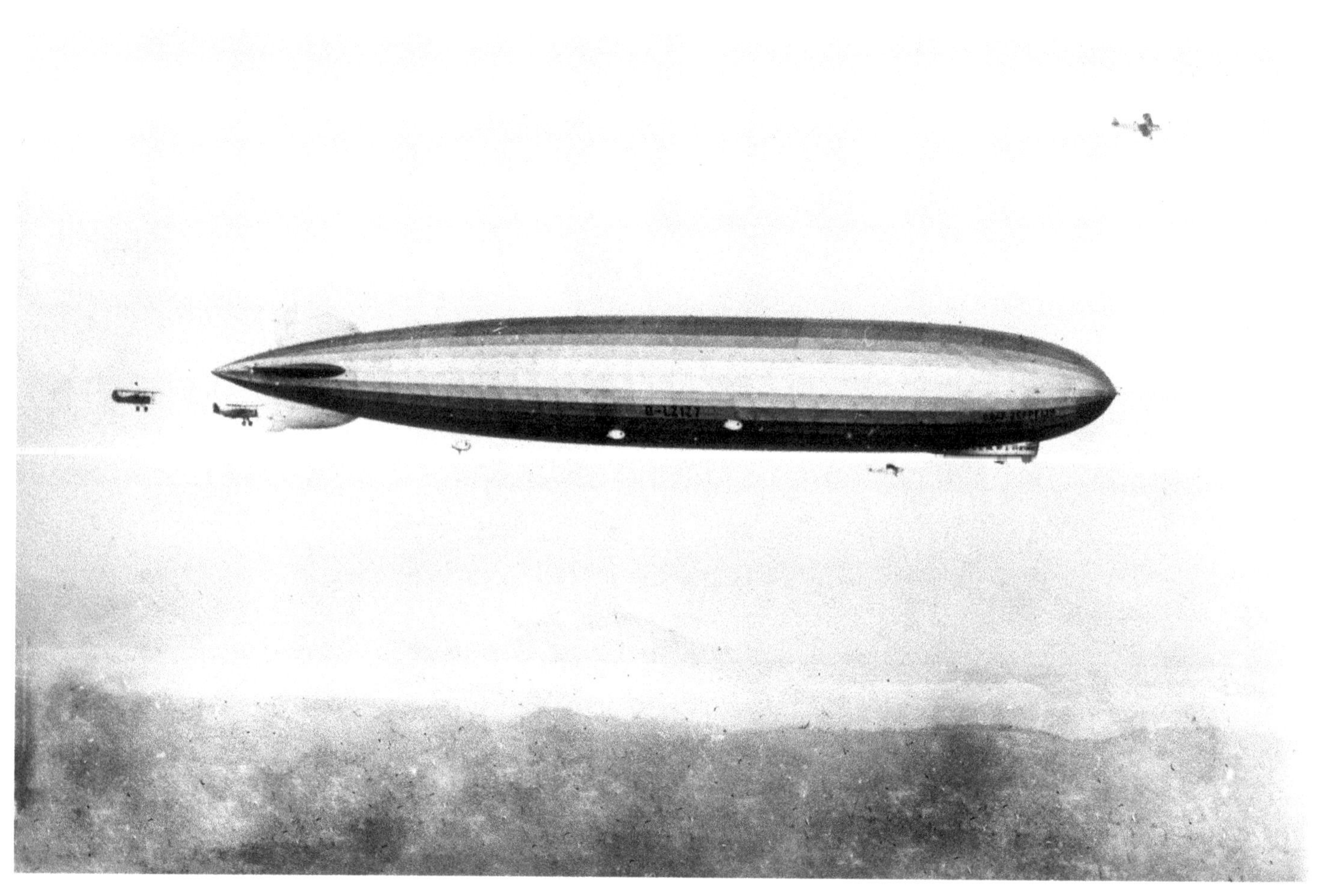

An armistice signed November 11, 1918, ended hostilities in Europe and ushered in an ambitious effort by the newly established German Republic to restore good will internationally. Oakland enjoyed the results of those efforts ten years later, when the *Graf Zeppelin* passed through the city in the skies overhead.

THE SECOND GOLD RUSH

(1929–1945)

Cycles of boom and bust have always characterized California's economy, but the bust following the stock market crash in 1929 was unlike any other. With Oakland's economy based on core industries like shipping and manufacturing, the Great Depression hit the city hard.

As always, Oaklanders found innovative ways to cope. A group of homeless men turned a large supply of unsold concrete sewer pipes into Pipe City, with an elected mayor and its own municipal code. Women in the Elmhurst district created a food bank, pooling funds to buy in bulk, offering surpluses to families in need. Reports of such responses to the crisis reached the White House and served as models for components of President Franklin Roosevelt's relief efforts.

Grand-scale public projects under Roosevelt's New Deal plan entered the long road back to prosperity. The San Francisco–Oakland Bay Bridge, the world's longest bridge at the time of its construction, now carries an average of 280,000 vehicles each day. The Alameda County Court House permanently changed the city's skyline. Large-scale subsidized housing projects at both ends of the city all contributed to an economic turnaround. But relief efforts alone could not fend off the decay in Oakland's neighborhoods, some already poor before the collapse of the economy. Large factories, some only a few years old, stood idle and vacant. Unemployment, which had peaked in 1933 at 25 percent nationwide, remained oppressively high at 19 percent by 1938, six years into the New Deal.

Another great war would reverse Oakland's decline completely, at least until peace was restored. Oakland's waterfront had been vital to the war effort during World War I, and the same was true when the Second World War erupted. Shipyards built and repaired ships. Tidelands were reclaimed for military bases used to move supplies and munitions to the fighting forces. The build-up demanded a large supply of workers and the city's population grew by one-third between 1940 and 1945, gaining nearly 100,000 new residents, with the growth spilling out into the suburbs.

Much of the mass migration westward began in the drought-ravaged and poverty-stricken regions west of New Orleans and south of Kansas City, bringing with it the cultural traditions and social values of those who now looked at California as their golden opportunity. Almost overnight, Oakland had become a much different place.

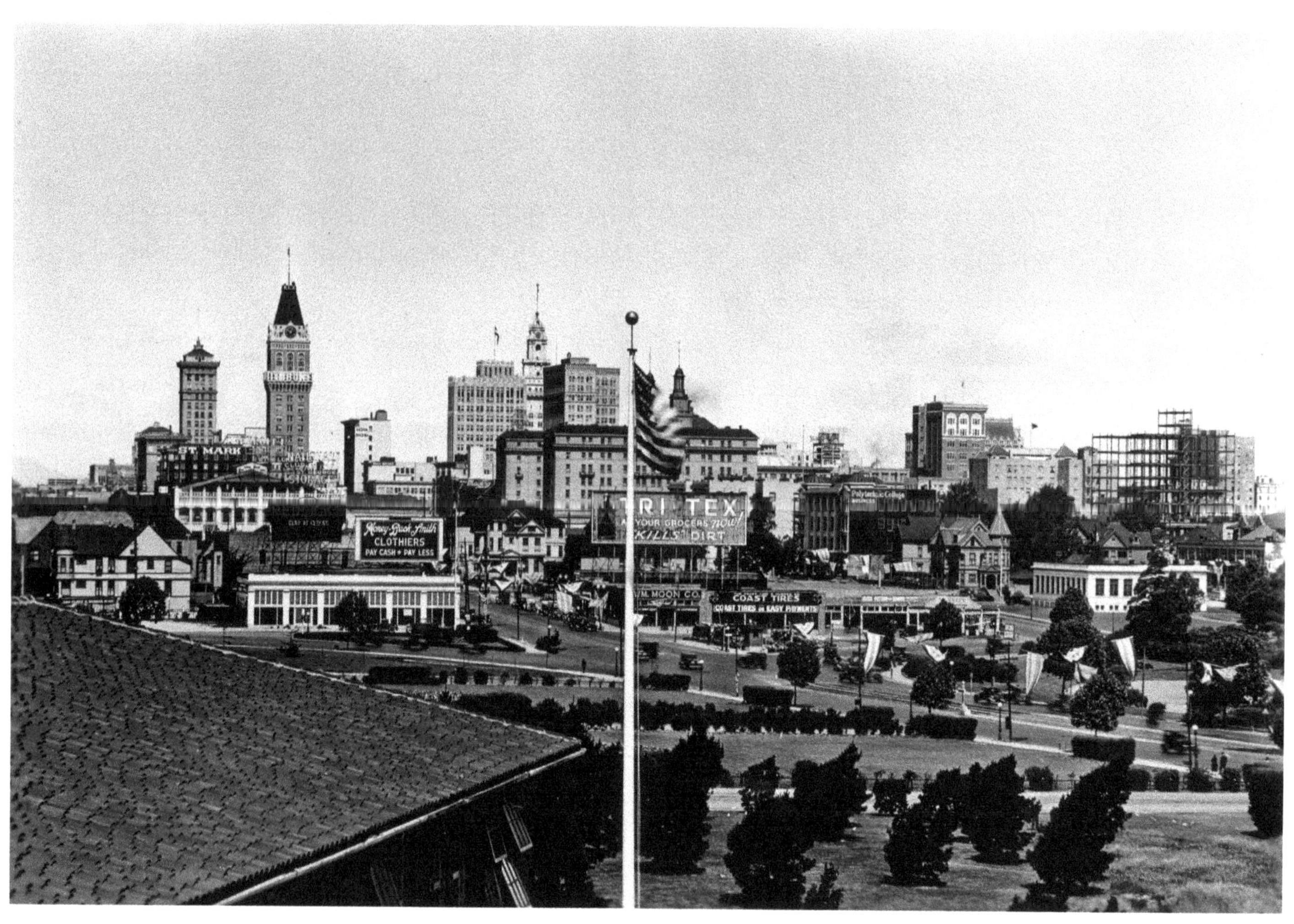

The boom in high-rise construction gave downtown Oakland a decidedly metropolitan appearance in this view facing west around 1930.

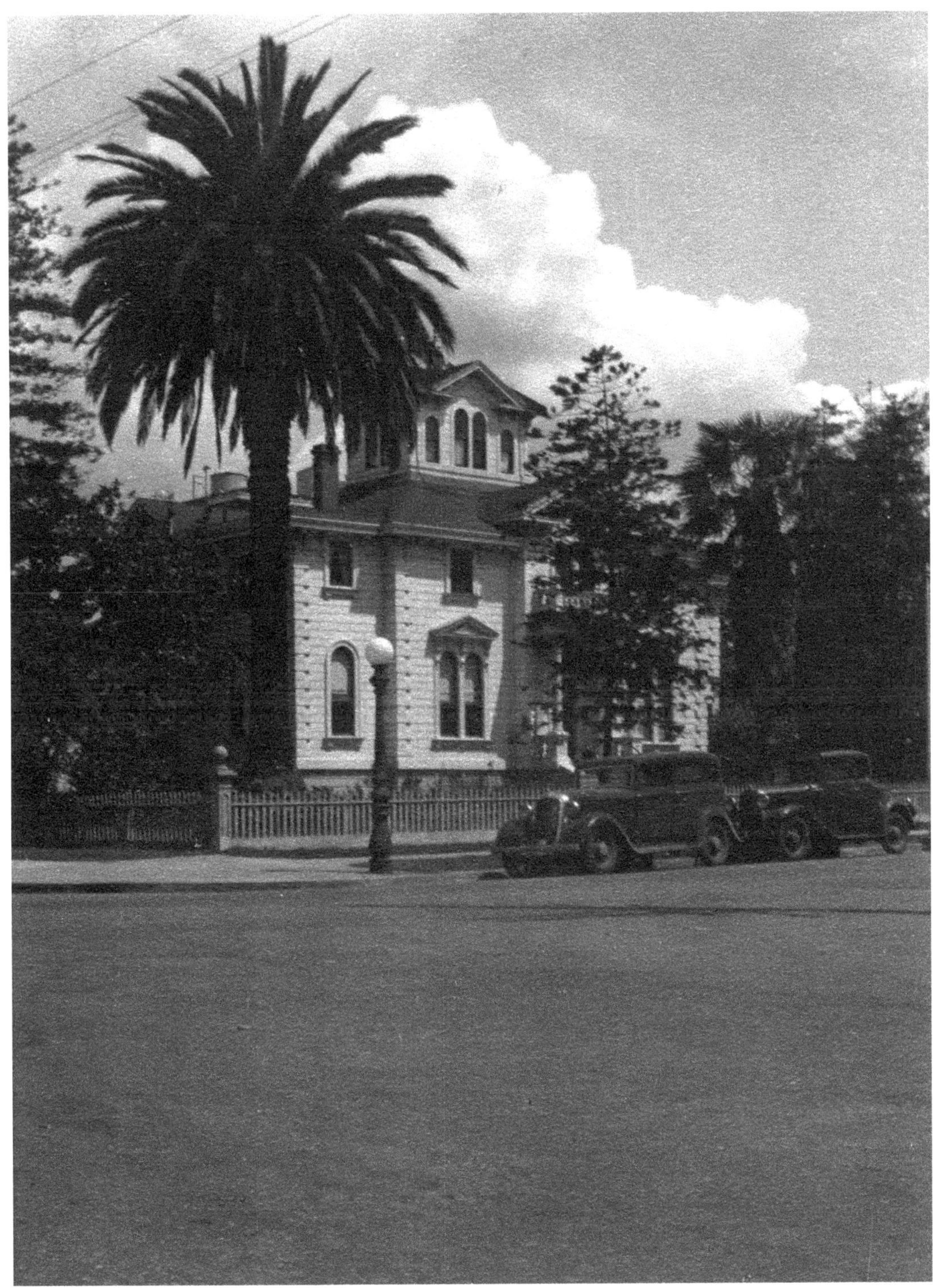

Governor George C. Pardee returned from Sacramento to his family home on the western edge of downtown Oakland and continued an active role in civic life. The house remains a museum commemorating the family's contributions to Oakland's early development and to California's political history.

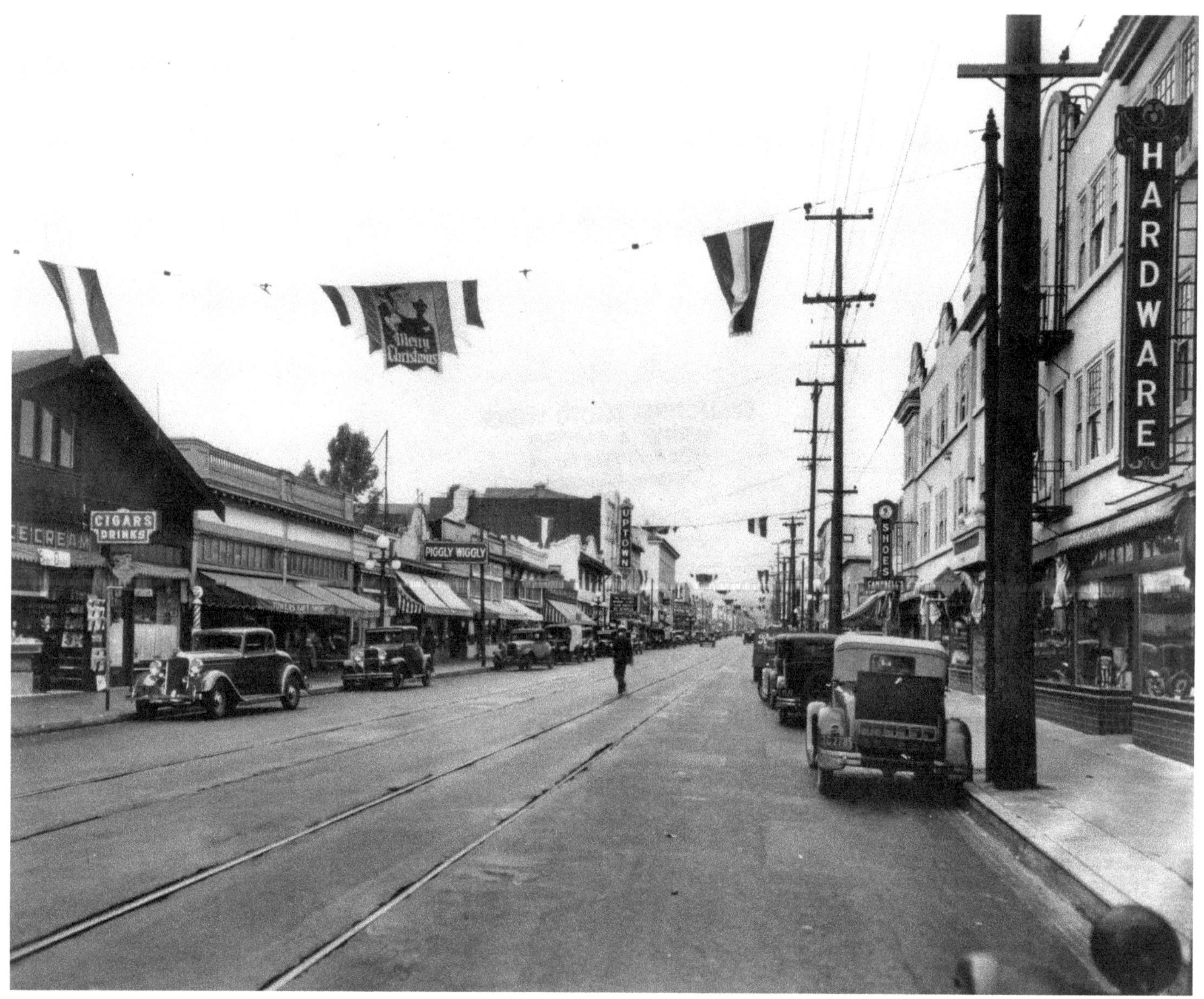

The growth and prosperity of the first decades of the twentieth century produced lively neighborhood commercial districts throughout the city. A stretch of College Avenue near the campus of the California College of Arts and Crafts is shown in this photograph from 1930. The tracks visible in the street carried streetcars bound for the University of California.

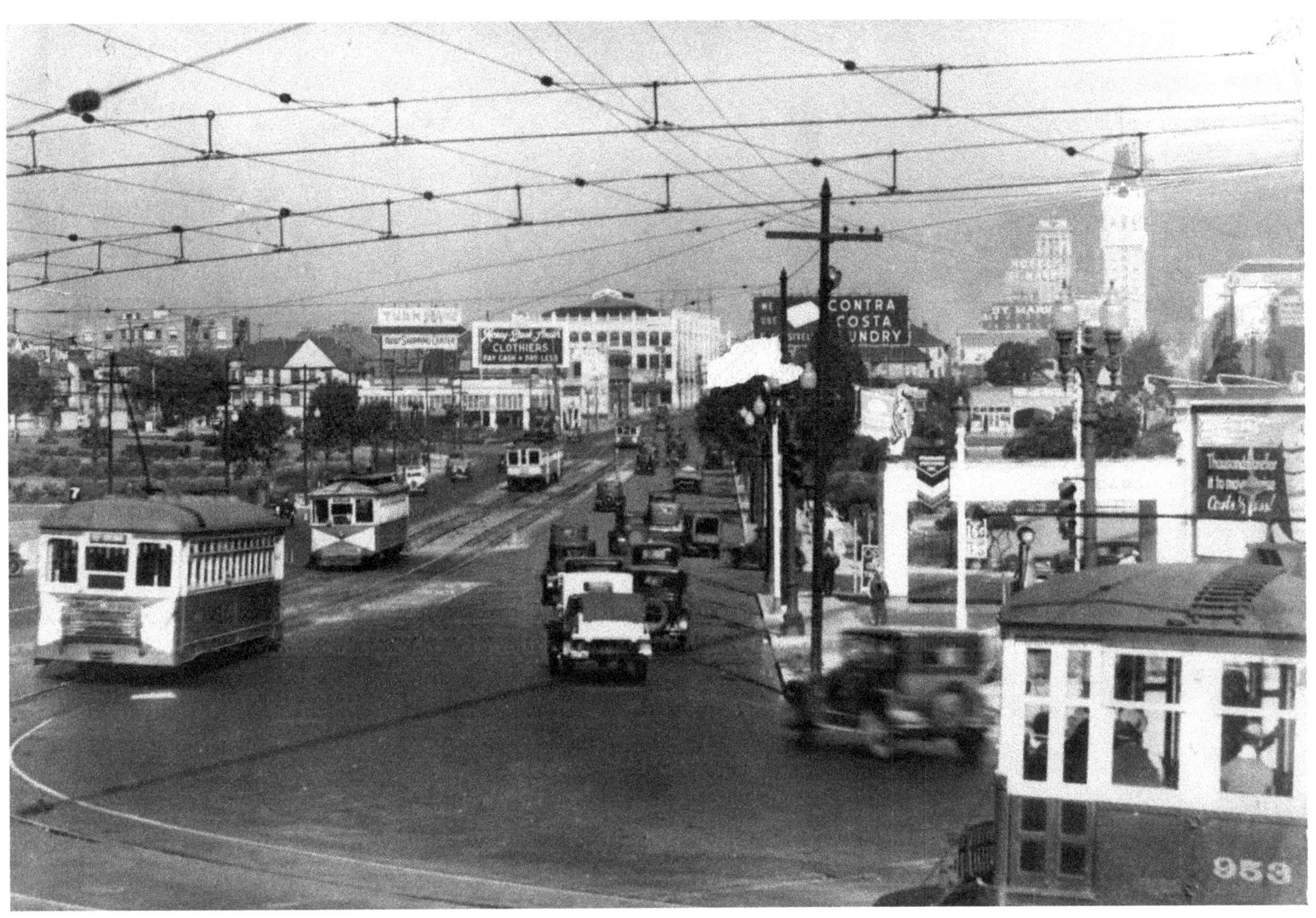

A rapidly growing population in East Oakland and in the suburbs beyond led to increasing congestion in the traffic bottleneck created by Lake Merritt's location at the heart of the commute. This view shows the approach from the dam into downtown from the east. Increased motor traffic would soon make the 12th Street Dam the most congested stretch of roadway in California.

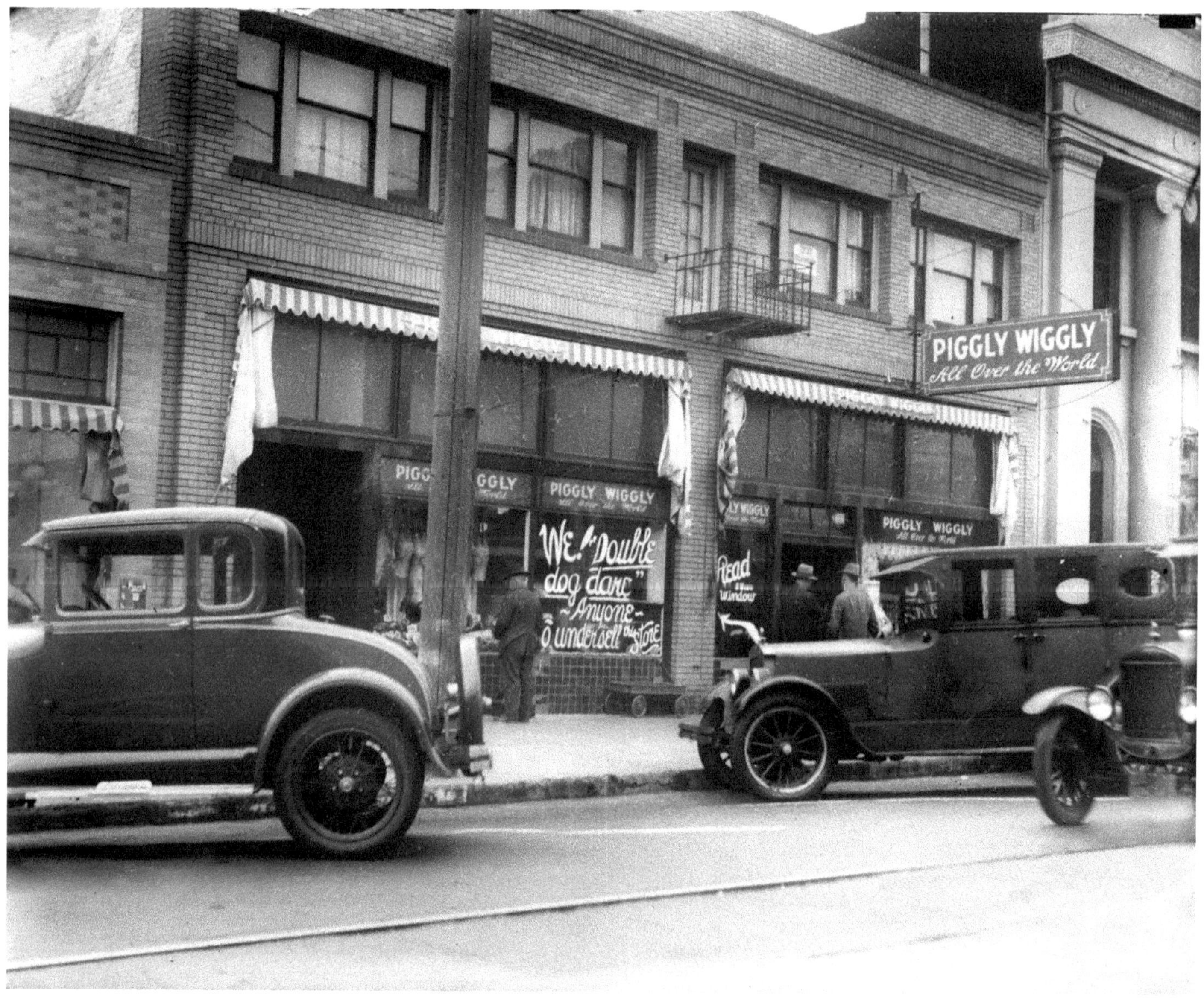

Piggly Wiggly stores came west from Memphis introducing the self-service grocery store to California. The local Piggly Wiggly stores would join with other smaller chains to form Safeway Stores, with its main offices in Oakland. This Piggly Wiggly on Piedmont Avenue is shown sometime before the conversion to Safeway in 1932.

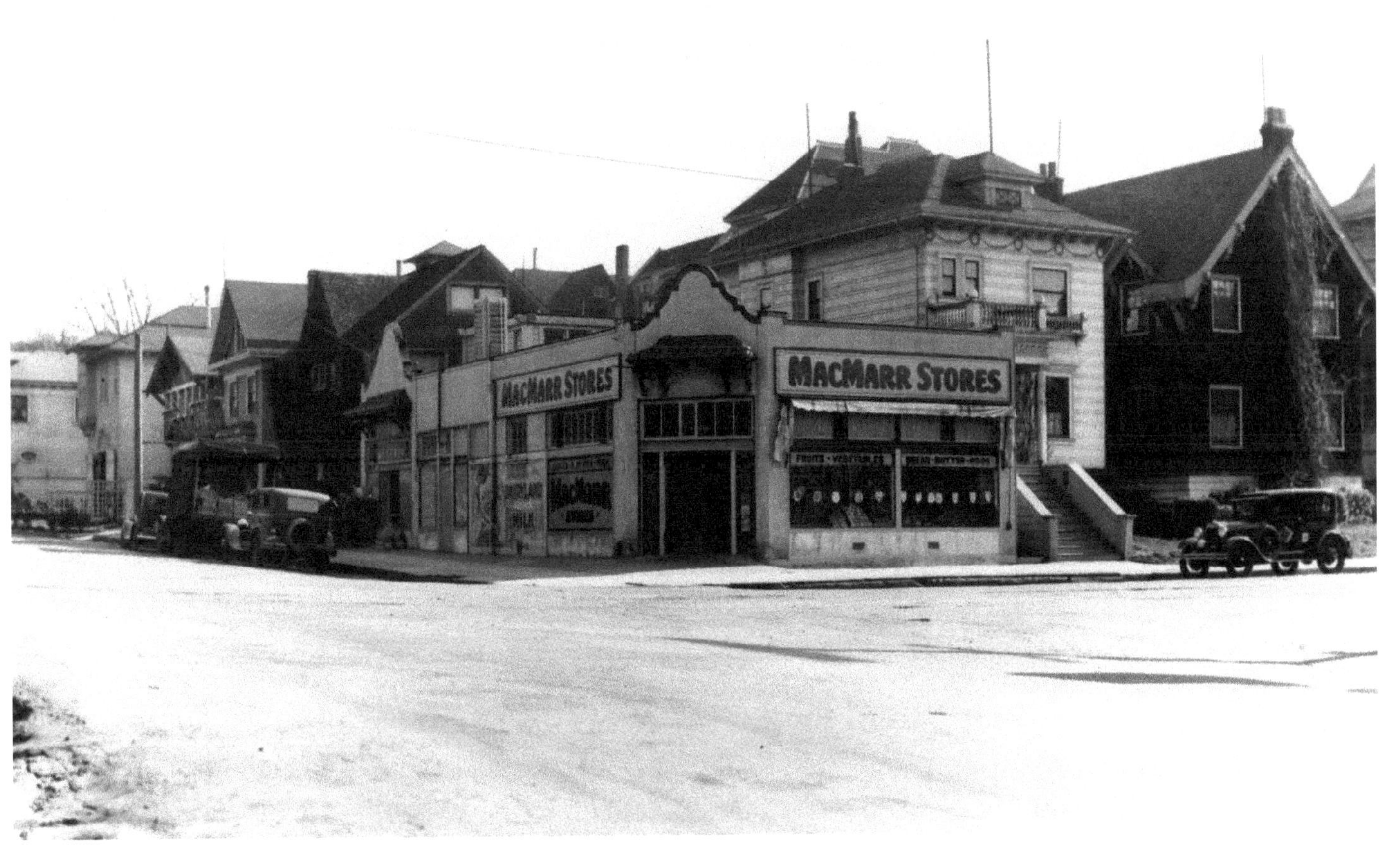

MacMarr Stores, another piece of the Safeway consolidation, operated this store on Oakland Avenue. The building sat directly in the path of the MacArthur Freeway.

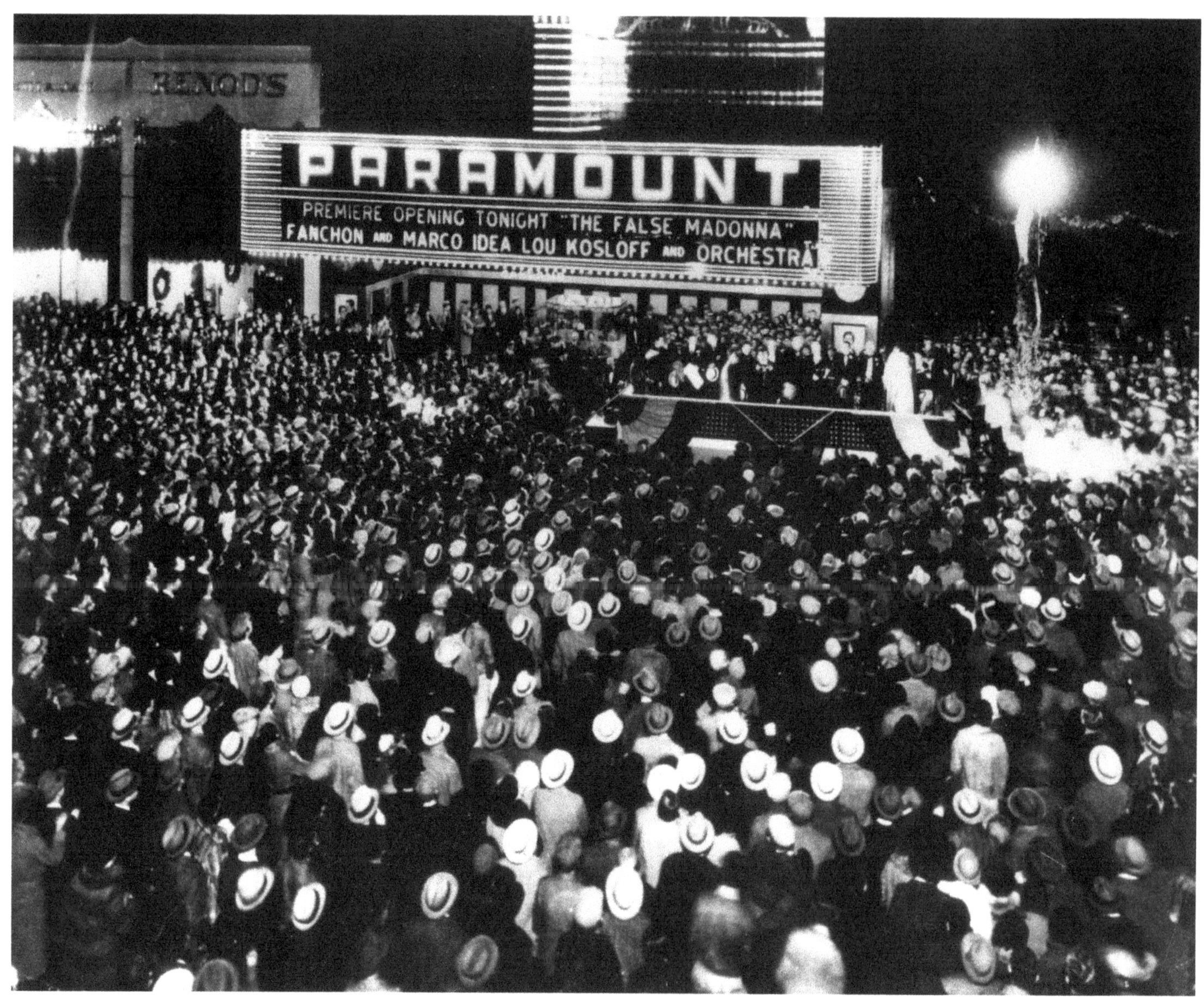

The last splash of Hollywood's Tinseltown era left a lasting monument in downtown Oakland with the spectacular Paramount Theatre, designed in the art deco style by architect Timothy Pfleuger. A large crowd gathered for its grand opening in 1931. The building has since been beautifully restored as a venue for touring entertainers and the local symphony.

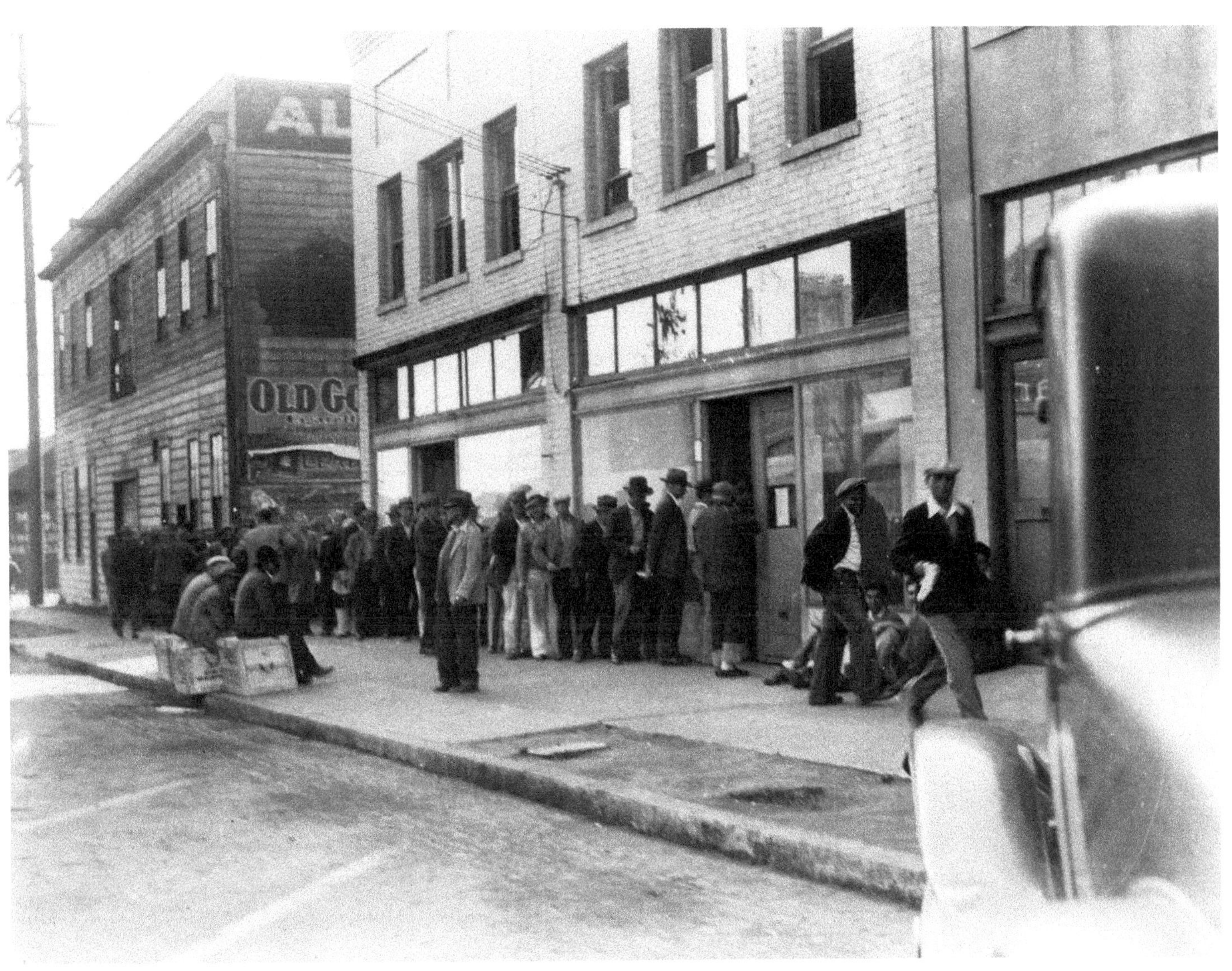

By 1934, with the economy mired in depression, many Oaklanders were too broke to buy groceries. A photographer captured a line of hungry men outside a free kitchen on Fourth Street.

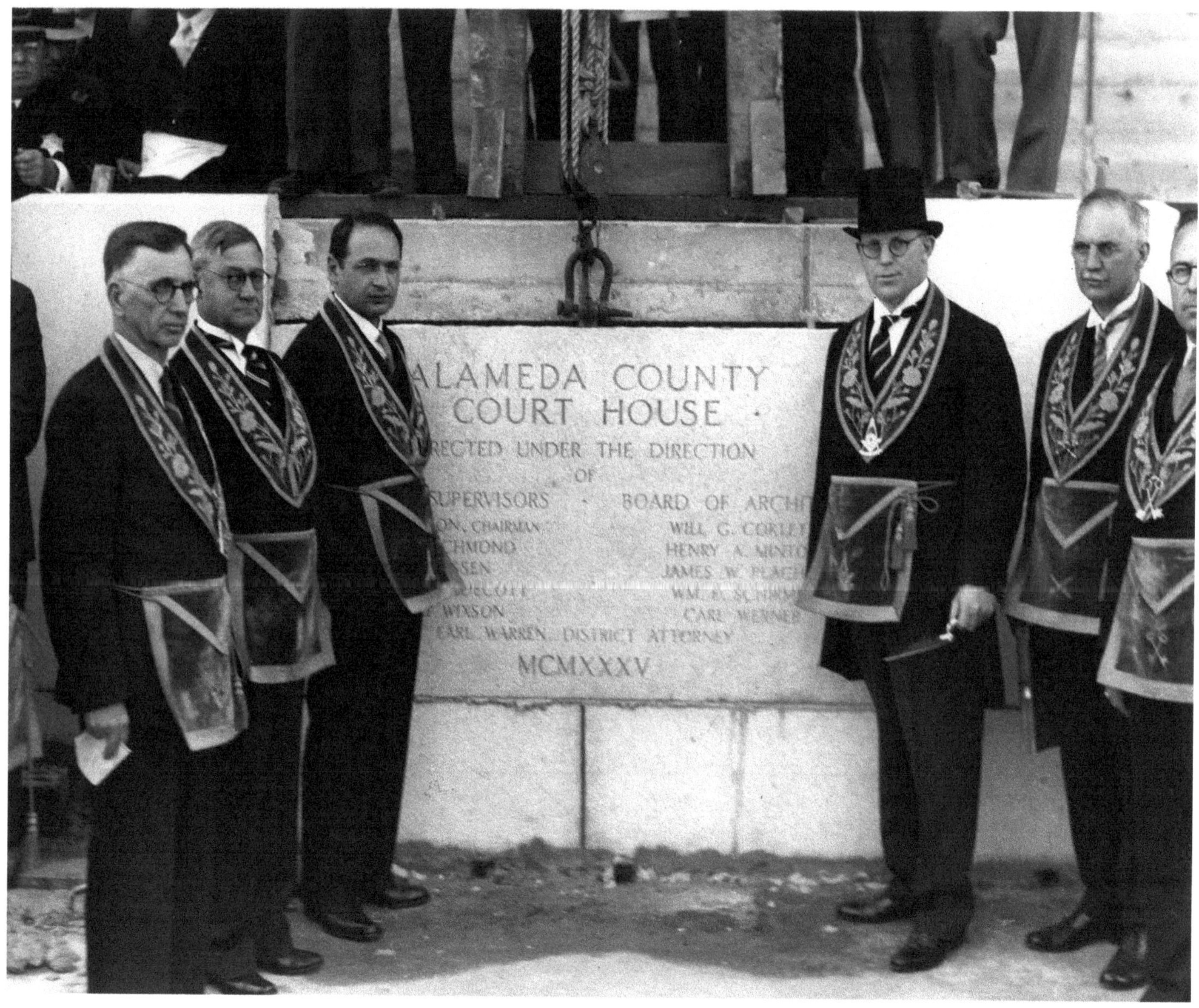

President Roosevelt's relief program appropriated funds to the County of Alameda to build a new courthouse. District Attorney Earl R. Warren, wearing the top hat, joined associates at the Scottish Rite Masonic temple for the laying of the cornerstone in 1935. Warren would go on to serve three terms as governor of California and later, as Chief Justice of the Supreme Court, oversaw the desegregation of the nation's public schools.

The new Alameda County Court House, completed in 1936, significantly changed the scene at Lake Merritt and added yet another architectural treasure to the city's built environment.

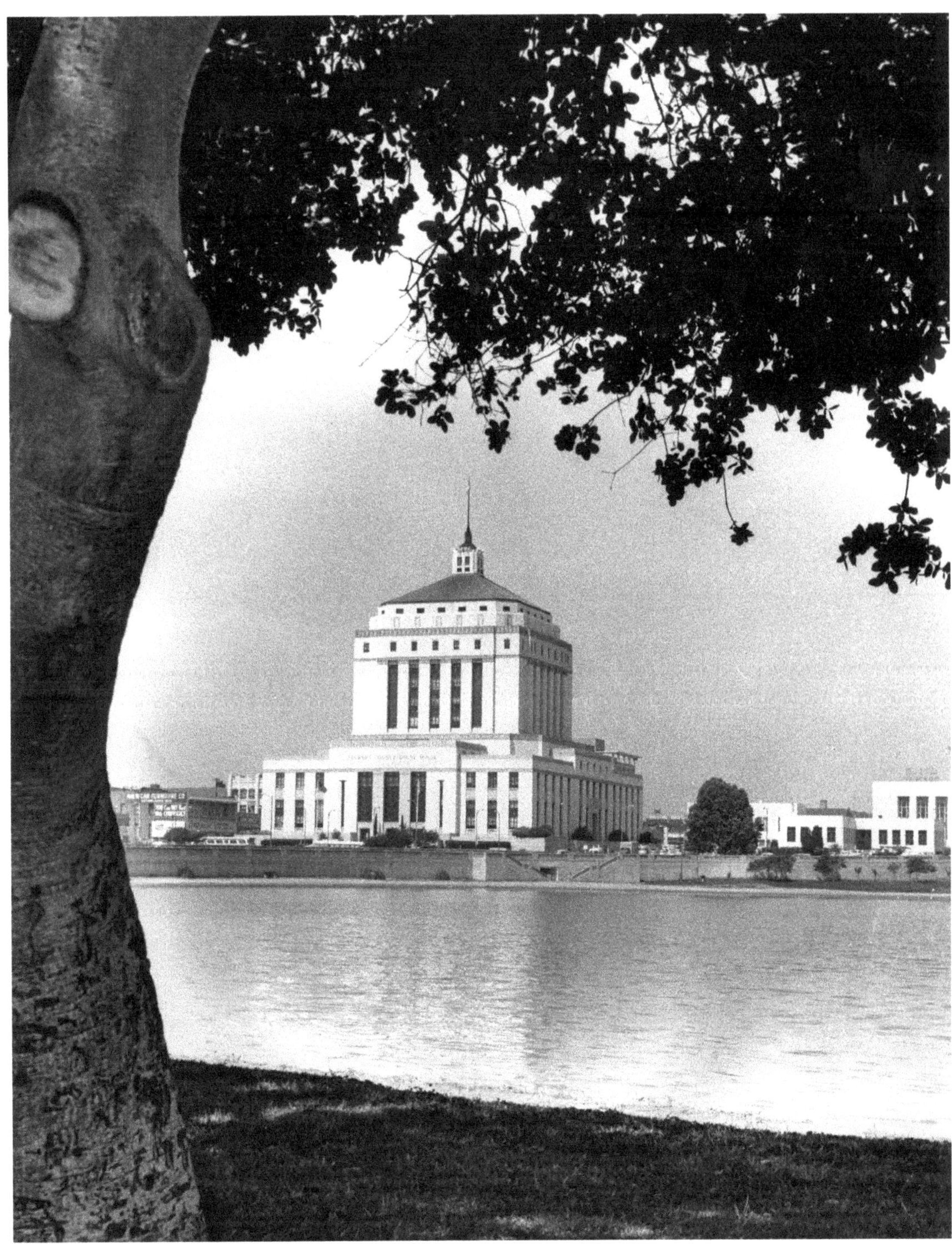

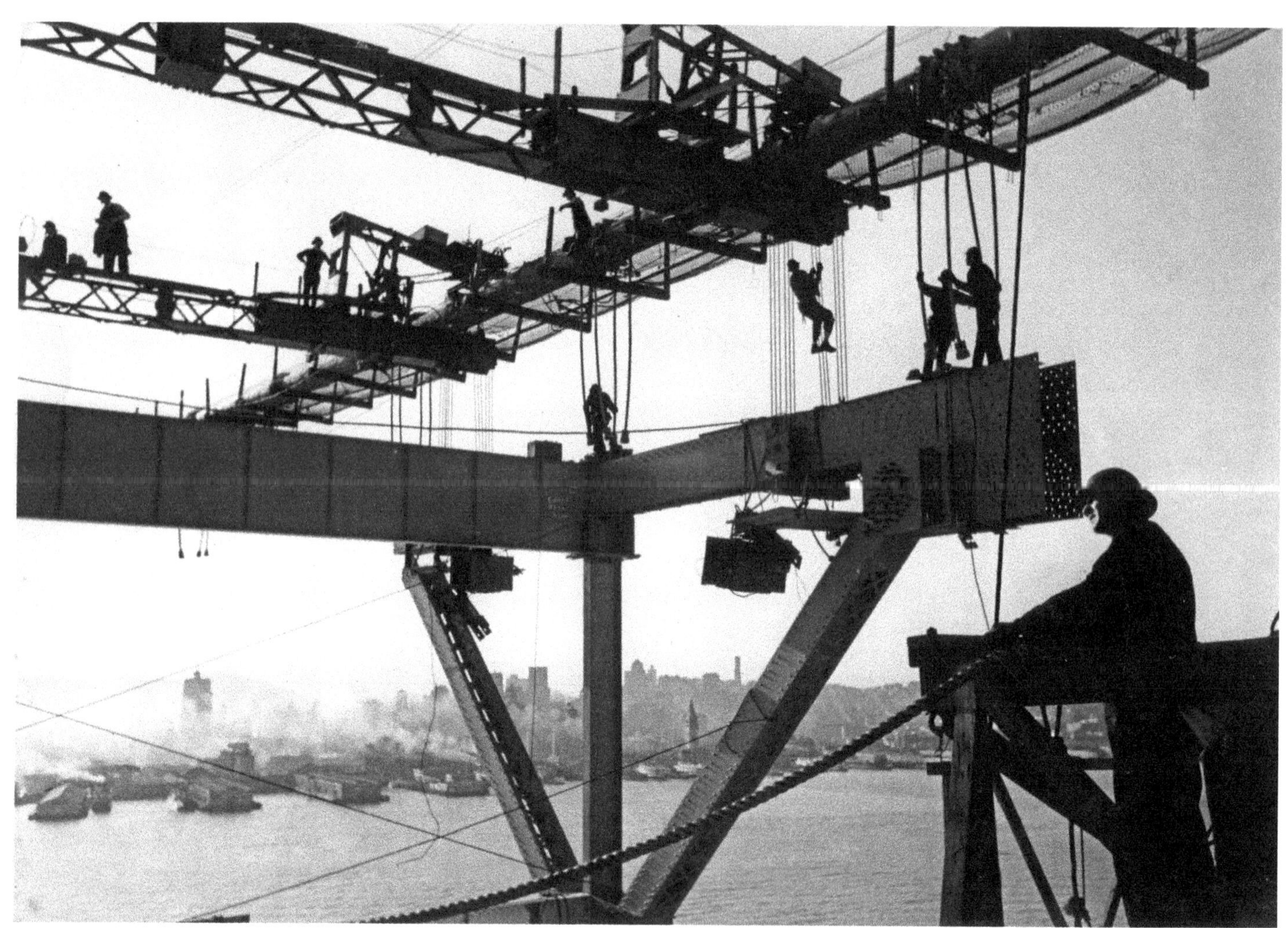

Jobs were a top priority for President Franklin Roosevelt in his ambitious campaign to end the Great Depression. Thousands of those jobs came with the building of the San Francisco–Oakland Bay Bridge. A photographer for the authority in charge of construction captured this image of work in progress on the suspension span of the bridge in 1935.

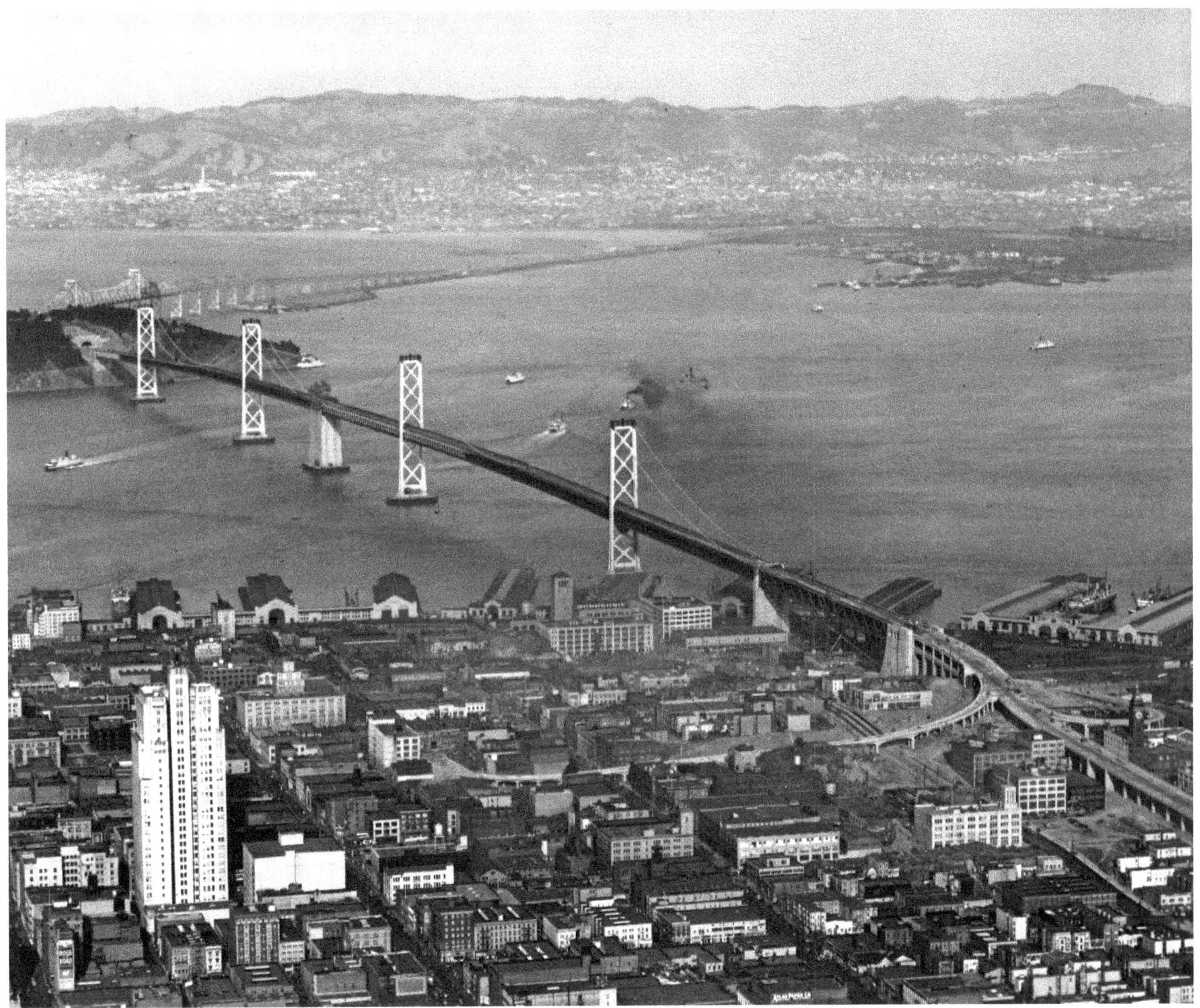

When the San Francisco–Oakland Bay Bridge opened in 1936, it was the world's longest vehicular bridge, covering nearly four miles. The top deck carried cars and trucks, and a lower deck carried the streetcars of the Key System transit service. The streetcars have since been removed. More than 280,000 vehicles cross the bridge daily.

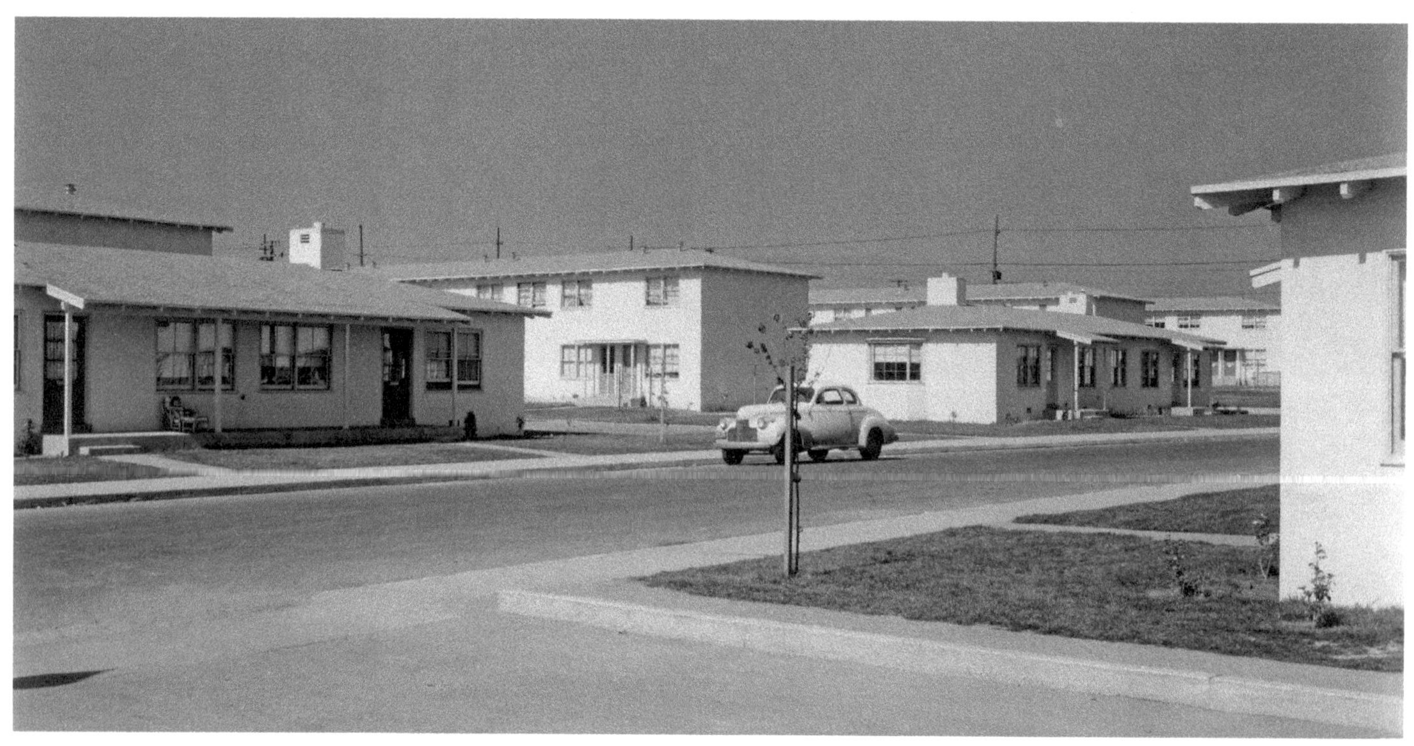

The housing crisis caused by the economic catastrophe took longer to solve than the hunger crisis. Political squabbles, financing, and administrative requirements delayed deployment of federal subsidized housing until the later years of the Great Depression. Lockwood Gardens, shown here, was one of the first of these projects in Oakland.

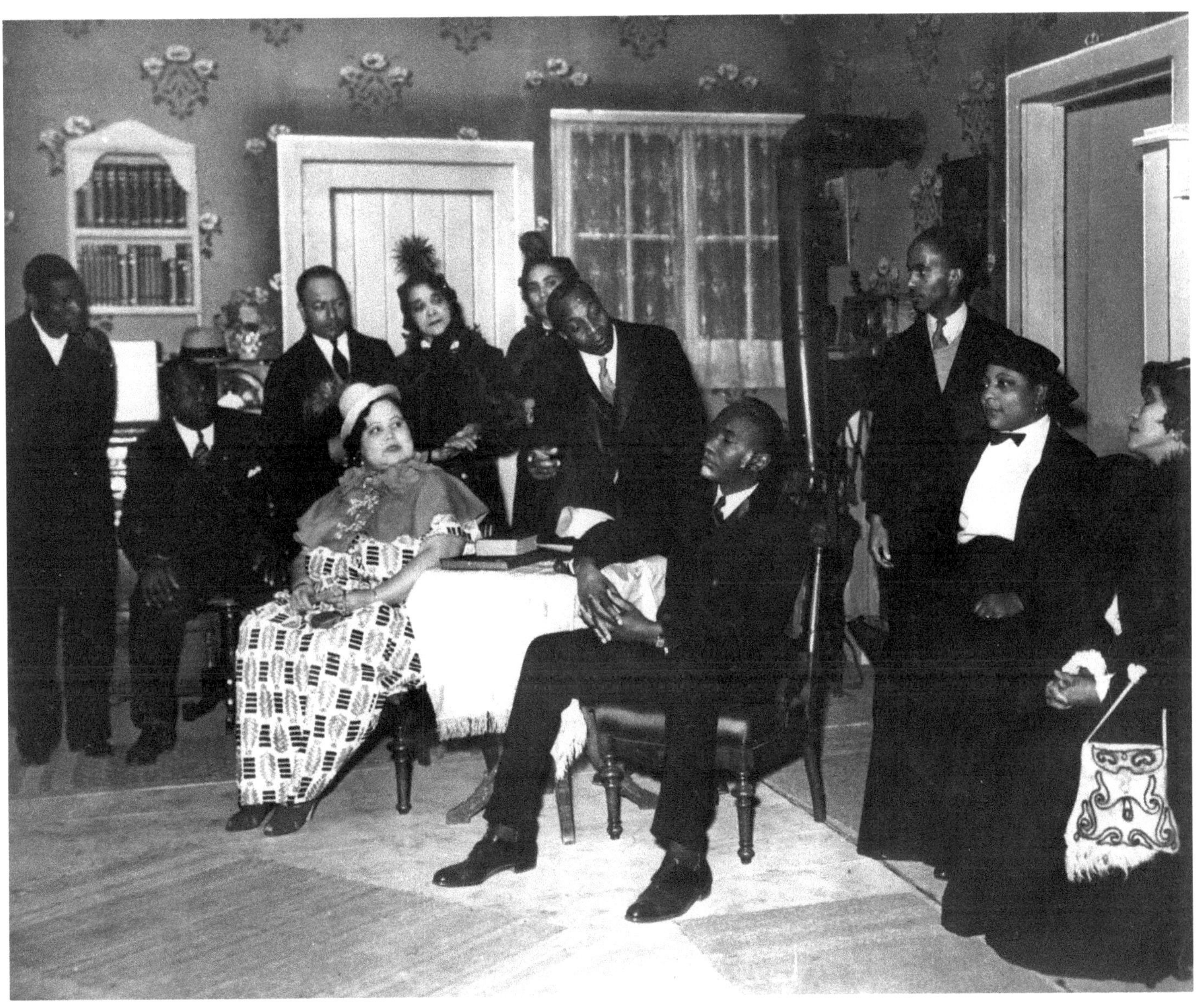

Local live theater reached a broad new audience during the Great Depression, with the help of New Deal arts programs. Keeton's Oakland Color Chorus, shown here in a performance at San Francisco's Alcazar Theatre, drew large audiences. Widespread dislike for the program by many Americans led to cuts in funding by 1939.

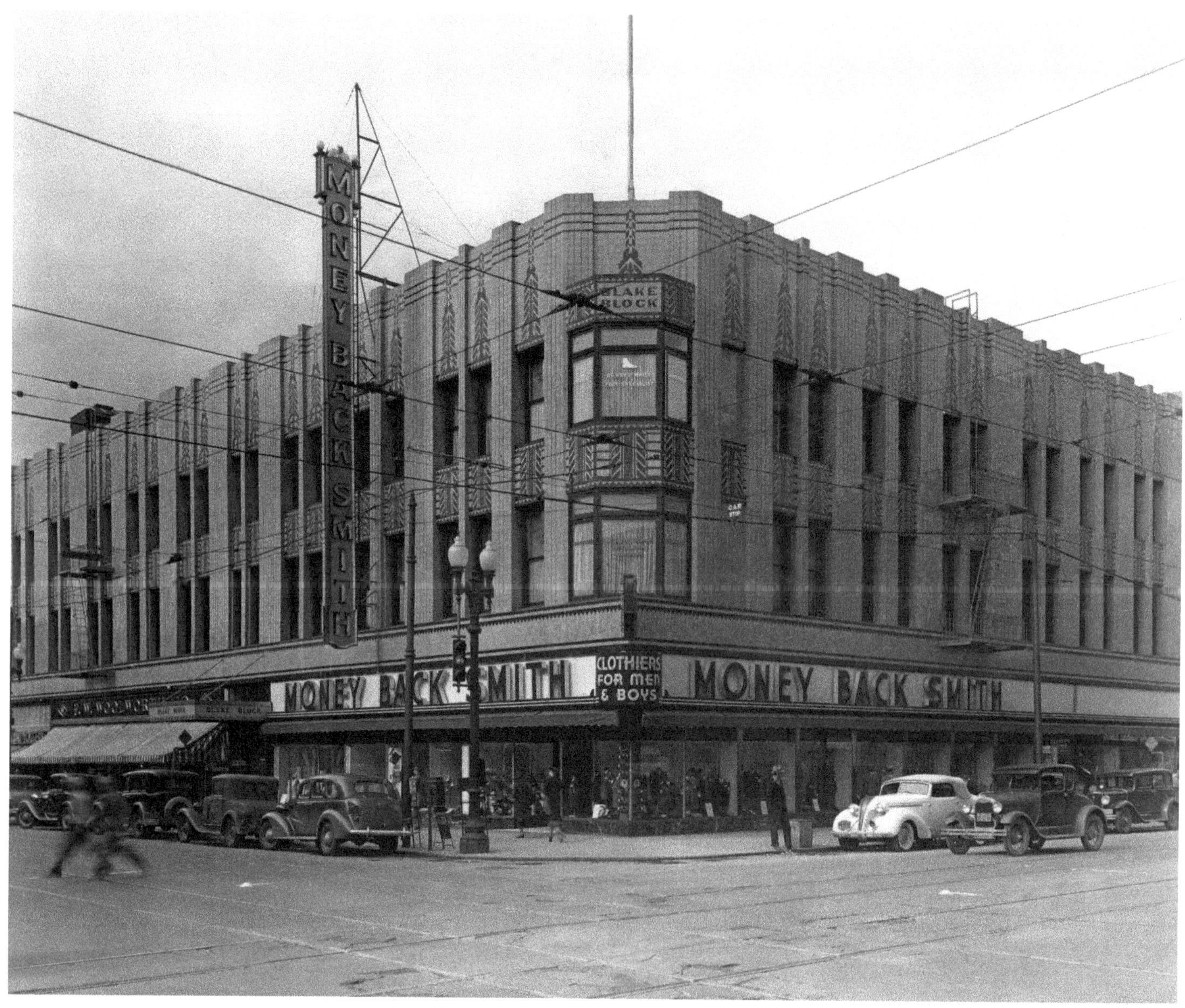

The large increase in the working population during World War II greatly bolstered the fortunes of Oakland's retailers, helping Oakland's Money Back Smith transform itself into Smith's Men's Wear, with a chain of stores across the west. The store earned its name for the unconditional guarantee its founder, William Smith, provided on any merchandise purchased at his store.

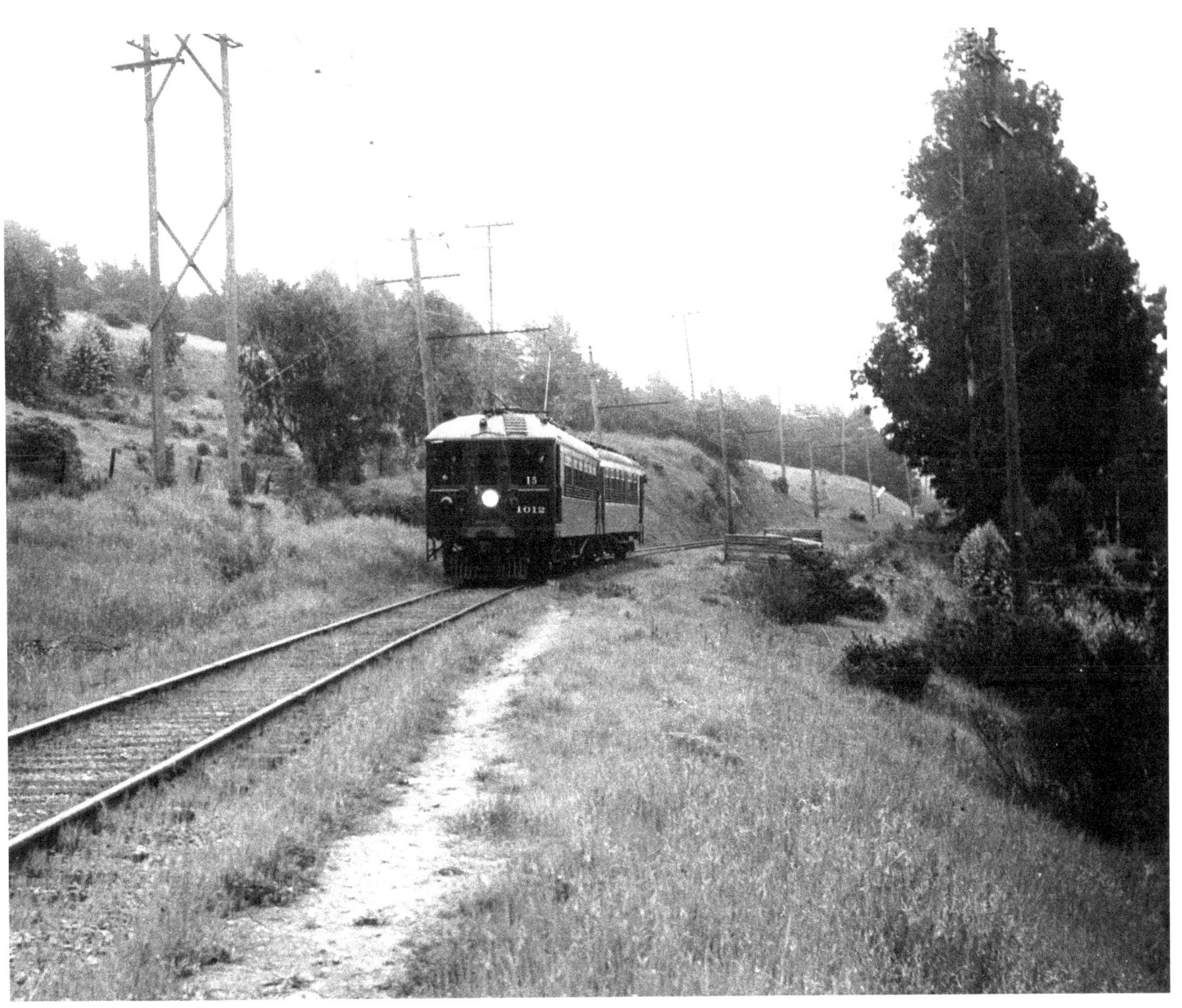

Running on electricity, a Sacramento Northern Railroad train approaches the Montclair station in this photograph from 1940. Passenger service on the railroad ceased the following year, ending the carrier's regular runs through scenic Contra Costa County and on to the state capital.

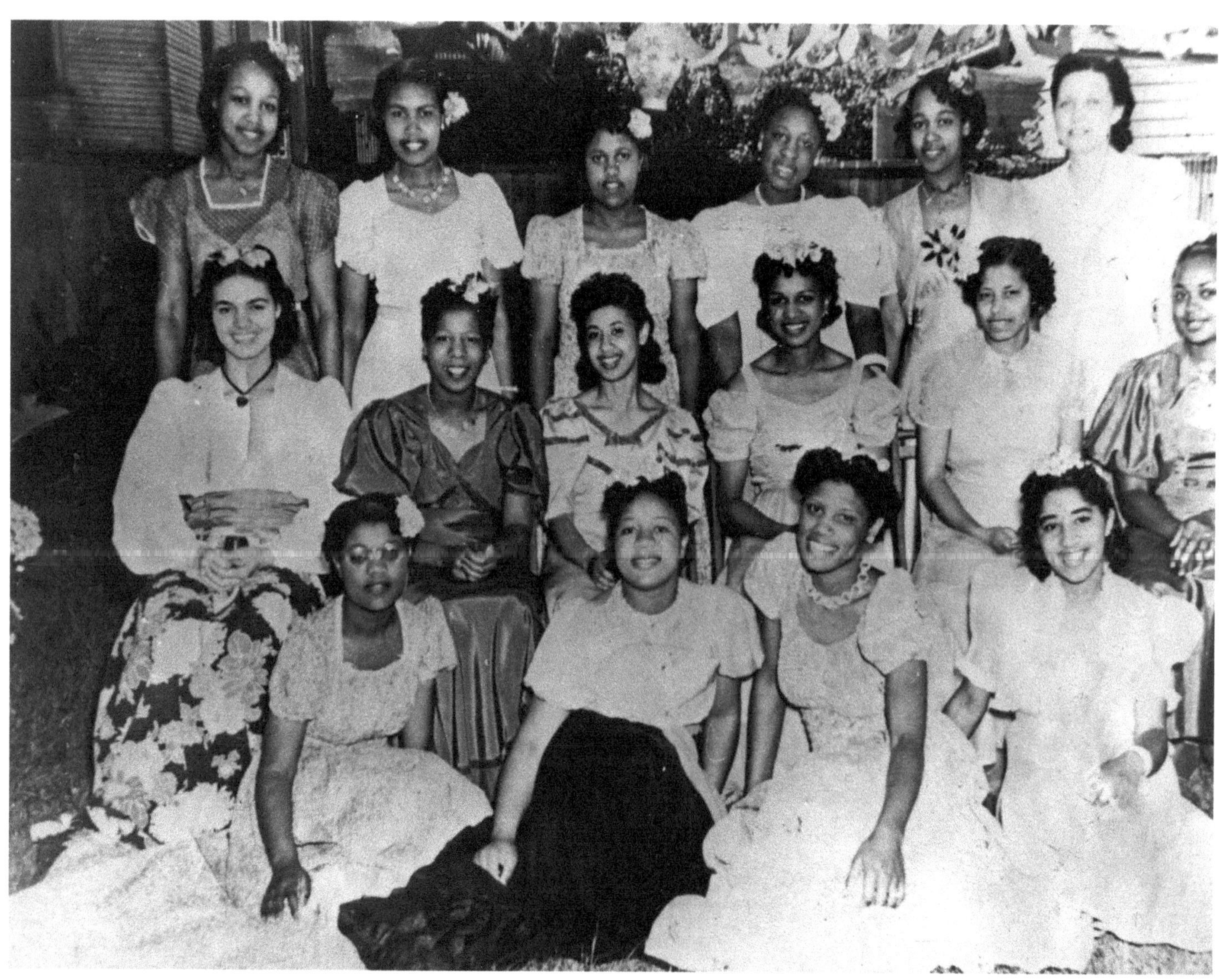

Rather than challenge admissions policies at the downtown branch of the Young Women's Christian Association, housed in a building designed by architect Julia Morgan, the girls of North Oakland organized their own branch on Linden Street. The impact of the Linden Y.W.C.A. on that community is still being felt. The earliest members pose for a photograph in 1940.

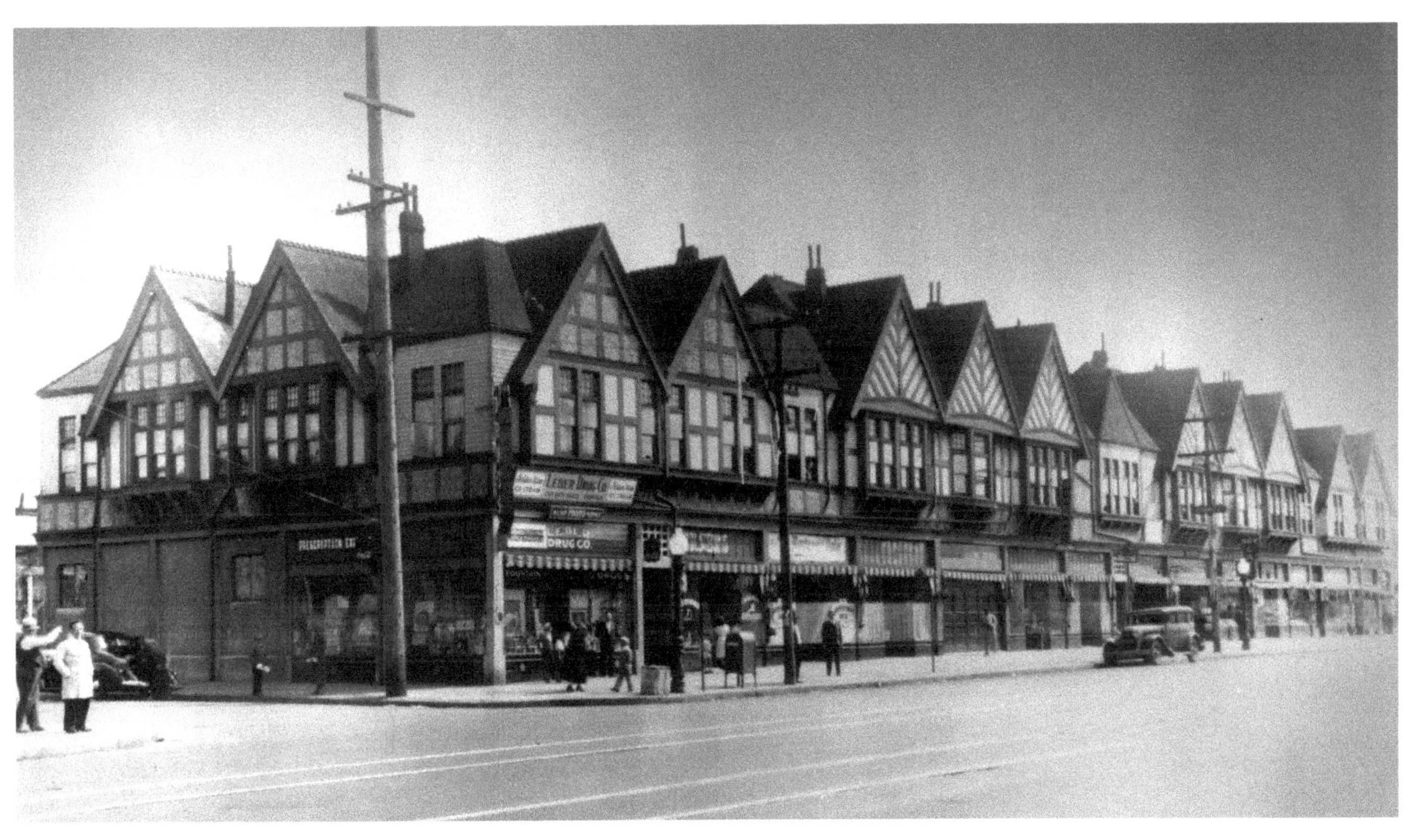

The scene along Seventh Street, captured here around 1940, would soon look very different. Nearly 100,000 defense-industry workers arrived in Oakland during World War II.

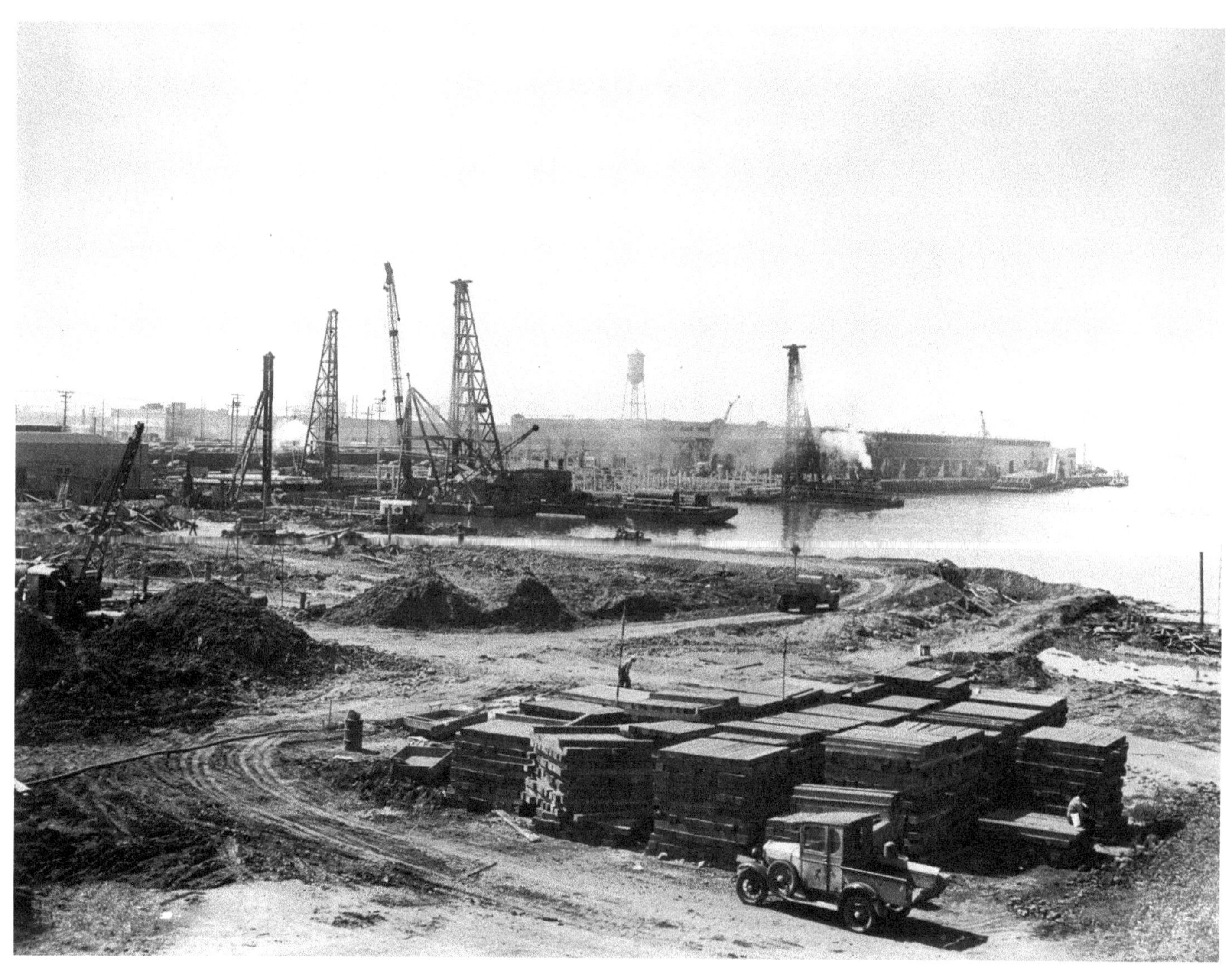

Expansionist ambitions of the imperial Japanese in the Far East justified the seizure of a prime stretch of Oakland's waterfront for use by the military. The Oakland Naval Supply Depot is shown here under development on September 25, 1941.

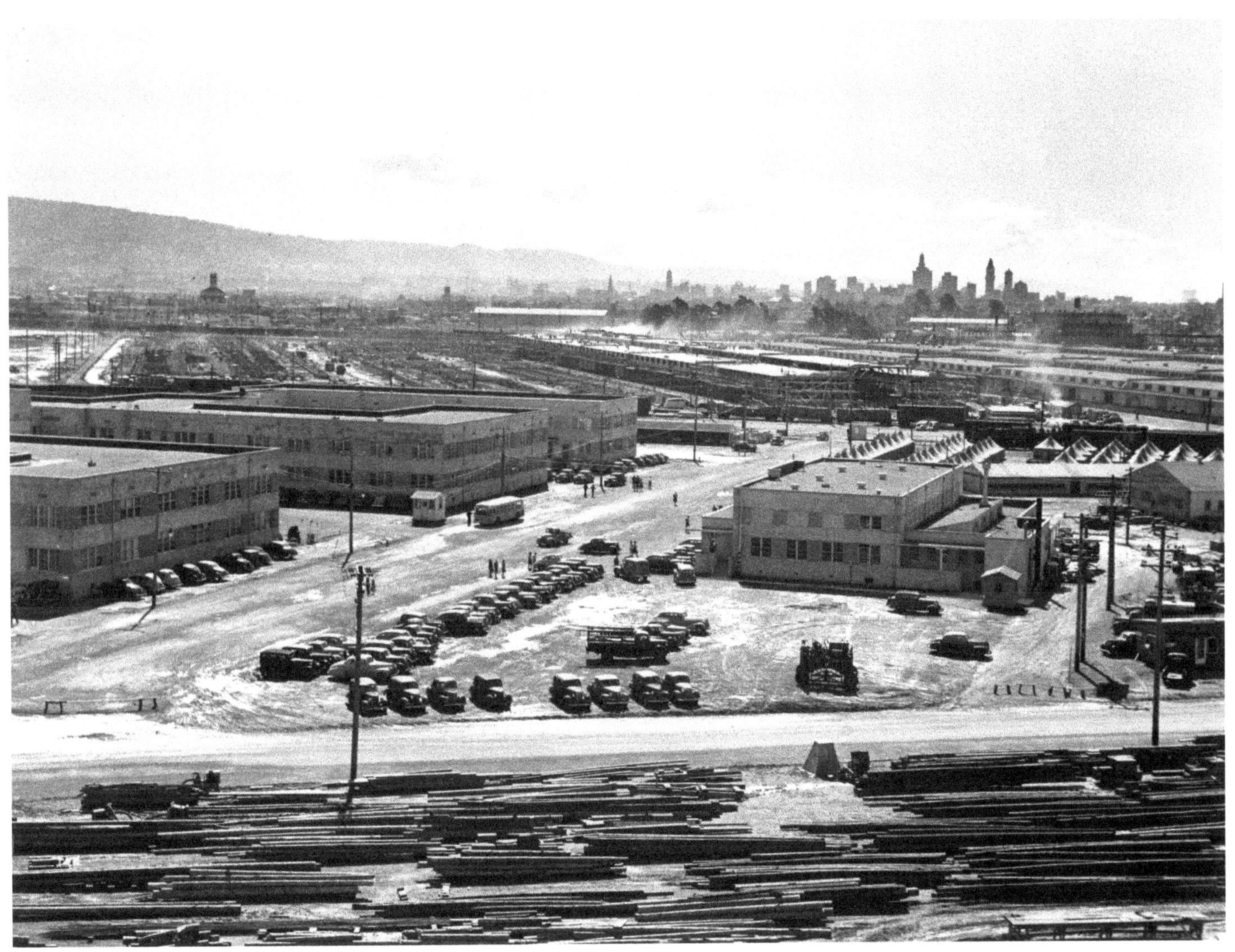

The Army acquired a site beside the naval depot for its own facility, the Oakland Port and General Depot. Both facilities would serve a vital role supplying Allied forces fighting in the Pacific during World War II. The Sequoyah Country Club was also seized for military purposes, for use in the construction of the Oakland Naval Hospital.

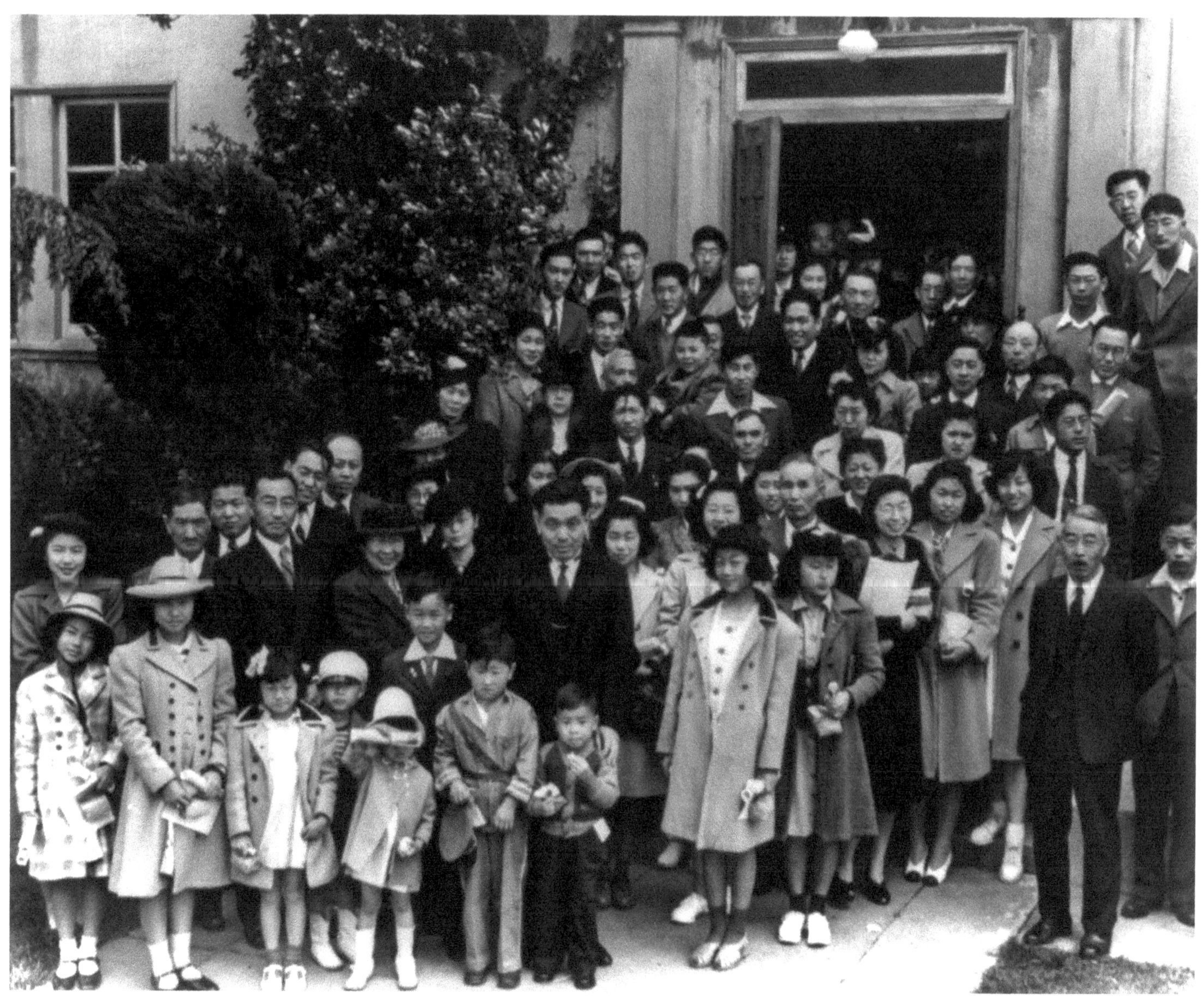

While newcomers arrived by the thousands, another part of Oakland's population evacuated. A presidential order required all persons of Japanese descent to report for relocation to remote internment camps. Oakland photographer Dorothea Lange was hired to document the relocation. Members of Oakland's Japanese Independent Congregational Church posed for her camera after farewell services in 1942.

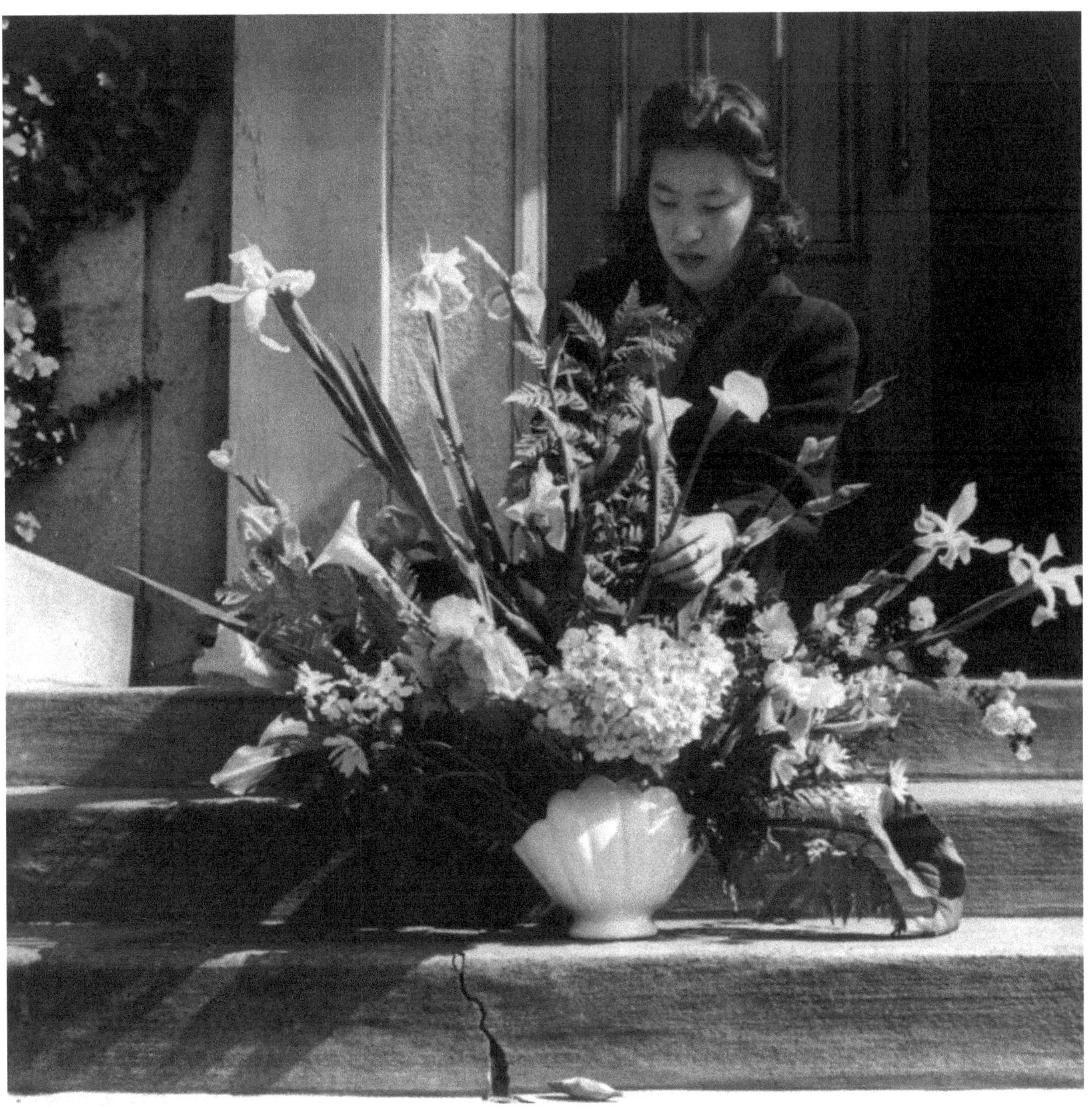

In this photograph by Dorothea Lange, a young member of the Japanese Independent Congregational Church arranges flowers for farewell ceremonies before reporting for evacuation to an internment camp.

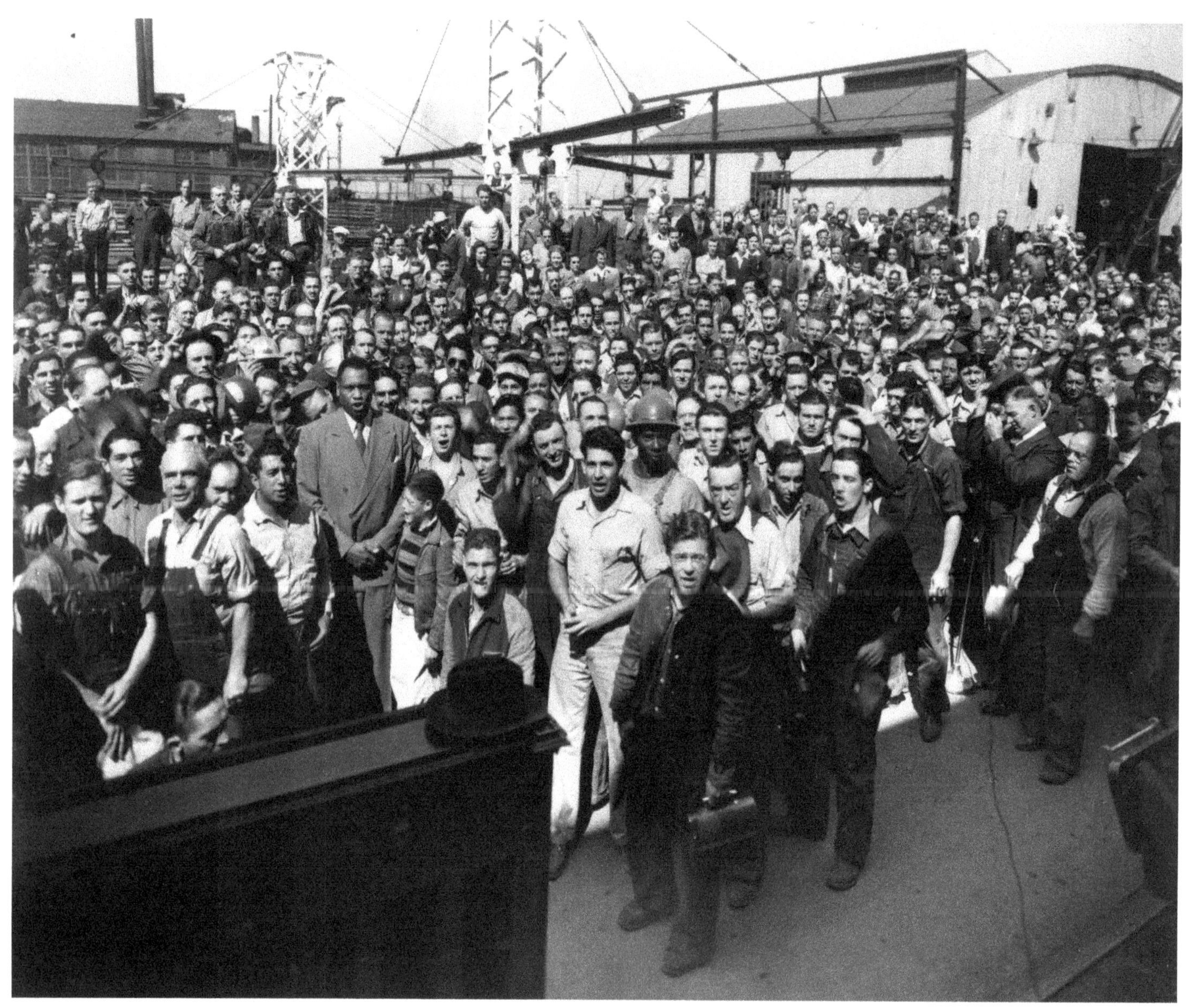

As it had during World War I, Moore Shipbuilding Company's Oakland dry dock absorbed much of the incoming workforce. Singer Paul Robeson hosted a morale-building sing-along for the shipyard workers in 1942, before his performance to a packed crowd at the Oakland Auditorium. A presidential decree ended long-standing policies of racial discrimination, a milestone event for the city's African-American community.

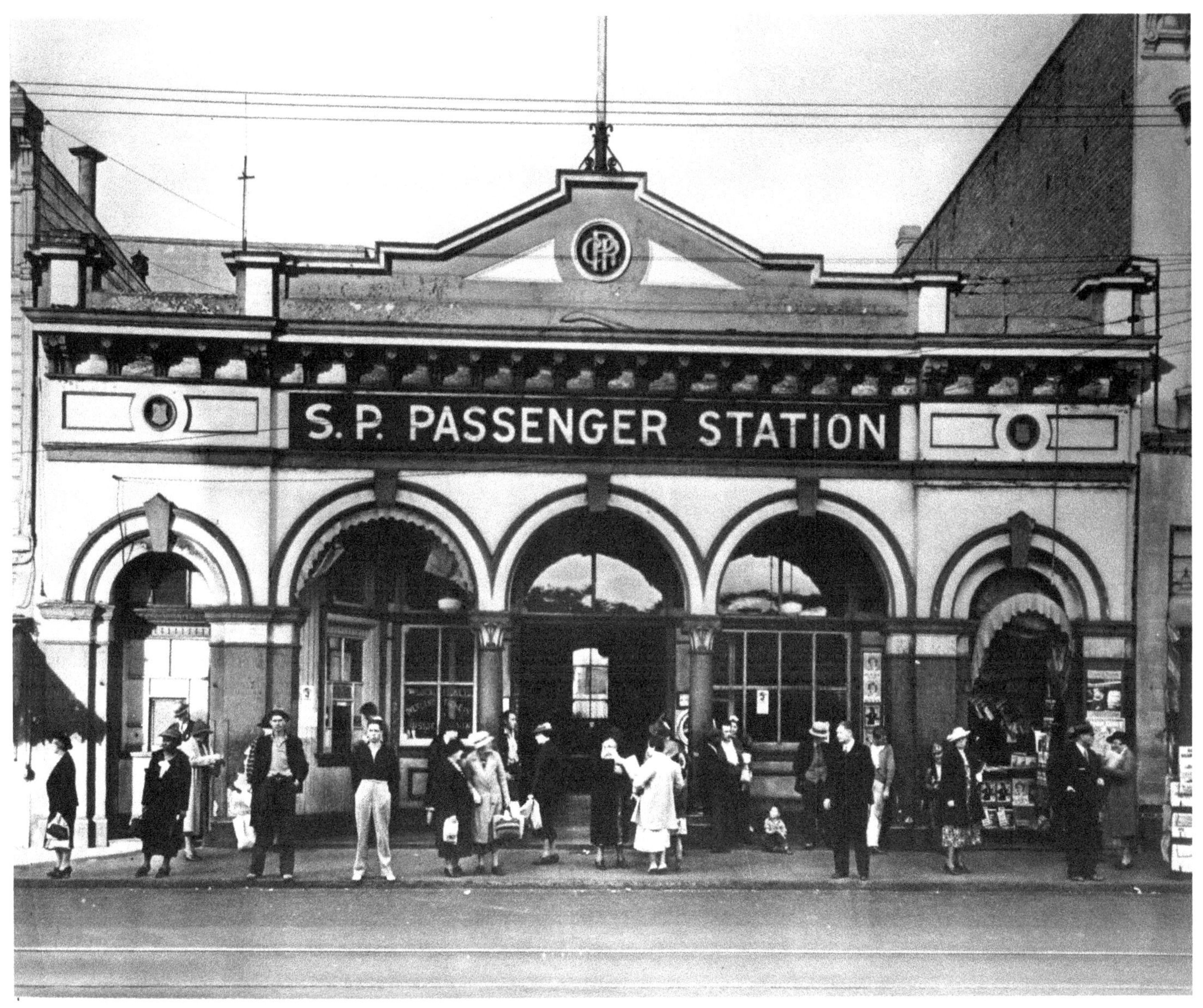

With workers arriving in Oakland on every incoming train, the passenger station on Seventh Street was seldom quiet. The city's population increased by one-third from 1940 to 1945, when Oakland added nearly 100,000 new residents.

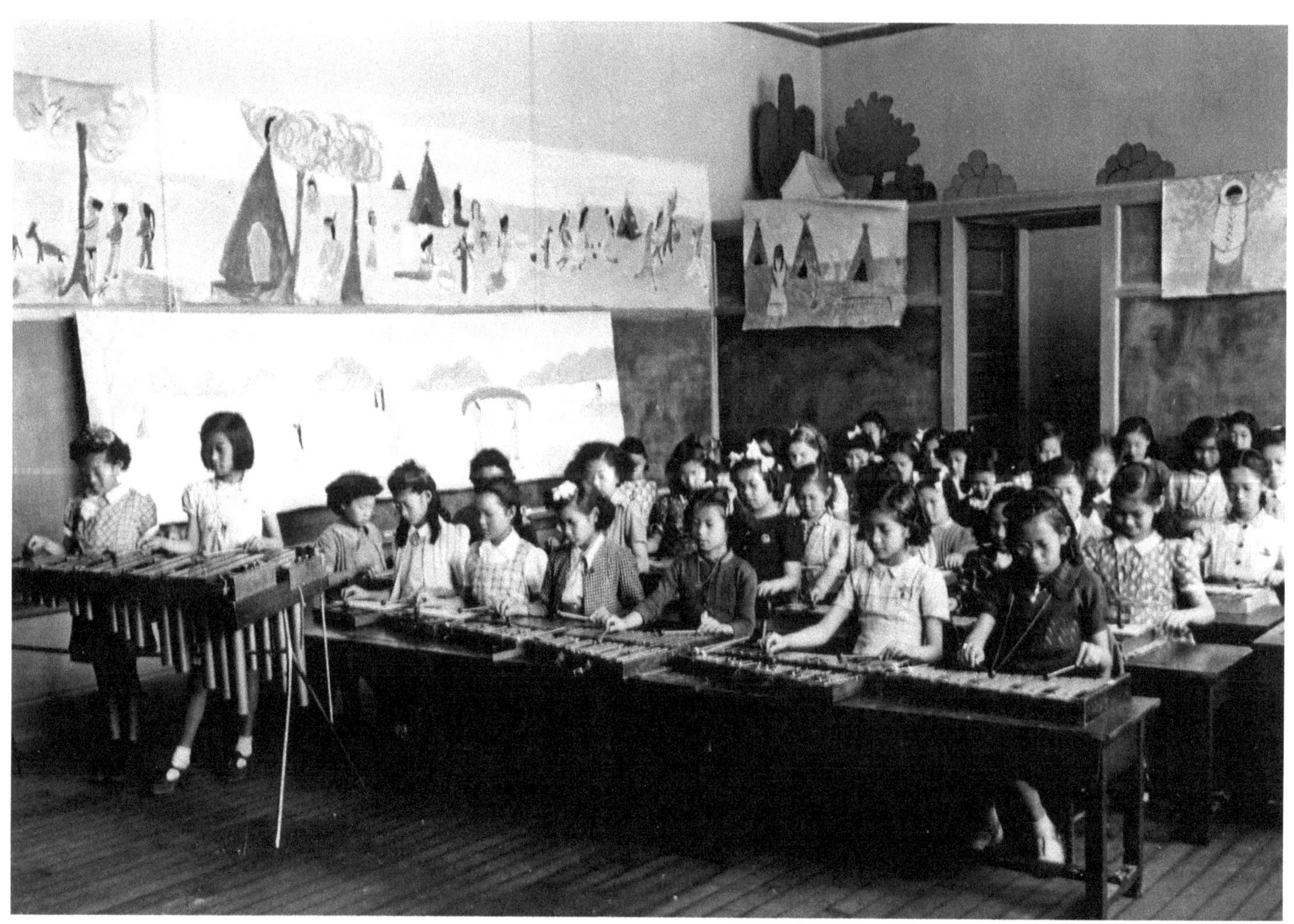

Americans of Chinese descent carried on with little disruption in the absence of their former Japanese-American neighbors, now residing in internment camps awaiting war's end. Students at Lincoln School are shown here practicing on their xylophones in a music class in 1943.

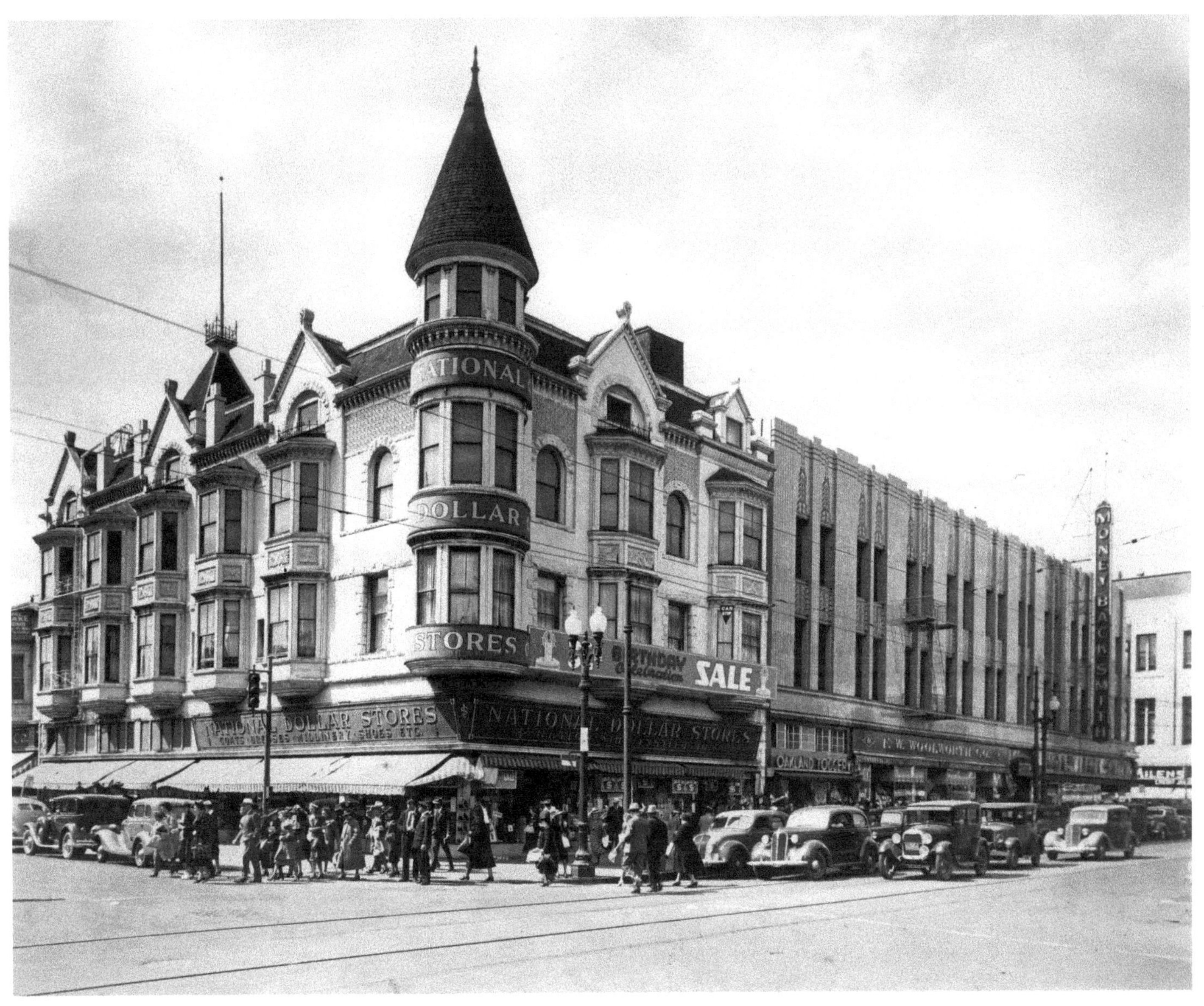

This building housed the flagship of one ubiquitous retail chain, National Dollar Stores, founded by Joe Shoong of Oakland. The stores helped make Shoong, an American whose parents had immigrated from China, one of California's wealthiest residents.

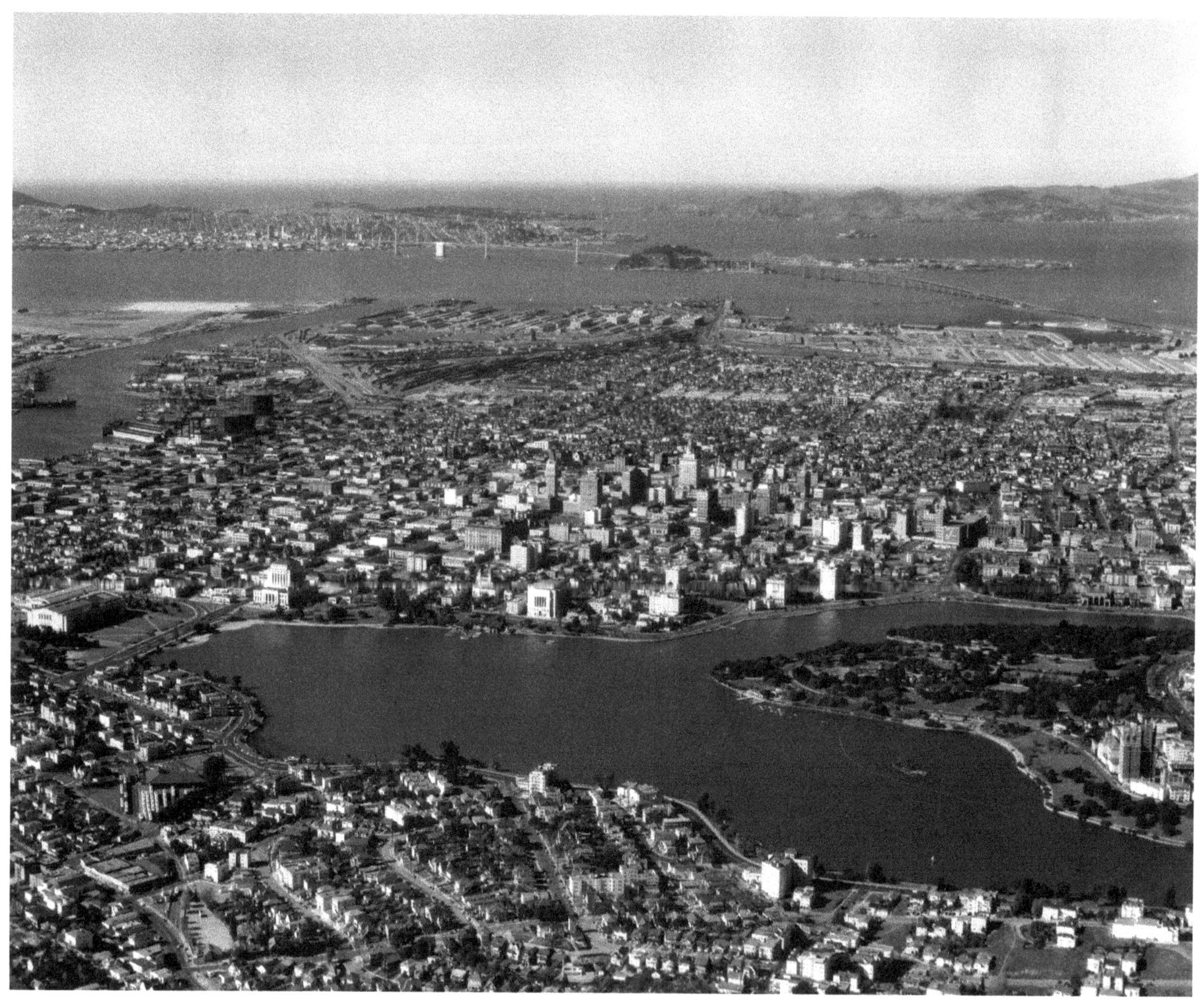

Facing west toward the Pacific Ocean, an aerial view of Oakland not long after World War II shows the East Bay's shoreline slowly pushing farther and farther into San Francisco Bay.

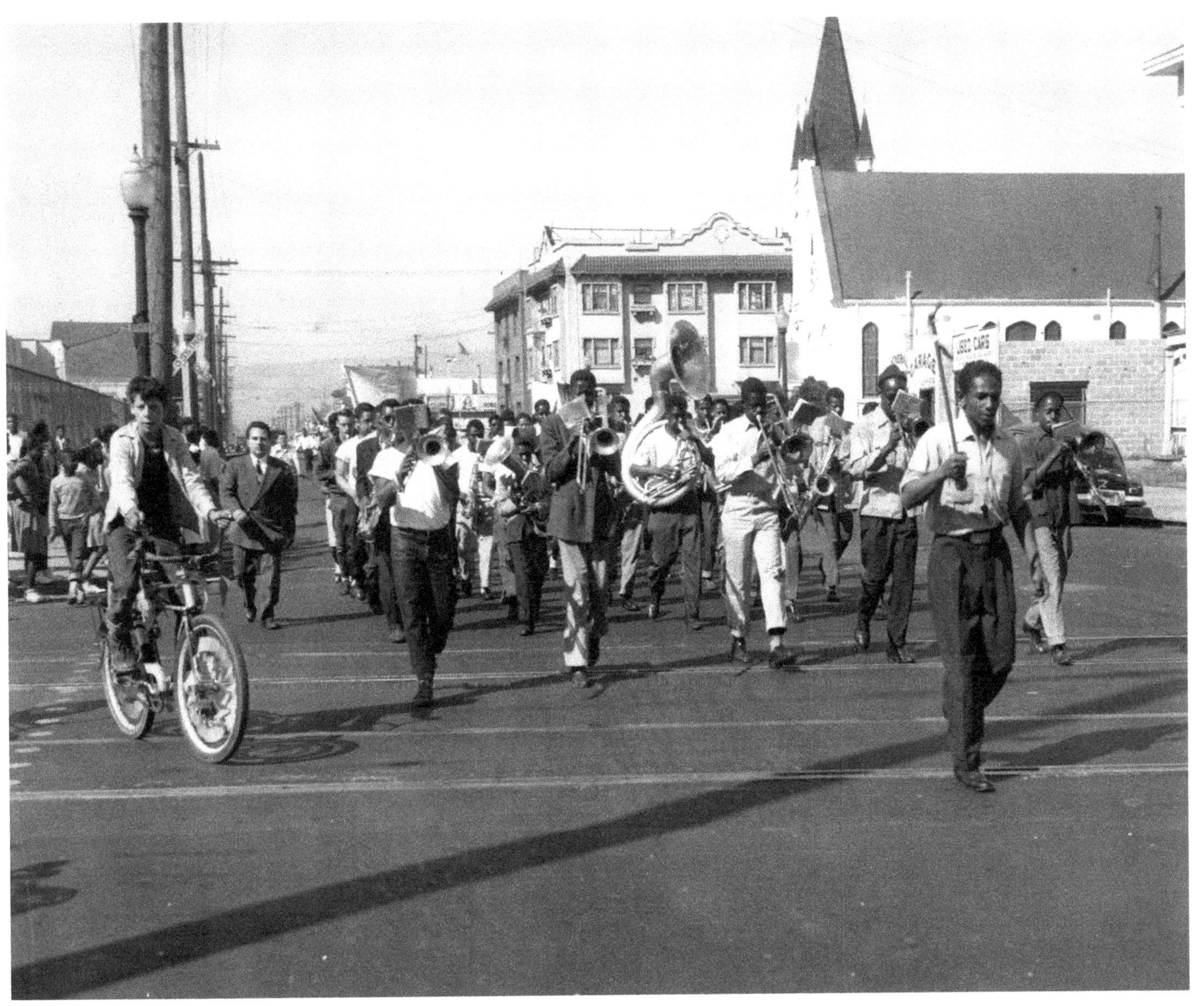

The war had a significant impact on the student bodies of many of Oakland's public schools, illustrated by this photograph of the McClymonds High School marching band, captured in 1946.

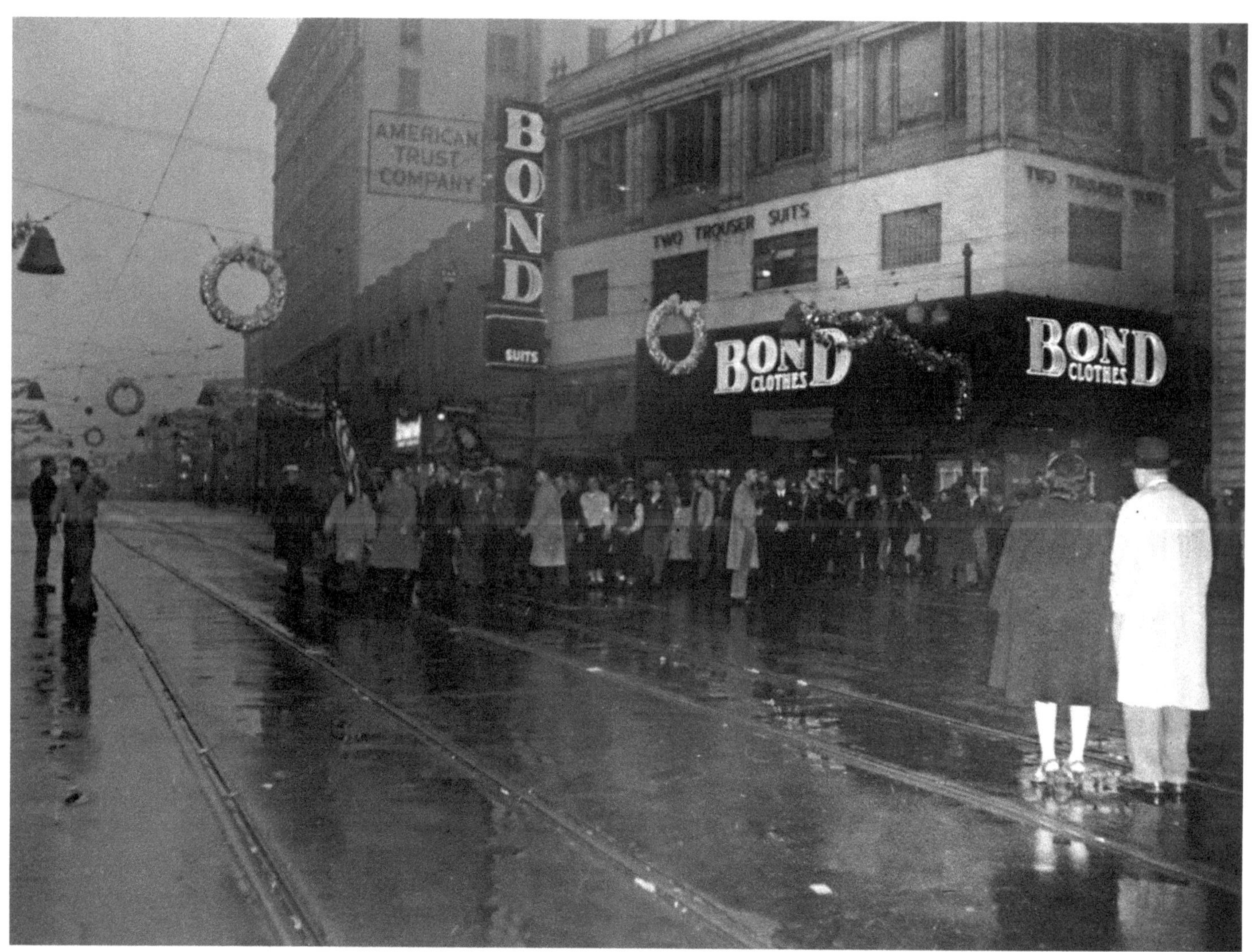

In this photograph, astonished workers gather as police officers make a delivery of merchandise to a downtown clothing store during a strike of retail clerks in 1946. Merchants had recruited the assistance of law enforcement after drivers refused deliveries to the affected stores to show support for the strikers. Outrage by the unions over the incident triggered a general strike that brought Oakland to a standstill for several days.

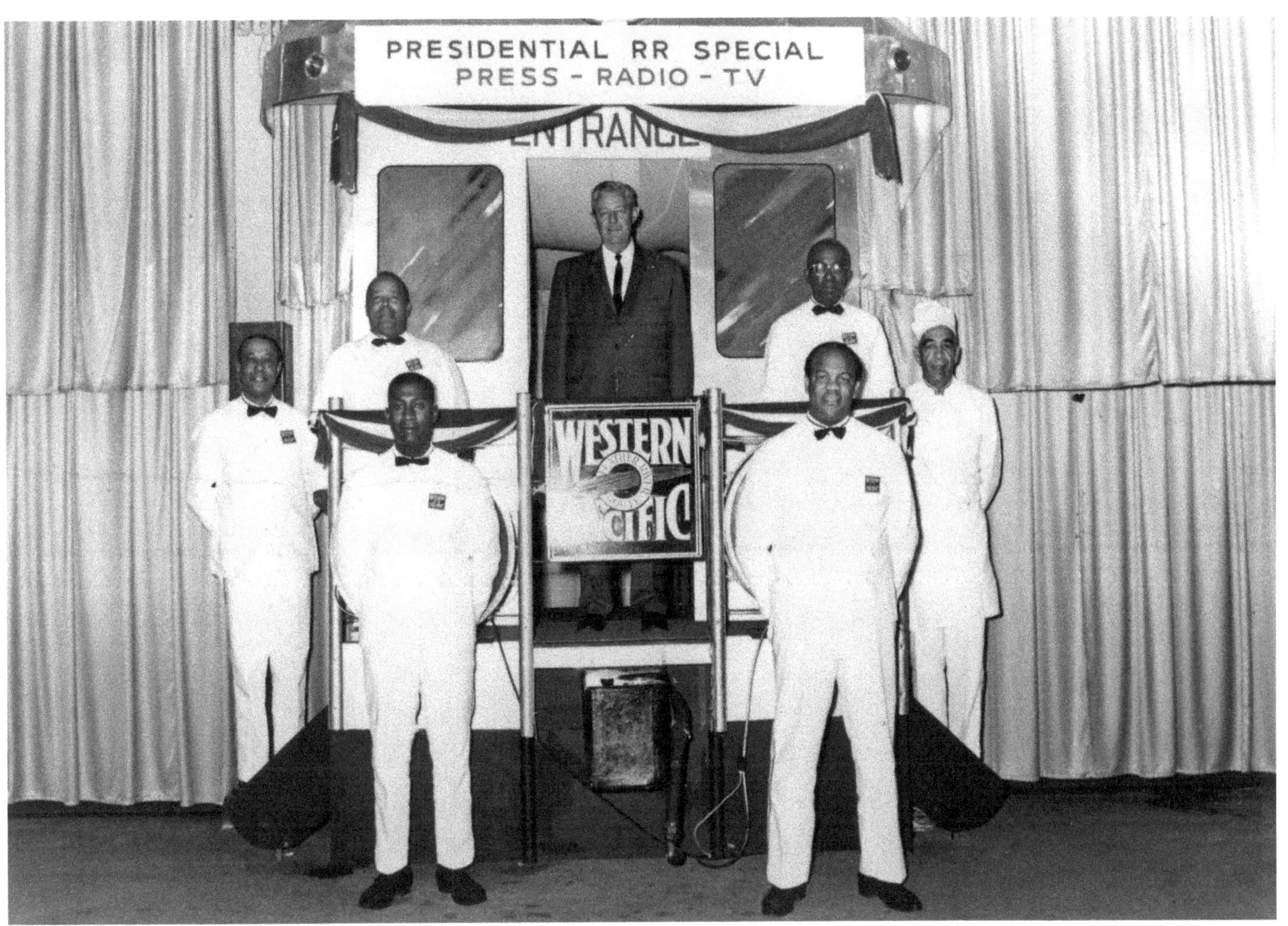

With the western headquarters of the International Brotherhood of Sleeping-car Porters located in Oakland, its members played a historic role in the local African-American community. Porters for the Western Pacific Railroad served as hosts for President Harry S. Truman on his visit to Oakland in 1948.

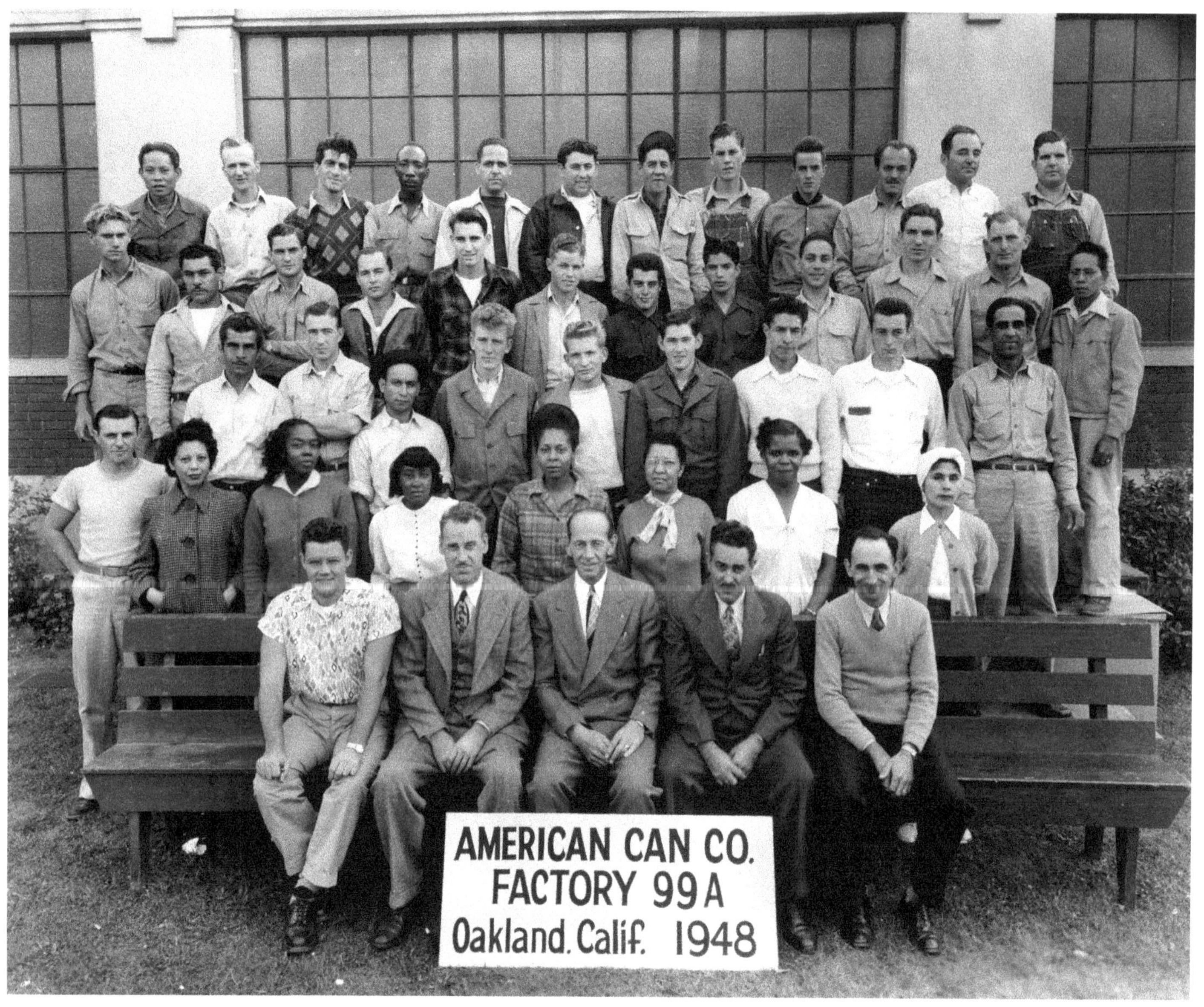

Serious labor shortages faced the canning industry during World War II and jobs held steady in the industry in the years that followed. Workers at the American Can Company, who made the can the industry depended on, pose for a group shot in 1948.

OUT OF THE SHADOWS

(1946–1970)

As the nation entered its longest and most expansive period of prosperity following World War II, its people had babies. Oakland made sure they would have somewhere to play. City officials commissioned a local sculptor to create for Oakland's children their own little world. He came up with Children's Fairyland, one of the very first theme parks and the inspiration for Disneyland. Opposite the lake, a local hobbyist built an exact replica of the overland train, which had brought passengers to early Oakland, as a popular attraction for children.

Local recreation programs were bringing local athletes, such as Frank Robinson in baseball and Bill Russell in basketball, to the highest levels of professional sports, even to the Hall of Fame. Robinson would be hired as the first African-American manager in Major League Baseball. Russell was selected as the first African-American coach in the National Basketball Association. Both men played together on the same high school basketball team in Oakland.

The older kids had cars. The hot rod craze that swept the country in the years following World War II reached Oakland early on. The city hosted the nation's first custom-car show, contributing some of the finest craftsmen to that hobby. Another new craze showed up in concerts by the leading acts of rock-and-roll and rhythm-and-blues, such as Elvis Presley and The Johnny Otis Show, whose leader got his start in the clubs and saloons of West Oakland and took what he learned there to help launch a new sound.

For a large part of Oakland's population, the postwar years saw a rapid return to the doldrums of the city before World War II. Wartime production jobs were gone, industrial output was declining, and major changes had come to the city's social fabric. City leaders acted aggressively to respond and federal programs began to address conditions shared by Oakland and cities across the country. The success of the Oakland Raiders and the arrival of the Oakland A's brought focus to the wealth of pride shared by Oaklanders in their city.

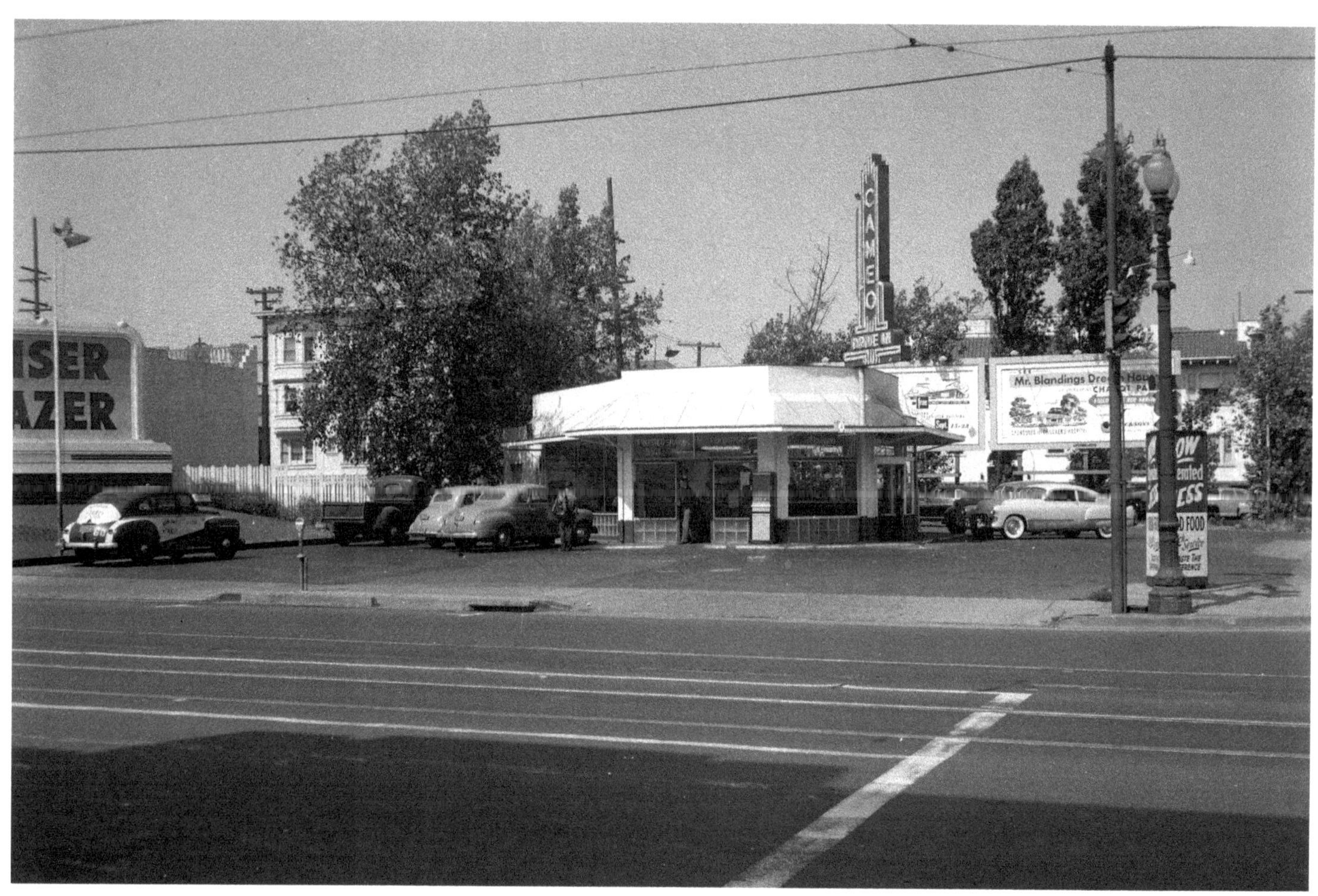

The drive-in restaurant provided a new kind of dining and a new destination for the nation's teenagers. Oakland, where cruising up and down the street in an automobile became a social phenomenon, was at the head of the trend. The Cameo on Foothill Boulevard near the Chevrolet factory sat at a midway point on a circuit of drive-in restaurants extending from Hayward to Richmond that cruising youngsters would tour on weekend evenings.

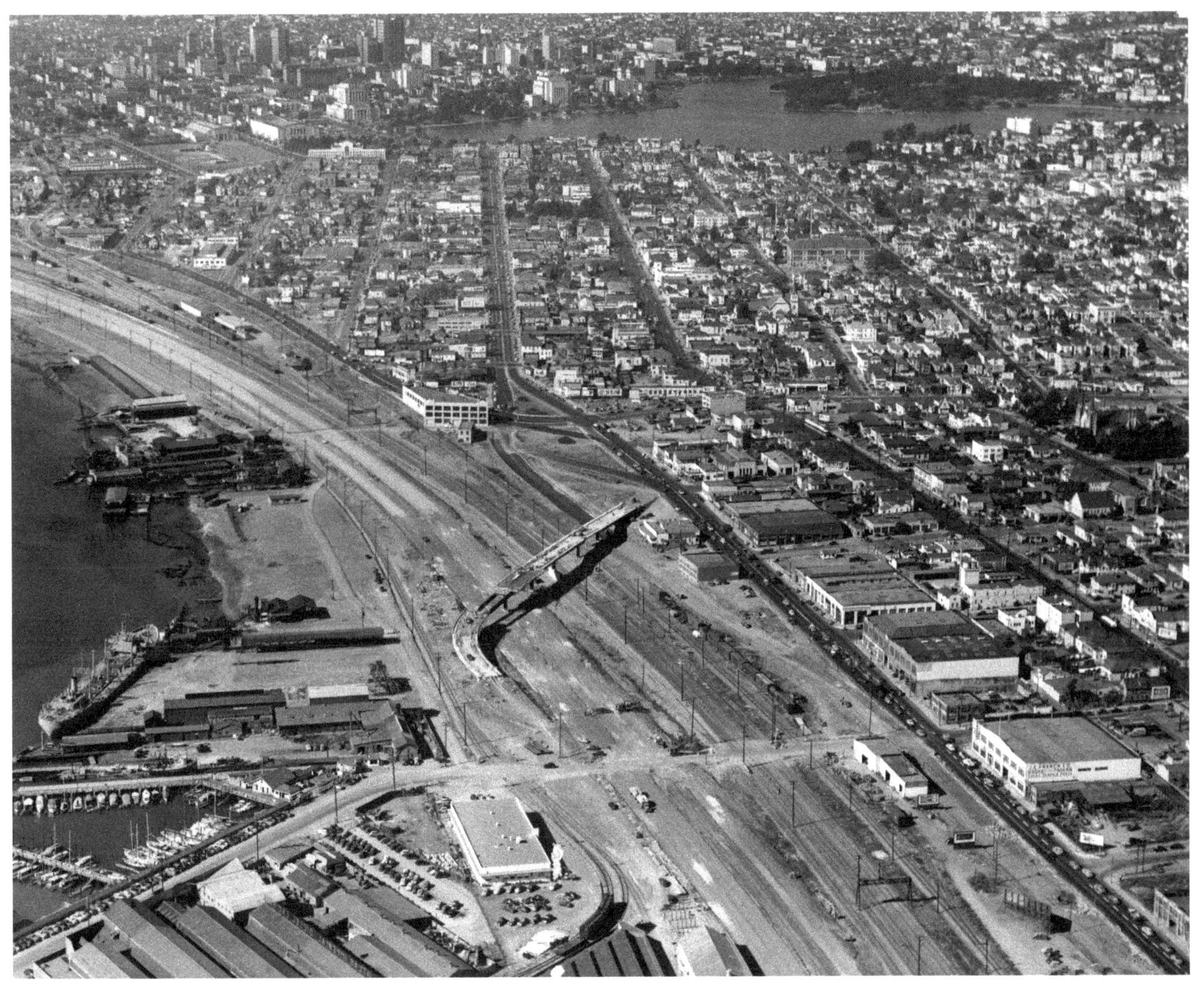

Traffic congestion reached intolerable levels by the late 1940s and the pressure was on public officials to take action. In 1947, construction began on a series of viaducts and bypass routes that would move the traffic off city streets and create the Bay Area's first freeway. Photographer Kayo Harris went up in the air to document progress on the early stages of that project.

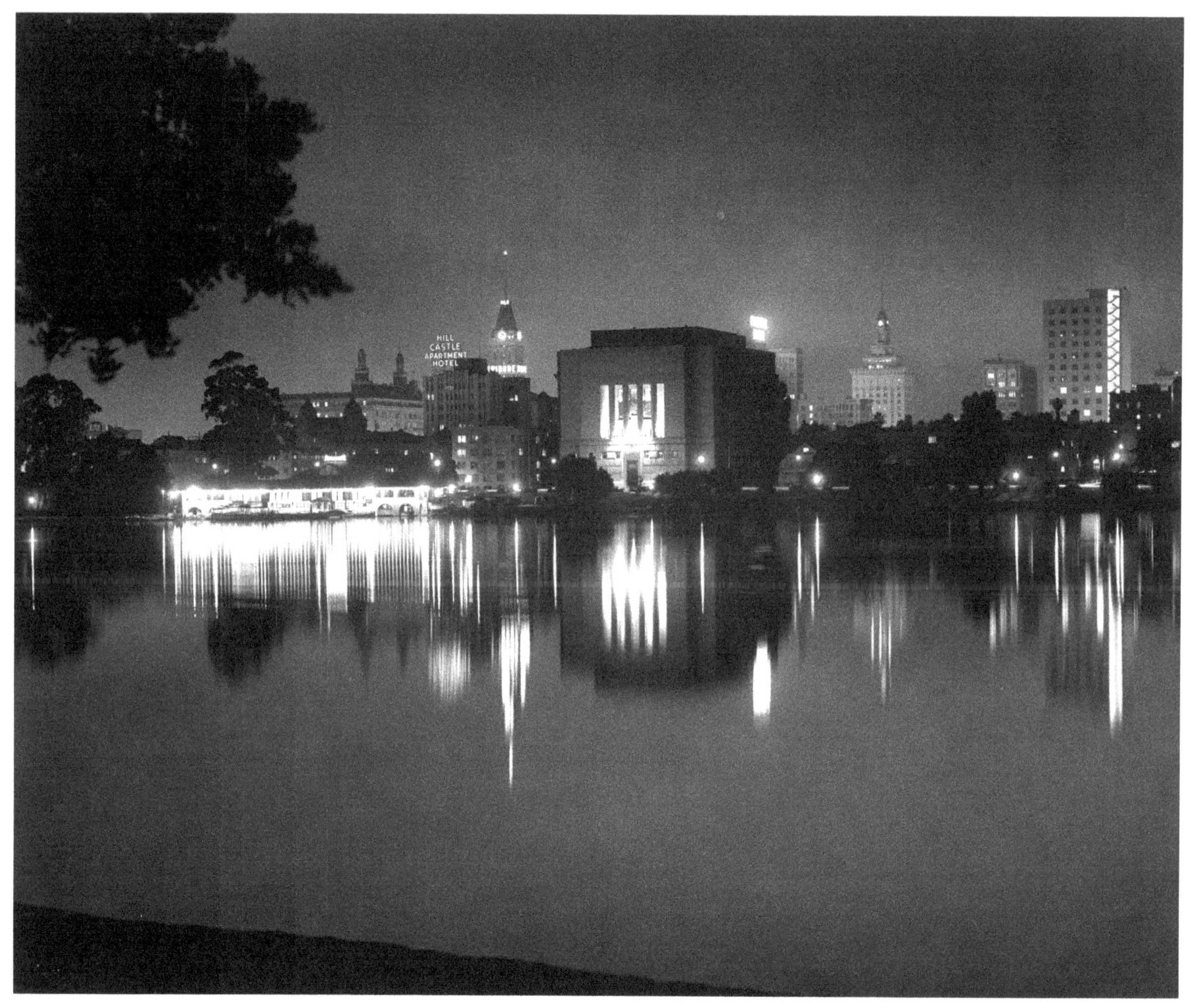

The Tribune Tower, with its brilliant neon sign, continued its dominance over the Oakland skyline as a new decade approached.

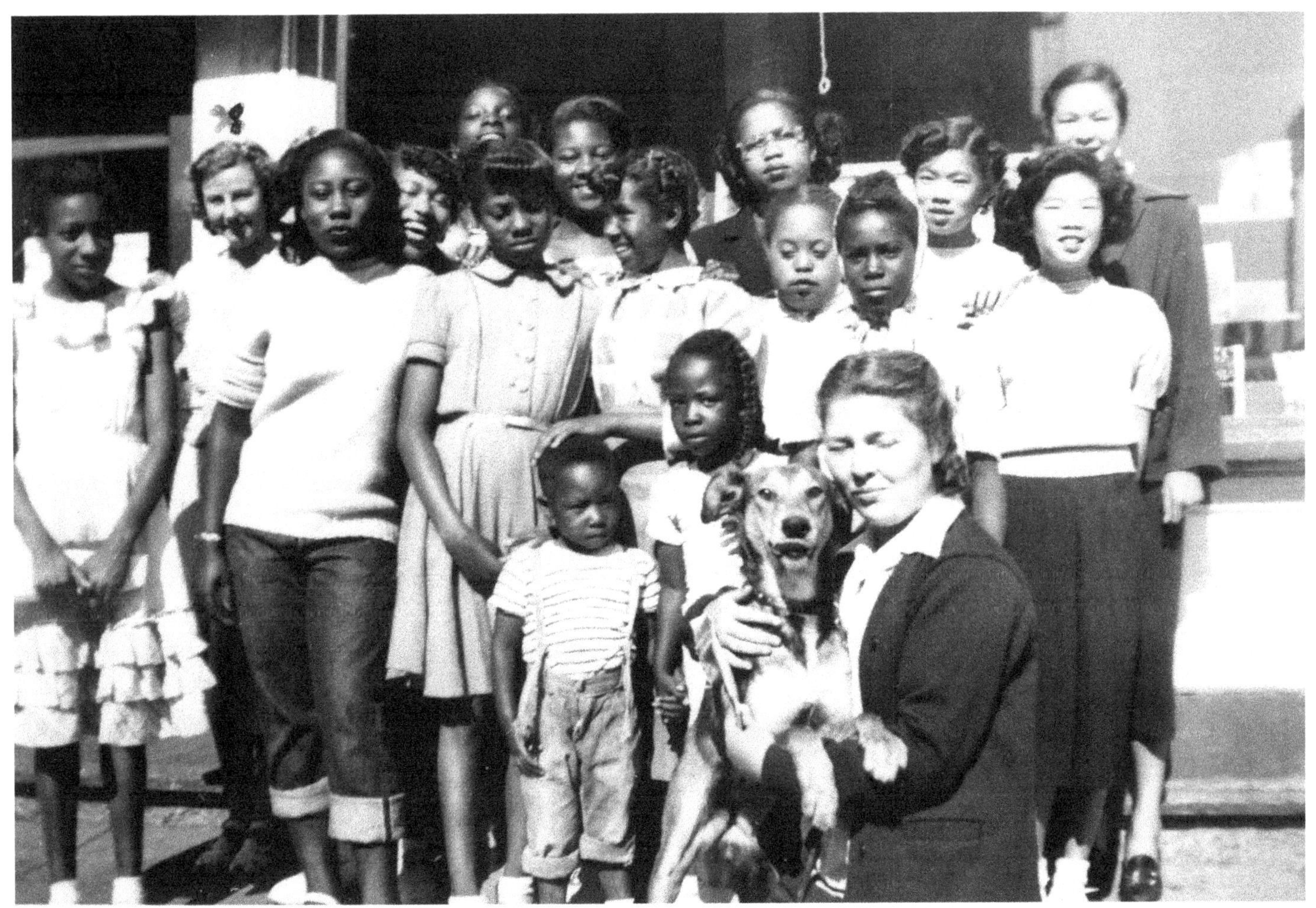

Young patrons of the North Oakland branch of the Collections of the Oakland History Room, Oakland Public Library formed the Charm Club in 1949, with Lady, one member's pet, serving as unofficial mascot.

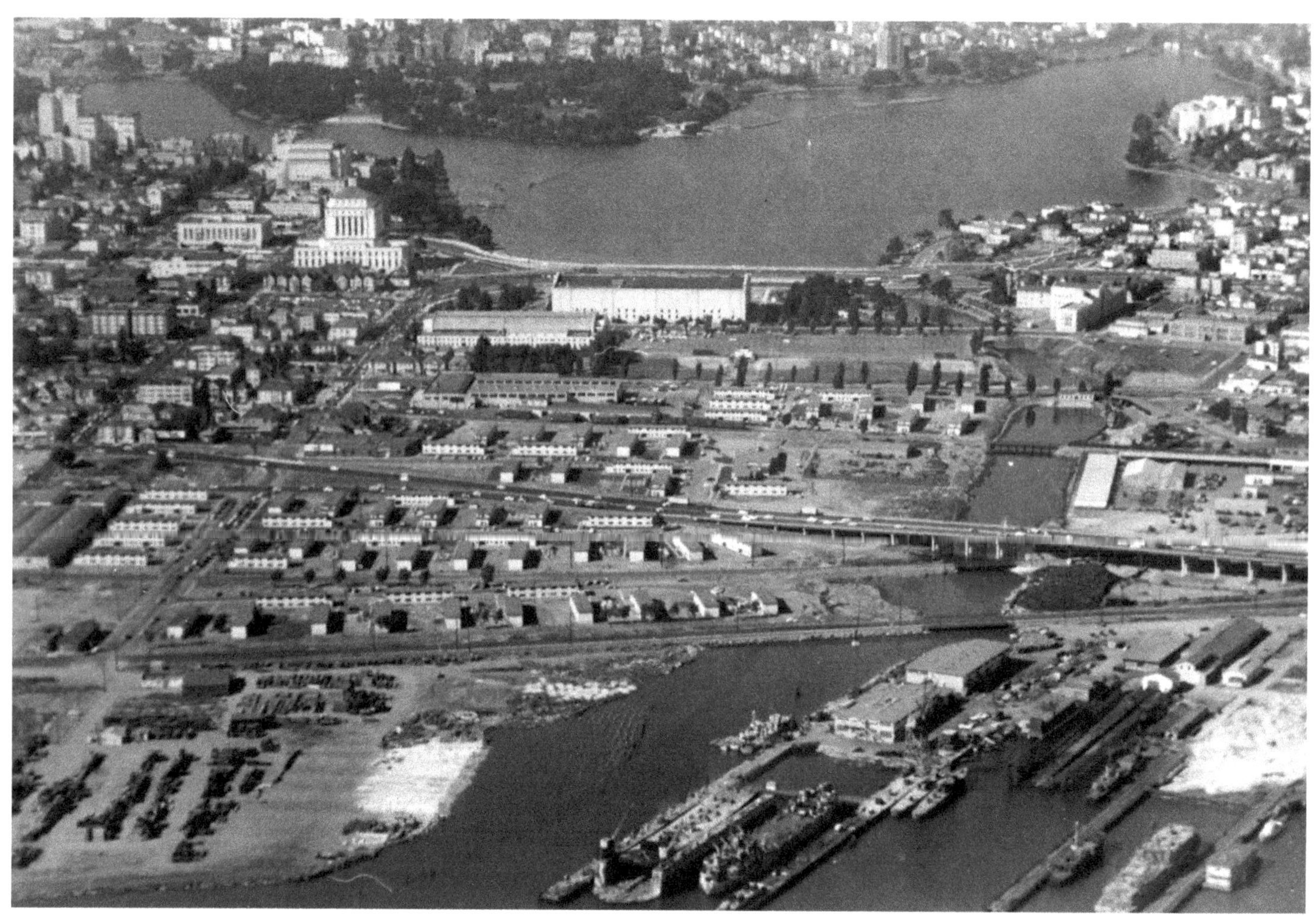

A housing emergency had resulted from the surge of war workers to Oakland, and temporary housing was erected wherever room could be spared. City-owned land south of the Oakland Auditorium and Exposition Center was used for Exposition Village, seen here in an aerial view around 1950. The site would later be cleared to make room for Laney College and the home football field of the Oakland Raiders.

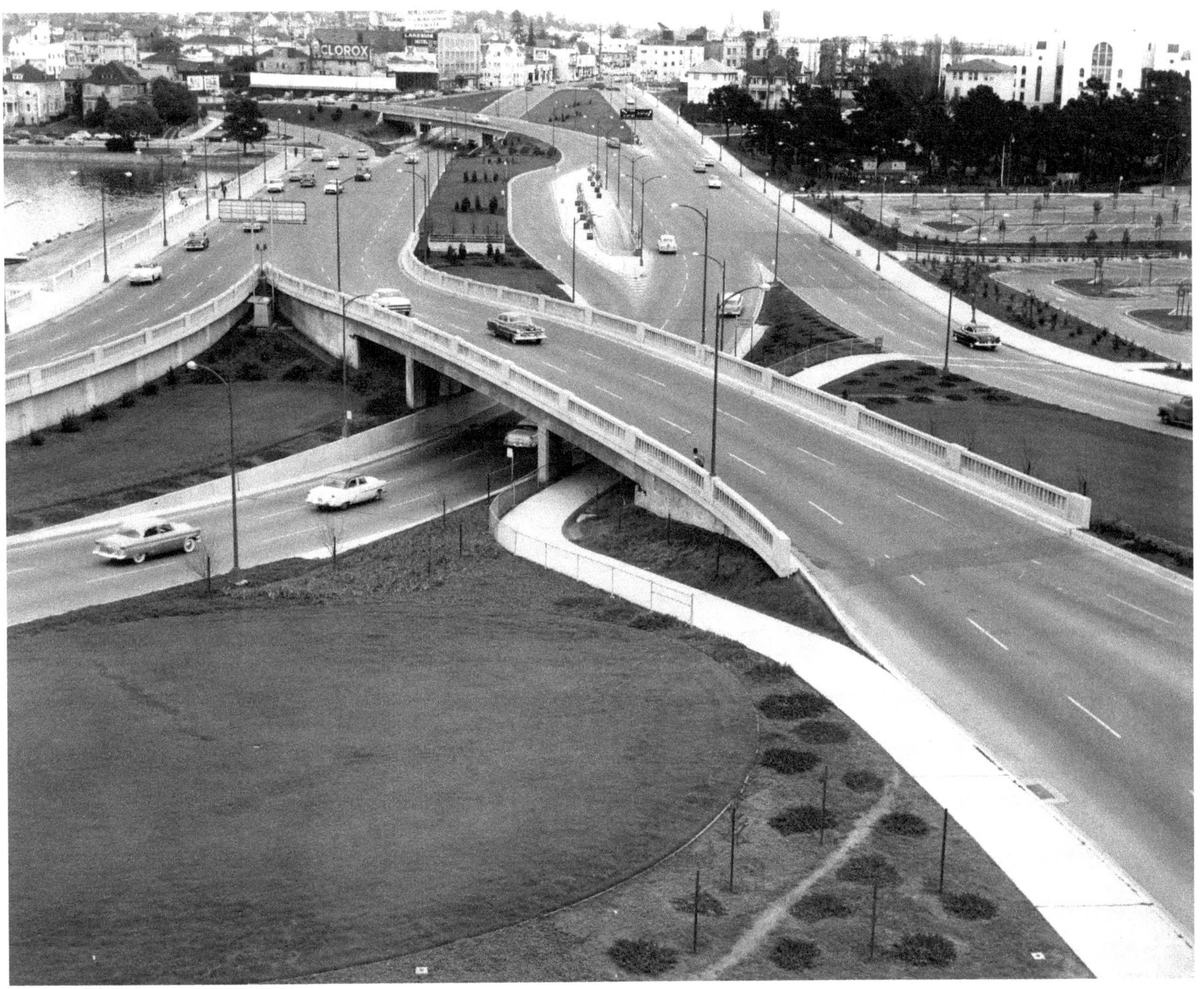

In response to public pressure to curb traffic congestion, city officials poured large sums of public money into an elaborate system of causeways and under-crossings designed to speed traffic over the 12th Street Dam. When the project was finally completed, much of the traffic was gone, traveling instead along a newly constructed freeway that bypassed Lake Merritt.

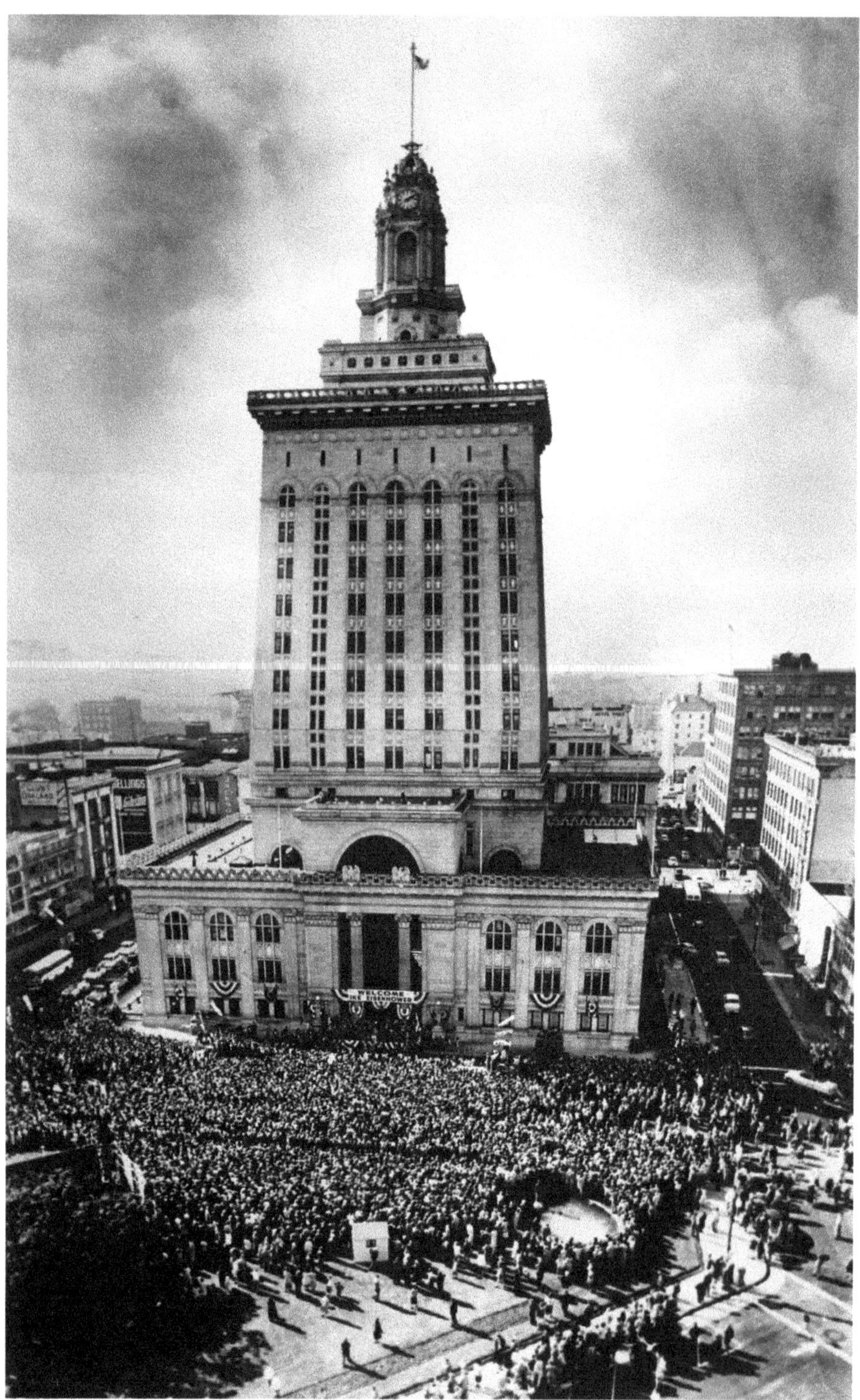

A large crowd filled City Hall Plaza for a visit by President Dwight D. Eisenhower in 1954.

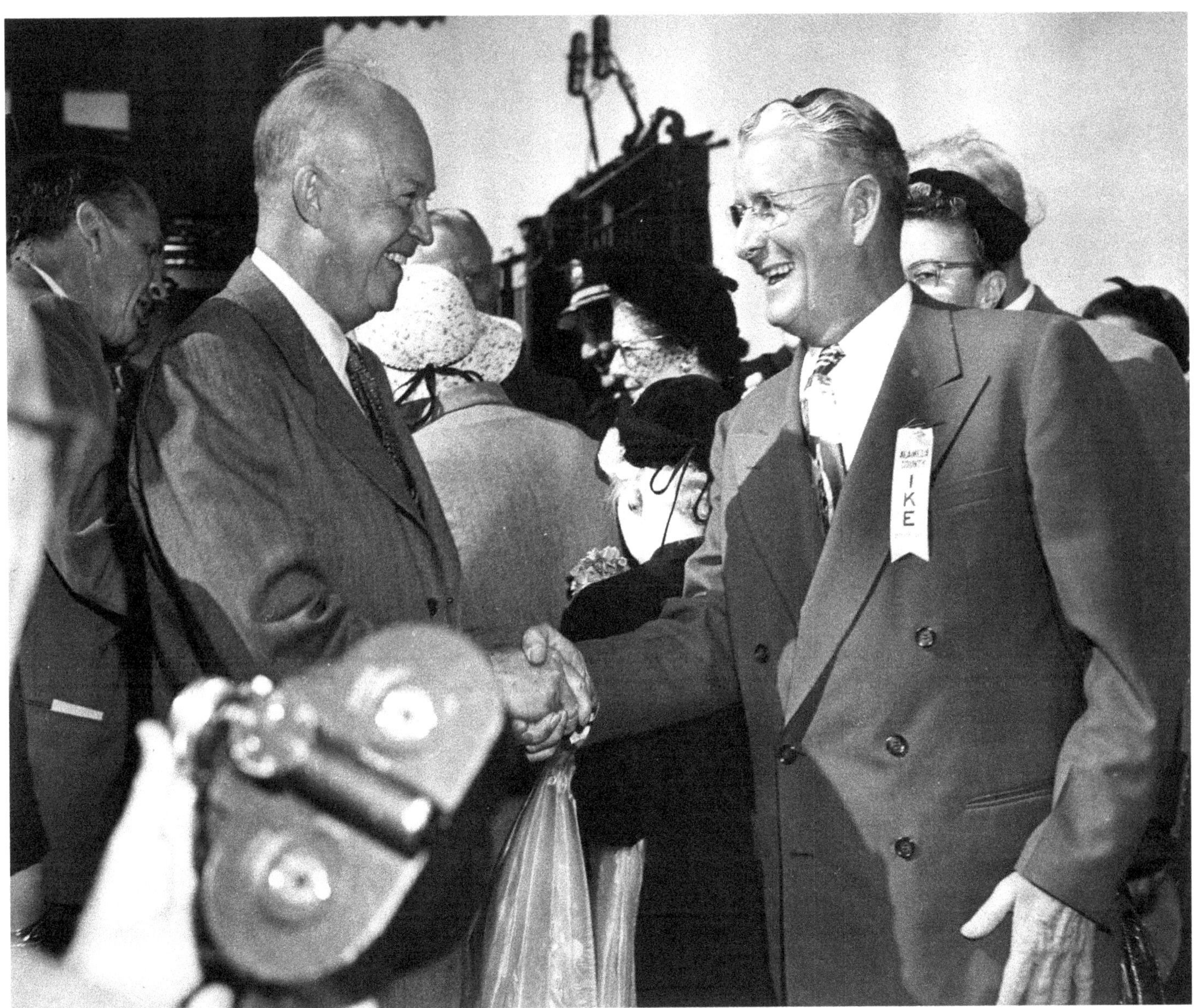

Mayor Clifford Rishell greeted fellow Republican Dwight Eisenhower in the lobby of City Hall during the president's visit in 1954. The visit came while Oakland's staunchly Republican political establishment enjoyed its greatest influence, with Earl Warren sitting as Chief Justice of the Supreme Court and William F. Knowland, son of the publisher of the *Oakland Tribune*, sitting as majority leader of the U.S. Senate. Warren's many controversial rulings, however, would lead Eisenhower to conclude that appointing Warren to the nation's highest court had been a mistake.

Oakland's newest attraction, Children's Fairyland, was attracting young visitors and their accompanying adults from throughout the region. Walt Disney attributed a visit to Children's Fairyland as inspiration for the creation of his own theme park.

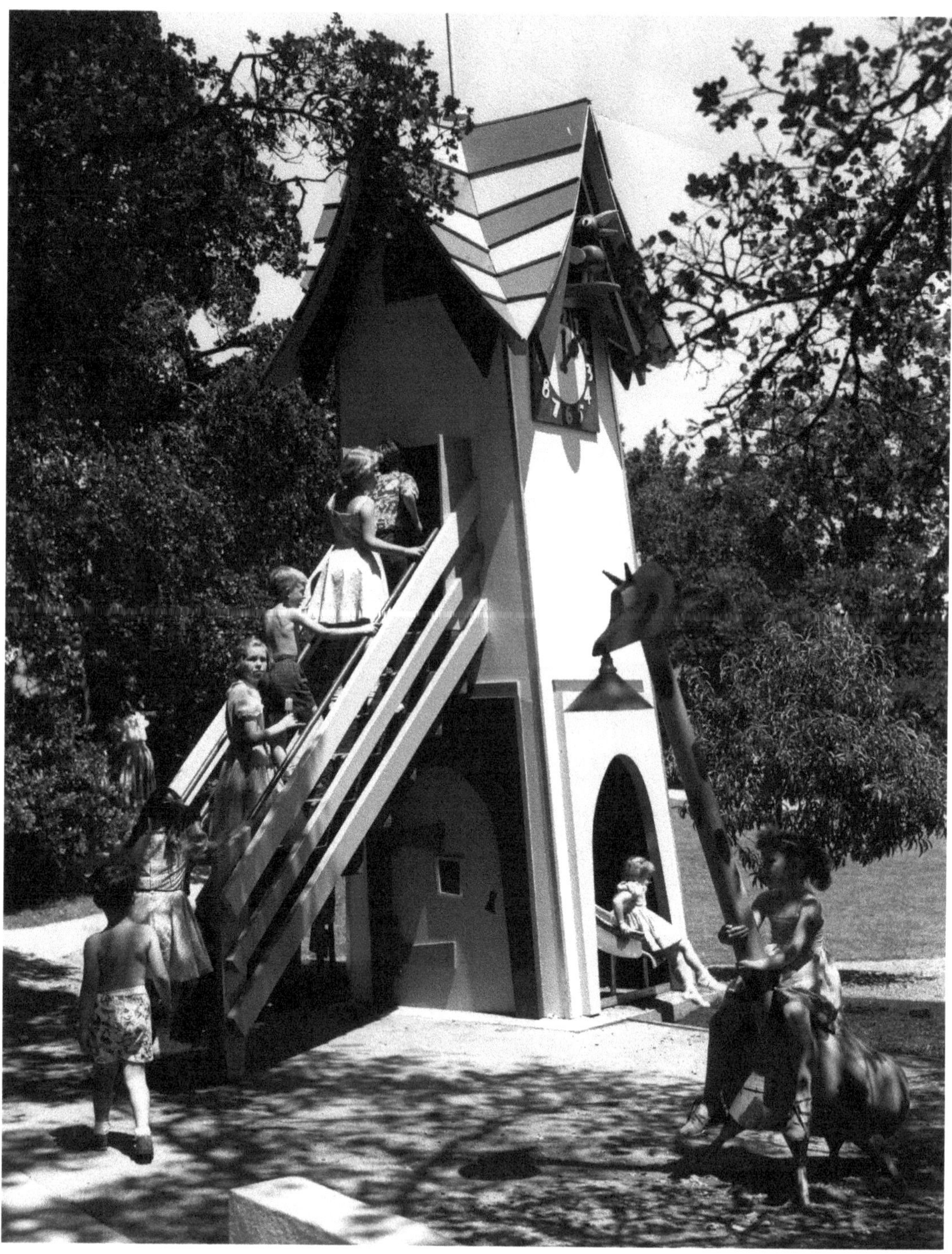

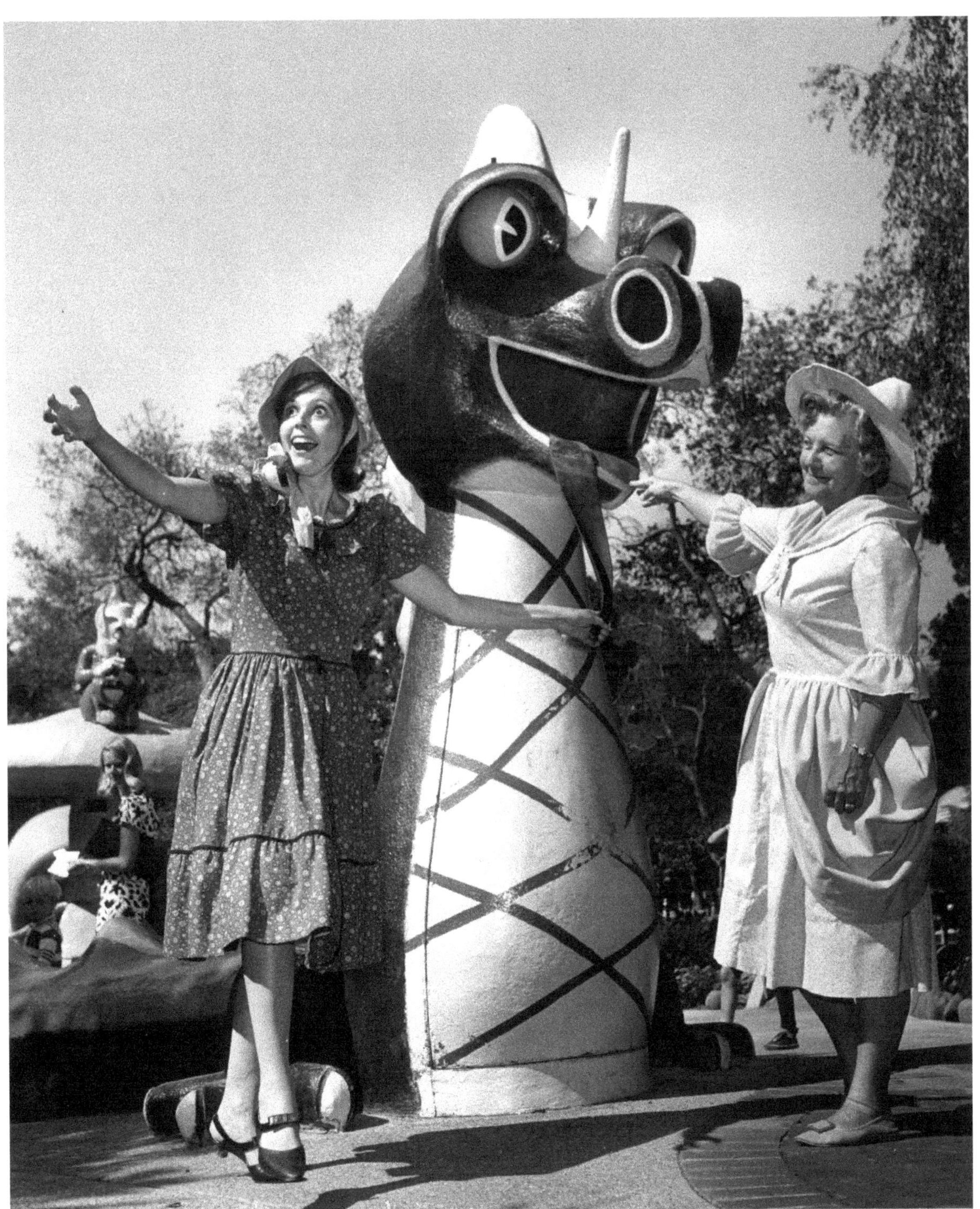

Live attractions at Children's Fairyland included actors and actresses roaming the grounds portraying characters from children's literature. Under the direction of Lewis Mahlmann, the puppet theater at Children's Fairyland would help to redefine puppetry for a new generation.

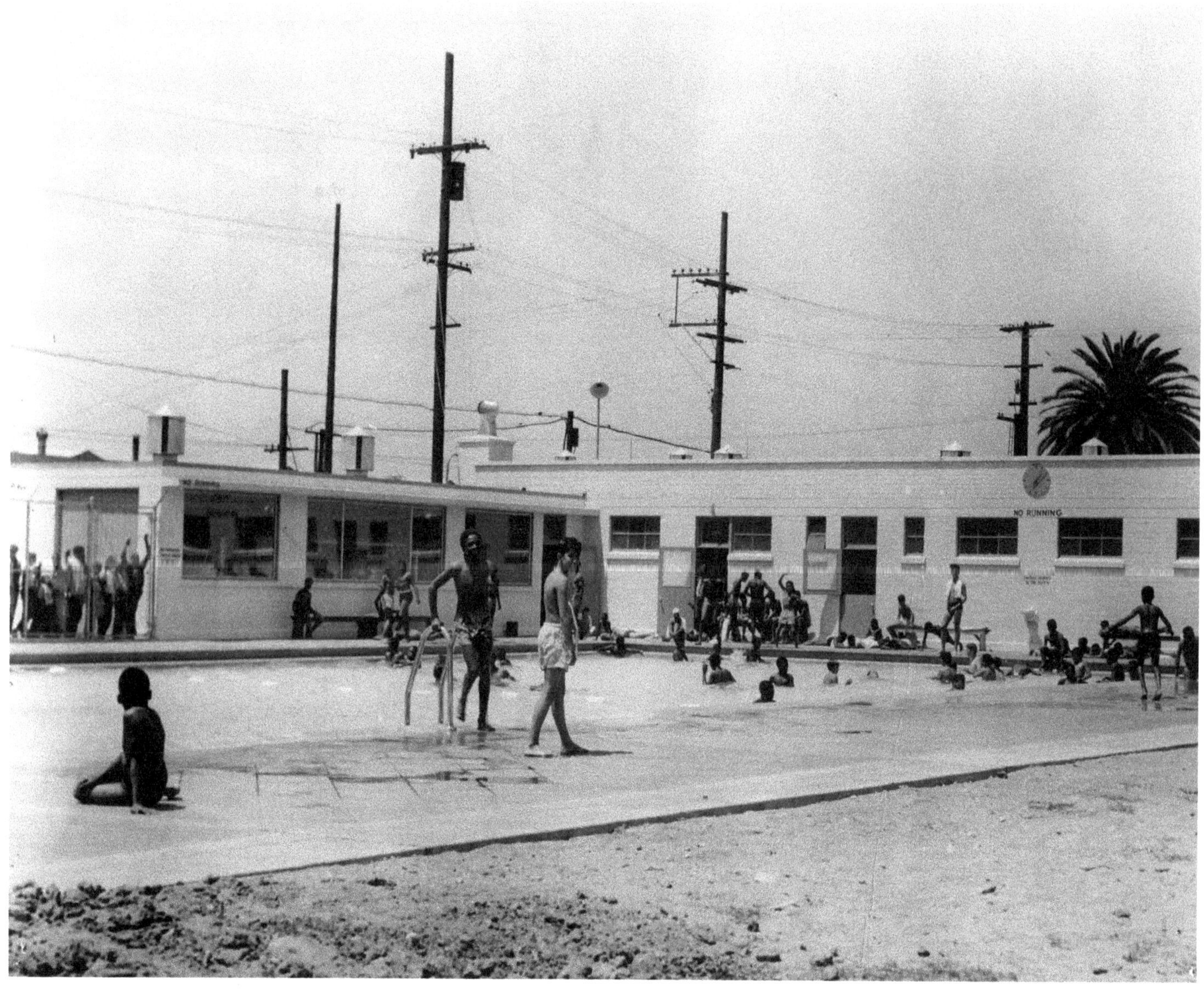

De Fremery Pool, shown here in the mid-1950s, is part of a park and recreation complex in West Oakland that enjoyed extraordinary success in the years after World War II. Leading musical artists, such as jazz saxophonist John Handy, and highly successful athletes such as Frank Robinson and Bill Russell, would emerge from the city's programs at the park.

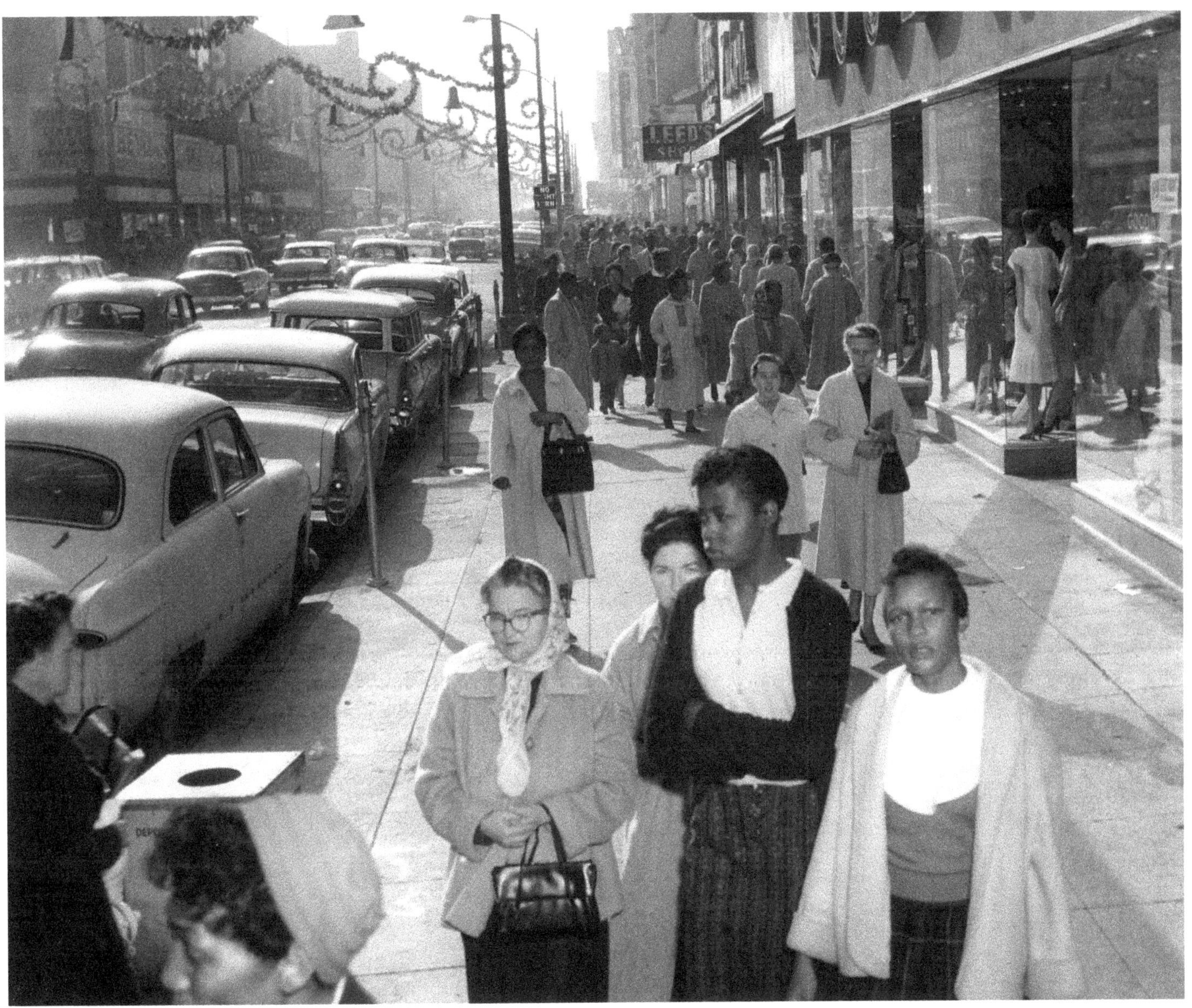

Broadway retained its hold on shoppers during the Christmas season, at least into the mid-1950s when this photograph was taken.

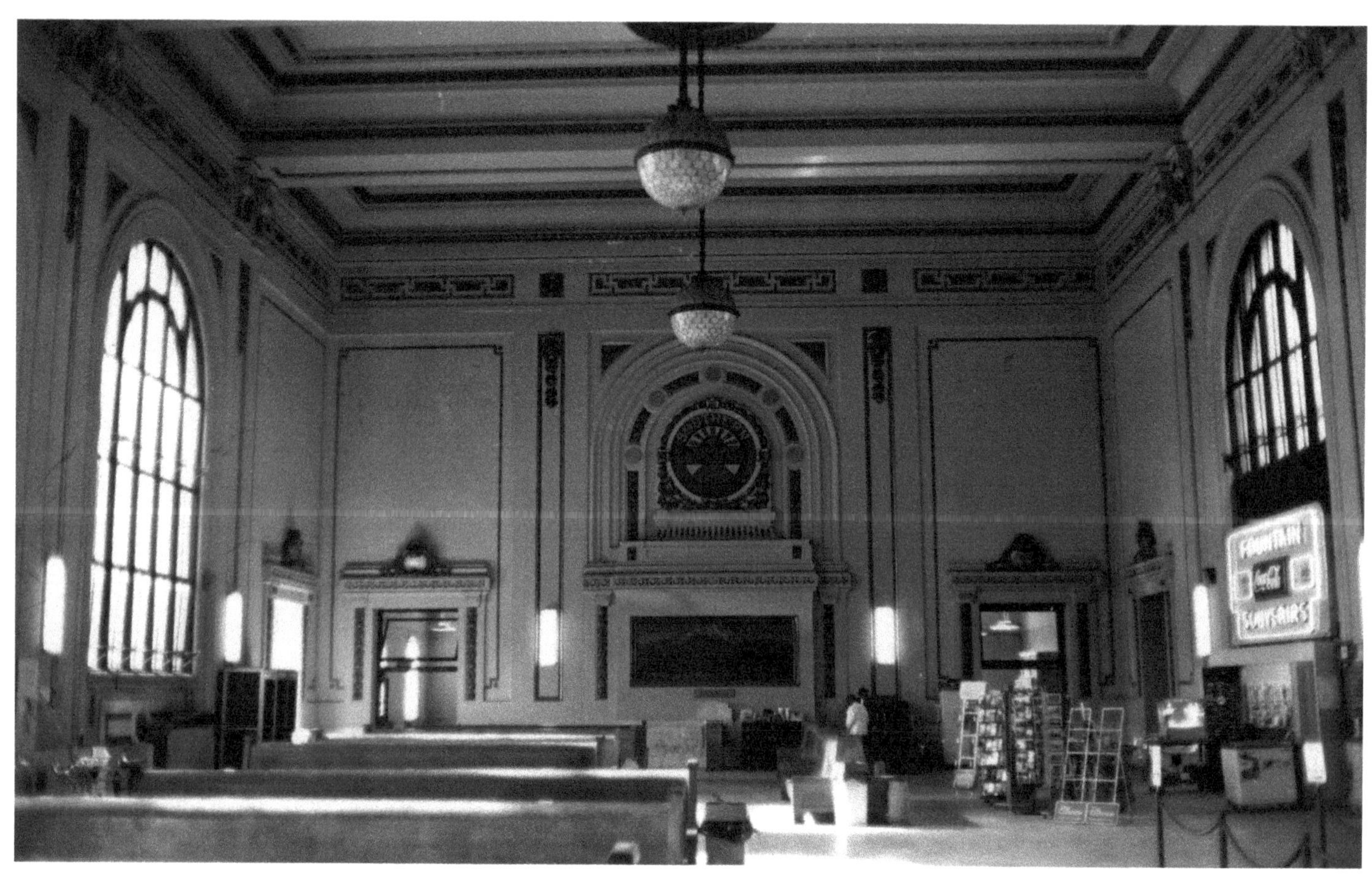

During the 1950s, passenger bookings on the railroads continued their steady decline. A photographer captured the lonely scene inside the Southern Pacific passenger station at 16th and Wood streets after the wartime travel frenzy had subsided. Although damaged by the 1989 Loma Prieta Earthquake, the station still stands and a restoration project is in progress.

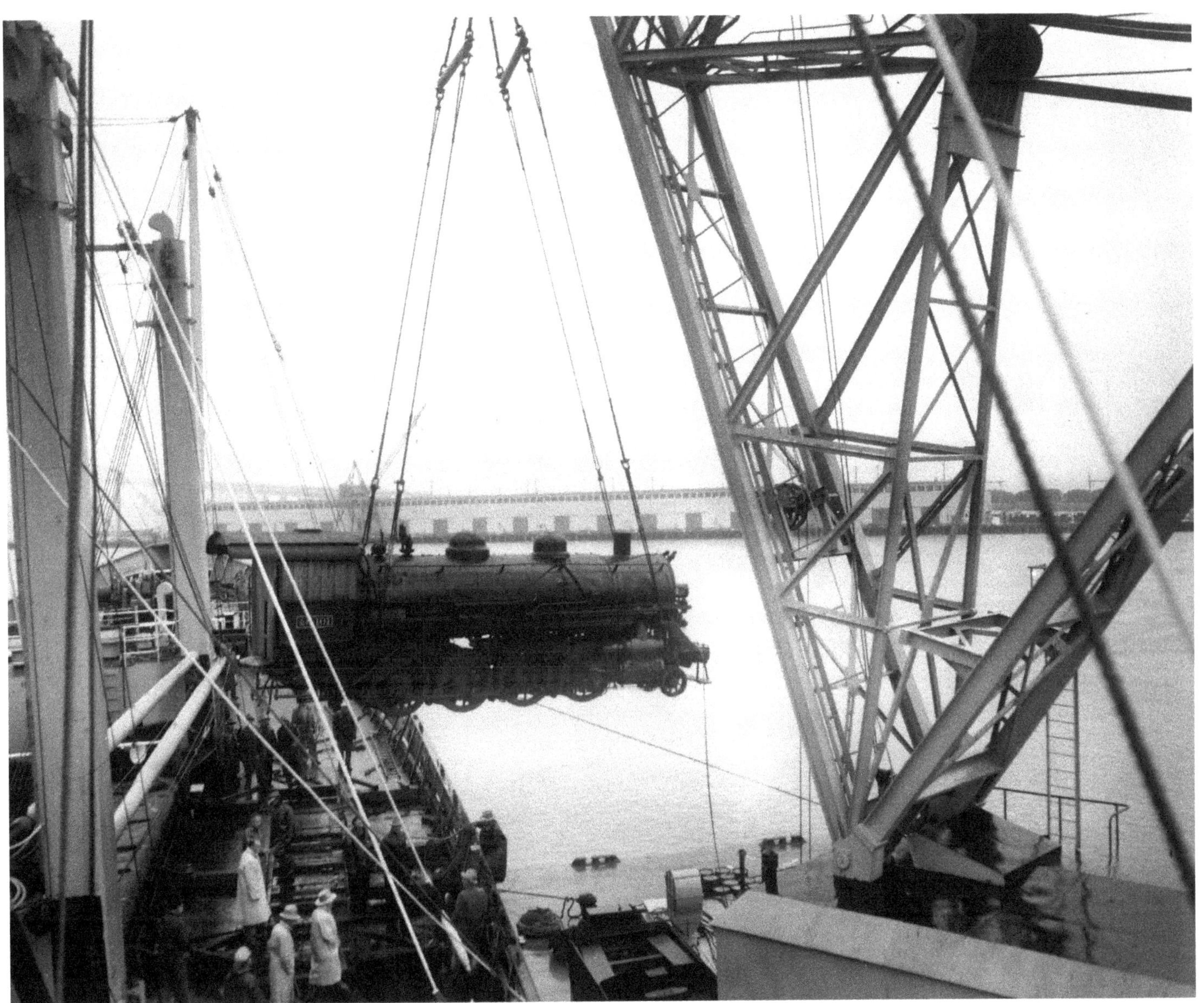

Oakland's military bases endured as permanent fixtures on the waterfront. In 1959, a Navy photographer documented the transfer of a historic freight locomotive from the ship that brought it from China, to a train that would take it to a railroad museum on the East Coast.

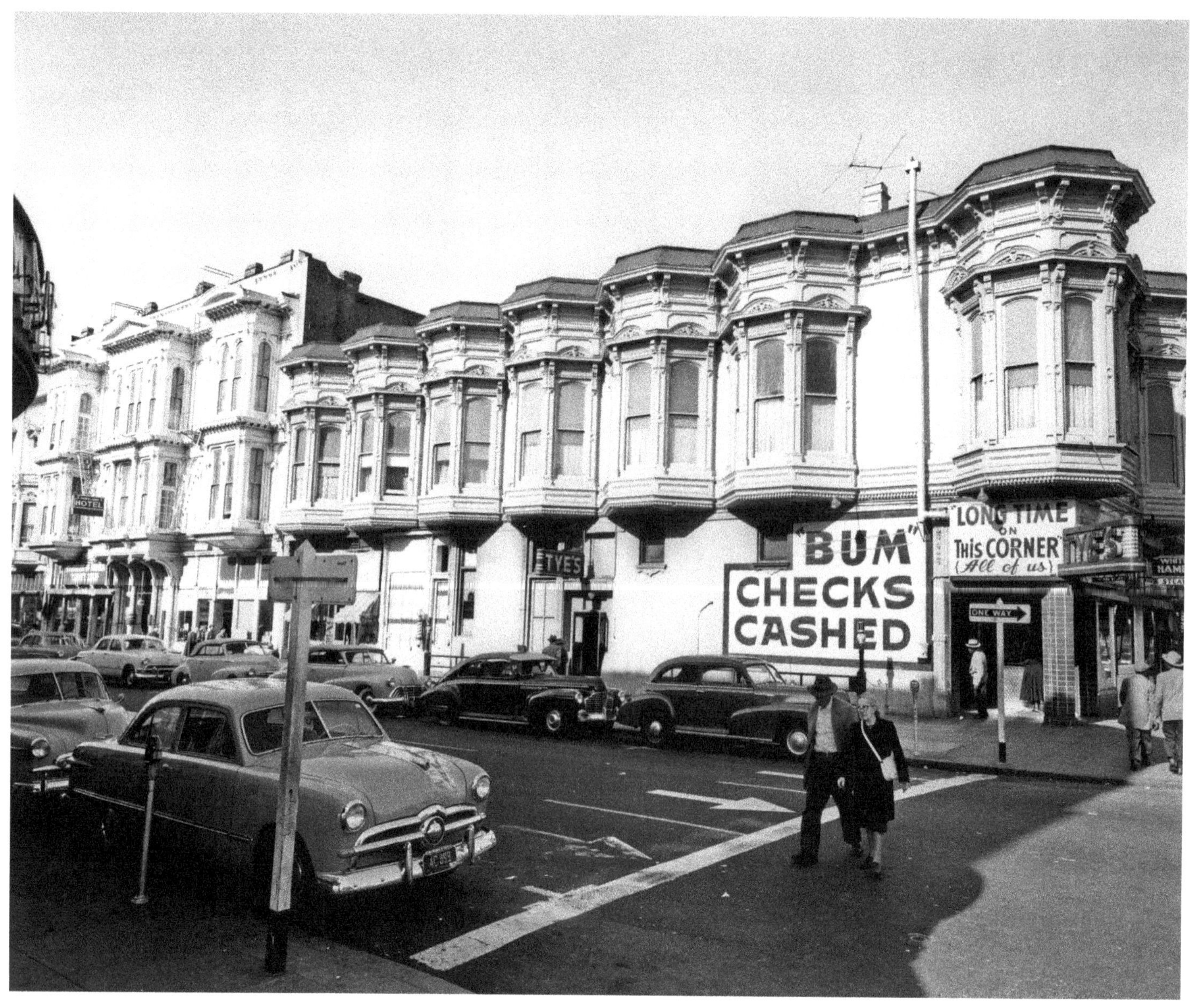

Some merchants held on as activity in downtown Oakland steadily declined with the expansion of the suburbs. Tye's Buffet at Tenth Street and Broadway advertised its stubborn loyalty to its inner-city corner.

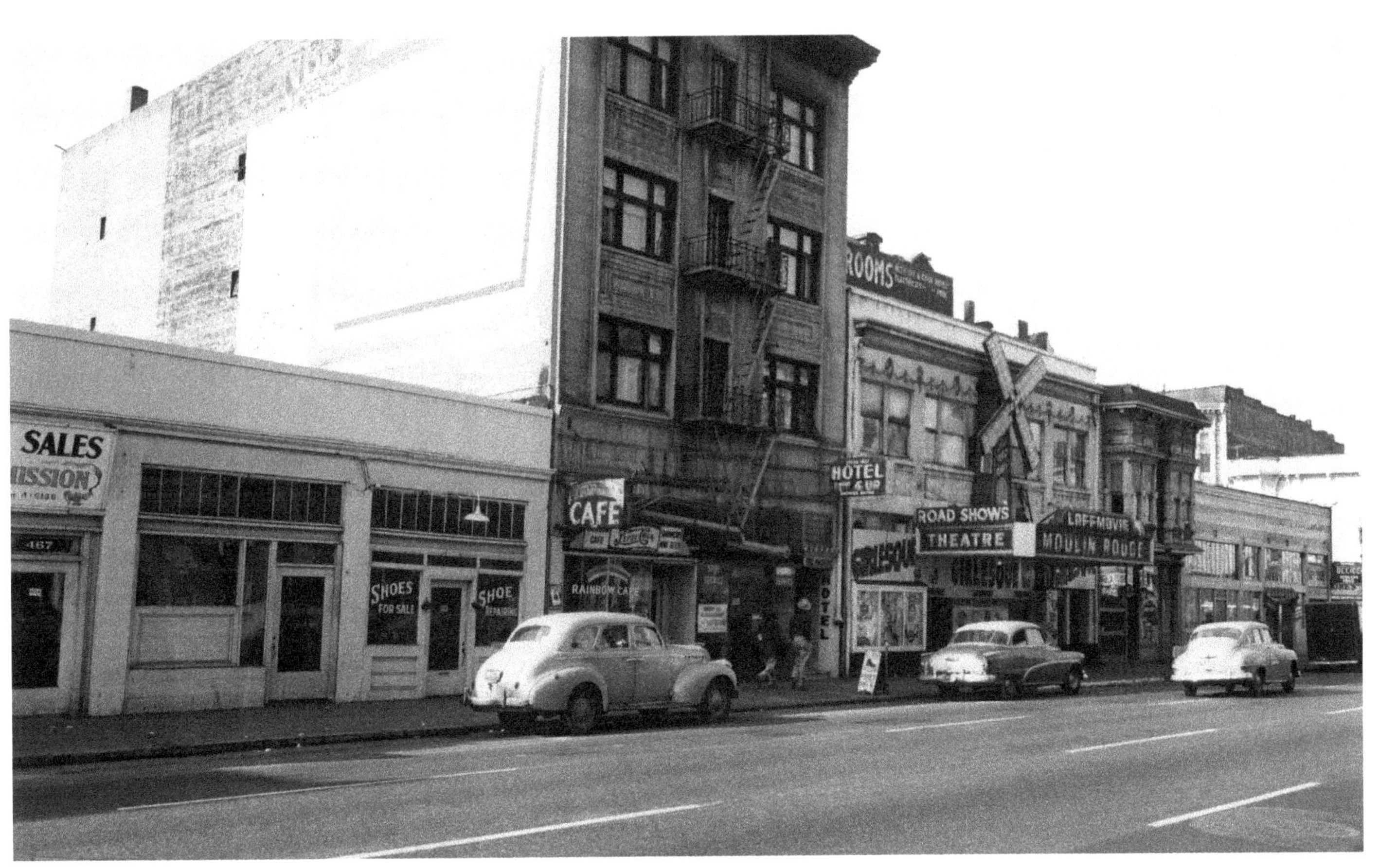

A three-dimensional representation of a windmill designated the Moulin Rouge, a run-down burlesque house on Eighth Street where Hollywood B-movie director Russ Meyer found his inspiration.

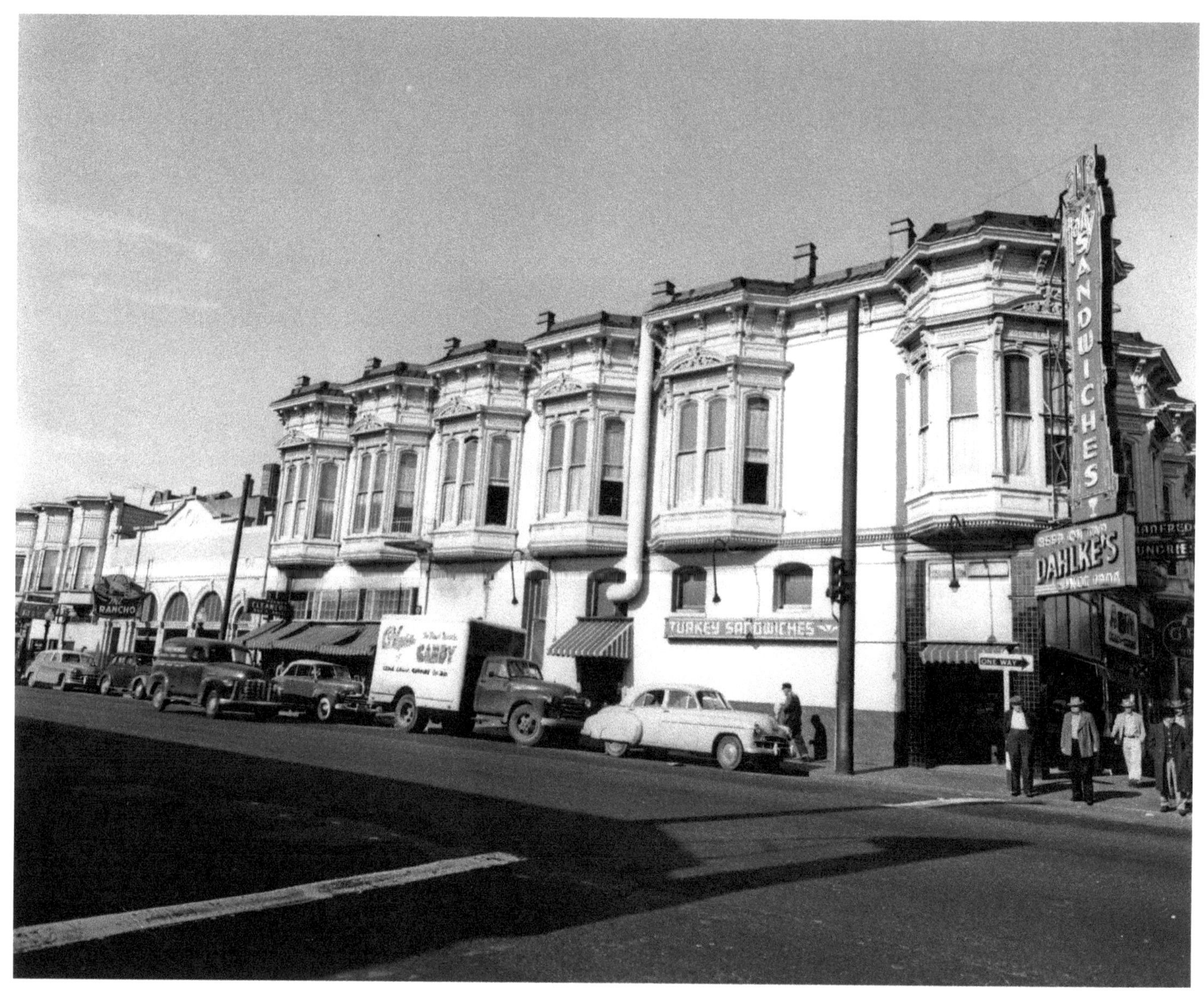

Dahlke's served sandwiches and beer over an ornately decorated antique bar to a mixed clientele of bail bondsmen, downtown denizens who were down on their luck, police officers, and hungry travelers from the train depot next door. When this photograph was taken in the mid-1950s, a Mexican market and tortilla factory occupied the former Seventh Street passenger station.

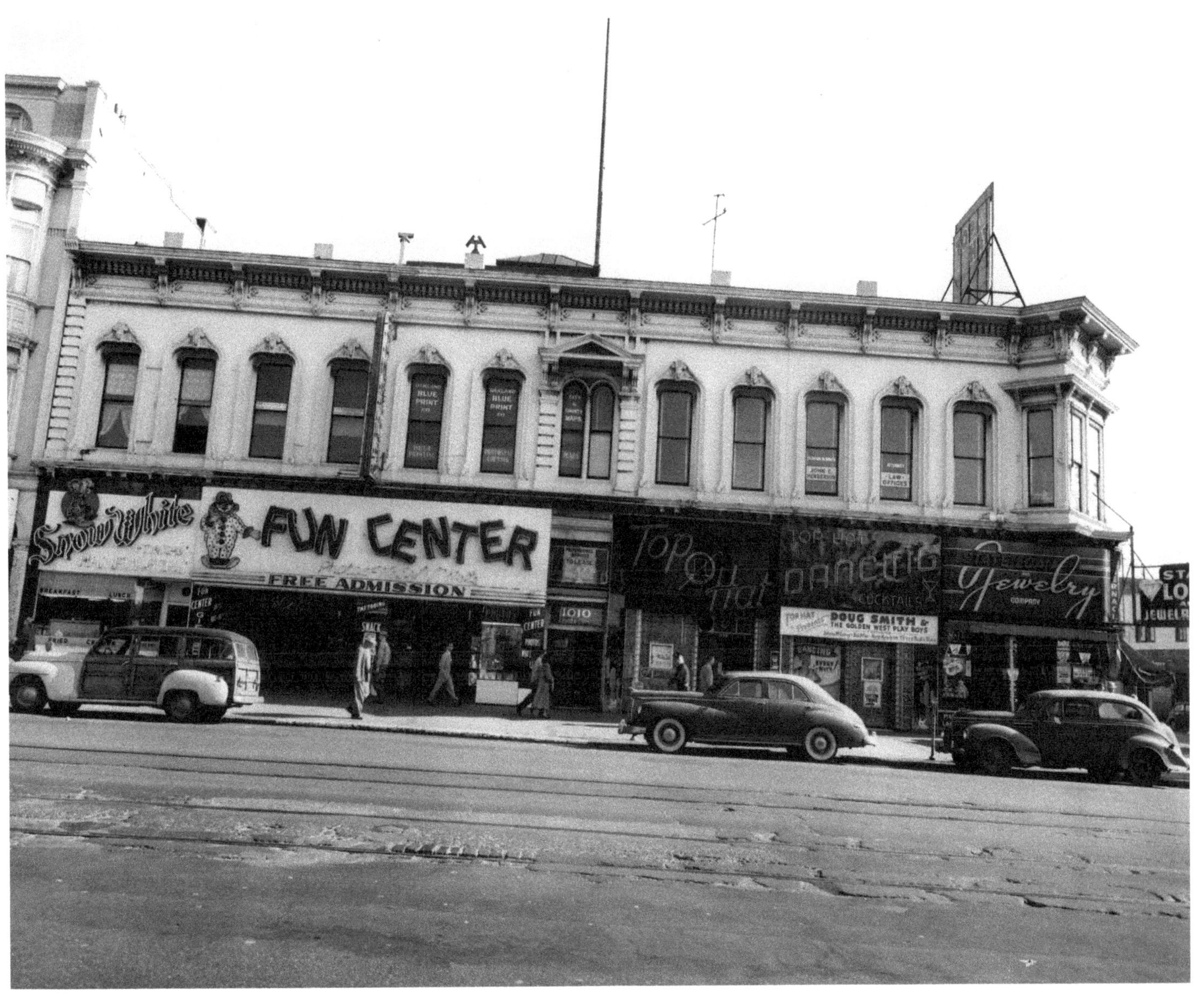

Pinball, Western swing, and taxi dancers provided the entertainment along this stretch of lower Broadway. Oakland was among the last cities in the country to operate dance halls in which women charged a fee in exchange for the privilege of a dance.

The fire department showed off its newly restored fireboat, the former USS *Hoga,* a vessel used to extinguish the flames after the bombing of Pearl Harbor in 1941.

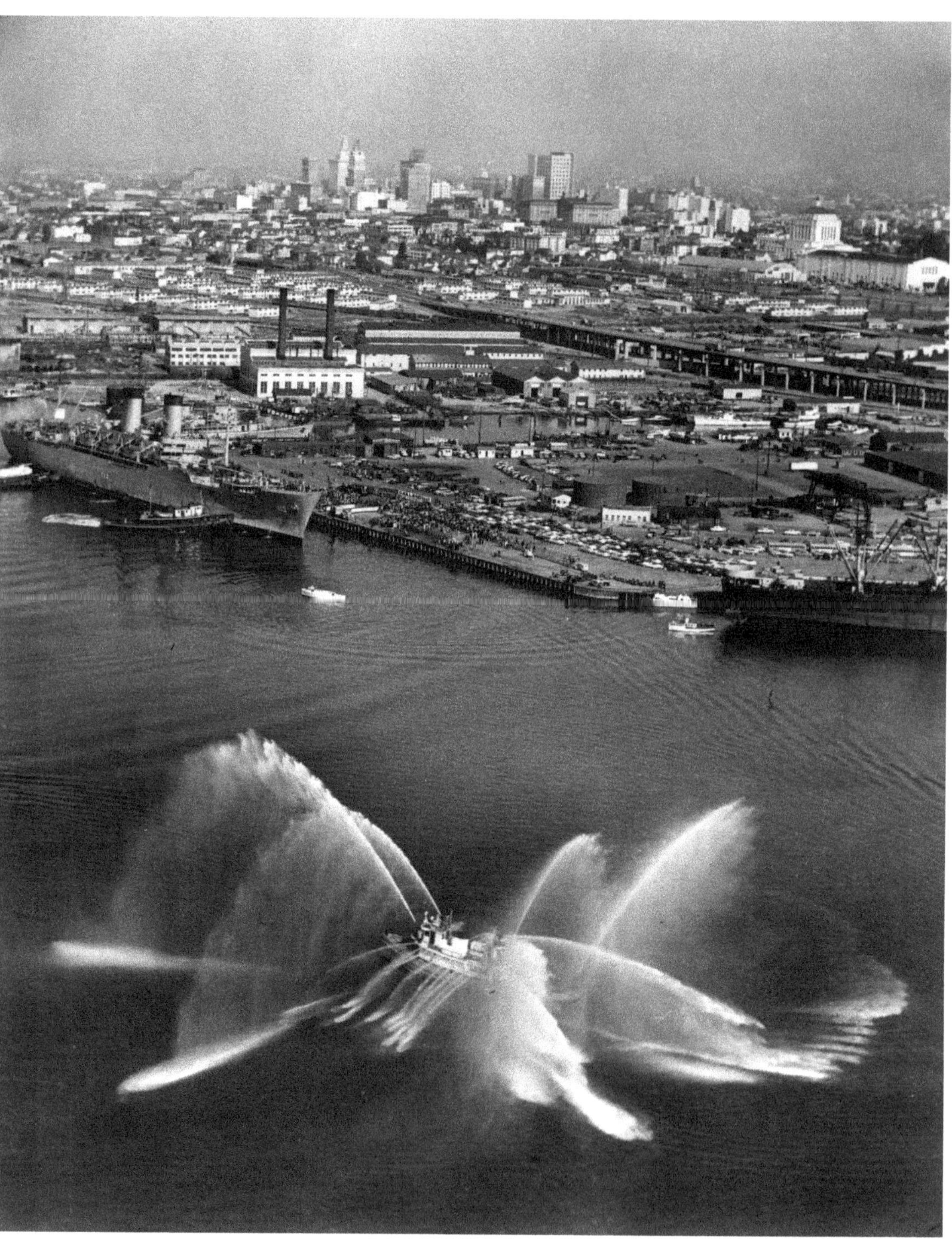

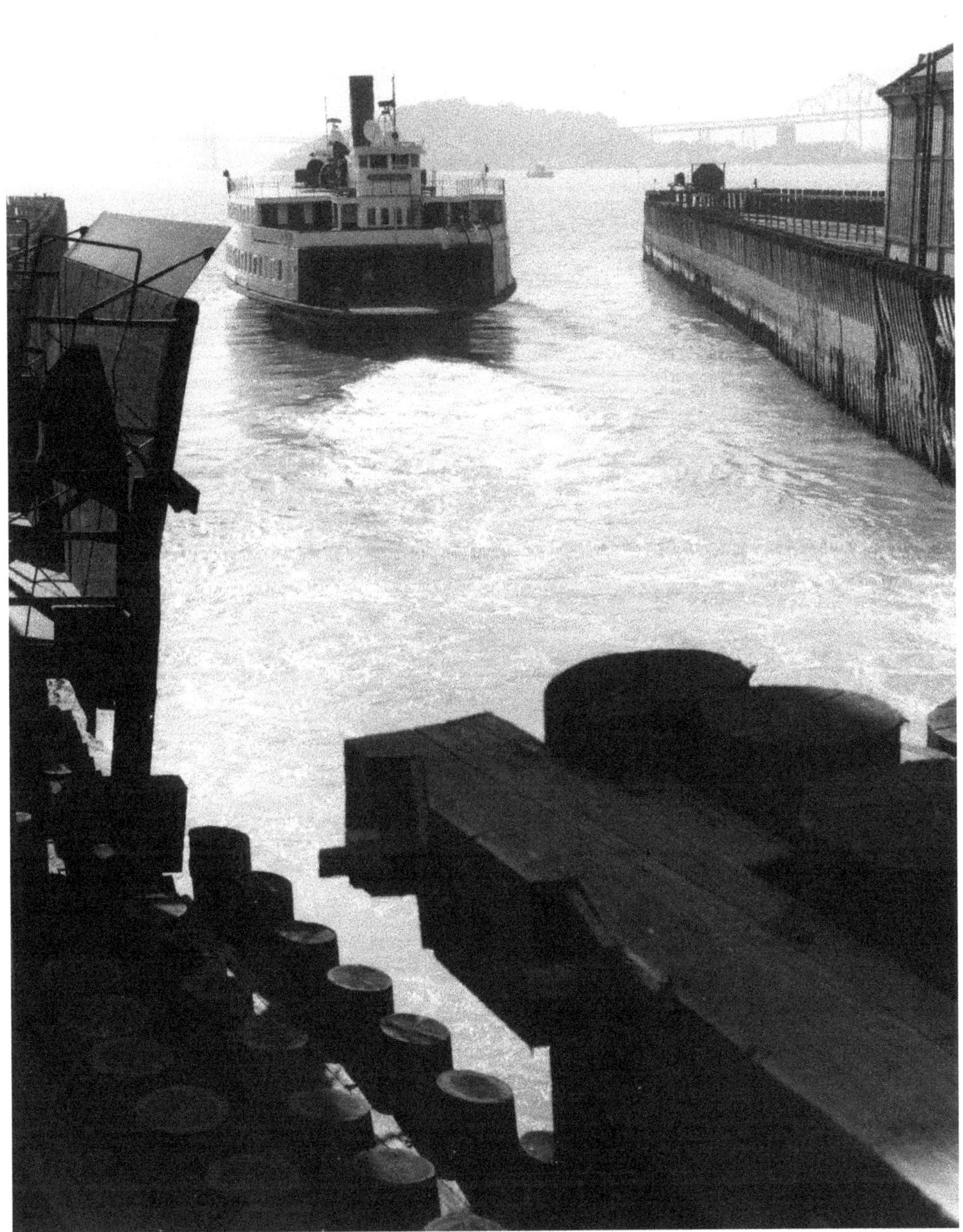

Commuter ferry service ended in 1941 after the completion of the Bay Bridge, but Southern Pacific ferries made the crossing until 1958 as an extension of rail service to San Francisco. Toward the end of that service, when this image was recorded, the ferry ride across the bay was very lonely.

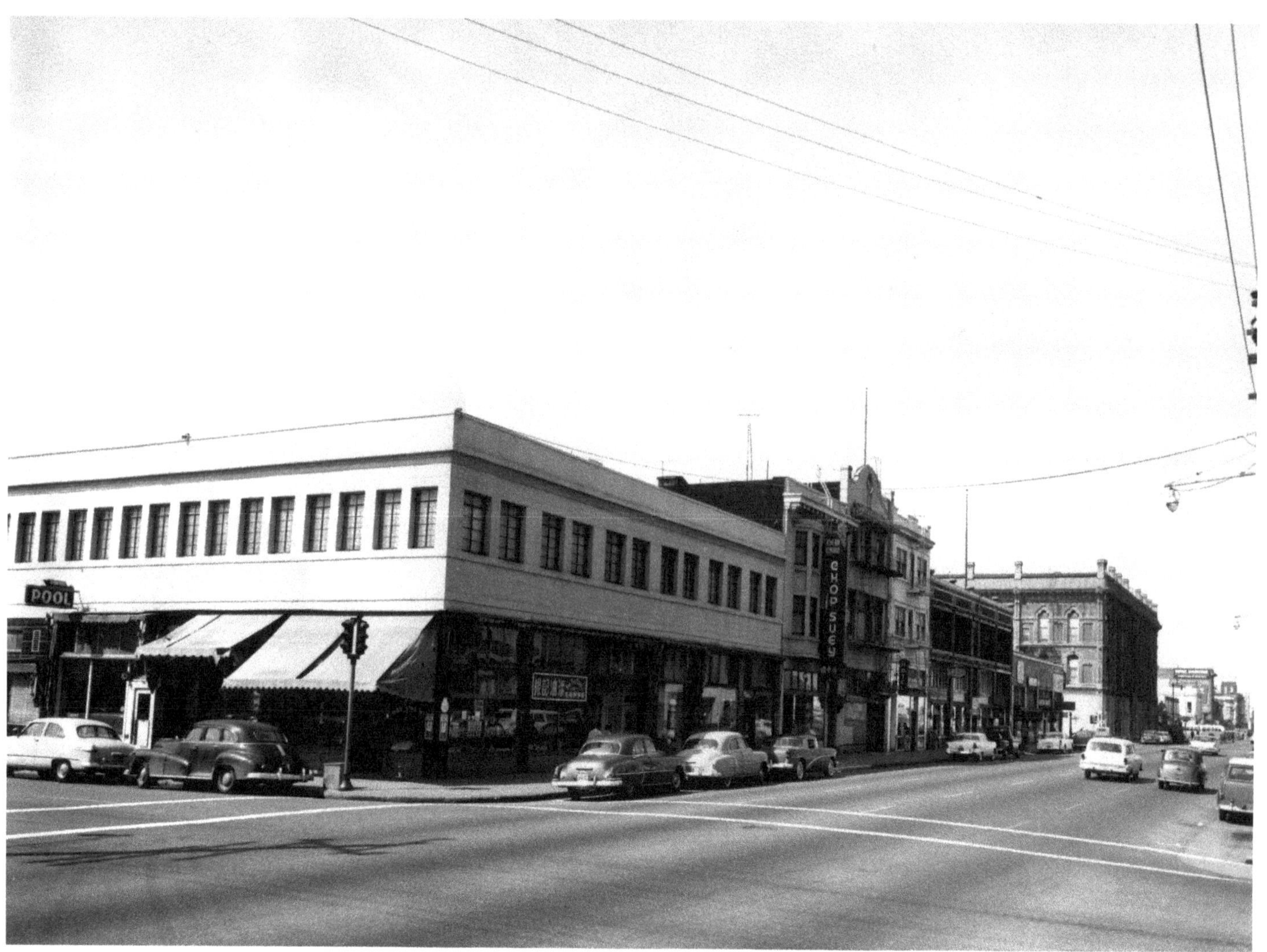

The city's historic Chinatown suffered the troubles typical to the inner cities of the late 1950s, enduring as an unpretentious and somewhat nondescript array of chop suey restaurants, shops, and fortune cookie factories. This would change dramatically after a surge in immigration renewed the vibrancy of this part of town.

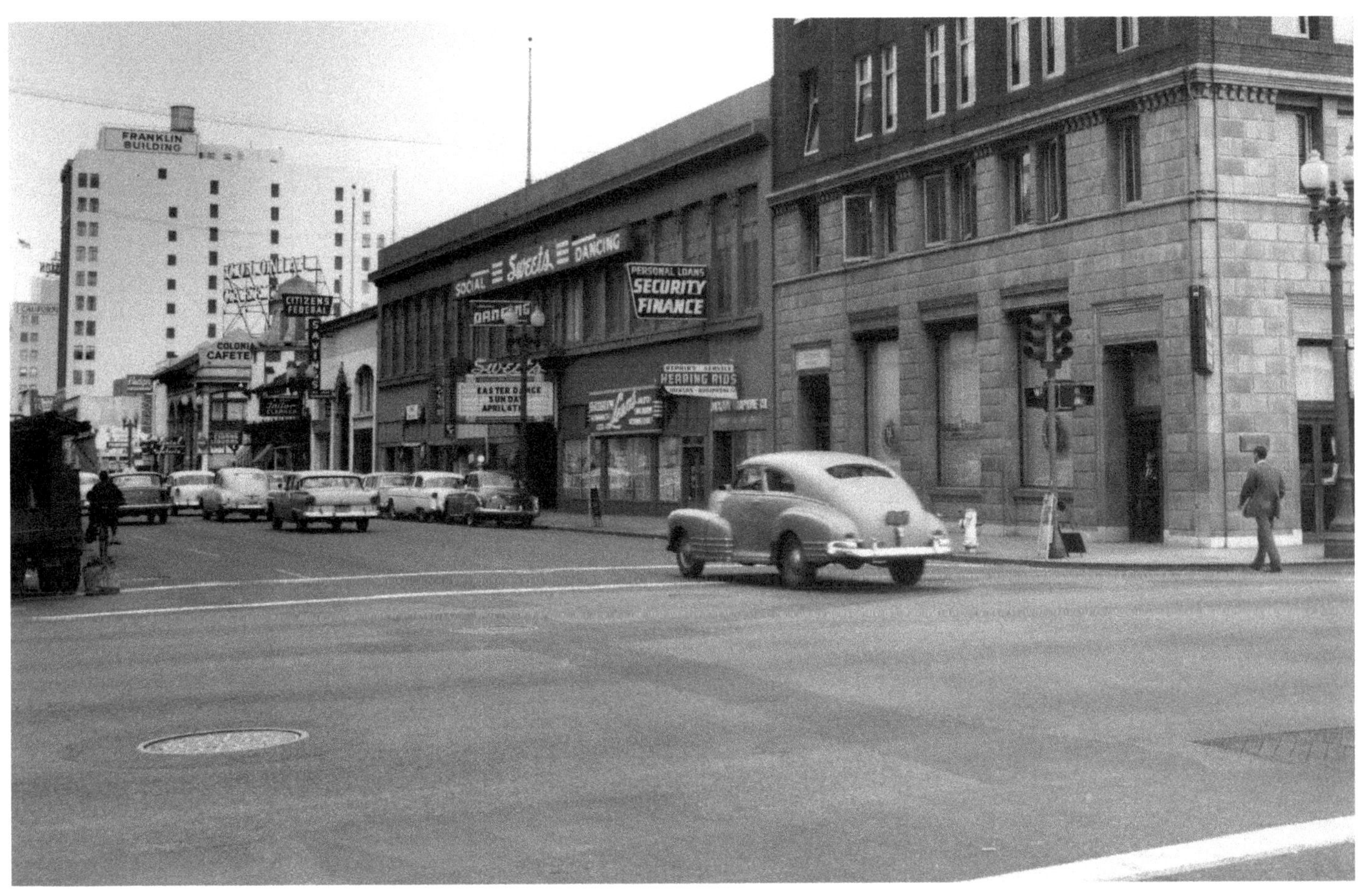

The glory days of Big Band jazz had long passed when a photographer captured this view up Franklin Street in 1958, with Sweet's ballroom visible on the left. Once the top venue in a lively downtown night life that brought many of musical entertainment's biggest names to an eager audience, Sweet's languished as the 1950s pressed on. Dave Brubeck, among many others, began his career in Oakland nightclubs.

High-rise construction moved to the center of downtown with the new tower of First Western Savings, an exceptional early example of the International style of architecture.

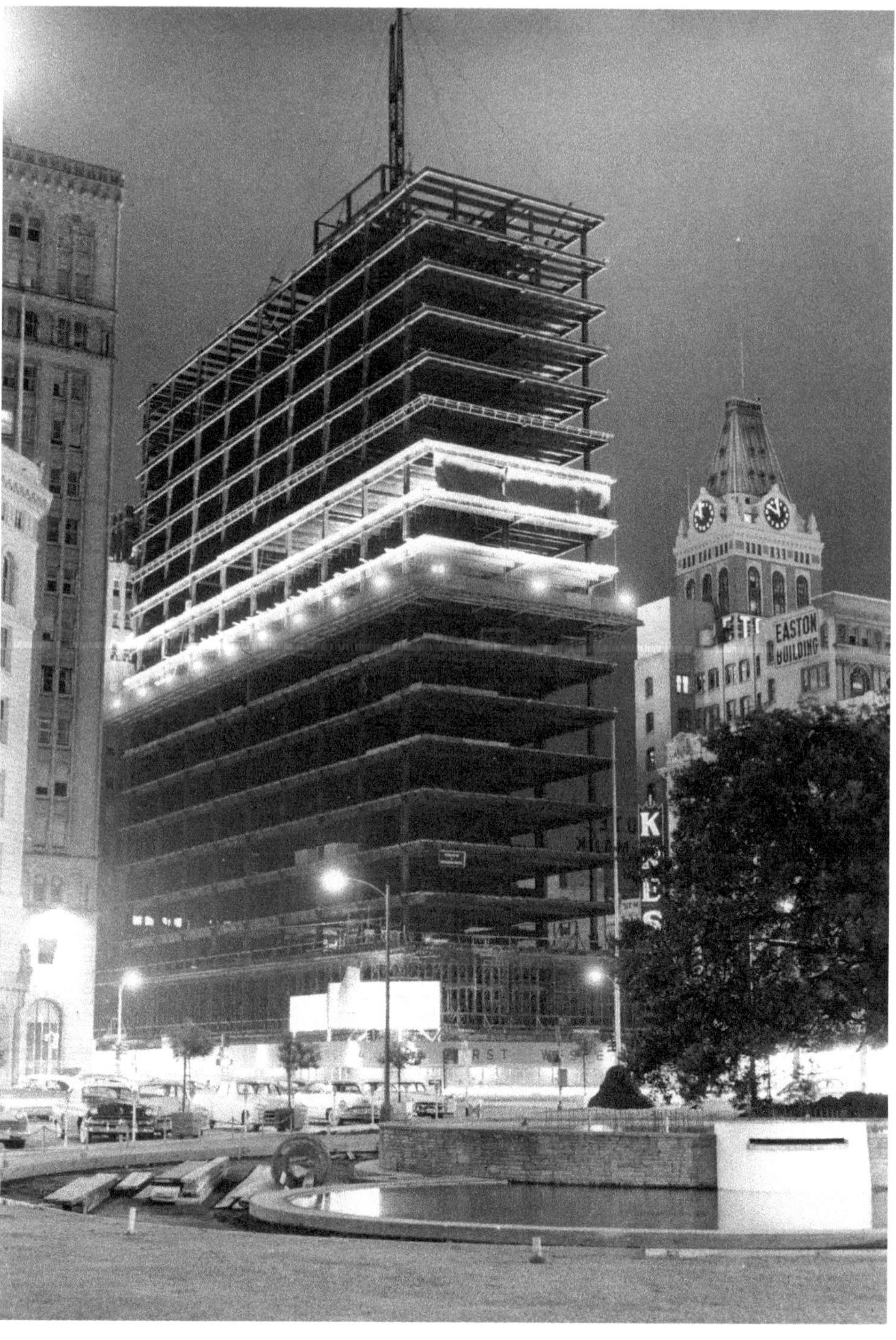

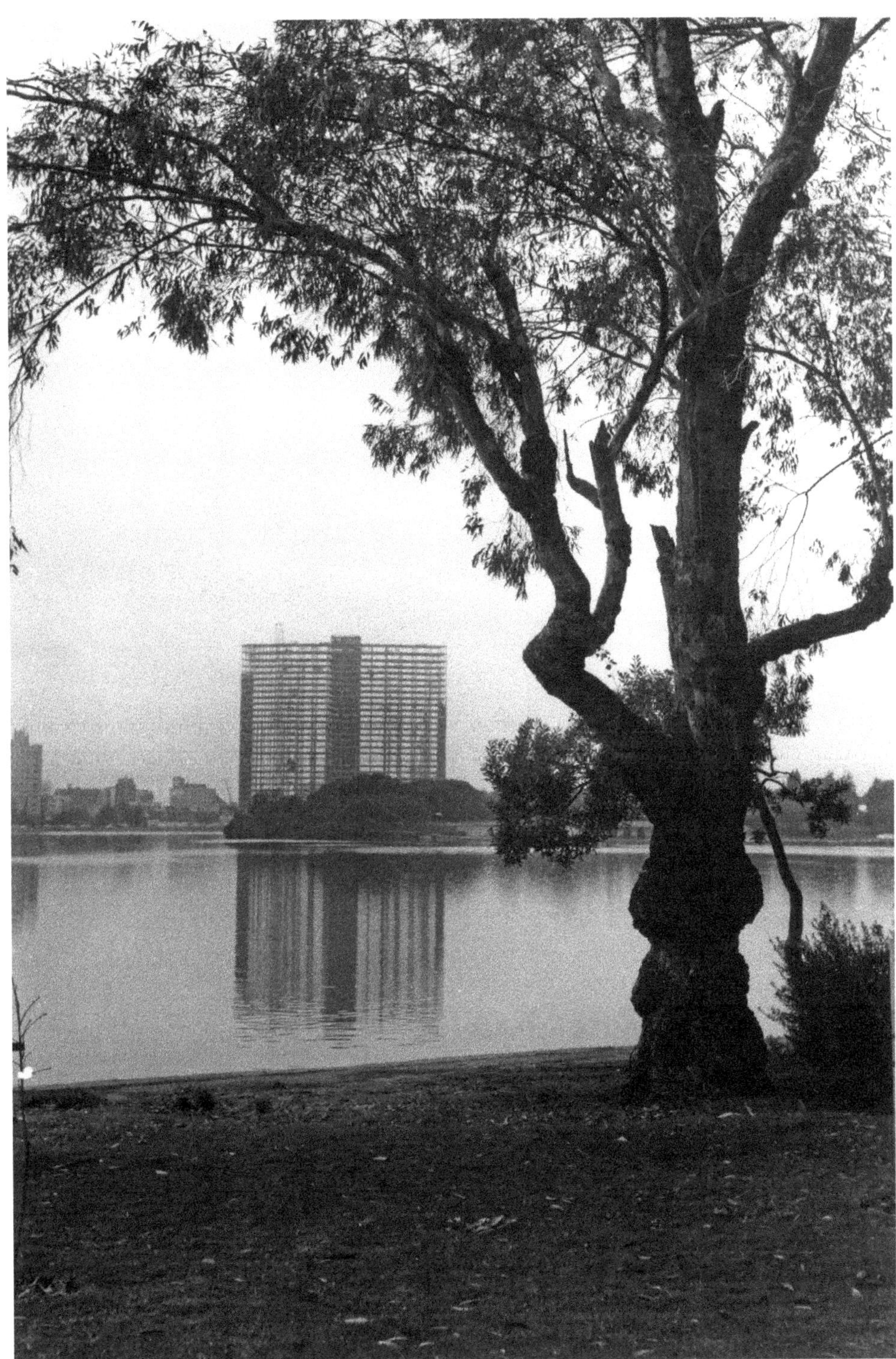

The rise of Kaiser Center on the shores of Lake Merritt was a great leap forward as Oakland struggled to shed its postwar doldrums. When it opened in 1958, the headquarters of Henry J. Kaiser's various companies was the largest office building west of Chicago. Materials for its construction were supplied almost entirely by one of the Kaiser subsidiaries.

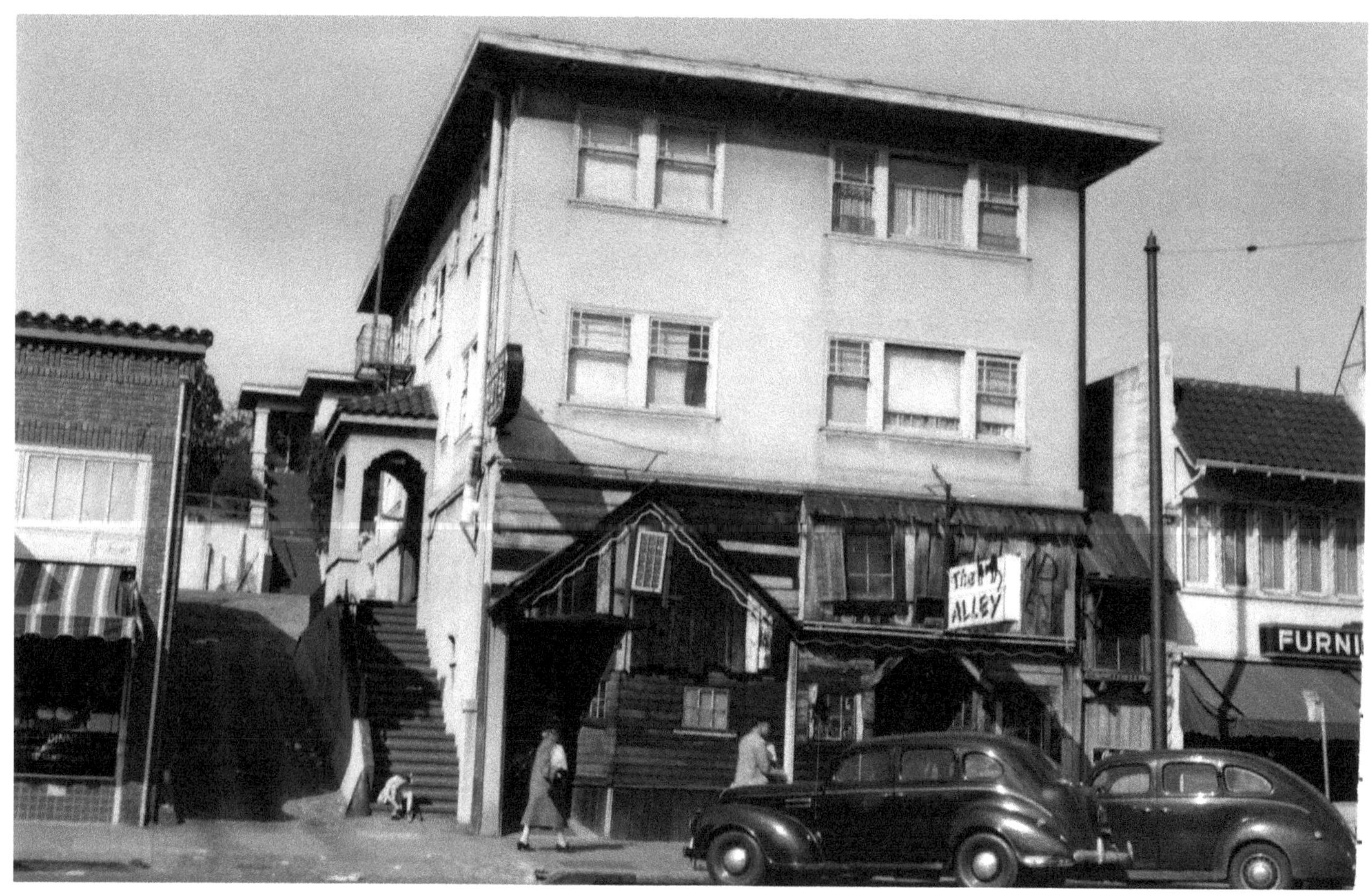

The proprietors of the Alley, an unassuming neighborhood tavern with an eccentric facade, put Rod Dibble behind the piano bar in 1960. He's been there ever since.

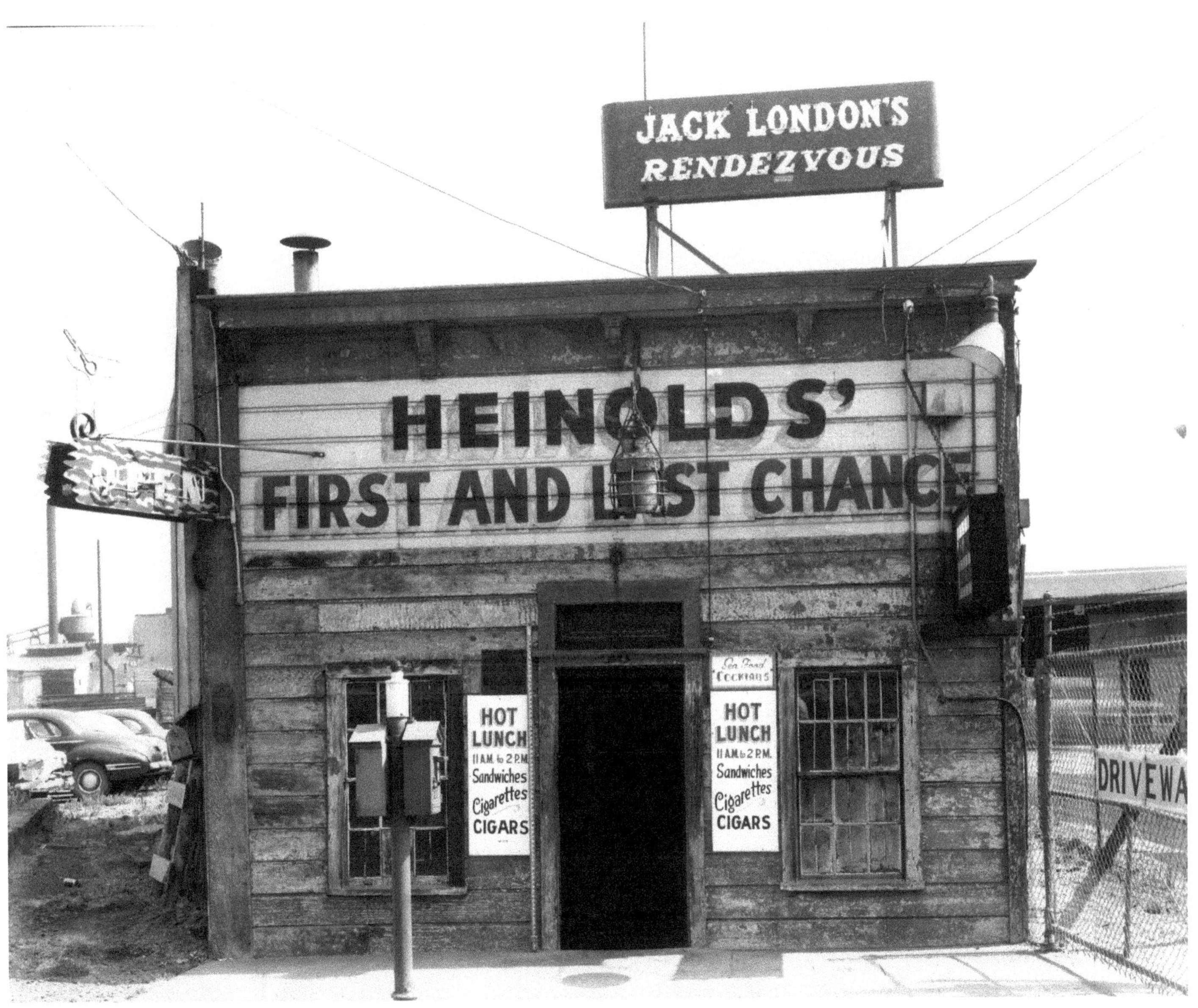

The combined efforts of city and port officials brought extensive redevelopment to the historic docks of Oakland's Inner Harbor. A rustic shack housing a sinking saloon was chosen as an anchor for Jack London Square, a mix of restaurants, shops, and public promenades that formed the central feature of the redevelopment plans.

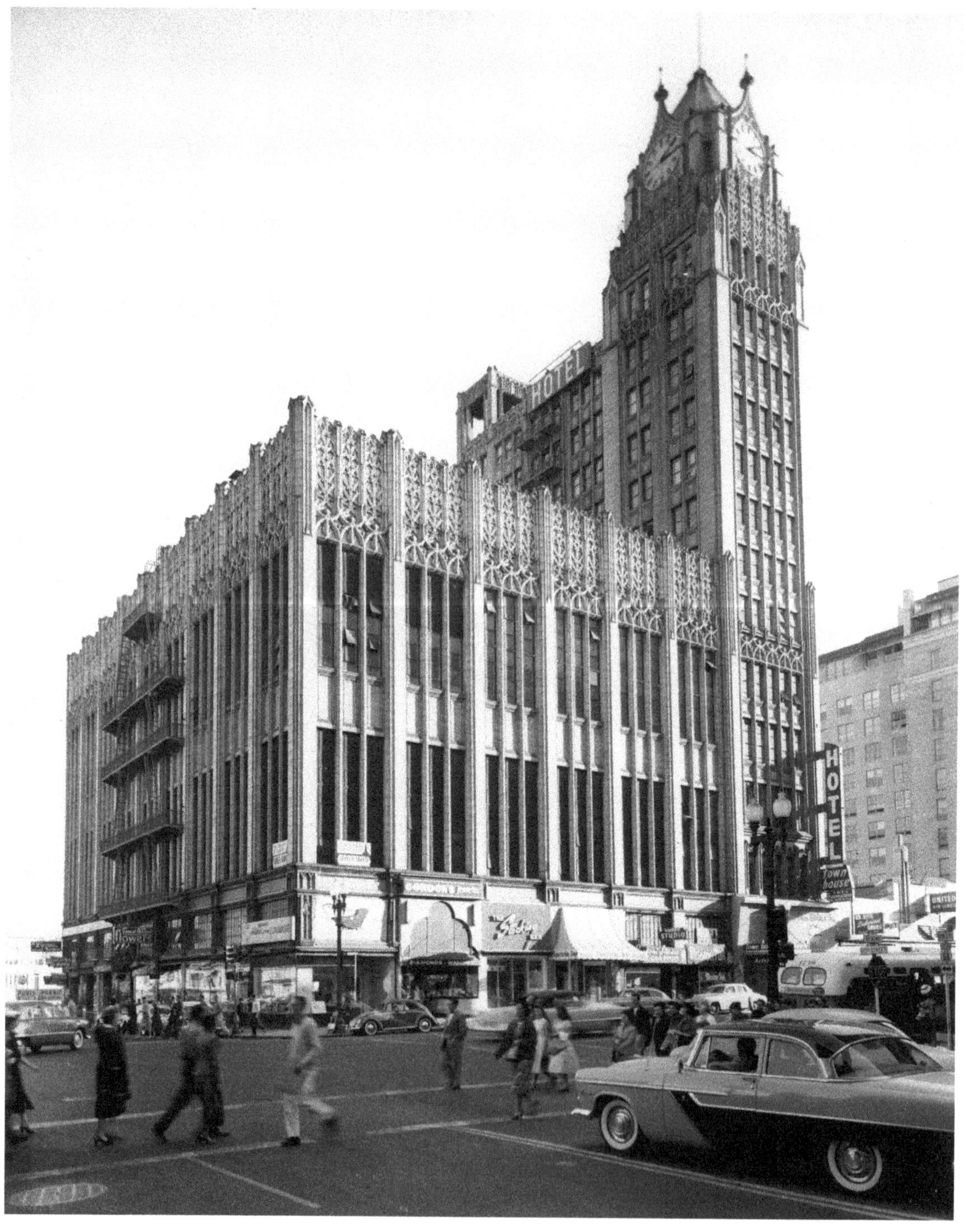

Some artifacts of the city's heritage met a much different fate in the redevelopment of the city's central core. The Hotel Carillon, built as an Elks clubhouse, was demolished. Nationwide, the federal Urban Renewal programs of the 1960s would have the same consequences for prime examples of period architecture in most cities.

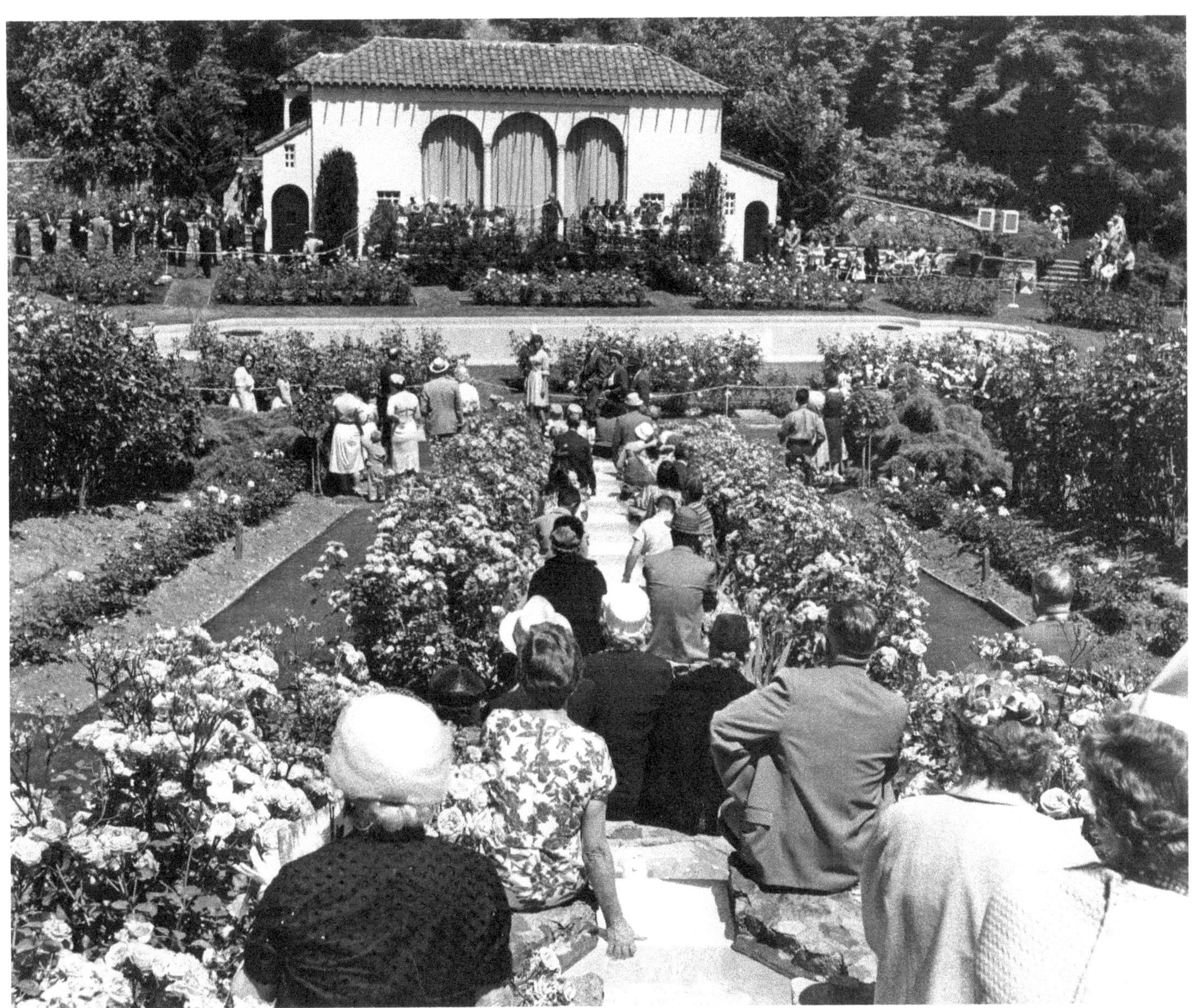

Oakland has recognized its "Mother of the Year" in ceremonies at its glorious Municipal Rose Garden since 1954. The Municipal Band, established in 1911, opens the Mother's Day ceremonies in 1961 shown here.

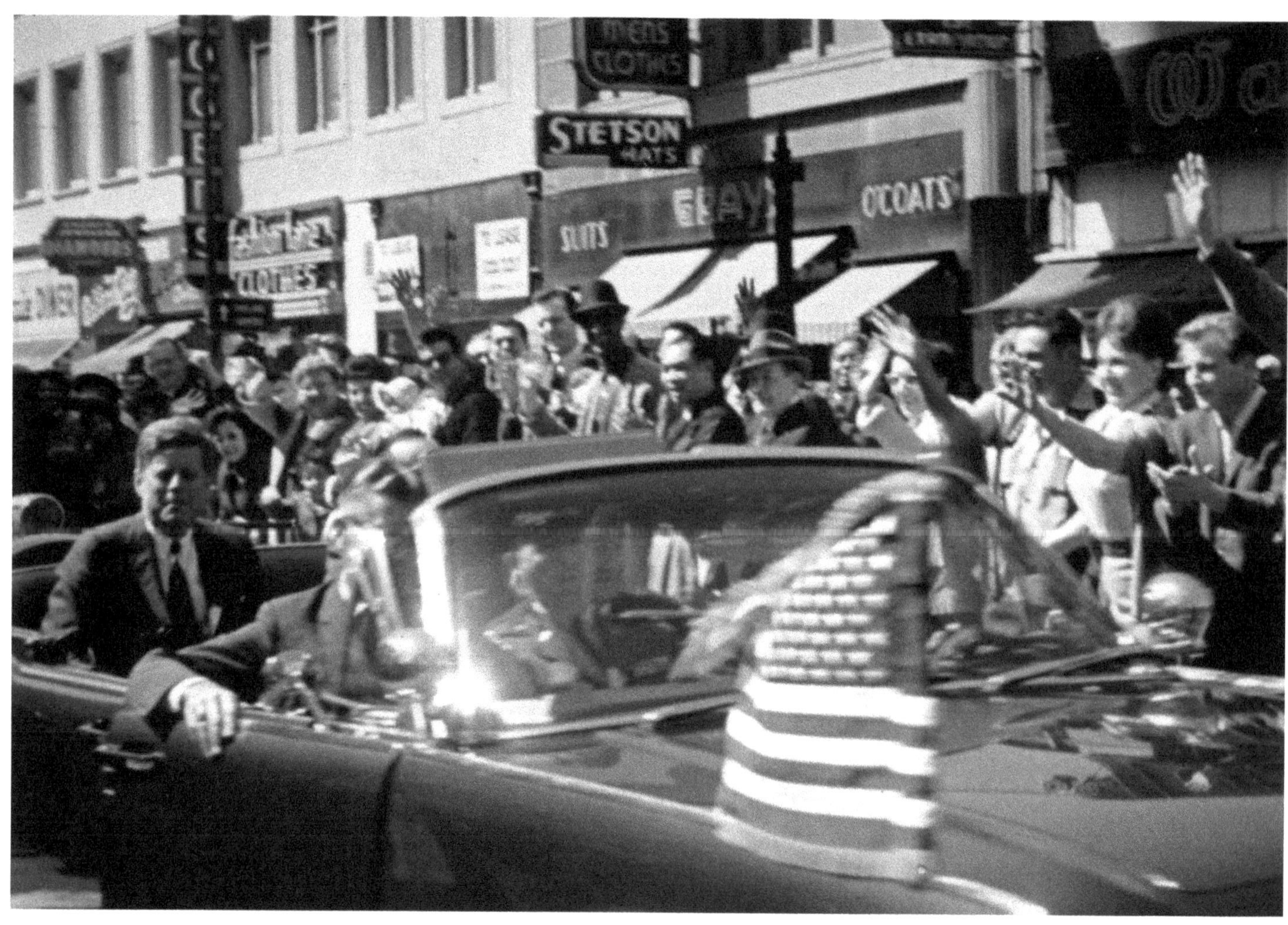

The election of John F. Kennedy brought a new sense of hope for progress to the nation's inner cities. Emil D. Miller caught this glimpse of the president on his motorcade through Oakland on March 23, 1962. Kennedy was in town for a speaking engagement at the University of California in Berkeley and a briefing on the hydrogen bomb with Edward Teller and other scientists at the Livermore National Laboratory.

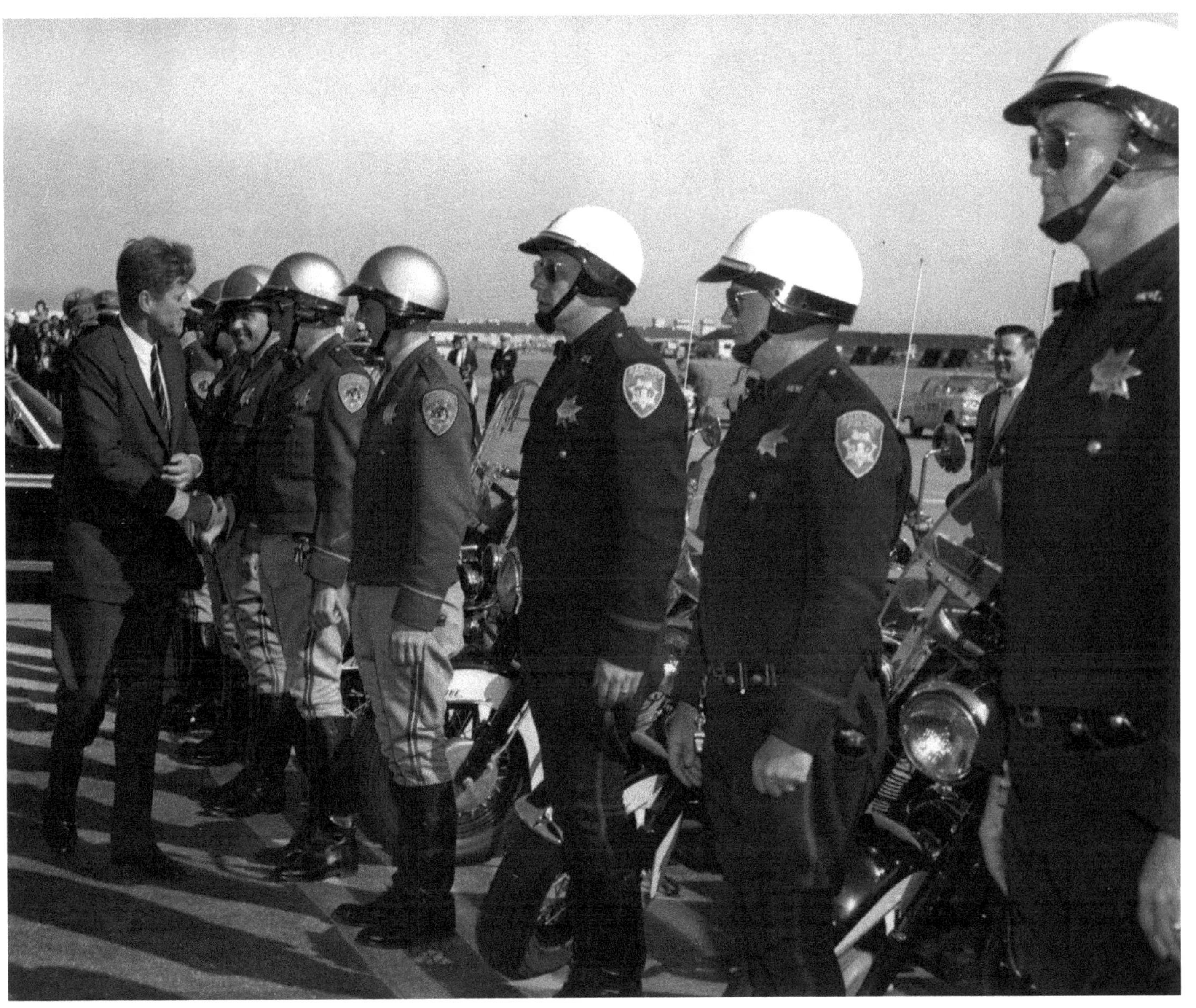

President Kennedy thanks officers from the California Highway Patrol and the Oakland Police Department for providing security during his visit in March 1962 before his departure aboard Air Force One from the Alameda Naval Air Station.

The Bermuda Building, shown here in 1962 shortly after its completion, typified the standards of the first phase of Oakland's urban renewal. The building was already struggling to lure tenants when it fell victim to the earthquake of 1989.

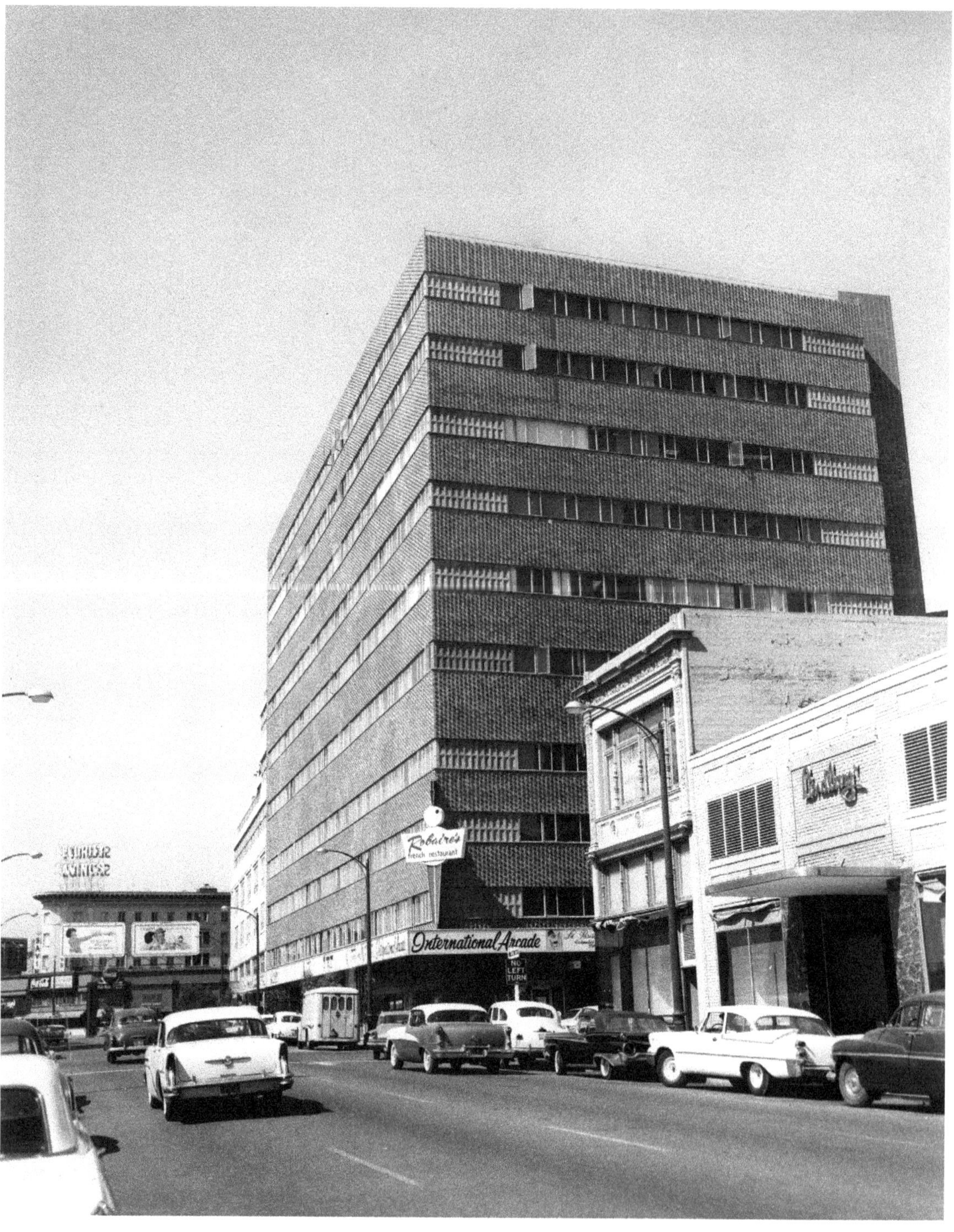

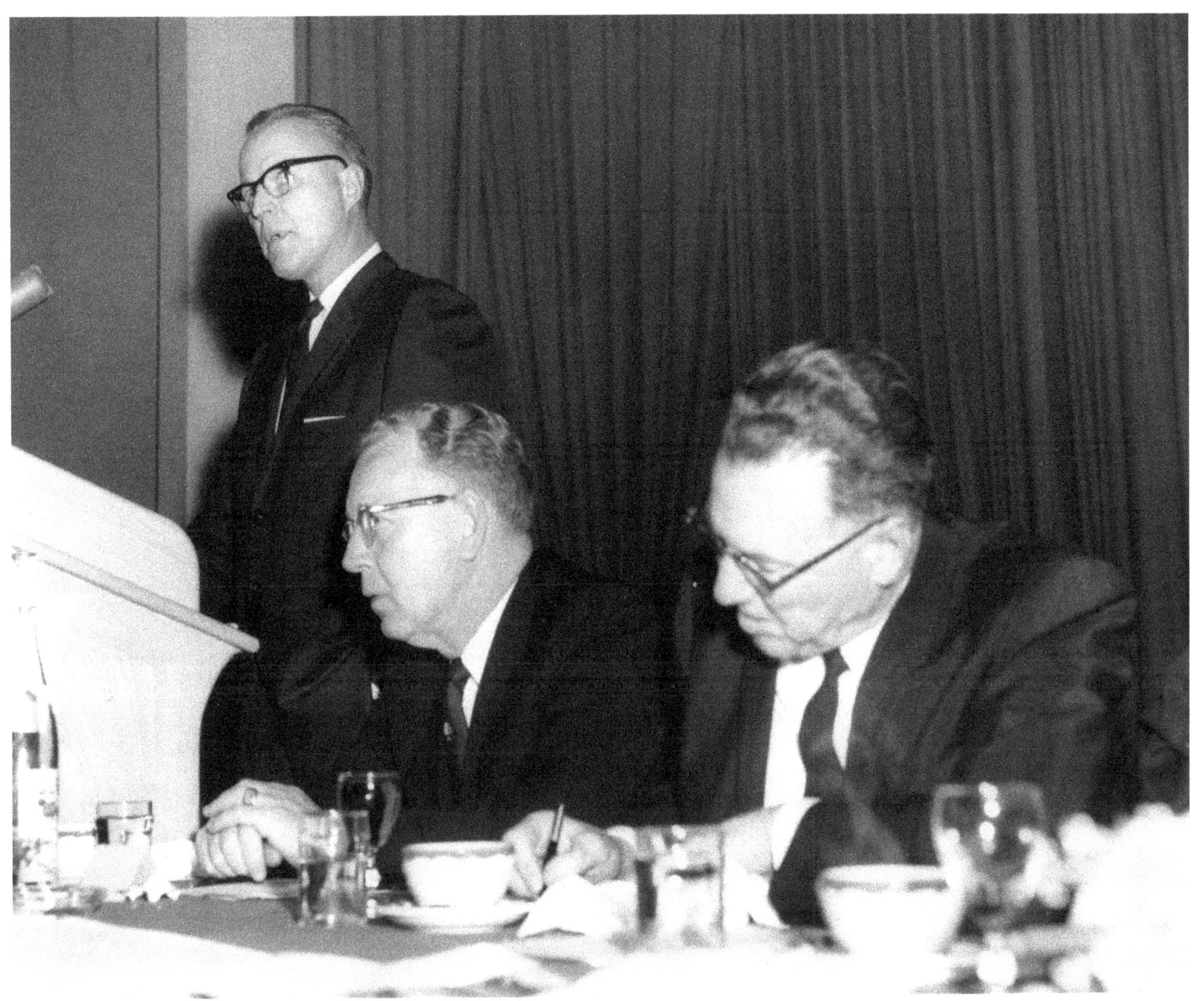

Oakland's ambitious revitalization plans stopped dead when scandal hit the mayor's office. In 1966, charges of embezzlement were filed against mayor John Houlihan, shown seated next to the speaker in this photograph from 1964. Houlihan admitted wrongdoing, blaming the low pay he received as mayor ($7,500 in 1964 dollars) for the problems that led to the crime.

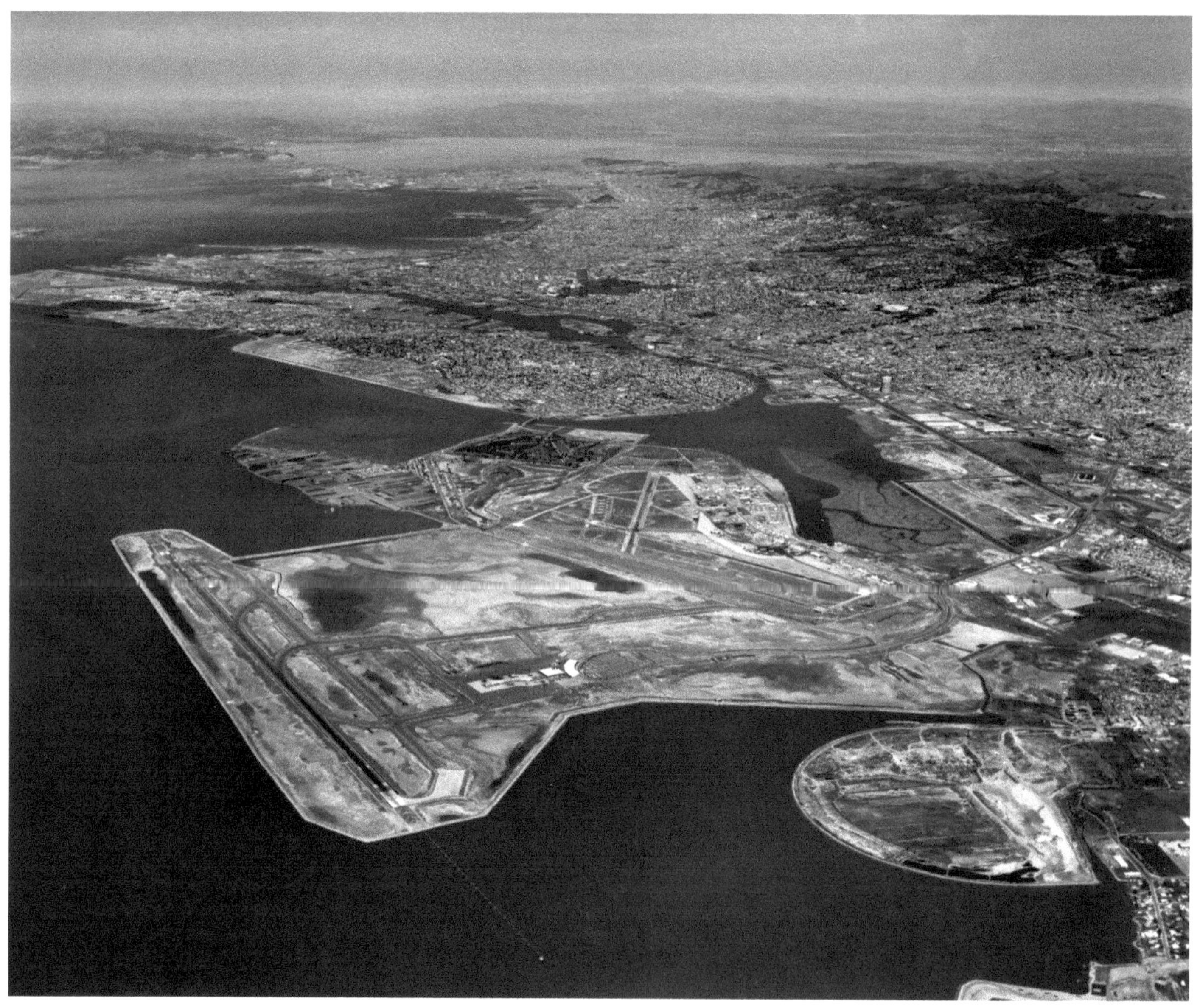

A great increase in the city's geographic dimensions, the result of major expansions of both Oakland harbor and its airport, is evident in this aerial photograph from 1964. The impacts of the shrinking San Francisco Bay would become a key issue to the growing environmental movement.

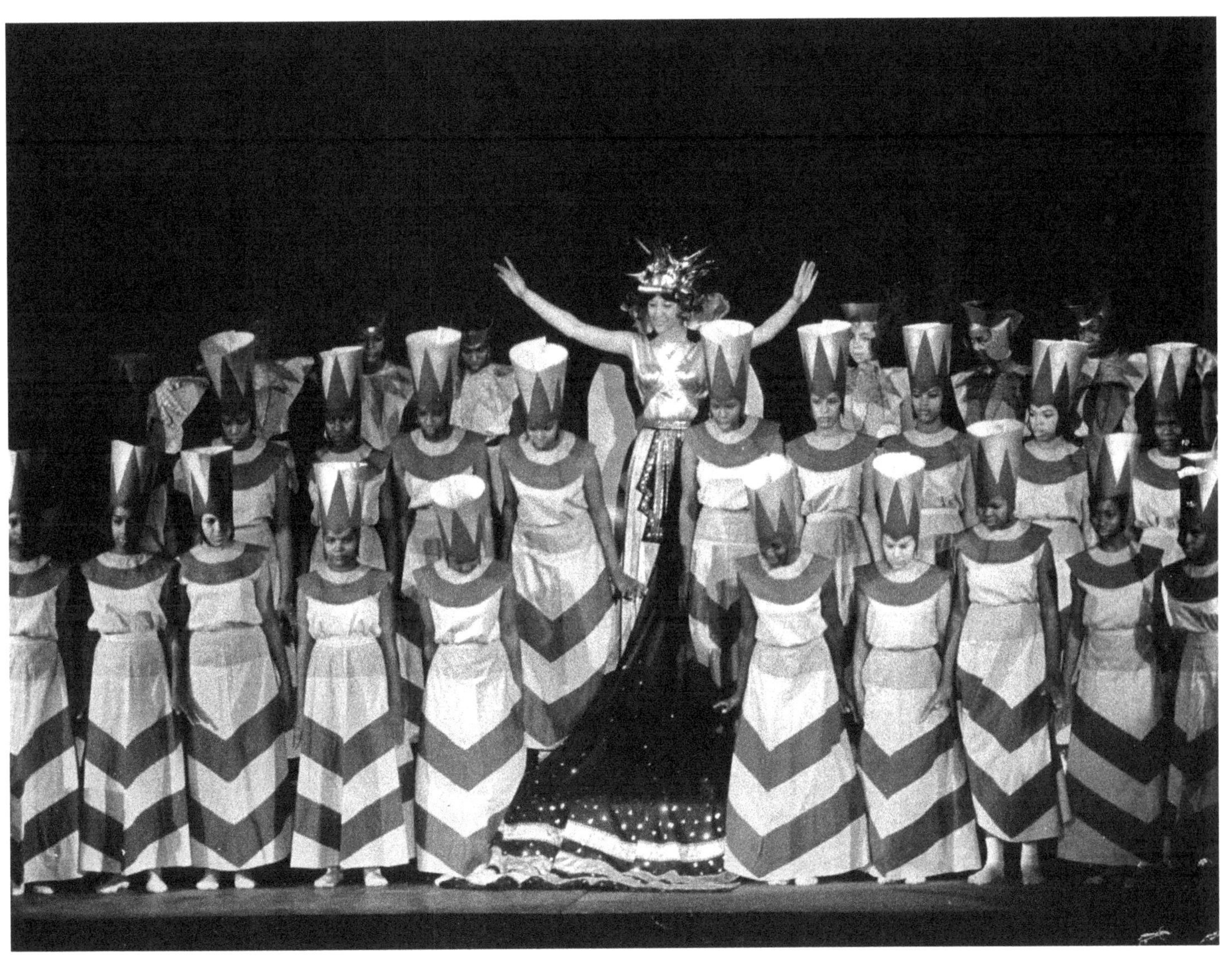

From its beginning in 1919, Oakland's annual Christmas Pageant hadn't missed a single holiday season, or a fashion trend. The trends of the times were on glorious display in the costumes for the pageant of 1967.

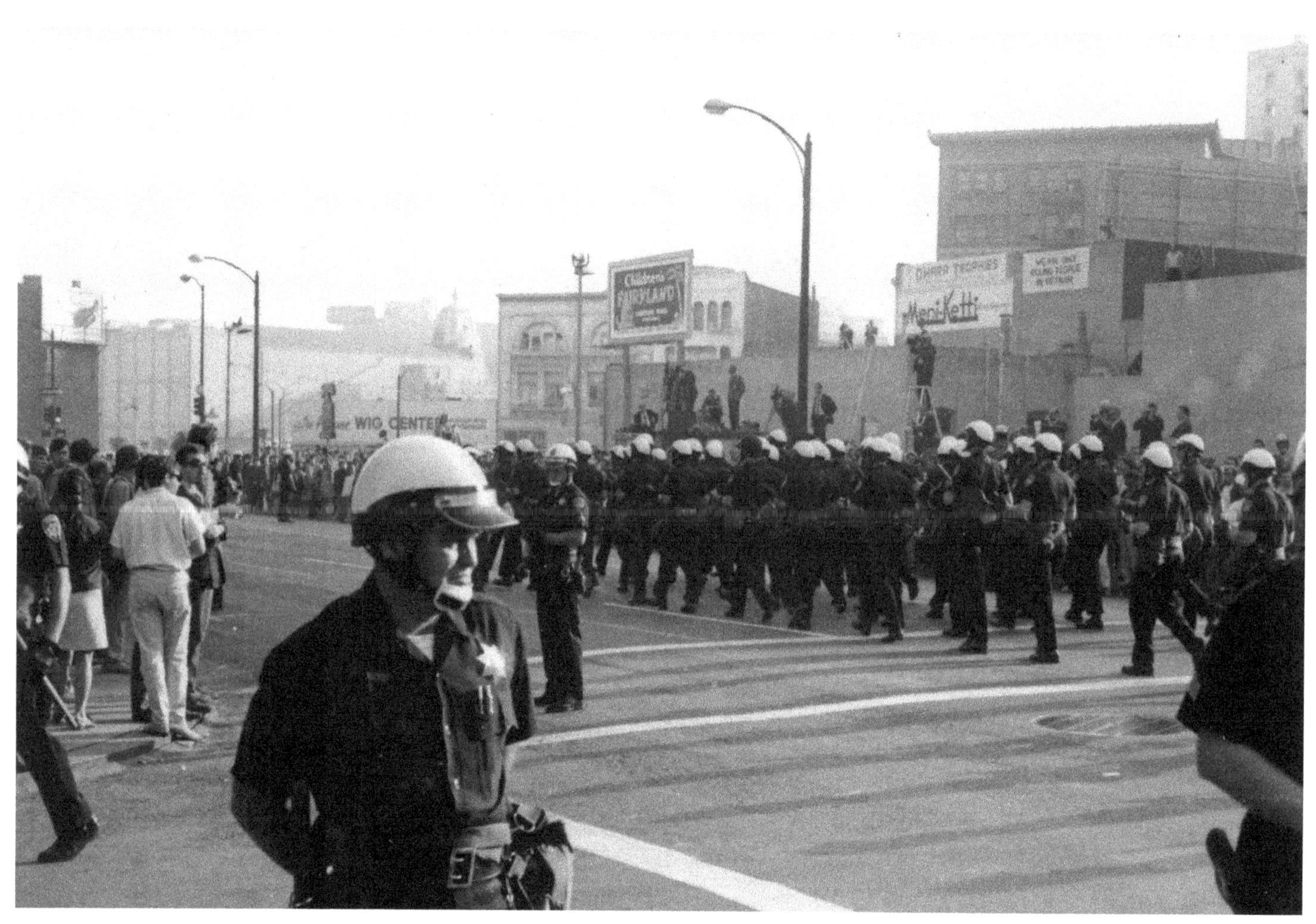

Oakland hosted the largest mass demonstration ever organized on the West Coast up to that time when activists converged on the local induction center for "Stop the Draft Week" in October 1967. As part of Governor Ronald Reagan's efforts "to clean up the mess at Berkeley," a legion of officers from the Oakland Police Department assembled to greet the arrival of student protesters, who marched down Telegraph Avenue from the campus of the University of California at Berkeley.

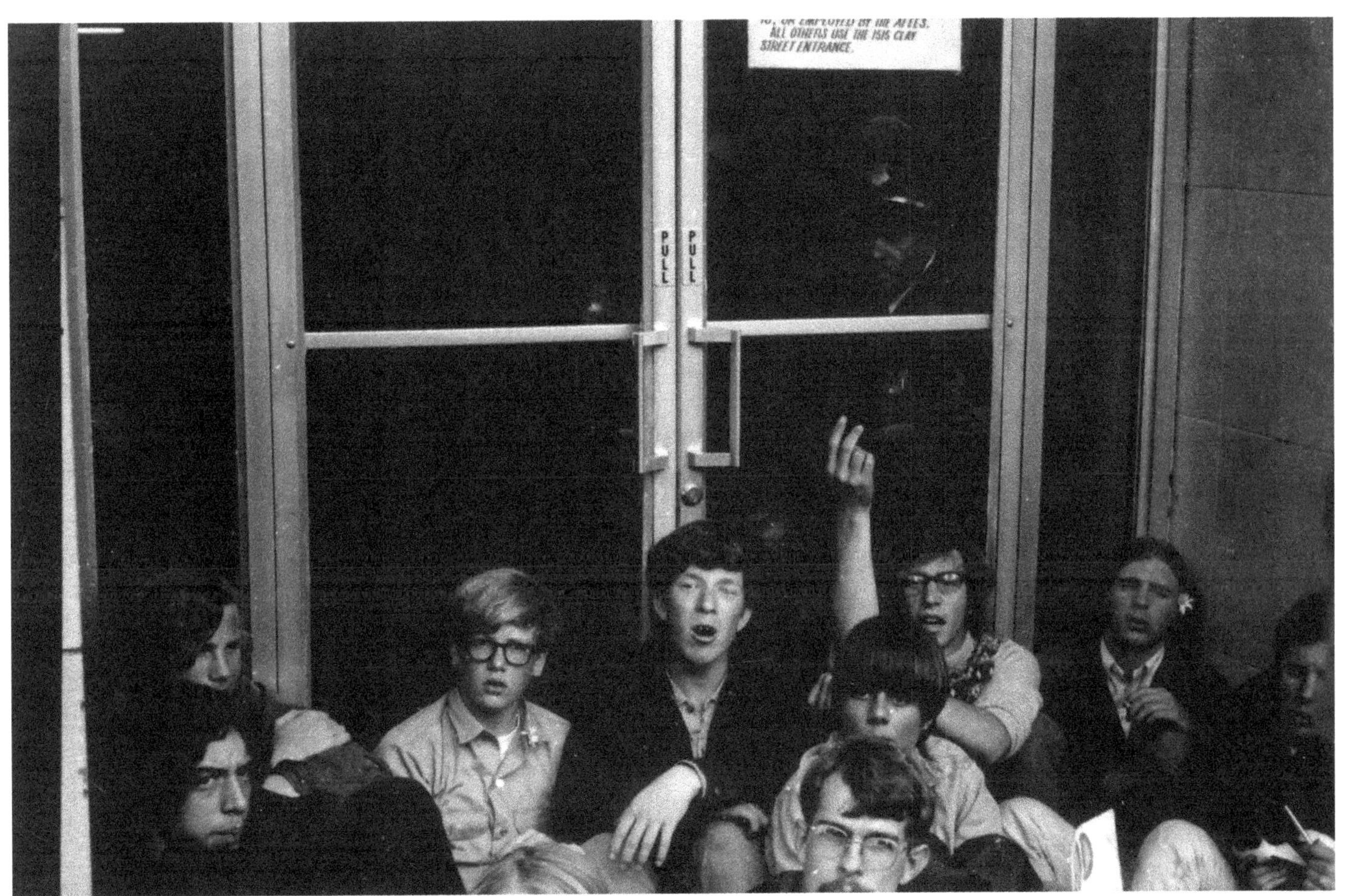

A police officer photographed demonstrators blocking the doorway to the induction center during the massive anti-draft protests of October 1967.

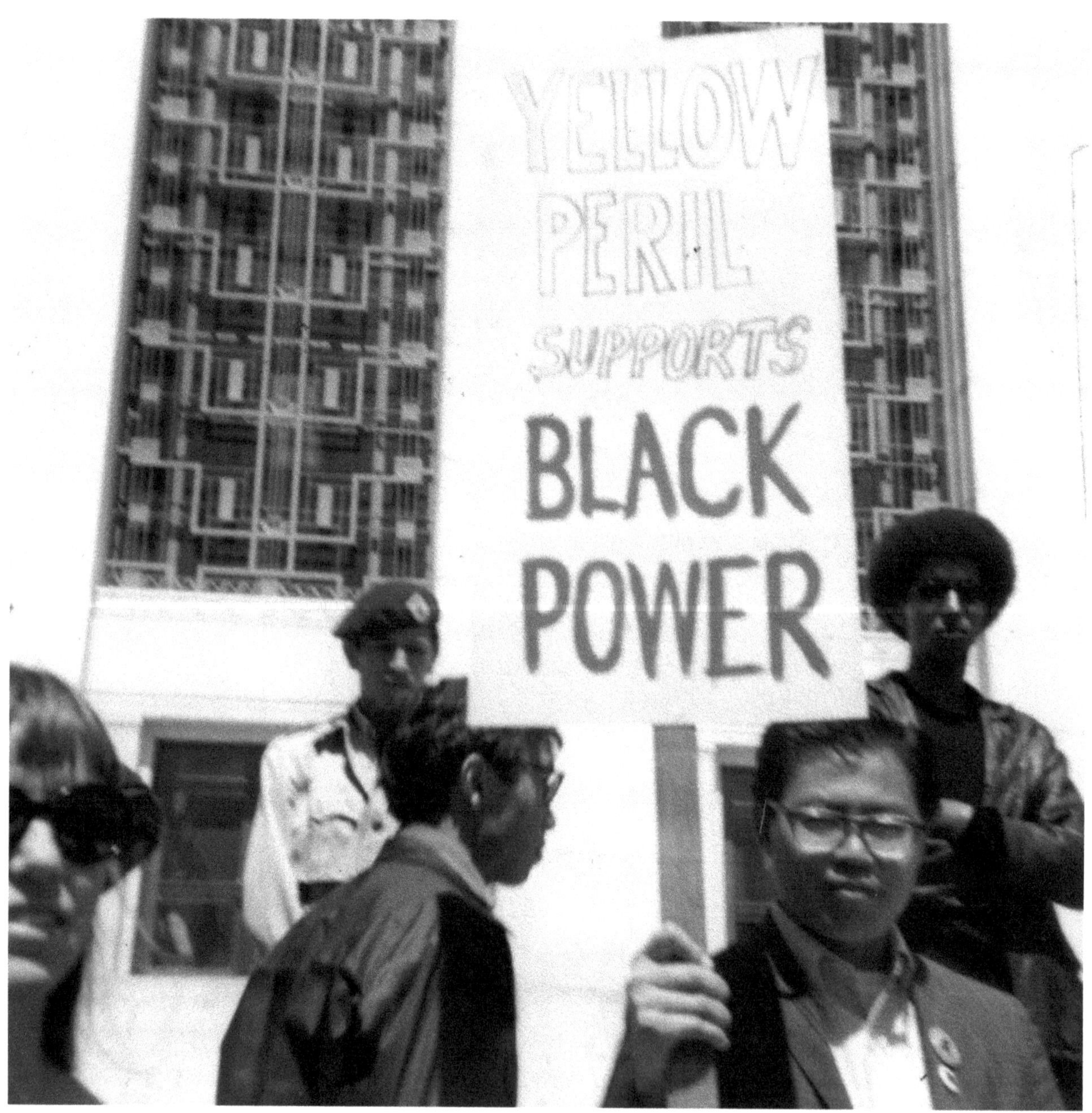

The Black Panther Party for Self Defense, established in Oakland in 1966 to challenge the treatment of African-Americans by the Oakland Police Department, grew quickly into a far-reaching organization in cities across the nation. In Oakland, its work to address issues of poverty and inequality greatly influenced other sectors of the local community. Founded on Marxist-inspired principles by Huey P. Newton and Bobby Seale, the organization adopted a militant strategy in pursuit of a socialist answer to the grievances of African-Americans.

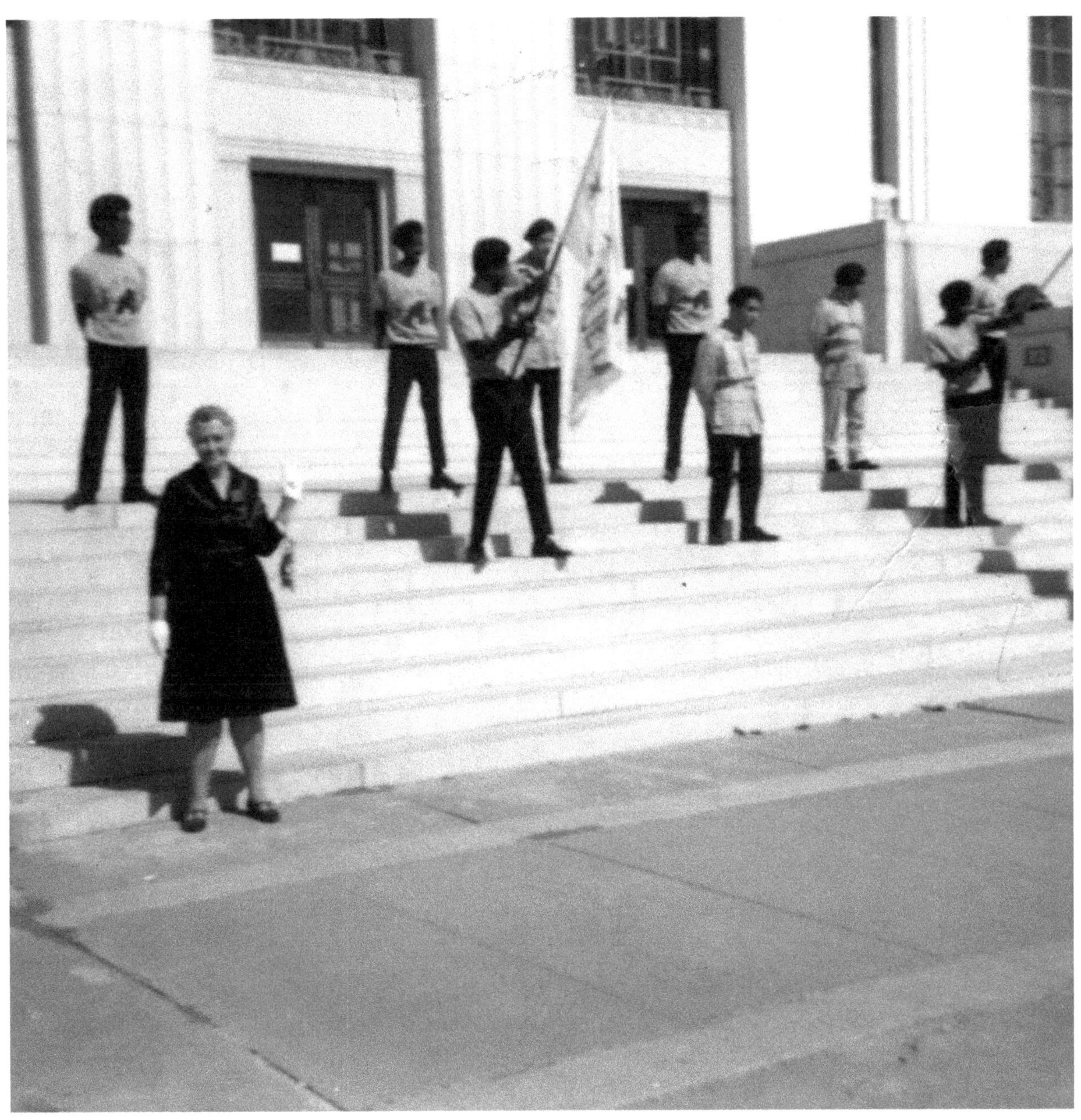

The Black Panther Party's vigil on the steps of the Alameda County Court House came to symbolize the turmoil that the 1960s have come to be known for.

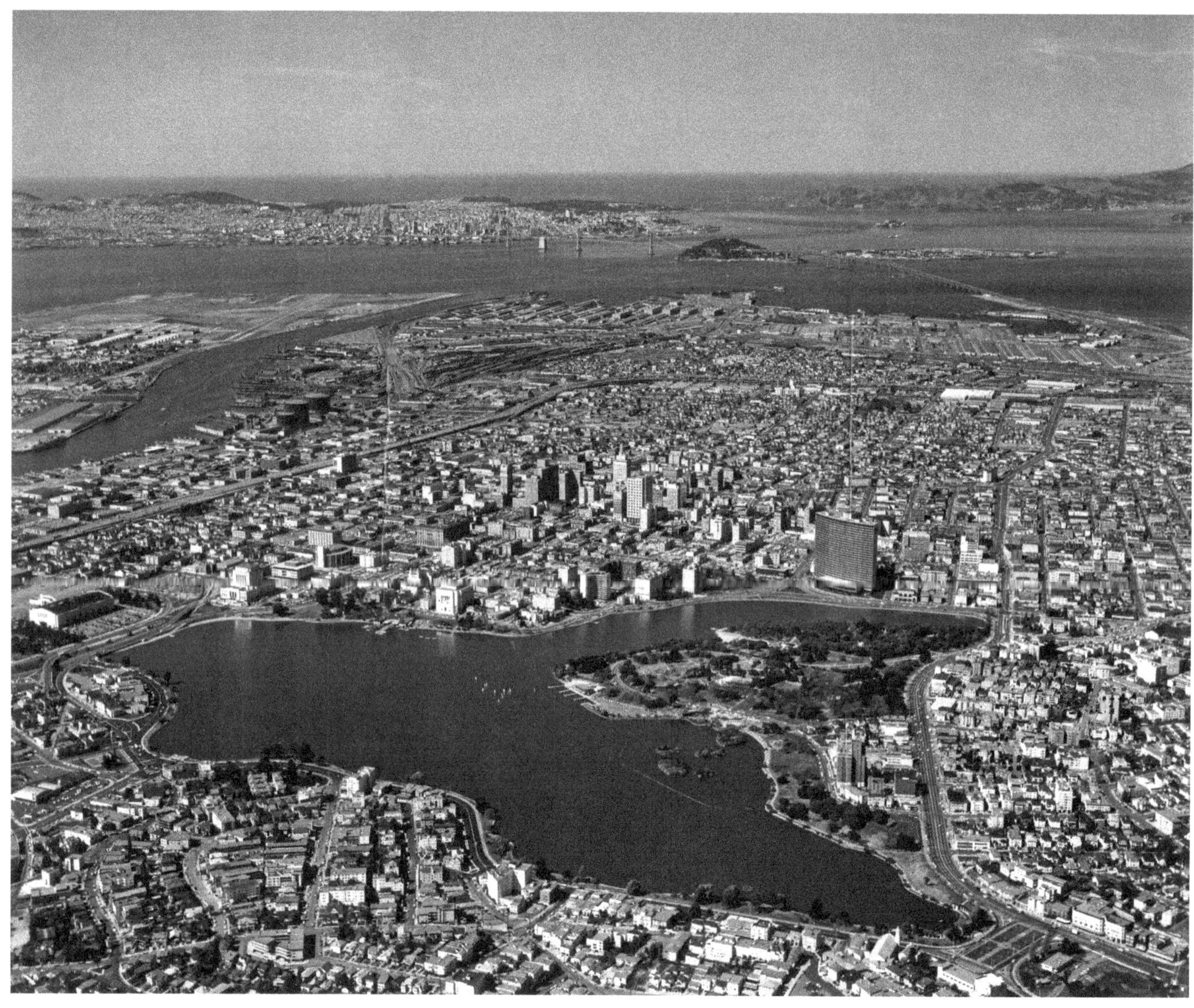

By 1970, Oakland appeared from the air as a bustling, modern metropolis. On the streets the city had finally begun to emerge from the long shadow cast over it by the city across the bay.

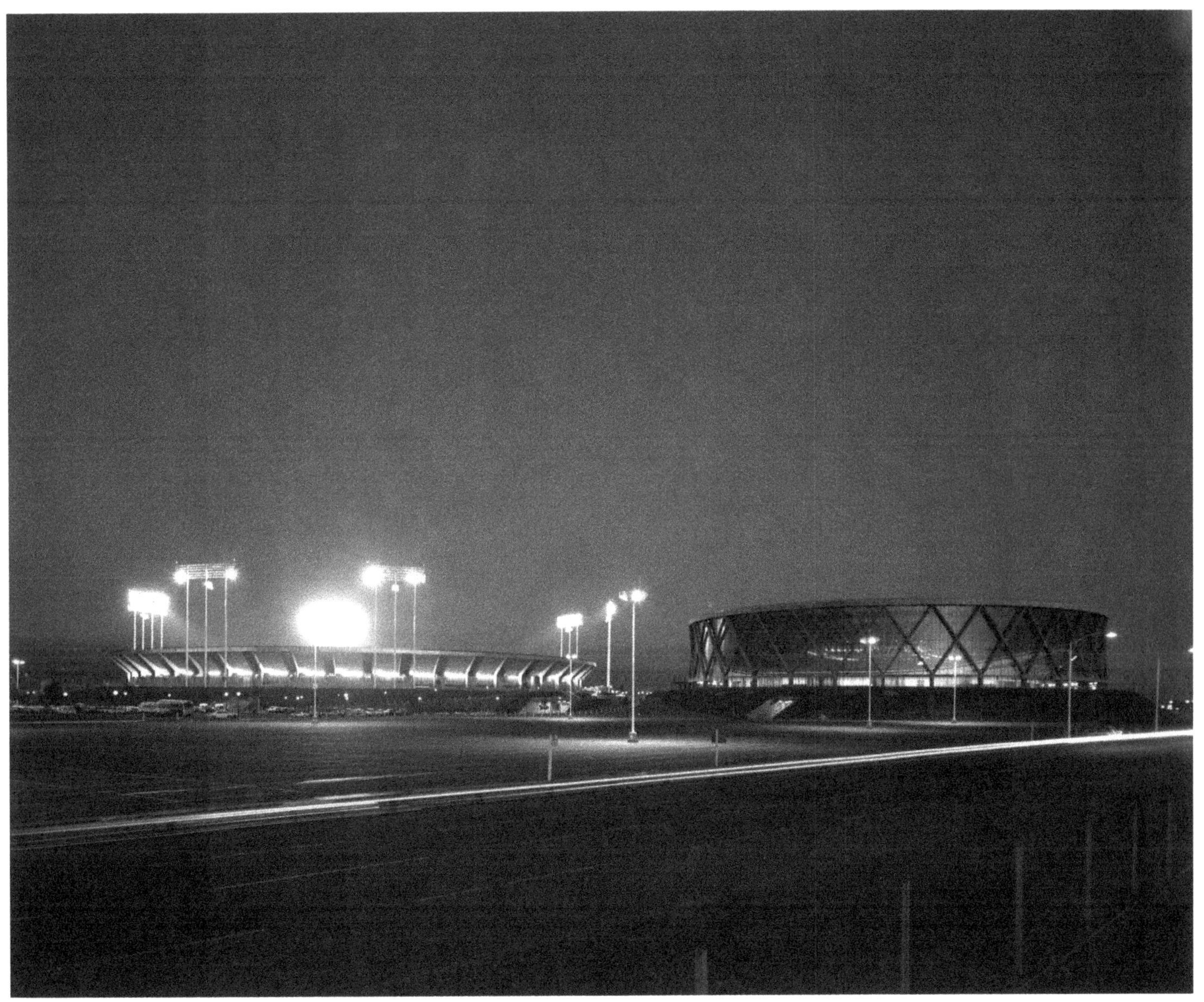

The public financing for construction of the Oakland–Alameda County Coliseum, primarily for the Oakland Raiders, was quickly rewarded with the arrival of major league baseball and basketball teams from other cities. The baseball team, the Oakland Athletics, would soon bring a string of World Series victories to the facility as the long-haired and cantankerous "Swingin' A's" of the 1970s.

Notes on the Photographs

These notes, listed by page number, attempt to include all aspects known of the photographs. Each of the photographs is identified by the page number, photograph's title or description, photographer and collection, archive, and call or box number when applicable. Although every attempt was made to collect all data, in some cases complete data was unavailable due to the age and condition of some of the photographs and records.

ii **Kelsey Nursery**
Collections of the Oakland History Room, Oakland Public Library

vi **Western Terminus of the Overland Train**
Collections of the Oakland History Room, Oakland Public Library

x **Samuel Merritt with the Stevensons**
Collections of the Oakland History Room, Oakland Public Library

2 **Broadway, Oakland, 1857**
Yale Collection of Western Americana, Beinecke Rare Book and Manuscript Library
Image ID no.: 4183117

3 **Sheriff Morse Home**
Library of Congress
LC-USZ62-27627

4 **Major Kirkham Estate**
Library of Congress
LC-USZ62-28137

5 **Oakland Oaks**
Collections of the Oakland History Room, Oakland Public Library

6 **Female College of the Pacific**
Library of Congress
LC-USZ62-27576

7 **Brayton College of California**
Collections of the Oakland History Room, Oakland Public Library

8 **City Streets, 1869**
Collections of the Oakland History Room, Oakland Public Library

9 **Victorian Houses on Lake Street**
Collections of the Oakland History Room, Oakland Public Library

10 **Poirier House, 1872**
Collections of the Oakland History Room, Oakland Public Library

11 **Transcontinental Railroad End of the Line**
Collections of the Oakland History Room, Oakland Public Library

12 **Mills College, 1873**
Collections of the Oakland History Room, Oakland Public Library
Behrmans Collection

13 **Palo Seco Creek Sawmill**
Collections of the Oakland History Room, Oakland Public Library

14 **Oakland Pier Train**
Library of Congress
HABS CAL,1-OAK,1-2

15 **Chabot Home at Lake Peralta**
Collections of the Oakland History Room, Oakland Public Library

16 **St. Mary's College**
Collections of the Oakland History Room, Oakland Public Library

17 **Marietta "Lizzie Bell" Stow**
Collections of the Oakland History Room, Oakland Public Library, and Oakland Museum

18 **The Thomas Hill Home**
Collections of the Oakland History Room, Oakland Public Library

19 **Eighth Street Bridge**
Collections of the Oakland History Room, Oakland Public Library

20 **Klinknerville**
Collections of the Oakland History Room, Oakland Public Library

21 **Charles Klinkner and Family**
Collections of the Oakland History Room, Oakland Public Library

22 **Greenhood & Moran Baseball Team**
Collections of the Oakland History Room, Oakland Public Library

23 **Lake Merritt and Dam**
Collections of the Oakland History Room, Oakland Public Library

24 **Children at Tenth and Washington Streets**
Collections of the Oakland History Room, Oakland Public Library

25 **San Antonio Wharf, 1885**
Collections of the Oakland History Room, Oakland Public Library

26 **Oakland Wharf from Yerba Buena**
Collections of the Oakland History Room, Oakland Public Library

27 **Live Oak Landmark**
Collections of the Oakland History Room, Oakland Public Library

28 **Convent of Our Lady of the Sacred Heart**
Collections of the Oakland History Room, Oakland Public Library

29 **Washington Street Retail**
Collections of the Oakland History Room, Oakland Public Library

30 **Oakland Point Exchange Hotel**
Collections of the Oakland History Room, Oakland Public Library

31 **Oakland Public High School**
Collections of the Oakland History Room, Oakland Public Library

32 **Lake View Cottage**
Collections of the Oakland History Room, Oakland Public Library

33 **Indian Gulch Trestle**
Collections of the Oakland History Room, Oakland Public Library

34 **Municipal Pier Nickel Ferry**
Collections of the Oakland History Room, Oakland Public Library

35 **Piedmont Springs**
Collections of the Oakland History Room, Oakland Public Library

36 **California Jute Mill**
Collections of the Oakland History Room, Oakland Public Library

37 **Oakland Lumber Company, 1894**
Collections of the Oakland History Room, Oakland Public Library

38 **Anthony Chabot Temescal Dam**
Collections of the Oakland History Room, Oakland Public Library

39 **Macdonough Theatre**
Collections of the Oakland History Room, Oakland Public Library

40 **California Cotton Mills**
Collections of the Oakland History Room, Oakland Public Library

41 **Dingee Nursery at Fernwood**
Collections of the Oakland History Room, Oakland Public Library

42 **Oakland Traction Company Streetcar**
Collections of the Oakland History Room, Oakland Public Library

43 **Peralta Adobe Ruins, 1899**
Collections of the Oakland History Room, Oakland Public Library

44 **Ferry Steamer Oakland**
Collections of the Oakland History Room, Oakland Public Library

46 **Dingee Real Estate**
Collections of the Oakland History Room, Oakland Public Library

47 **William Shorey and Family**
Collections of the Oakland History Room, Oakland Public Library

48 **Lusk Canning Company**
Collections of the Oakland History Room, Oakland Public Library

49 **Hickmott Asparagus Canning Company**
Collections of the Oakland History Room, Oakland Public Library

50 **Downtown Oakland, Early 1900s**
Collections of the Oakland History Room, Oakland Public Library

52 **Oakland's Carnegie Library**
Collections of the Oakland History Room, Oakland Public Library

53 **Carnegie Library Interior**
Collections of the Oakland History Room, Oakland Public Library

54 **Jack London, Charmian, and the Snark**
Collections of the Oakland History Room, Oakland Public Library

55 **Jack and Charmian**
Collections of the Oakland History Room, Oakland Public Library

56 **Schilling Home at Lake Merritt**
Collections of the Oakland History Room, Oakland Public Library

57 **Arbor Villa**
Collections of the Oakland History Room, Oakland Public Library

58 **McKinley Visit**
Collections of the Oakland History Room, Oakland Public Library

59 **McKinley Speech**
Collections of the Oakland History Room, Oakland Public Library

60 **Roosevelt Train**
Collections of the Oakland History Room, Oakland Public Library

61 **A.T.&S.F. Train at Emeryville**
Collections of the Oakland History Room, Oakland Public Library

62 **Parade with Dragon**
Collections of the Oakland History Room, Oakland Public Library

63 **Earthquake Aftermath no. 1**
Collections of the Oakland History Room, Oakland Public Library

64 **Earthquake Aftermath no. 2**
Collections of the Oakland History Room, Oakland Public Library

65 **Earthquake Aftermath no. 3**
Collections of the Oakland History Room, Oakland Public Library

67 **Earthquake Aftermath no. 4**
Collections of the Oakland History Room, Oakland Public Library

68 **National Guard Earthquake Relief Drill**
Library of Congress LC-USZ62-55716

69 **Overland Railroad Train En Route**
Library of Congress LC-USZ62-89508

70 **Charles Tepper Resort**
Collections of the Oakland History Room, Oakland Public Library

71 **Hopkins Street at Tepper's**
Collections of the Oakland History Room, Oakland Public Library

72 **Sausal Creek Swimming Hole**
Collections of the Oakland History Room, Oakland Public Library

73 **Temescal Horseshoe Shop**
Collections of the Oakland History Room, Oakland Public Library

74 **Hotel Oakland Interior**
Collections of the Oakland History Room, Oakland Public Library

75 **Idora Park**
Collections of the Oakland History Room, Oakland Public Library

76 **Streets to the Hills**
Collections of the Oakland History Room, Oakland Public Library

77 **Arrival of the Western Pacific**
Collections of the Oakland History Room, Oakland Public Library

78 **First Skeins from the Imperial Valley**
Collections of the Oakland History Room, Oakland Public Library

79 **Portola Festival Auto Race, 1909**
Collections of the Oakland History Room, Oakland Public Library

80 **Bird's-eye View of Melrose**
Collections of the Oakland History Room, Oakland Public Library

81 **Buffalo Bill and Company**
Collections of the Oakland History Room, Oakland Public Library

82 **City of Oakland Hot-air Balloon and Onlookers**
Collections of the Oakland History Room, Oakland Public Library

83 **23rd Avenue, Around 1910**
Collections of the Oakland History Room, Oakland Public Library

84 **View Down Broadway**
Collections of the Oakland History Room, Oakland Public Library

85 **Vandershoot's "Butchertown" Livestock**
Collections of the Oakland History Room, Oakland Public Library

86 **Ostrich Feather Fashions**
Collections of the Oakland History Room, Oakland Public Library

87 **Chris Klein on His Melrose Ranch**
Collections of the Oakland History Room, Oakland Public Library

88 **Seventh and Myrtle Streets, 1913**
Collections of the Oakland History Room, Oakland Public Library

89 **Construction of Municipal Auditorium**
Collections of the Oakland History Room, Oakland Public Library

90 **Office of Realty Union**
Collections of the Oakland History Room, Oakland Public Library

91 **Southern Pacific Railroad Station**
Collections of the Oakland History Room, Oakland Public Library

92 **Boatbuilder's Companions**
Collections of the Oakland History Room, Oakland Public Library

93 **Home Construction in Elmhurst**
Collections of the Oakland History Room, Oakland Public Library

94 **Stella Aydlott and Her Dogmobile**
Collections of the Oakland History Room, Oakland Public Library

95 **Federal Realty Company Headquarters**
Collections of the Oakland History Room, Oakland Public Library

96 **Coxey's Second March**
Collections of the Oakland History Room, Oakland Public Library

97 **Scenic Lake Merritt**
Collections of the Oakland History Room, Oakland Public Library

98 **A View South from the Foothills**
Collections of the Oakland History Room, Oakland Public Library

99 **City Hall Dedication, 1914**
Collections of the Oakland History Room, Oakland Public Library, and Oakland Museum

100 **Northern Waterfront Wharf**
Collections of the Oakland History Room, Oakland Public Library

101 **Convention of Colored Women's Clubs**
Collections of the Oakland History Room, Oakland Public Library

102 **Moore Shipbuilding Band**
Collections of the Oakland History Room, Oakland Public Library

103 **Shredded Wheat Grand Opening**
Collections of the Oakland History Room, Oakland Public Library

104 **General Motors Publicity Shot**
Collections of the Oakland History Room, Oakland Public Library

105 **Street Dance for Doughboys**
Collections of the Oakland History Room, Oakland Public Library

106 **The Influenza Pandemic, 1918**
Collections of the Oakland History Room, Oakland Public Library

107 **Victims of the Influenza Pandemic**
Collections of the Oakland History Room, Oakland Public Library

108 **Heroes' Welcome for the 159th Infantry**
Collections of the Oakland History Room, Oakland Public Library

109 **Aerial View of the Inner Harbor**
Collections of the Oakland History Room, Oakland Public Library

110 **Arrival of First Airmail at Durant Field**
Collections of the Oakland History Room, Oakland Public Library

111 **Montgomery Ward and Company at Fruitvale**
Collections of the Oakland History Room, Oakland Public Library

112 **Temescal Creek Canyon**
Collections of the Oakland History Room, Oakland Public Library

113 **View of the Golden Gate from the Oakland Hills**
Collections of the Oakland History Room, Oakland Public Library

114 **First Car Off the Assembly Line**
Collections of the Oakland History Room, Oakland Public Library

115 First Trust and Savings Bank
Collections of the Oakland History Room, Oakland Public Library

116 The Tribune Tower
Collections of the Oakland History Room, Oakland Public Library

117 Aerial View of City
Collections of the Oakland History Room, Oakland Public Library

118 A Most Festive Columbus Day
Collections of the Oakland History Room, Oakland Public Library

119 Construction of Athens Athletic Club Facility
Collections of the Oakland History Room, Oakland Public Library

120 Grand Lake Theatre
Collections of the Oakland History Room, Oakland Public Library

121 "Our Gang" Stars with Mayor Davie
Collections of the Oakland History Room, Oakland Public Library

122 Women's Rowing Club
Collections of the Oakland History Room, Oakland Public Library

123 Oakland Municipal Airport
Collections of the Oakland History Room, Oakland Public Library

124 To Honolulu by Air
Collections of the Oakland History Room, Oakland Public Library

126 Lindbergh Visit
Collections of the Oakland History Room, Oakland Public Library

127 Retail at 20th and Broadway
Collections of the Oakland History Room, Oakland Public Library

128 Graf Zeppelin, 1928
Collections of the Oakland History Room, Oakland Public Library

130 City Skyline, 1930
Collections of the Oakland History Room, Oakland Public Library

131 Governor Pardee Home
Collections of the Oakland History Room, Oakland Public Library

132 Stretch of College Avenue
Collections of the Oakland History Room, Oakland Public Library

133 Traffic Congestion at the 12th Street Dam
Collections of the Oakland History Room, Oakland Public Library

134 Piggly Wiggly on Piedmont
Collections of the Oakland History Room, Oakland Public Library

135 MacMarr Stores
Collections of the Oakland History Room, Oakland Public Library

136 Crowd at the Paramount Theatre
Collections of the Oakland History Room, Oakland Public Library

137 Depression-era Soup Line
Collections of the Oakland History Room, Oakland Public Library

138 Courthouse Cornerstone Ceremony
Collections of the Oakland History Room, Oakland Public Library

139 Alameda County Court House, 1936
Collections of the Oakland History Room, Oakland Public Library

140 Bay Bridge Construction, 1935
Collections of the Oakland History Room, Oakland Public Library

141 Aerial View of the Completed Bay Bridge
Collections of the Oakland History Room, Oakland Public Library

142 Lockwood Gardens Housing Project
Collections of the Oakland History Room, Oakland Public Library

143 New Deal Arts Program
Collections of the Oakland History Room, Oakland Public Library

144 Money Back Smith
Collections of the Oakland History Room, Oakland Public Library

145 Approach of Northern Railroad Train
Collections of the Oakland History Room, Oakland Public Library

146 Linden Street Y.W.C.A.
Collections of the Oakland History Room, Oakland Public Library

147 Along Seventh Street, 1940
Collections of the Oakland History Room, Oakland Public Library

148 Naval Supply Depot Construction
Collections of the Oakland History Room, Oakland Public Library

149 The Port and General Depot
Collections of the Oakland History Room, Oakland Public Library

150 Independent Congregational Church Group Portrait
Library of Congress
LC-USZ62-41599

151 Flowers for Farewell Ceremonies
Library of Congress
LC-USZ62-17120

152 World War II Shipyard Workers
Collections of the Oakland History Room, Oakland Public Library

153 New Arrivals at the Southern Pacific Station
Collections of the Oakland History Room, Oakland Public Library

154 Students at Lincoln School During Wartime
Collections of the Oakland History Room, Oakland Public Library

155 Shoong National Dollar Stores
Collections of the Oakland History Room, Oakland Public Library

156 Aerial View Following the War
Collections of the Oakland History Room, Oakland Public Library

157 McClymonds High School Band
Collections of the Oakland History Room, Oakland Public Library

158 Retail Clerk Strike
Collections of the Oakland History Room, Oakland Public Library

159 Porters Hosting Truman
Collections of the Oakland History Room, Oakland Public Library

160 American Can Company Workers
Collections of the Oakland History Room, Oakland Public Library

162 Cameo Drive-in
Collections of the Oakland History Room, Oakland Public Library

163 First Freeway Construction
Collections of the Oakland History Room, Oakland Public Library

164 Skyline at Night
Collections of the Oakland History Room, Oakland Public Library

165 Public Library Charm Club Members
Collections of the Oakland History Room, Oakland Public Library

166 Exposition Village, 1950
Collections of the Oakland History Room, Oakland Public Library

167 New Roads Over the 12th Street Dam
Collections of the Oakland History Room, Oakland Public Library

168 Eisenhower Visit to City Hall
Collections of the Oakland History Room, Oakland Public Library

169 Rishell and Eisenhower at City Hall
Collections of the Oakland History Room, Oakland Public Library

170 Children's Fairyland
Collections of the Oakland History Room, Oakland Public Library

171 Fairyland Actresses
Collections of the Oakland History Room, Oakland Public Library

172 De Fremery Pool
Collections of the Oakland History Room, Oakland Public Library

173 Broadway Christmas Shoppers
Collections of the Oakland History Room, Oakland Public Library

174 Southern Pacific Station Interior
Collections of the Oakland History Room, Oakland Public Library

175 Museum-bound Steam Locomotive
Collections of the Oakland History Room, Oakland Public Library

176 Tye's Buffet at Tenth and Broadway
Collections of the Oakland History Room, Oakland Public Library

177 Moulin Rouge on Eighth Street
Collections of the Oakland History Room, Oakland Public Library

178 Dahlke's Sandwiches and Beer
Collections of the Oakland History Room, Oakland Public Library

179 Lower Broadway, 1950s
Collections of the Oakland History Room, Oakland Public Library

180 USS Hoga
Collections of the Oakland History Room, Oakland Public Library

181 Final Days for Ferry Service
Collections of the Oakland History Room, Oakland Public Library

182 Chinatown
Collections of the Oakland History Room, Oakland Public Library

183 Sweets Ballroom on Franklin Street
Collections of the Oakland History Room, Oakland Public Library

184 First Western Savings Under Construction
Collections of the Oakland History Room, Oakland Public Library

185 Rise of Kaiser Center
Collections of the Oakland History Room, Oakland Public Library

186 The Alley
Collections of the Oakland History Room, Oakland Public Library

187 Historic Docks Redevelopment
Collections of the Oakland History Room, Oakland Public Library

188 Hotel Carillon
Collections of the Oakland History Room, Oakland Public Library

189 Assembly at Municipal Rose Garden
Collections of the Oakland History Room, Oakland Public Library

190 Kennedy Motorcade
Collections of the Oakland History Room, Oakland Public Library

191 Kennedy Greeting Officers, 1962
Collections of the Oakland History Room, Oakland Public Library

192 The Bermuda Building
Collections of the Oakland History Room, Oakland Public Library

193 Mayor Houlihan
Collections of the Oakland History Room, Oakland Public Library

194 Oakland Harbor from the Air
Collections of the Oakland History Room, Oakland Public Library

195 The Annual Christmas Pageant
Collections of the Oakland History Room, Oakland Public Library

196 Student Protests
Collections of the Oakland History Room, Oakland Public Library

197 Student Protesters
Collections of the Oakland History Room, Oakland Public Library

198 Black Panther Protest
Collections of the Oakland History Room, Oakland Public Library

199 Black Panther Protest, no. 2
Collections of the Oakland History Room, Oakland Public Library

200 Oakland from the Air, 1970
Collections of the Oakland History Room, Oakland Public Library

201 Oakland–Alameda County Coliseum
Collections of the Oakland History Room, Oakland Public Library

HISTORIC PHOTOS OF OAKLAND

Its place directly opposite San Francisco Bay from one of the world's most visited cities has left Oakland to struggle against comparison from the start. It has greeted that challenge by asserting its identity as an effervescent international port city with a richly diverse, uniquely creative, and highly resilient population.

Oakland consistently finds itself at the forefront of the rapid pace of change that California has helped to drive, with its history of daring experiments in social, scientific, and cultural innovation.

The camera has preserved glimpses into the impacts of that change—and the ways in which Oakland has adapted to sustain itself as a charming and welcoming gateway to the Pacific. *Historic Photos of Oakland* collects a small fraction of the record the cameras have left behind, providing a compelling view of the colorful past of the "second" City by the Bay.

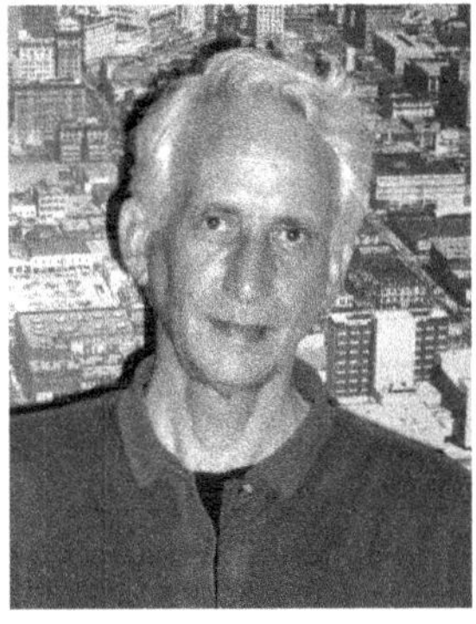

Steven Lavoie is librarian in the Oakland History Room of the Oakland Public Library, the source of most of the photographs published in this book. He formerly served that function at the *Oakland Tribune,* where he contributed columns, features, and editorials. Lavoie holds two degrees from the University of California, Berkeley and has lived in Oakland since he relocated here from a remote northern suburb to shorten the trip to Oakland A's games.

WWW.TURNERPUBLISHING.COM

www.ingramcontent.com/pod-product-compliance
Lightning Source LLC
LaVergne TN
LVHW060612110826
845154LV00003B/73
* 9 7 8 1 6 8 4 4 2 0 8 5 8 *